FLIPSIDE

STORY & ART:
BRION
FOULKE

FLIPSIDE VOL. 1

Visit Flipside online and read the latest storylines at:
flipside.keenspot.com

Story & Art by Brion Foulke

Cover Coloring by Del "Delusion" Borovic
Book Design and Additional Coloring by Jennifer Brazas
Additional Coloring by Karla Groth

Flipside © 2000 by Brion Foulke

Sixth Printing, November 2014
Printed in the United States of America

FLIPSIDE 1

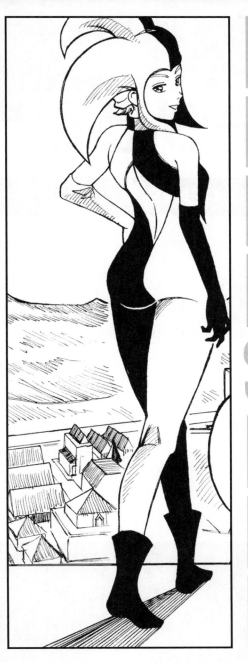

FLIPSIDE

CONTENTS

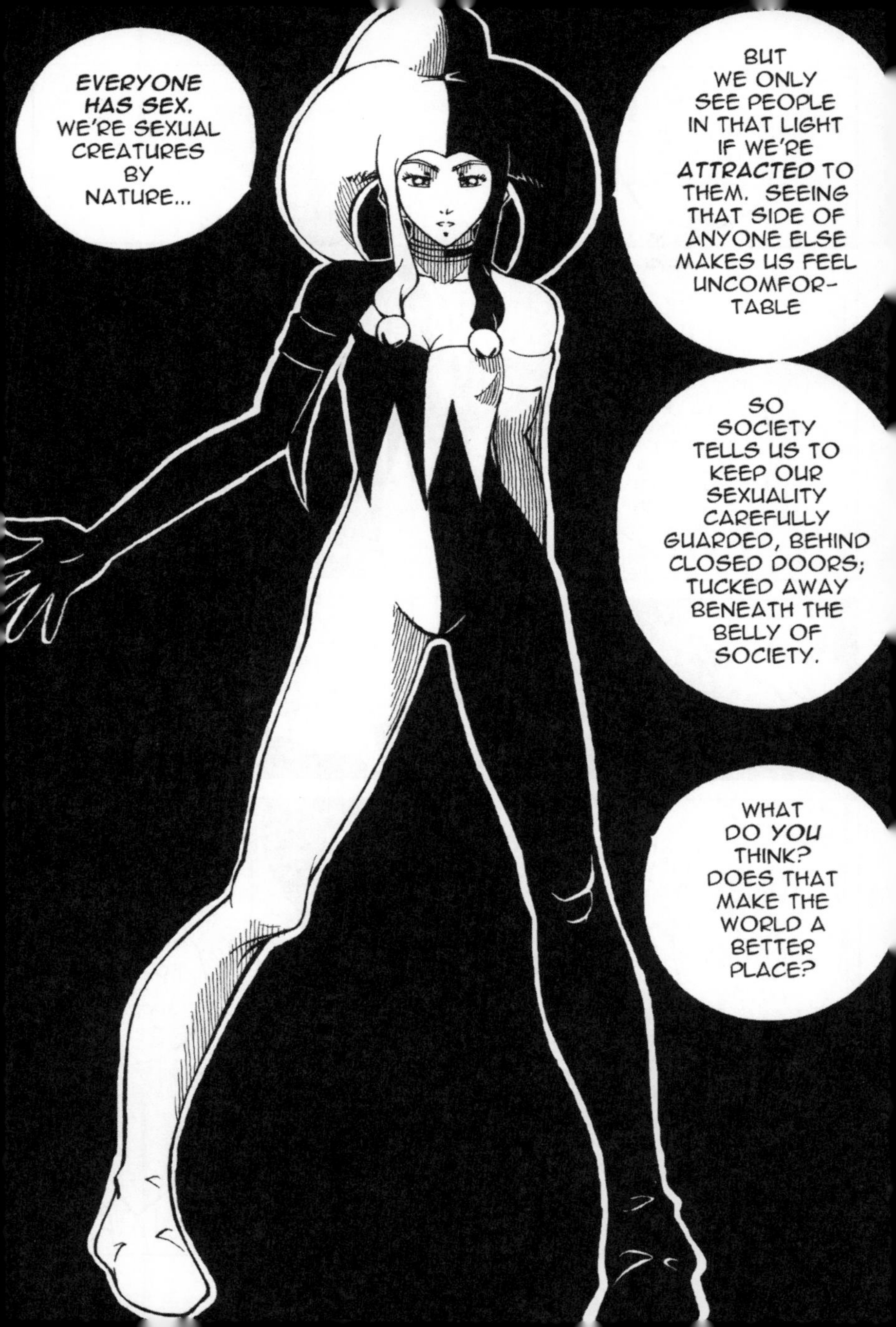
EVERYONE HAS SEX. WE'RE SEXUAL CREATURES BY NATURE...
BUT WE ONLY SEE PEOPLE IN THAT LIGHT IF WE'RE ATTRACTED TO THEM. SEEING THAT SIDE OF ANYONE ELSE MAKES US FEEL UNCOMFOR-TABLE
SO SOCIETY TELLS US TO KEEP OUR SEXUALITY CAREFULLY GUARDED, BEHIND CLOSED DOORS; TUCKED AWAY BENEATH THE BELLY OF SOCIETY.
WHAT DO YOU THINK? DOES THAT MAKE THE WORLD A BETTER PLACE?

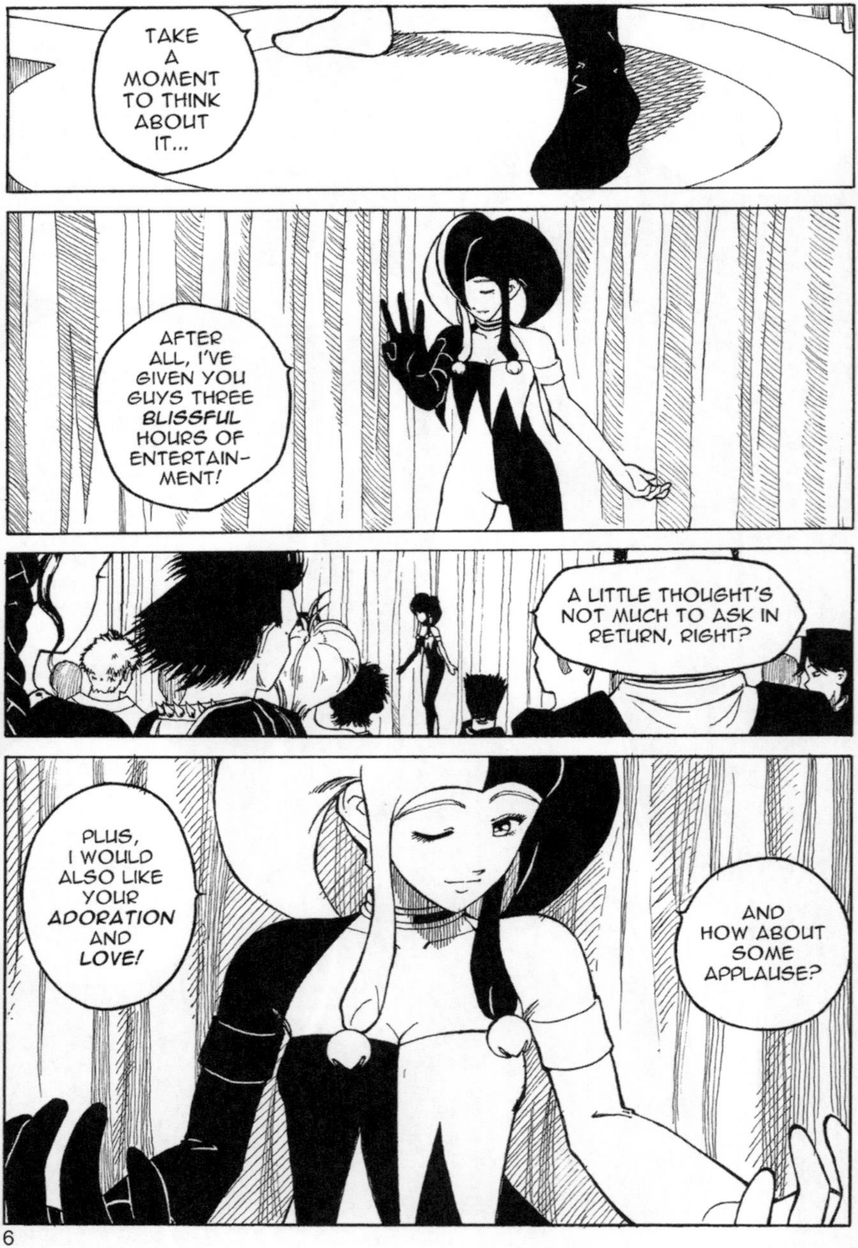
TAKE A MOMENT TO THINK ABOUT IT...
AFTER ALL, I'VE GIVEN YOU GUYS THREE *BLISSFUL* HOURS OF ENTERTAIN-MENT!
A LITTLE THOUGHT'S NOT MUCH TO ASK IN RETURN, RIGHT?
AND HOW ABOUT SOME APPLAUSE?
PLUS, I WOULD ALSO LIKE YOUR *ADORATION* AND *LOVE!*

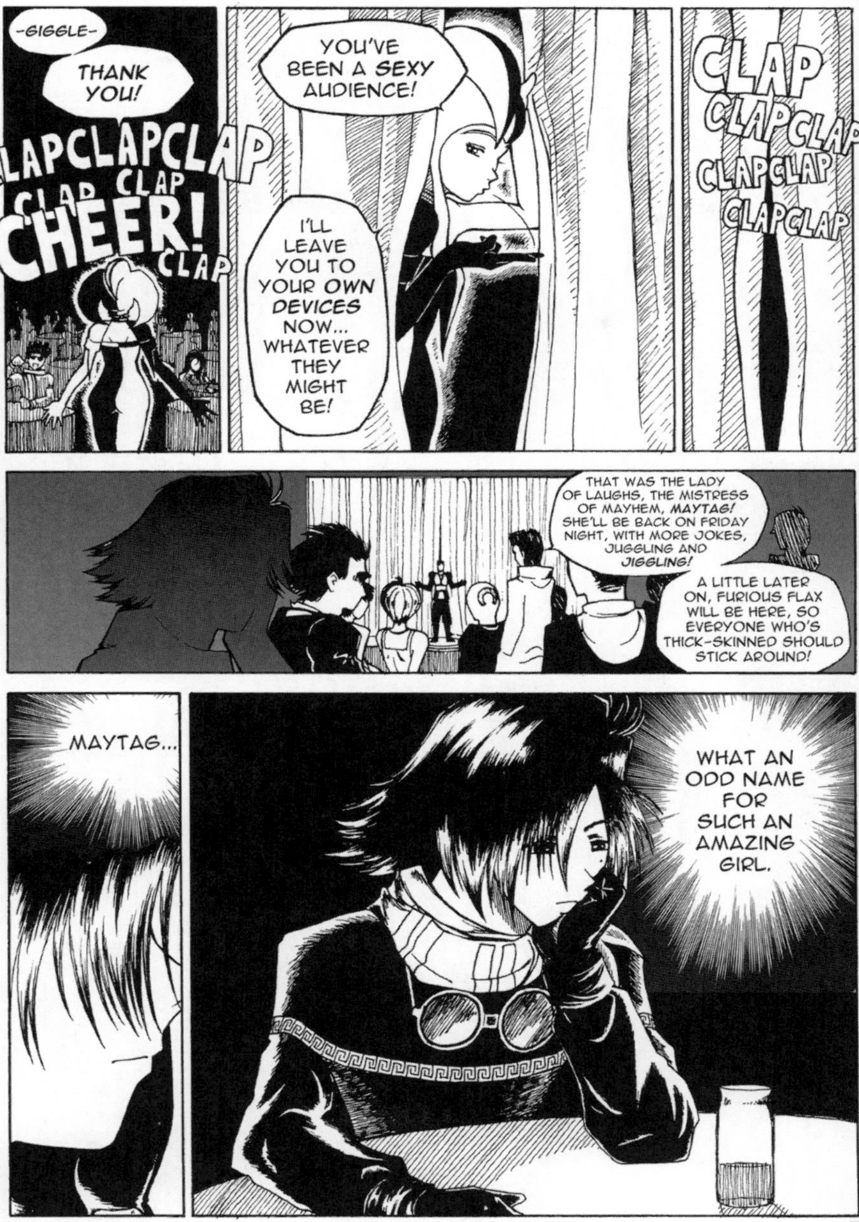
-GIGGLE-
THANK YOU!
CLAPCLAPCLAP
CLAP CLAP
CHEER!
CLAP
YOU'VE BEEN A SEXY AUDIENCE!
I'LL LEAVE YOU TO YOUR OWN DEVICES NOW... WHATEVER THEY MIGHT BE!
CLAP
CLAPCLAP
CLAPCLAP
CLAPCLAP
THAT WAS THE LADY OF LAUGHS, THE MISTRESS OF MAYHEM, MAYTAG! SHE'LL BE BACK ON FRIDAY NIGHT, WITH MORE JOKES, JUGGLING AND JIGGLING!
A LITTLE LATER ON, FURIOUS FLAX WILL BE HERE, SO EVERYONE WHO'S THICK-SKINNED SHOULD STICK AROUND!
MAYTAG...
WHAT AN ODD NAME FOR SUCH AN AMAZING GIRL.

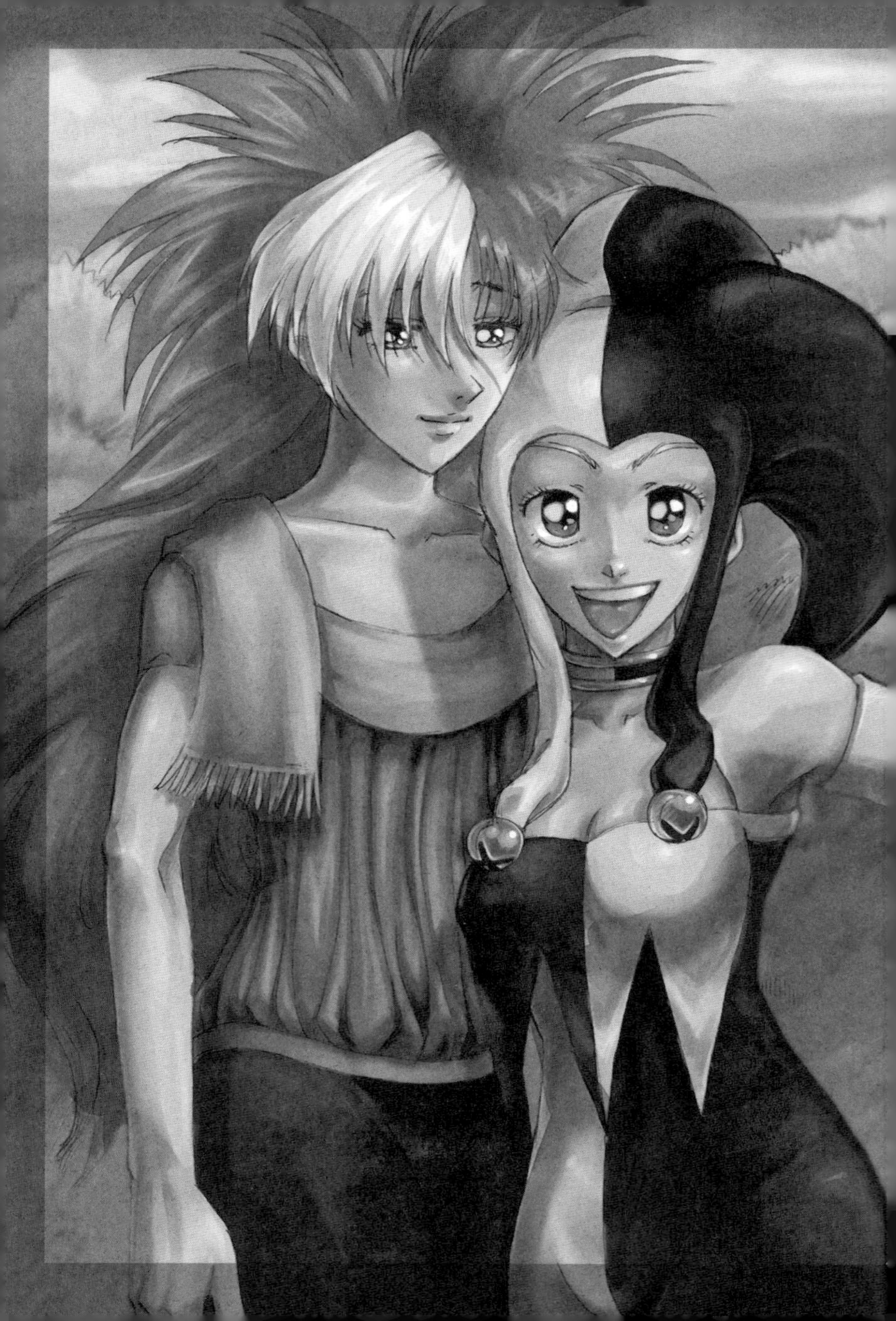

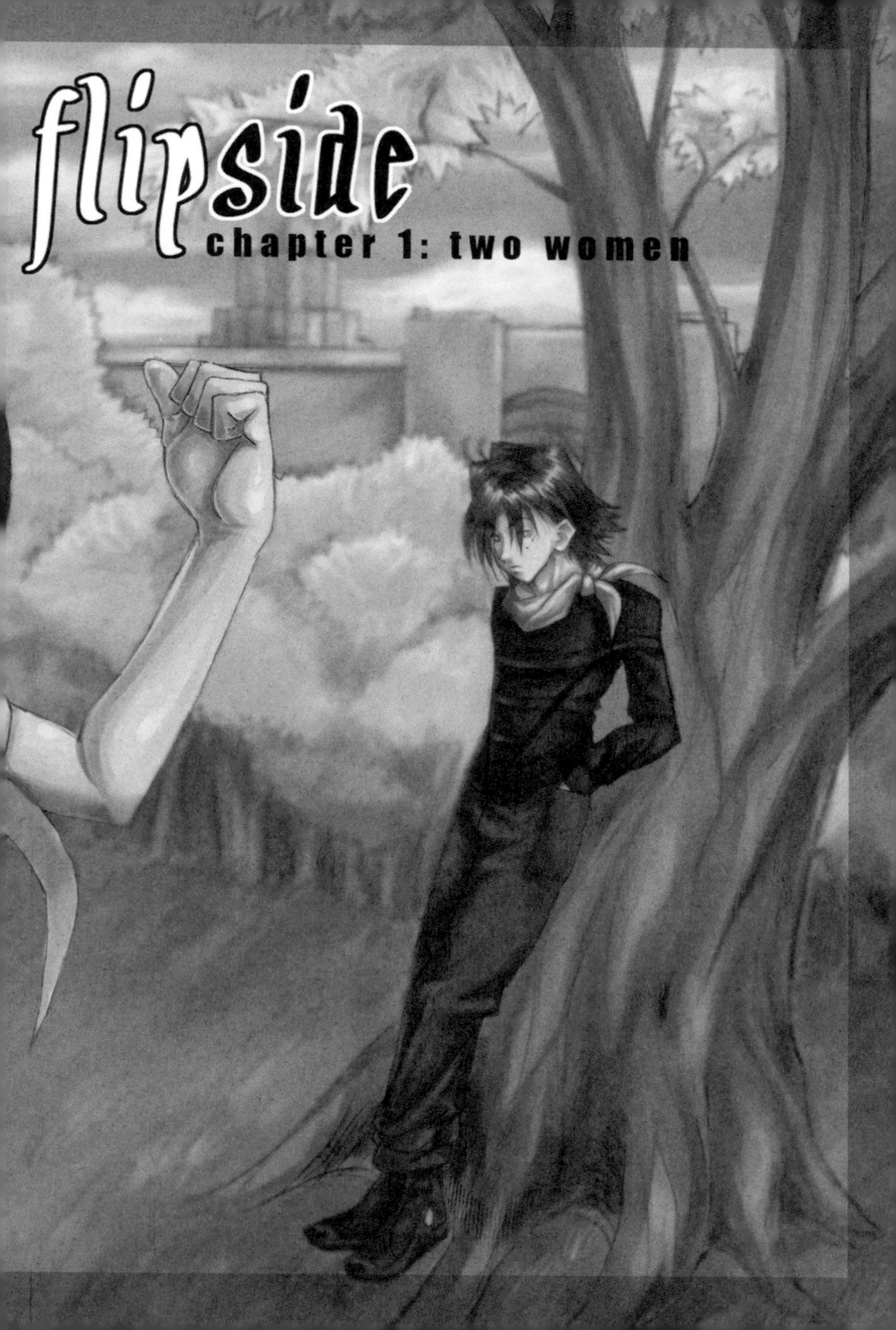
flipside
chapter 1: two women

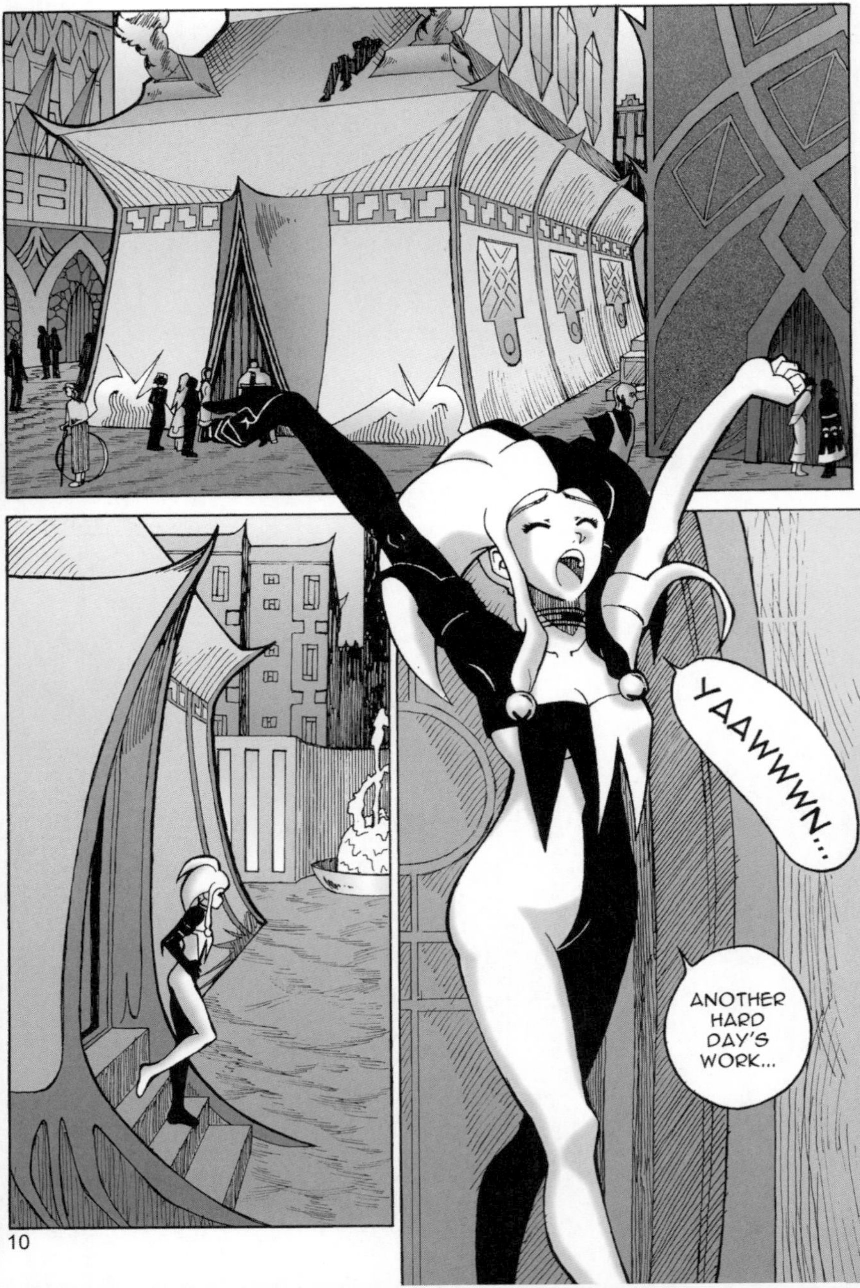
YAAWWWN...
ANOTHER HARD DAY'S WORK...

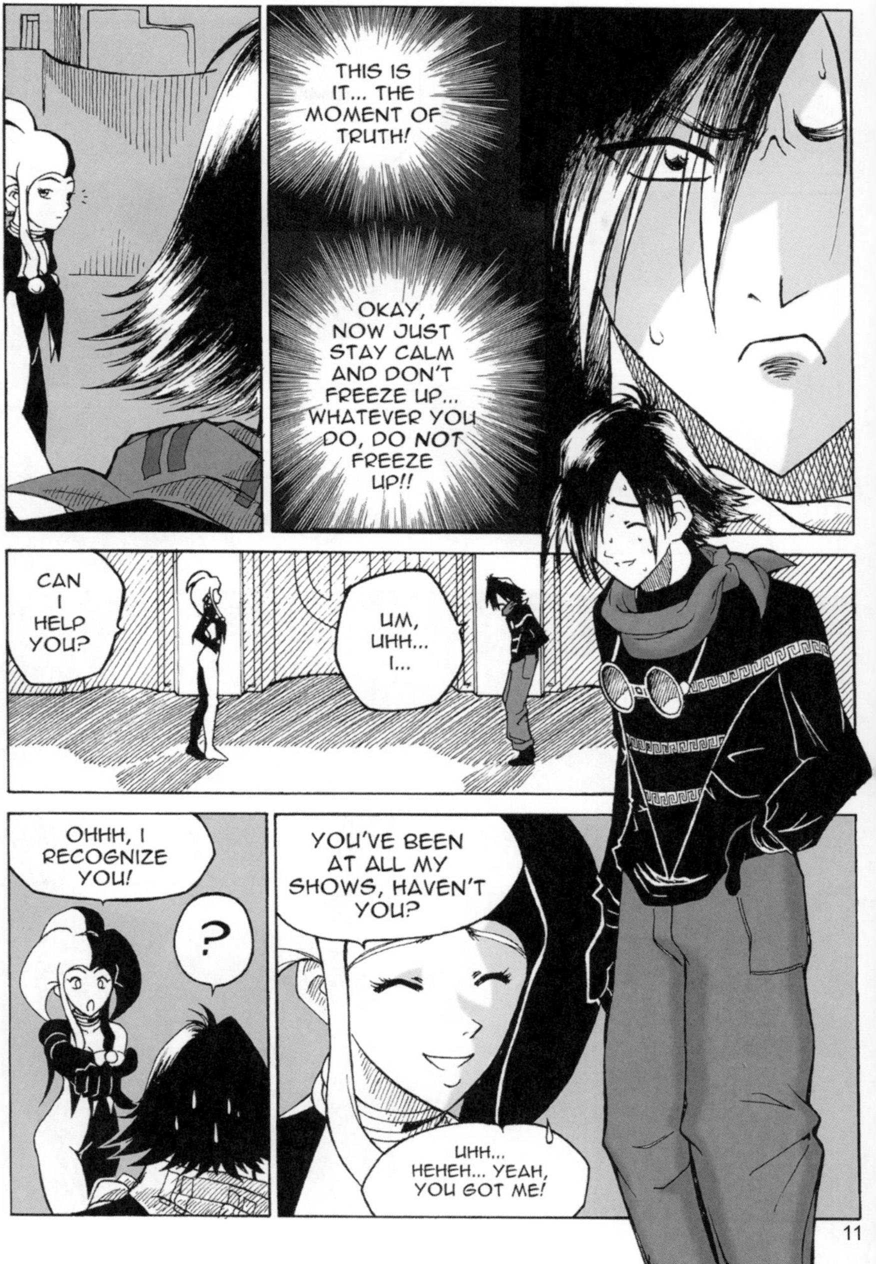
THIS IS IT... THE MOMENT OF TRUTH!
OKAY, NOW JUST STAY CALM AND DON'T FREEZE UP... WHATEVER YOU DO, DO NOT FREEZE UP!!
CAN I HELP YOU?
UM, UHH... I...
OHHH, I RECOGNIZE YOU!
?
YOU'VE BEEN AT ALL MY SHOWS, HAVEN'T YOU?
UHH... HEHEH... YEAH, YOU GOT ME!

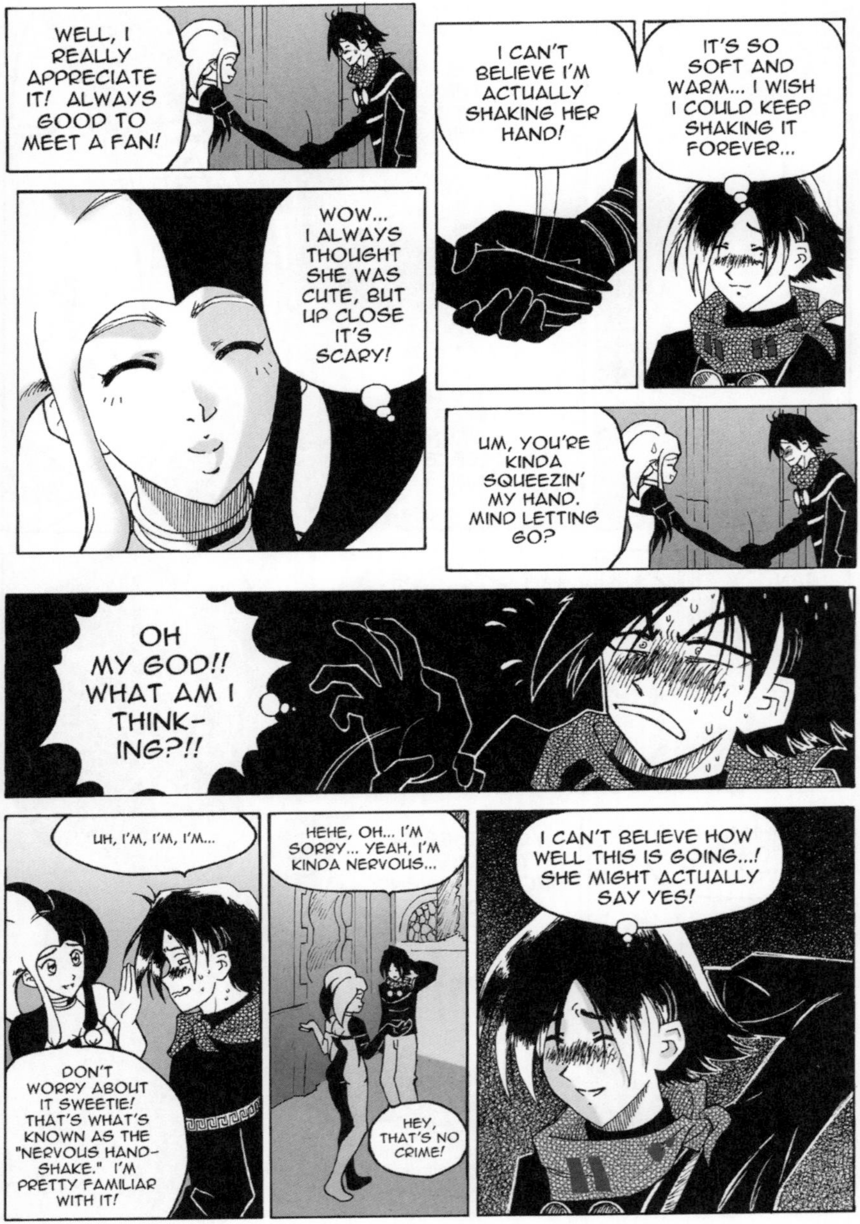

WELL, I REALLY APPRECIATE IT! ALWAYS GOOD TO MEET A FAN!
I CAN'T BELIEVE I'M ACTUALLY SHAKING HER HAND!
IT'S SO SOFT AND WARM... I WISH I COULD KEEP SHAKING IT FOREVER...
WOW... I ALWAYS THOUGHT SHE WAS CUTE, BUT UP CLOSE IT'S SCARY!
UM, YOU'RE KINDA SQUEEZIN' MY HAND. MIND LETTING GO?
OH MY GOD!! WHAT AM I THINK-ING?!!
UH, I'M, I'M, I'M...
DON'T WORRY ABOUT IT SWEETIE! THAT'S WHAT'S KNOWN AS THE "NERVOUS HAND-SHAKE." I'M PRETTY FAMILIAR WITH IT!
HEHE, OH... I'M SORRY... YEAH, I'M KINDA NERVOUS...
HEY, THAT'S NO CRIME!
I CAN'T BELIEVE HOW WELL THIS IS GOING...! SHE MIGHT ACTUALLY SAY YES!

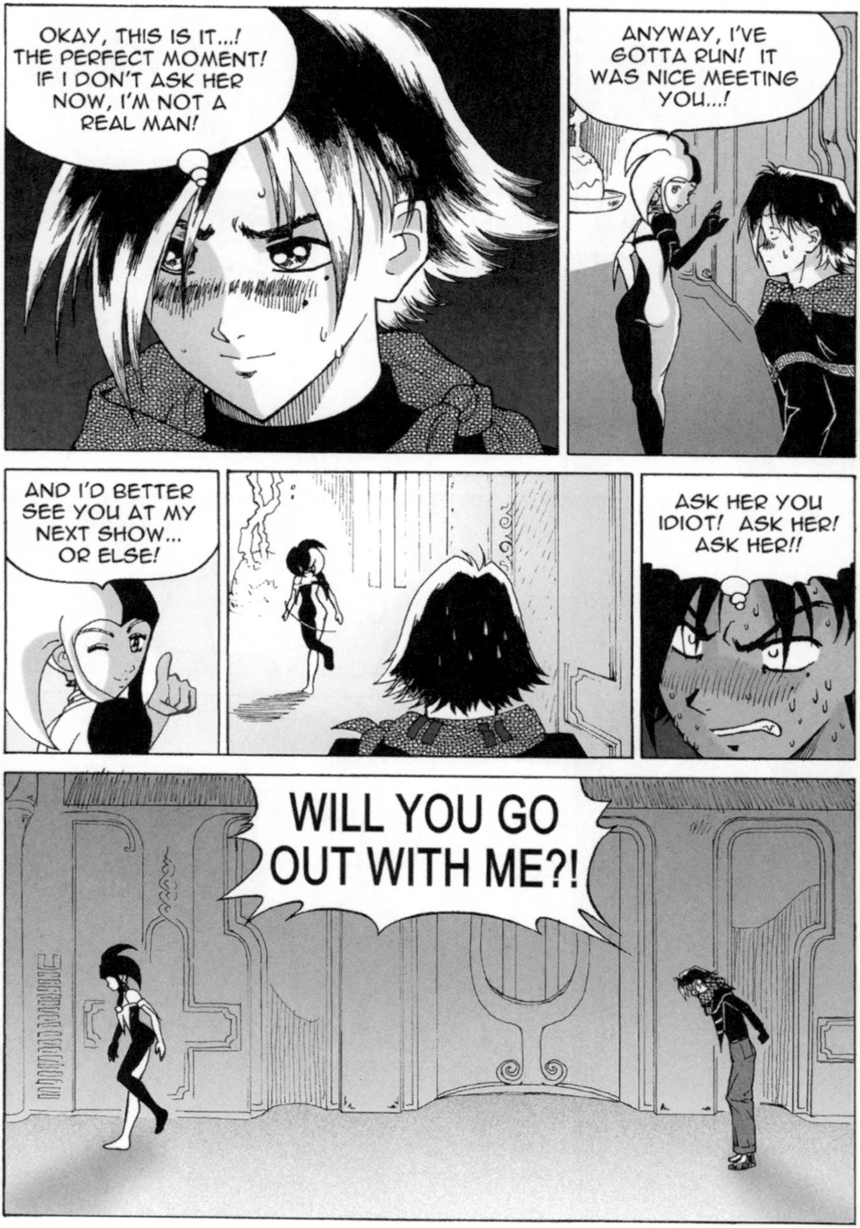
OKAY, THIS IS IT...! THE PERFECT MOMENT! IF I DON'T ASK HER NOW, I'M NOT A REAL MAN!
ANYWAY, I'VE GOTTA RUN! IT WAS NICE MEETING YOU...!
AND I'D BETTER SEE YOU AT MY NEXT SHOW... OR ELSE!
ASK HER YOU IDIOT! ASK HER! ASK HER!!
WILL YOU GO OUT WITH ME?!

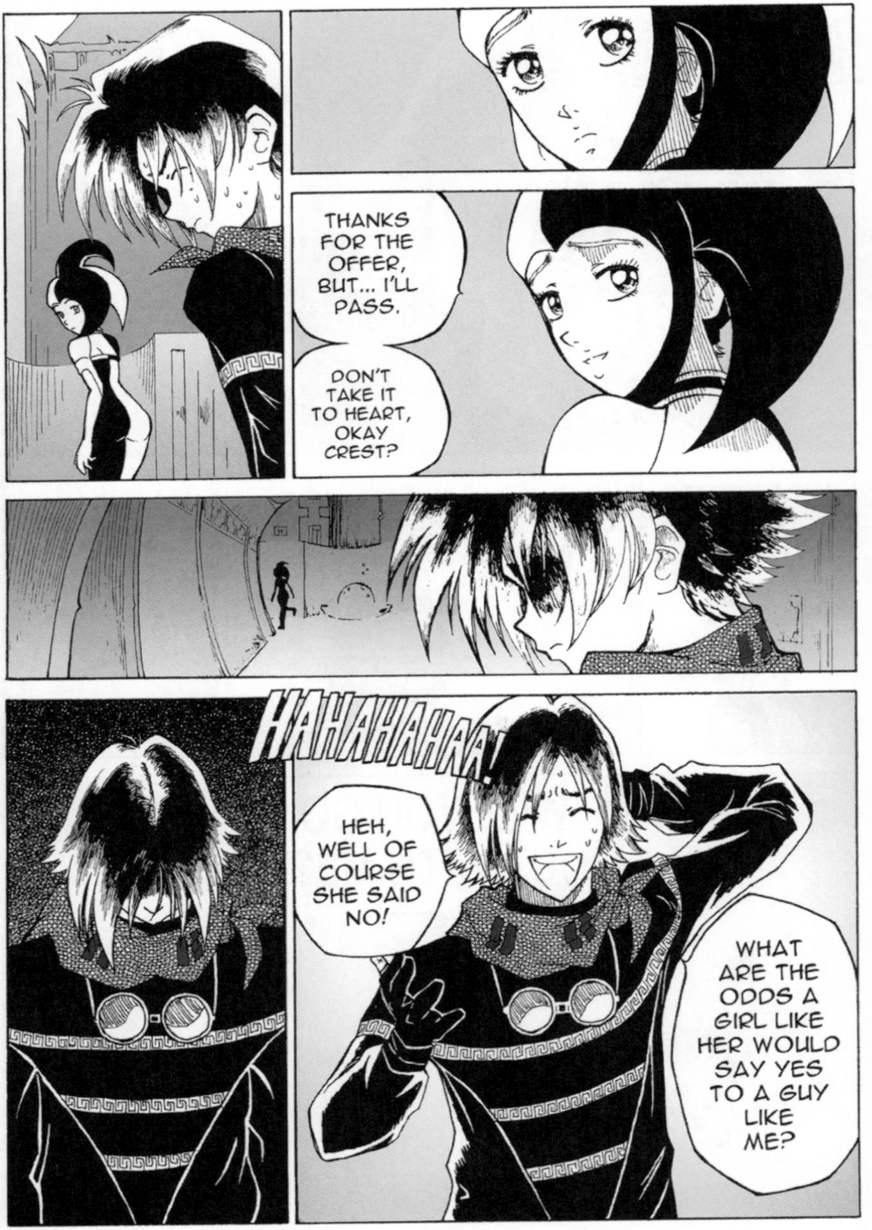
THANKS FOR THE OFFER, BUT... I'LL PASS.
DON'T TAKE IT TO HEART, OKAY CREST?
HAHAHAHAHAA!
HEH, WELL OF COURSE SHE SAID NO!
WHAT ARE THE ODDS A GIRL LIKE HER WOULD SAY YES TO A GUY LIKE ME?

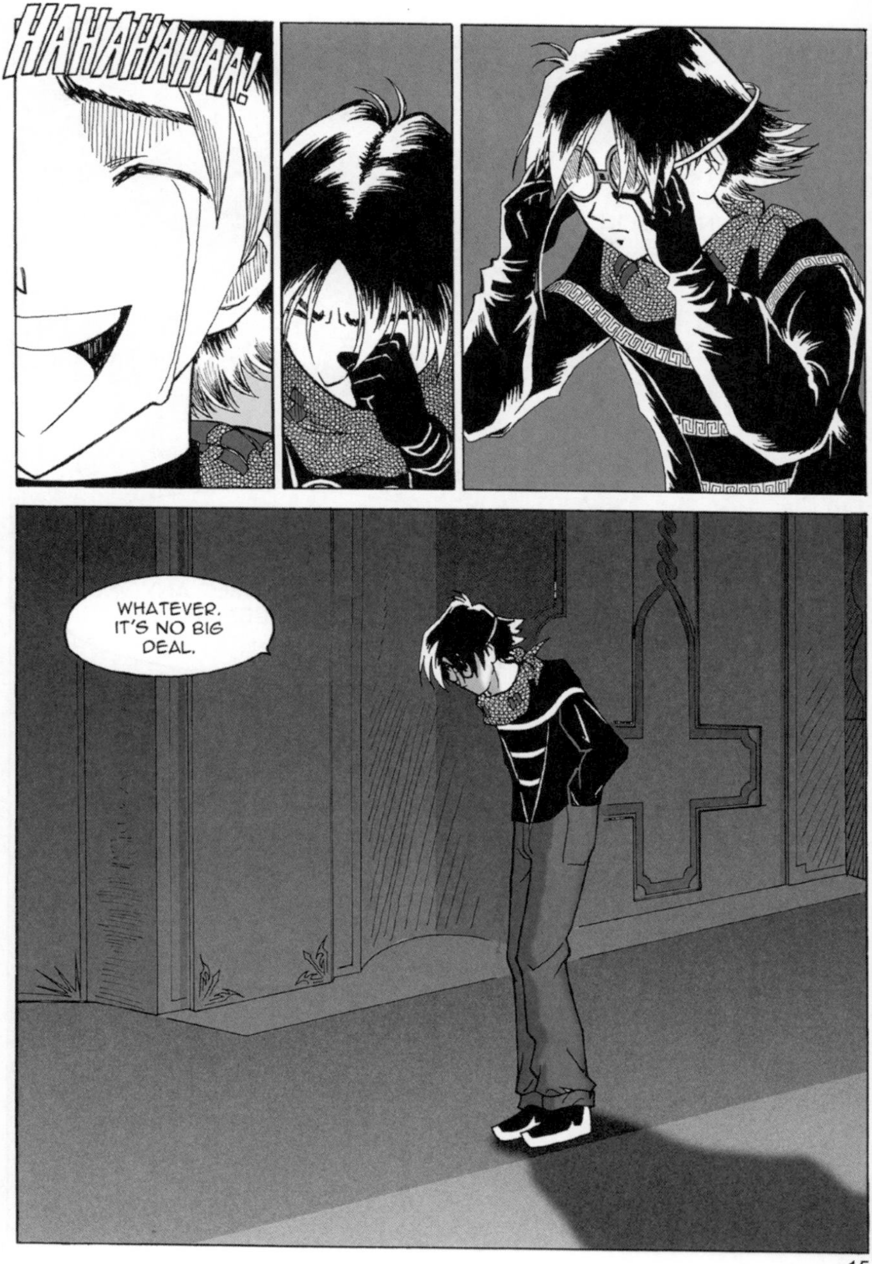
HAHAHAHAHAA!
WHATEVER. IT'S NO BIG DEAL.

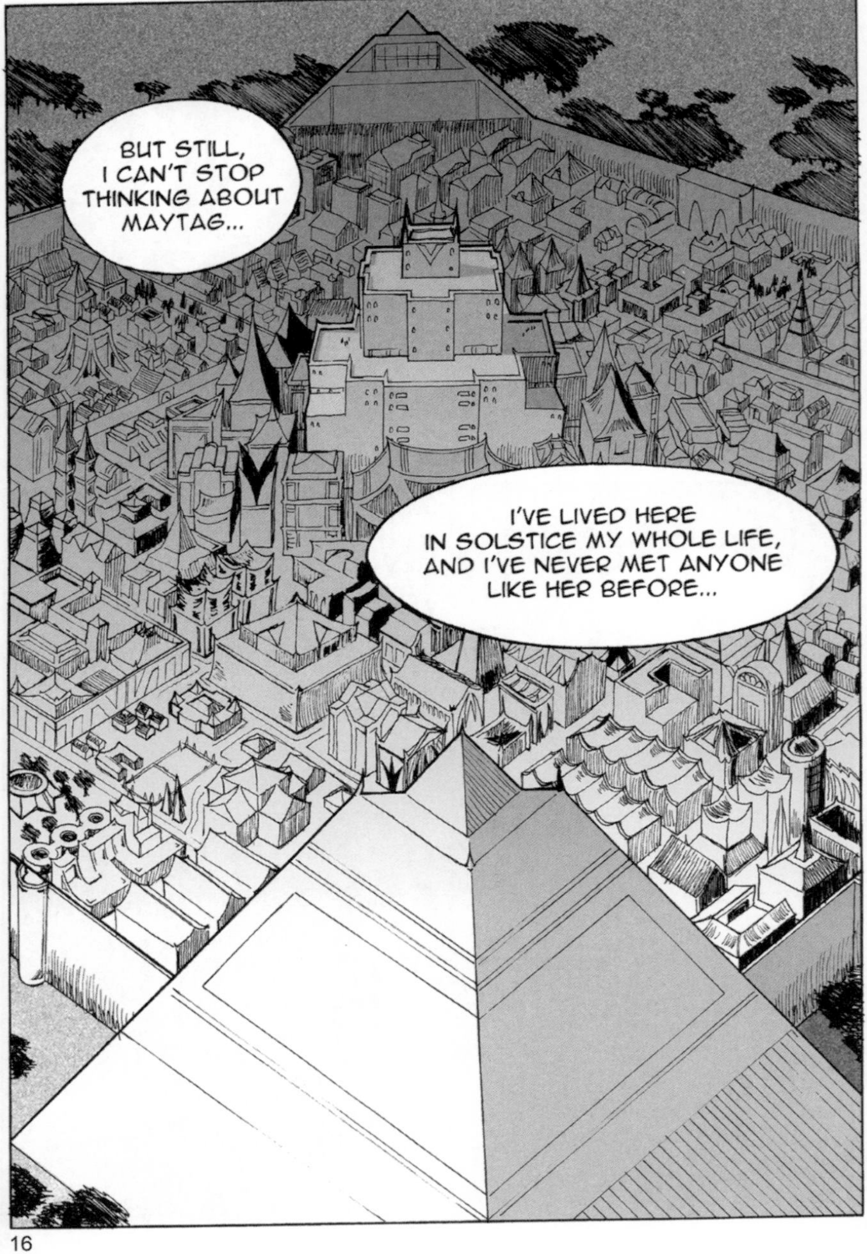
BUT STILL, I CAN'T STOP THINKING ABOUT MAYTAG...
I'VE LIVED HERE IN SOLSTICE MY WHOLE LIFE, AND I'VE NEVER MET ANYONE LIKE HER BEFORE...

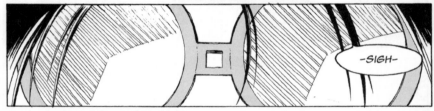

-SIGH-

WHERE YA BEEN, BOY? UP TO NO GOOD AGAIN?

NO SIR.

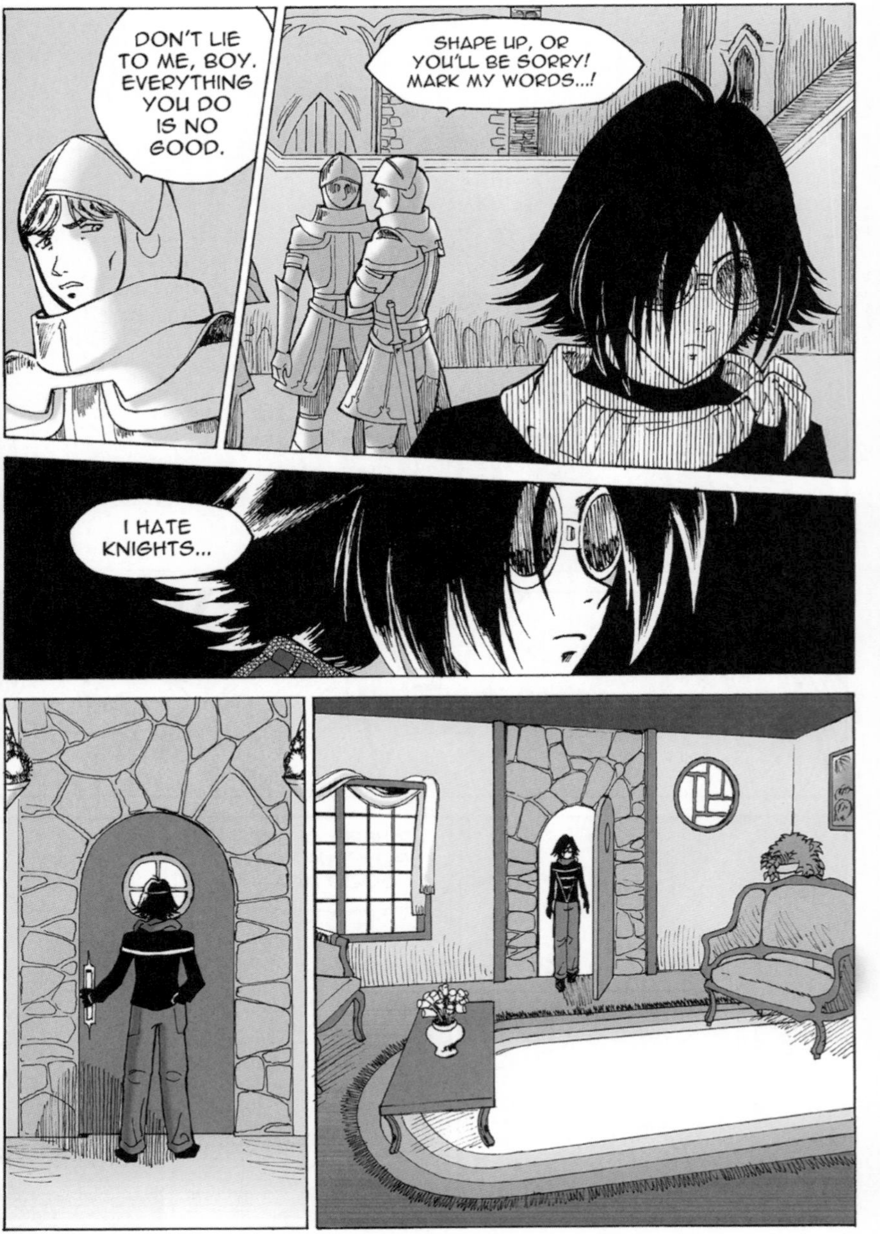
DON'T LIE TO ME, BOY. EVERYTHING YOU DO IS NO GOOD.
SHAPE UP, OR YOU'LL BE SORRY! MARK MY WORDS...!
I HATE KNIGHTS...

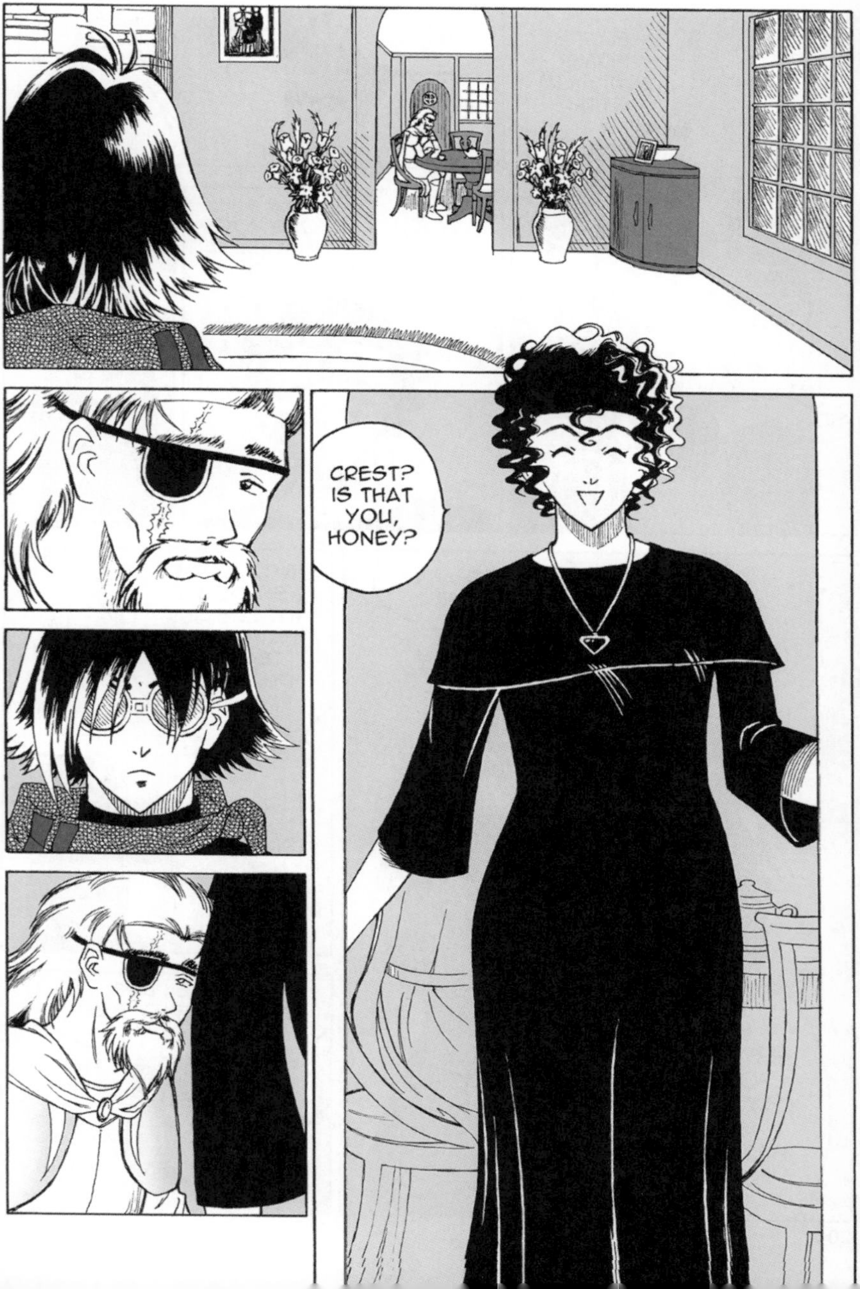
CREST? IS THAT YOU, HONEY?

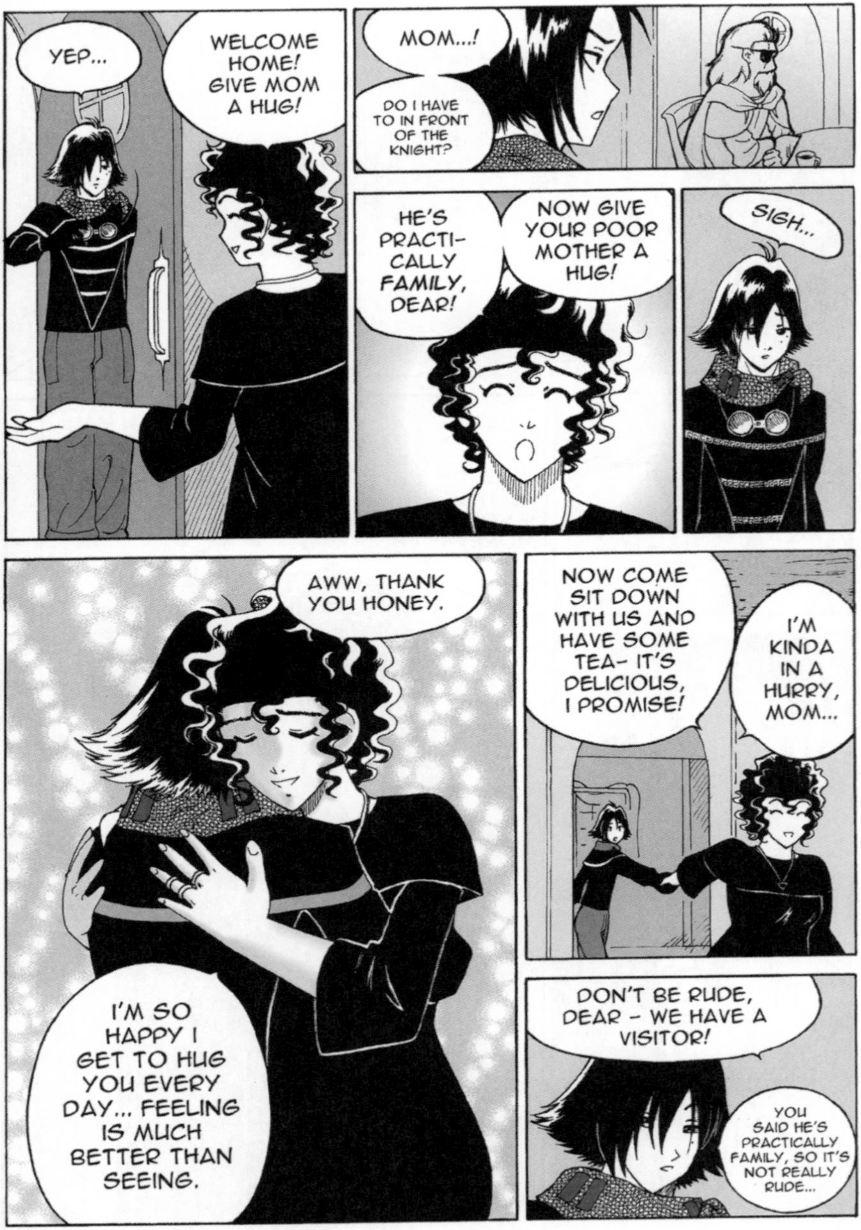

WELCOME HOME! GIVE MOM A HUG!
YEP...
MOM...!
DO I HAVE TO IN FRONT OF THE KNIGHT?
HE'S PRACTI-CALLY FAMILY, DEAR!
NOW GIVE YOUR POOR MOTHER A HUG!
SIGH...
AWW, THANK YOU HONEY.
I'M SO HAPPY I GET TO HUG YOU EVERY DAY... FEELING IS MUCH BETTER THAN SEEING.
NOW COME SIT DOWN WITH US AND HAVE SOME TEA– IT'S DELICIOUS, I PROMISE!
I'M KINDA IN A HURRY, MOM...
DON'T BE RUDE, DEAR – WE HAVE A VISITOR!
YOU SAID HE'S PRACTICALLY FAMILY, SO IT'S NOT REALLY RUDE...

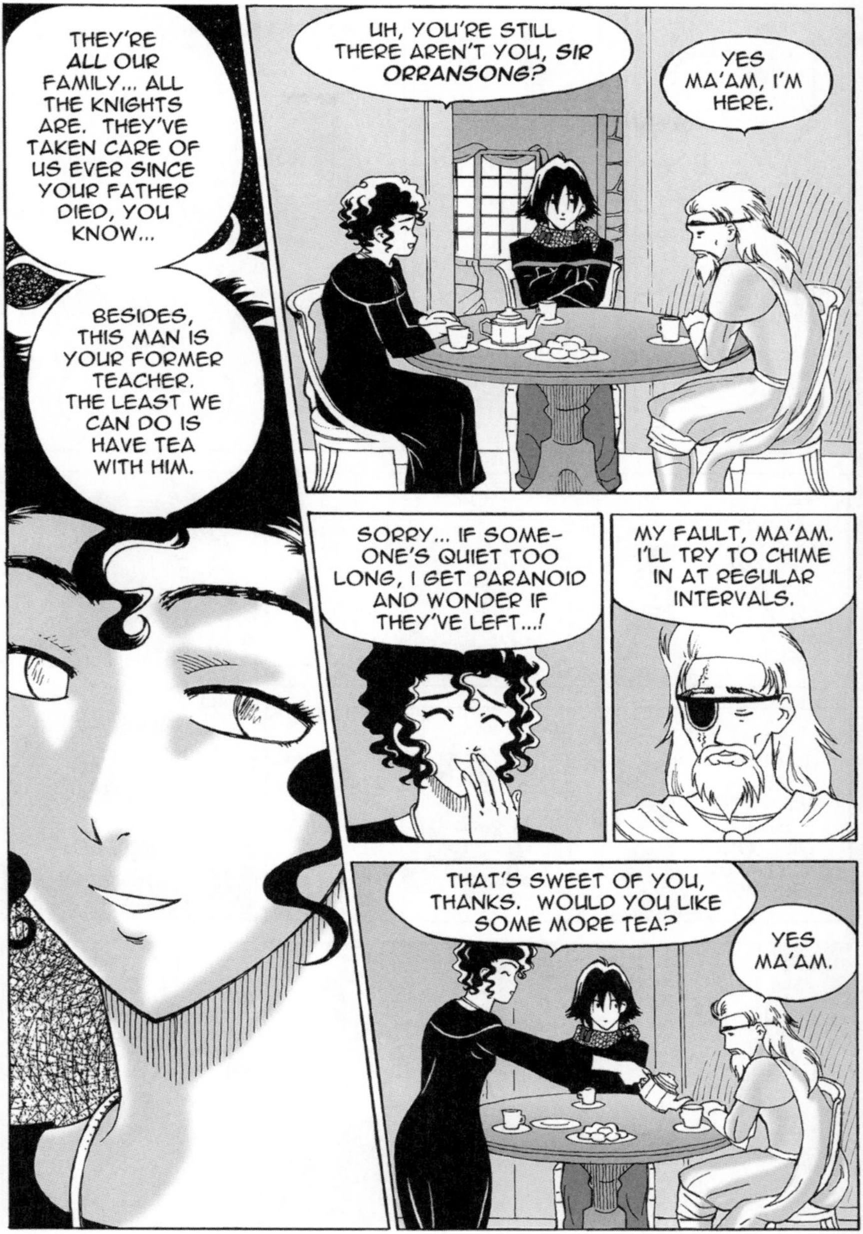
THEY'RE ALL OUR FAMILY... ALL THE KNIGHTS ARE. THEY'VE TAKEN CARE OF US EVER SINCE YOUR FATHER DIED, YOU KNOW...
BESIDES, THIS MAN IS YOUR FORMER TEACHER. THE LEAST WE CAN DO IS HAVE TEA WITH HIM.
UH, YOU'RE STILL THERE AREN'T YOU, SIR ORRANSONG?
YES MA'AM, I'M HERE.
SORRY... IF SOME-ONE'S QUIET TOO LONG, I GET PARANOID AND WONDER IF THEY'VE LEFT...!
MY FAULT, MA'AM. I'LL TRY TO CHIME IN AT REGULAR INTERVALS.
THAT'S SWEET OF YOU, THANKS. WOULD YOU LIKE SOME MORE TEA?
YES MA'AM.

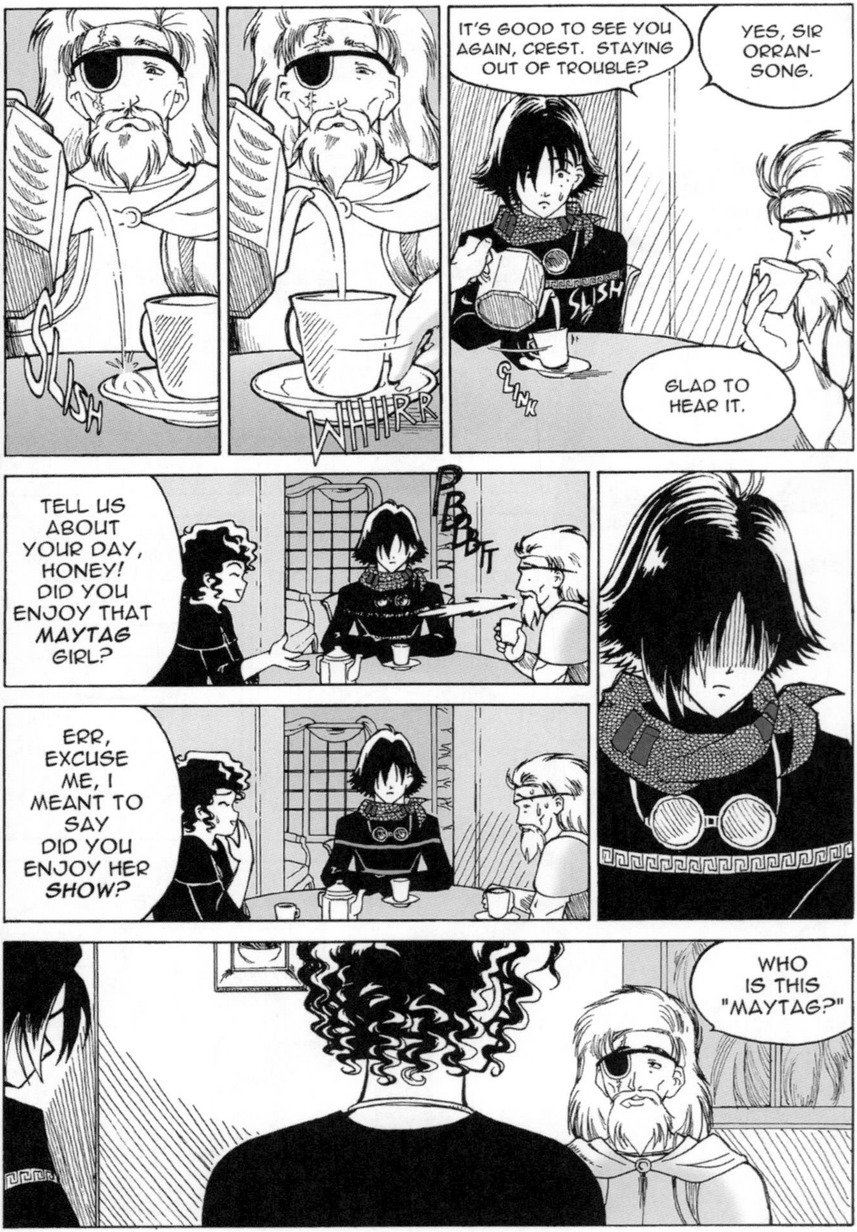
SLISH
WHIRRR
IT'S GOOD TO SEE YOU AGAIN, CREST. STAYING OUT OF TROUBLE?
YES, SIR ORRAN-SONG.
SLISH
CLINK
GLAD TO HEAR IT.
TELL US ABOUT YOUR DAY, HONEY! DID YOU ENJOY THAT MAYTAG GIRL?
PBBBFT
ERR, EXCUSE ME, I MEANT TO SAY DID YOU ENJOY HER SHOW?
WHO IS THIS "MAYTAG?"

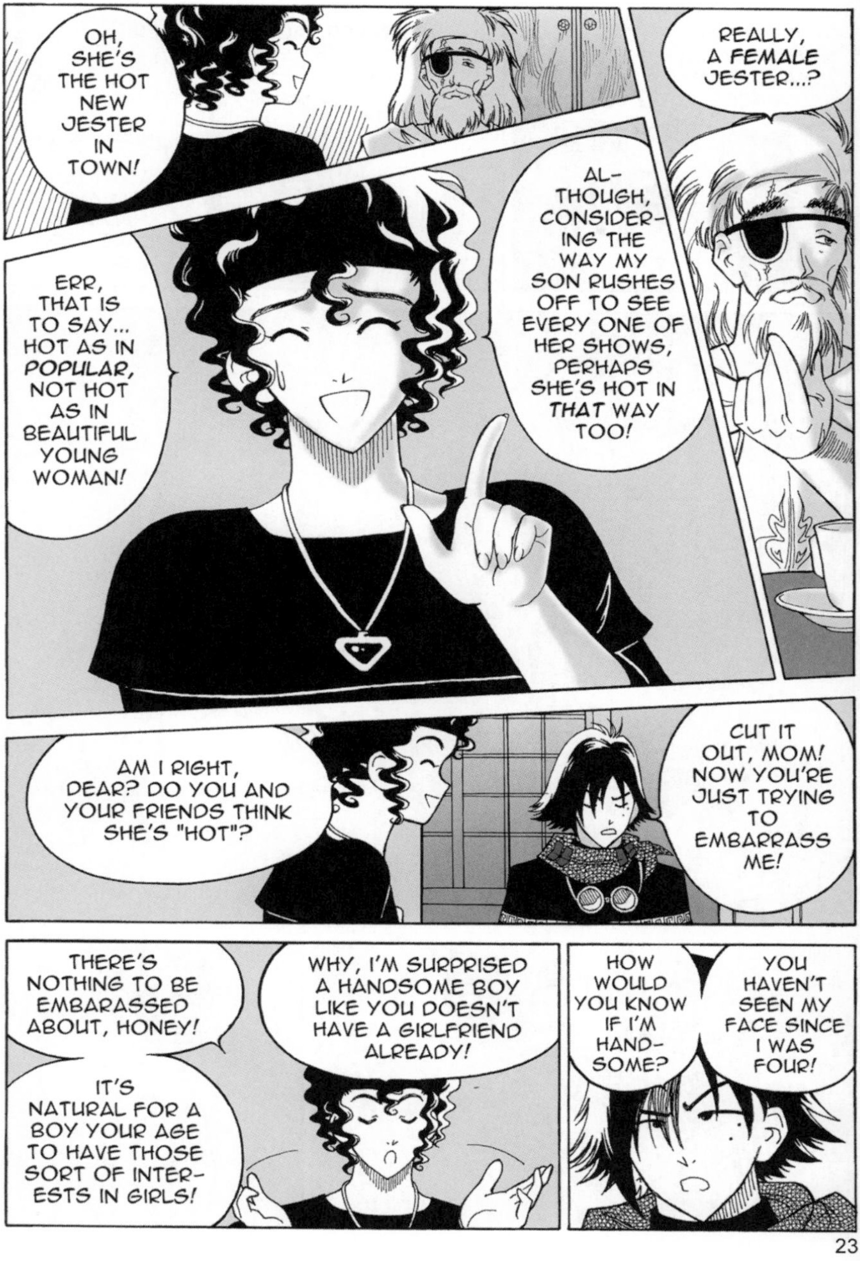

OH, SHE'S THE HOT NEW JESTER IN TOWN!
REALLY, A *FEMALE* JESTER...?
ERR, THAT IS TO SAY... HOT AS IN *POPULAR*, NOT HOT AS IN BEAUTIFUL YOUNG WOMAN!
AL-THOUGH, CONSIDER-ING THE WAY MY SON RUSHES OFF TO SEE EVERY ONE OF HER SHOWS, PERHAPS SHE'S HOT IN *THAT* WAY TOO!
AM I RIGHT, DEAR? DO YOU AND YOUR FRIENDS THINK SHE'S "HOT"?
CUT IT OUT, MOM! NOW YOU'RE JUST TRYING TO EMBARRASS ME!
THERE'S NOTHING TO BE EMBARASSED ABOUT, HONEY!
WHY, I'M SURPRISED A HANDSOME BOY LIKE YOU DOESN'T HAVE A GIRLFRIEND ALREADY!
IT'S NATURAL FOR A BOY YOUR AGE TO HAVE THOSE SORT OF INTER-ESTS IN GIRLS!
HOW WOULD YOU KNOW IF I'M HAND-SOME?
YOU HAVEN'T SEEN MY FACE SINCE I WAS FOUR!

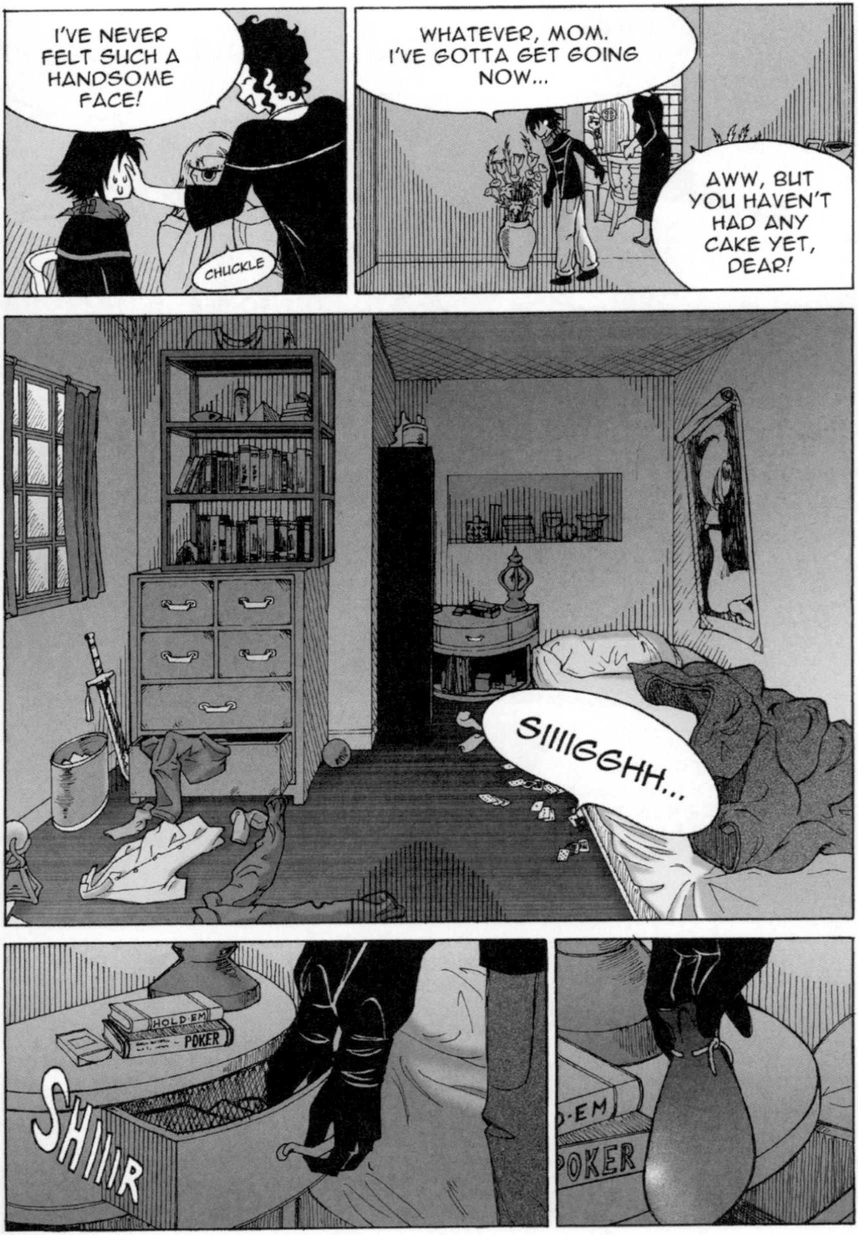
I'VE NEVER FELT SUCH A HANDSOME FACE!
CHUCKLE
WHATEVER, MOM. I'VE GOTTA GET GOING NOW...
AWW, BUT YOU HAVEN'T HAD ANY CAKE YET, DEAR!
SIIIIGGHH...
HOLD·EM
POKER
SHIIIR
D·EM
POKER

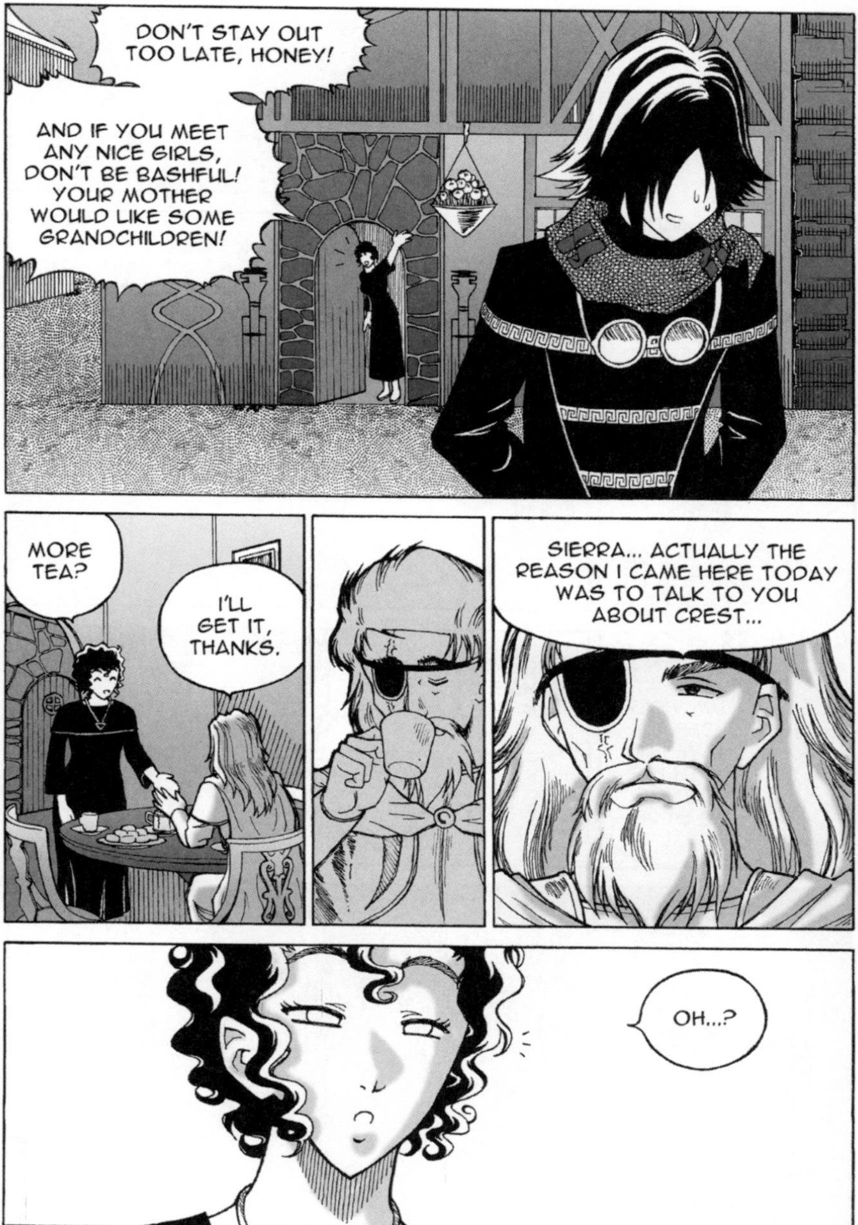
DON'T STAY OUT TOO LATE, HONEY!
AND IF YOU MEET ANY NICE GIRLS, DON'T BE BASHFUL! YOUR MOTHER WOULD LIKE SOME GRANDCHILDREN!
MORE TEA?
I'LL GET IT, THANKS.
SIERRA... ACTUALLY THE REASON I CAME HERE TODAY WAS TO TALK TO YOU ABOUT CREST...
OH...?

DO YOU HAPPEN TO KNOW WHERE HE WAS RUSHING OFF TO, JUST NOW?

I SEE.

KLINK

I'M CONCERNED HE MIGHT BE HANGING AROUND WITH THE WRONG FRIENDS...

WHAT DO YOU MEAN?

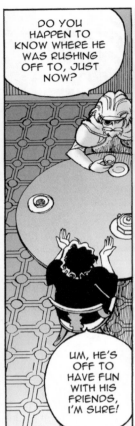

UM, HE'S OFF TO HAVE FUN WITH HIS FRIENDS, I'M SURE!

WE BOTH KNOW HE HAS A HISTORY OF STEALING...

BUT THAT WAS YEARS AGO...!

....
....

TRUE. BUT I'VE HEARD A RUMOR... THAT HE'S BEEN SEEN HANGING OUT IN "SICKLE ALLEY"...

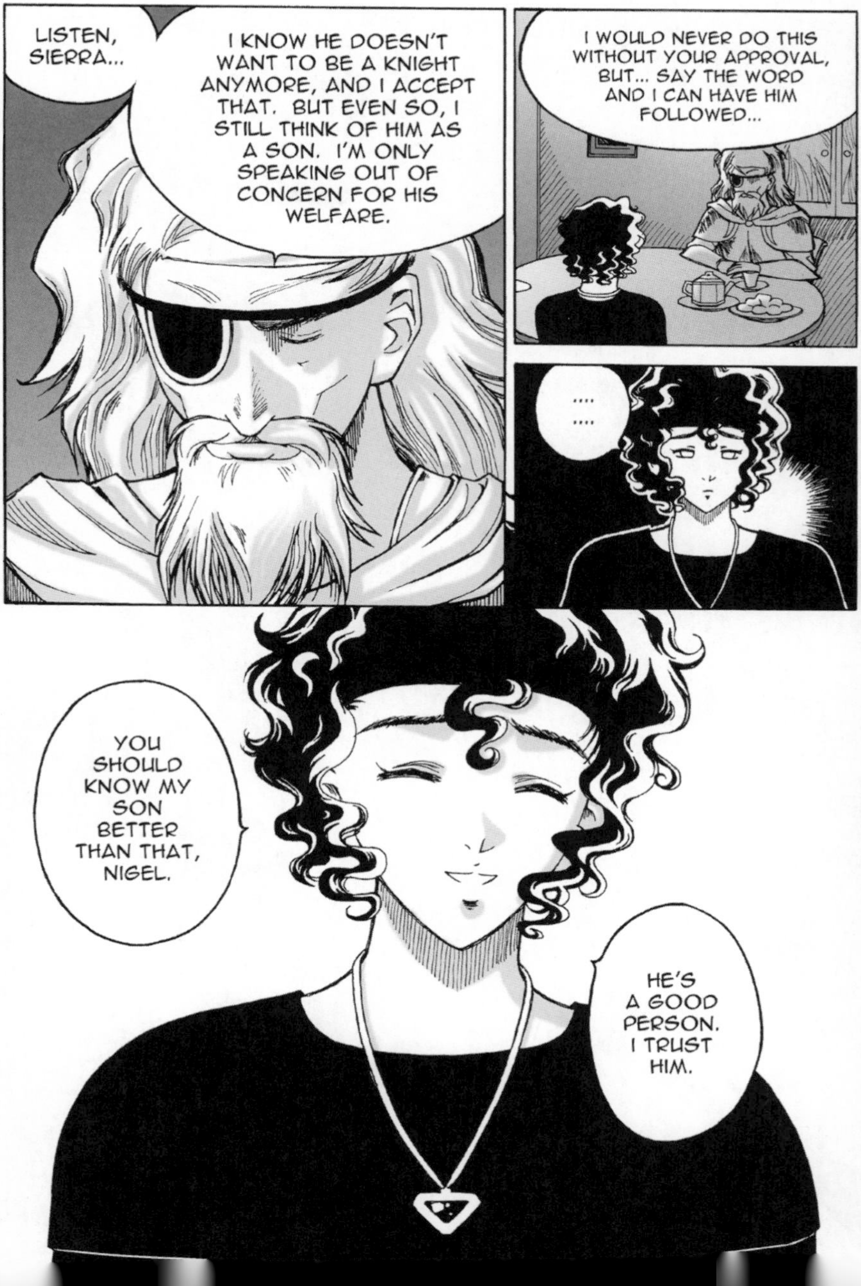
LISTEN, SIERRA...
I KNOW HE DOESN'T WANT TO BE A KNIGHT ANYMORE, AND I ACCEPT THAT. BUT EVEN SO, I STILL THINK OF HIM AS A SON. I'M ONLY SPEAKING OUT OF CONCERN FOR HIS WELFARE.
I WOULD NEVER DO THIS WITHOUT YOUR APPROVAL, BUT... SAY THE WORD AND I CAN HAVE HIM FOLLOWED...
....
YOU SHOULD KNOW MY SON BETTER THAN THAT, NIGEL.
HE'S A GOOD PERSON. I TRUST HIM.

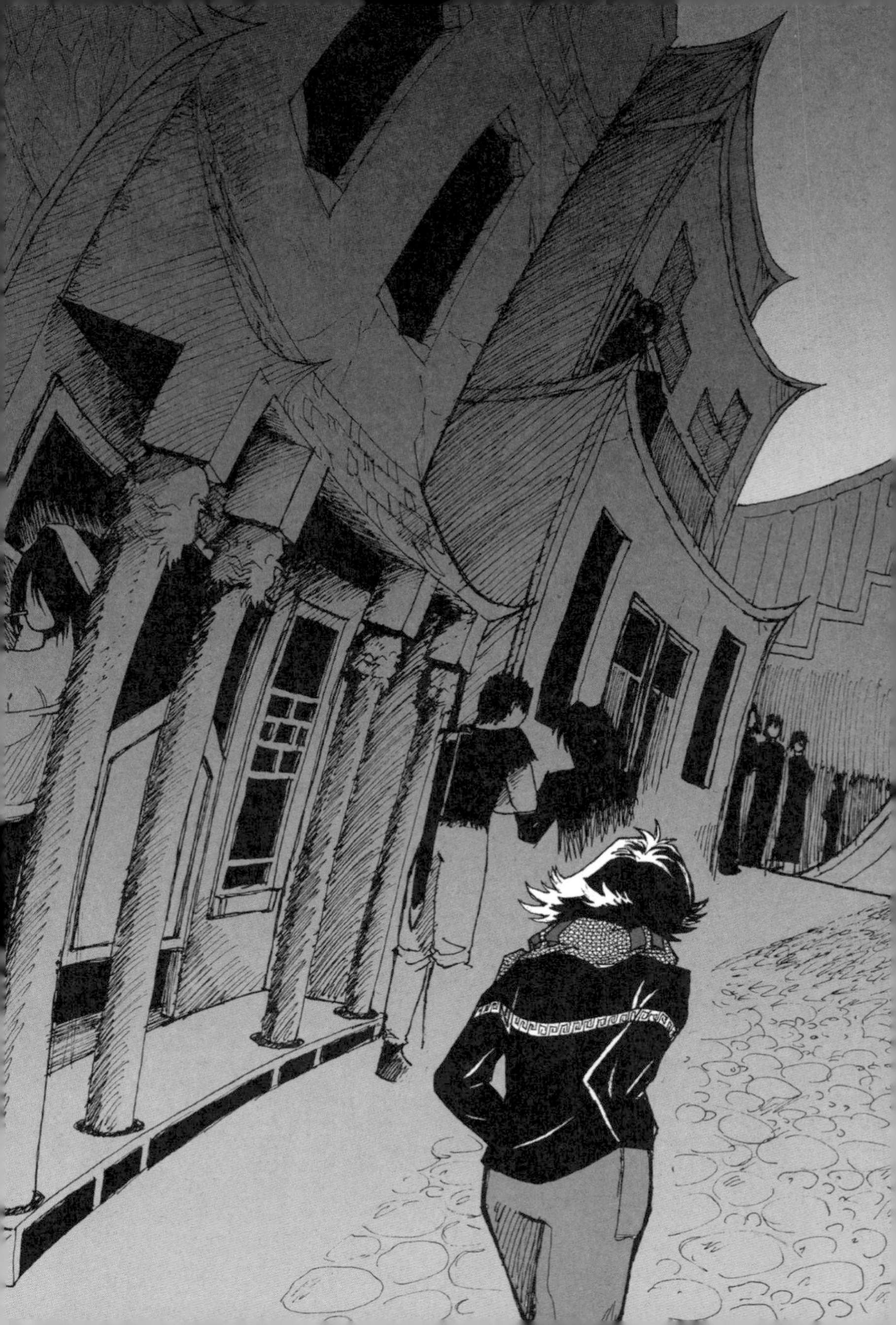

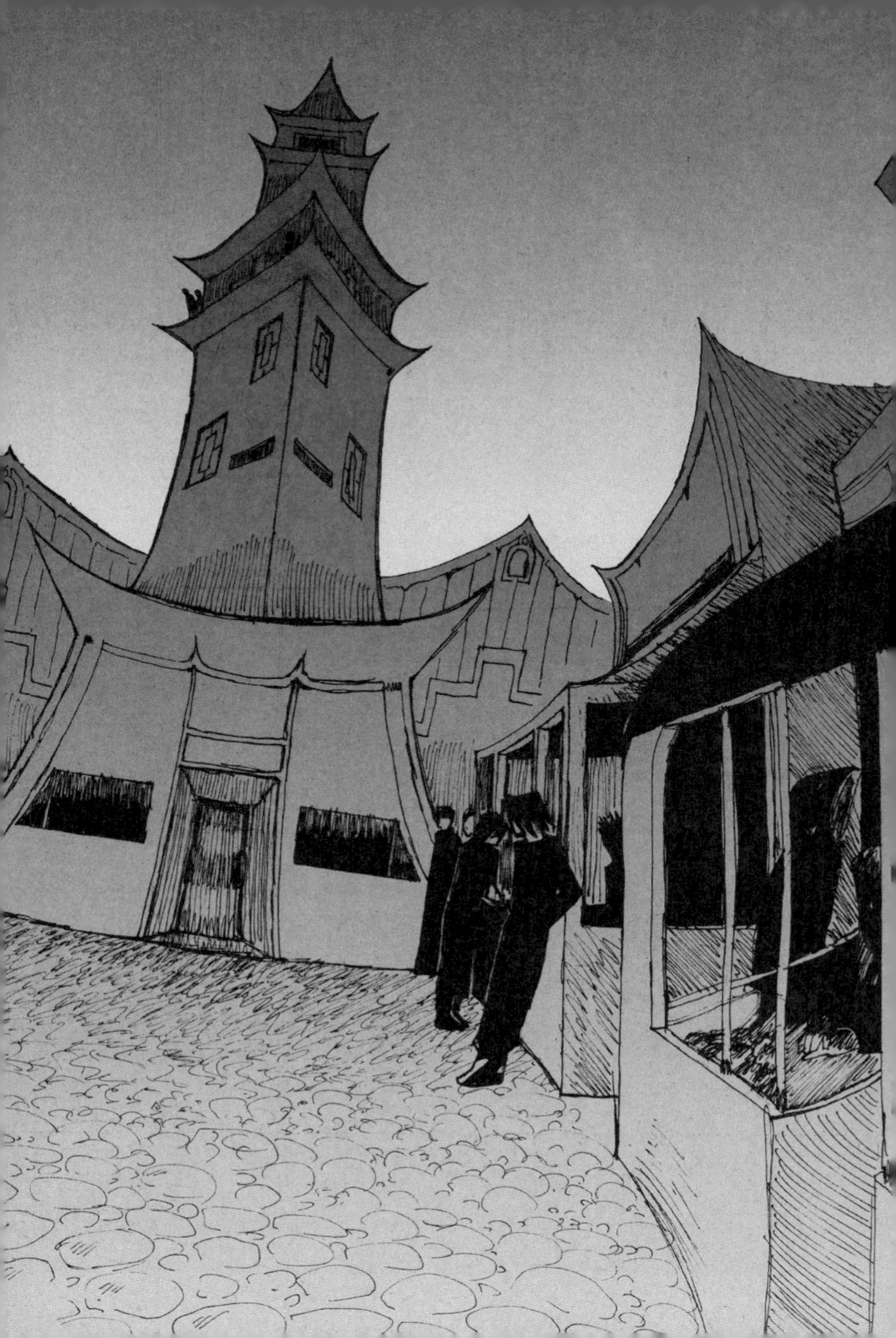

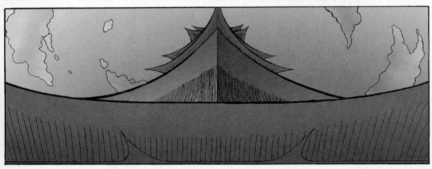

NOK
NOK

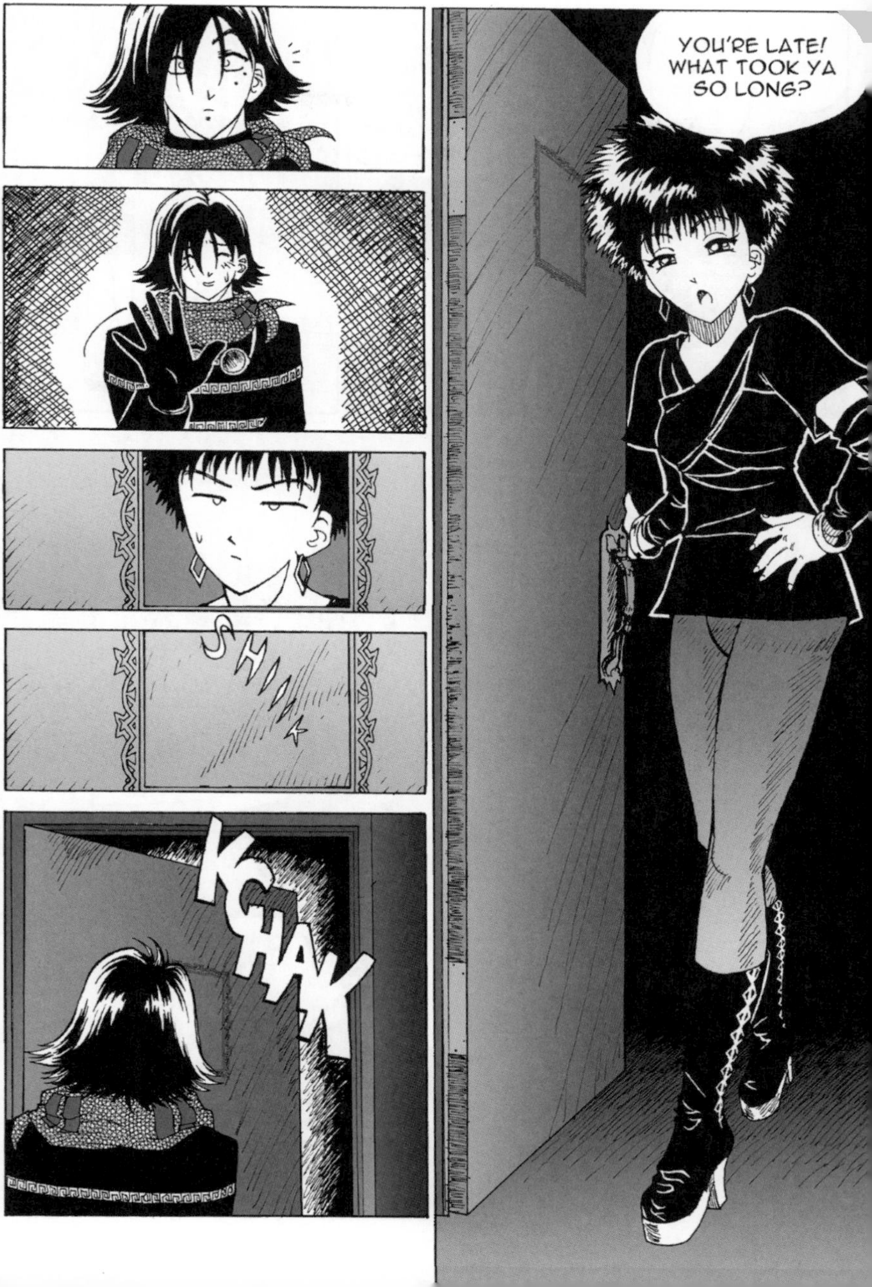
SHIIIK
KCHAK
YOU'RE LATE! WHAT TOOK YA SO LONG?

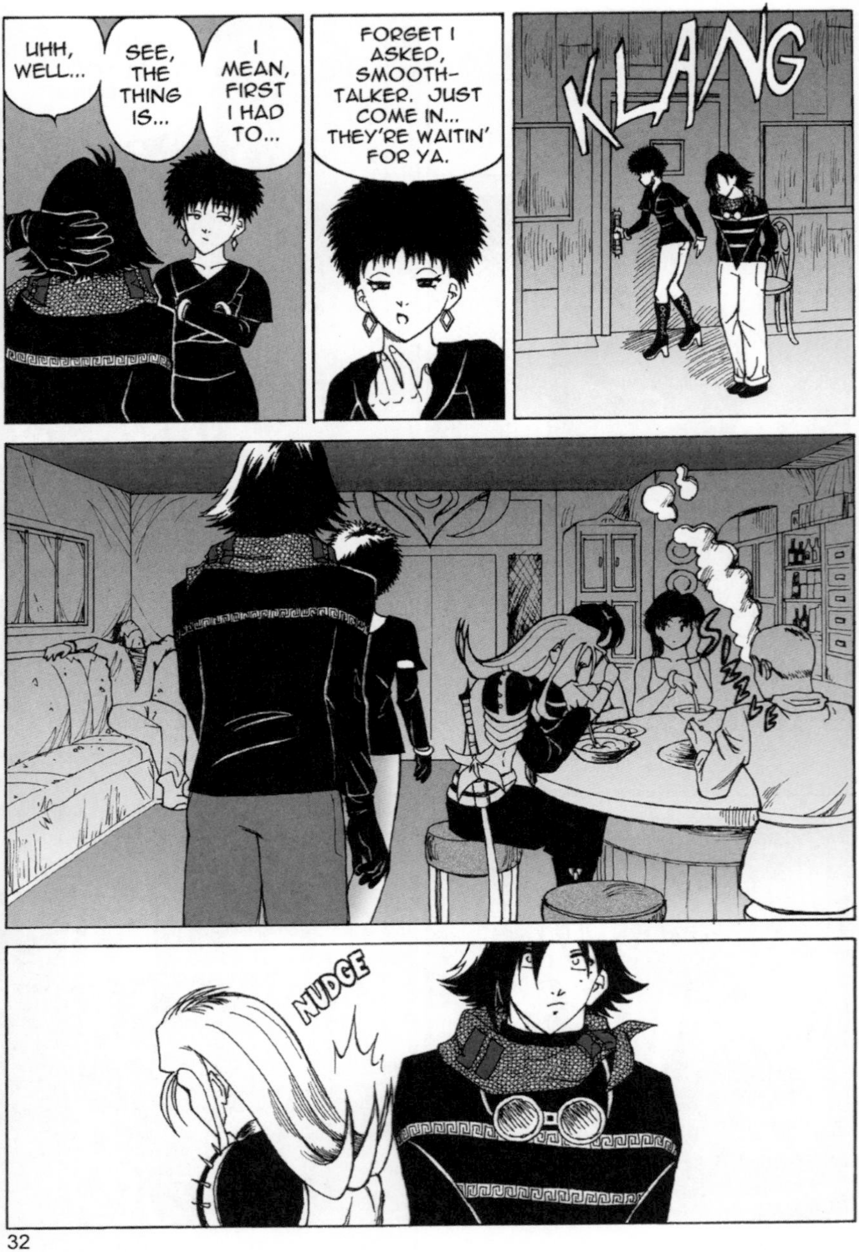
UHH, WELL...
SEE, THE THING IS...
I MEAN, FIRST I HAD TO...
FORGET I ASKED, SMOOTH-TALKER. JUST COME IN... THEY'RE WAITIN' FOR YA.
KLANG
NUDGE

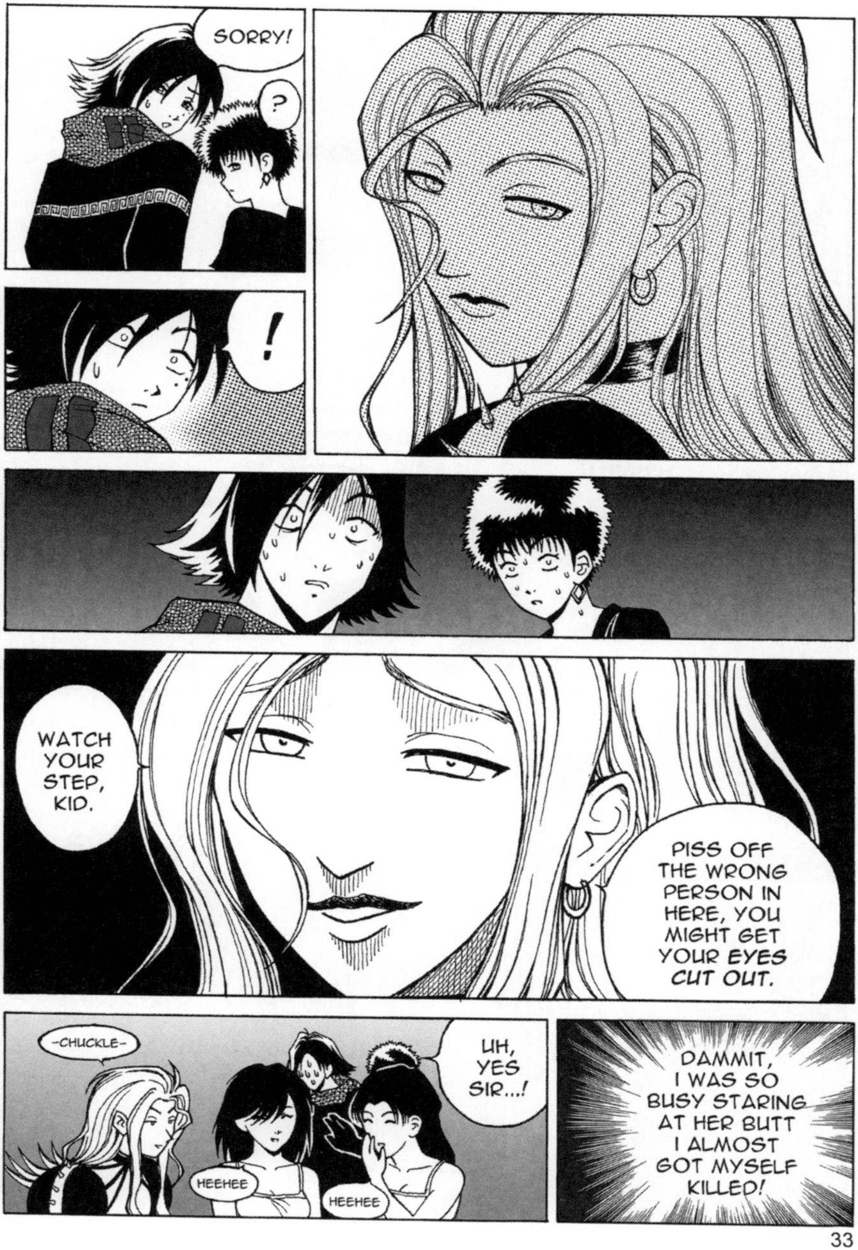
SORRY!
?
!
WATCH YOUR STEP, KID.
PISS OFF THE WRONG PERSON IN HERE, YOU MIGHT GET YOUR EYES CUT OUT.
-CHUCKLE-
UH, YES SIR...!
HEEHEE
HEEHEE
DAMMIT, I WAS SO BUSY STARING AT HER BUTT I ALMOST GOT MYSELF KILLED!

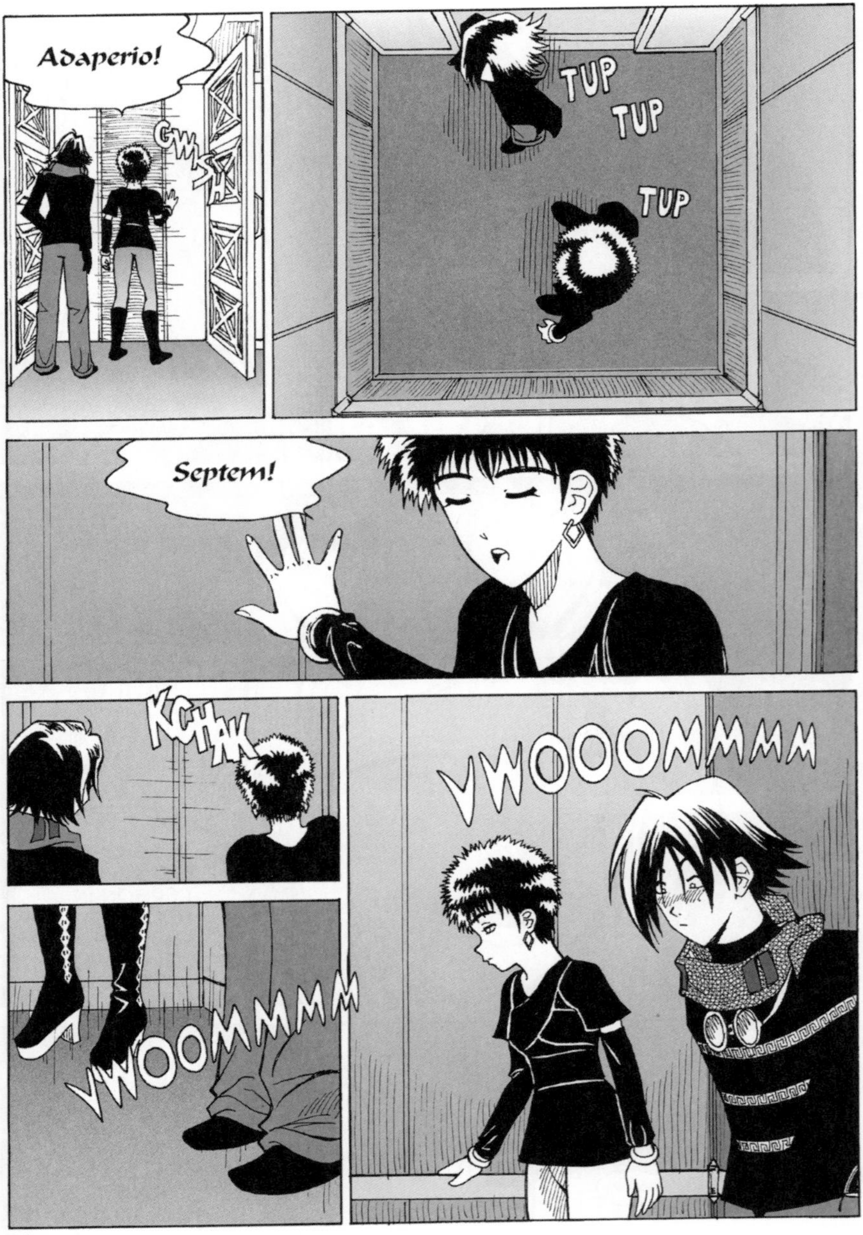
Adaperio!
GWISH
TUP
TUP
TUP
Septem!
KCHAK
VWOOOMMMM
VWOOMMMM

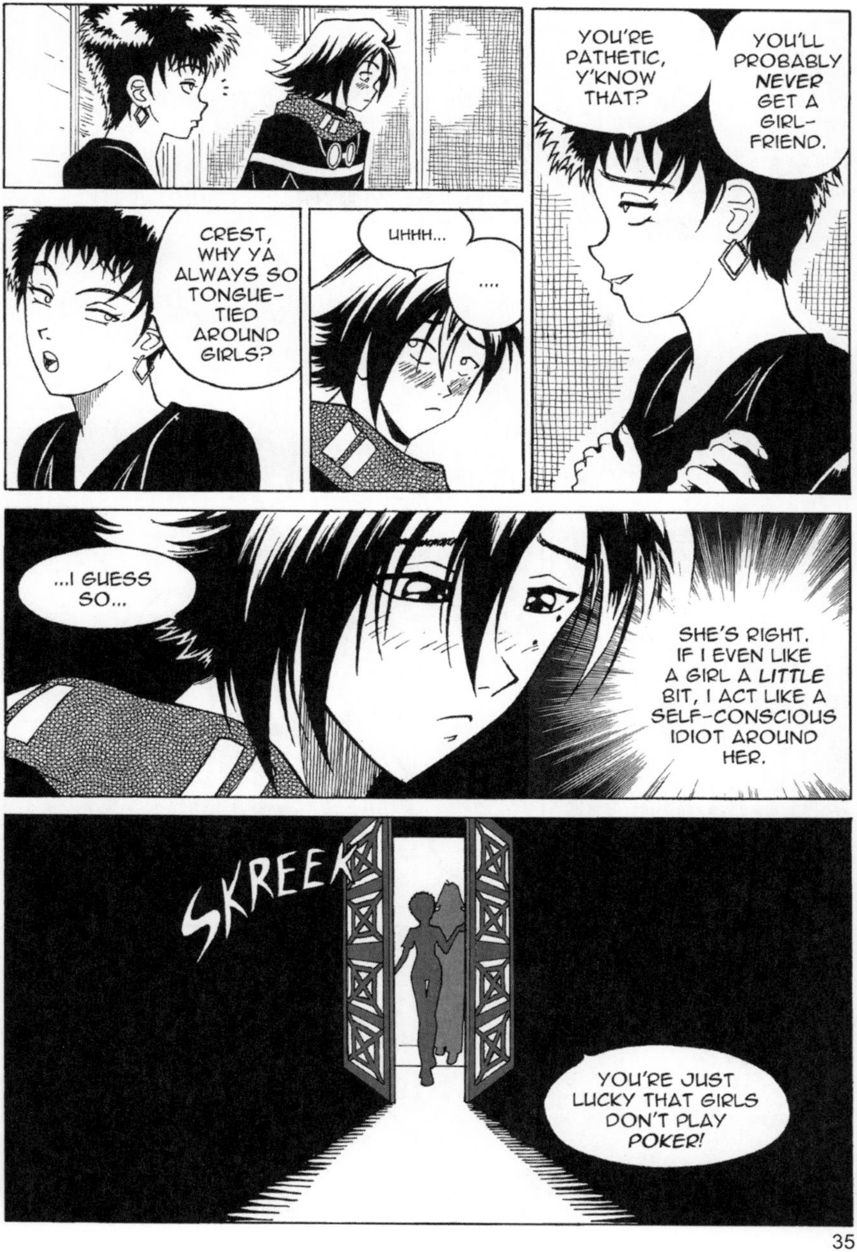
YOU'RE PATHETIC, Y'KNOW THAT?
YOU'LL PROBABLY NEVER GET A GIRL-FRIEND.
CREST, WHY YA ALWAYS SO TONGUE-TIED AROUND GIRLS?
UHHH...
....
...I GUESS SO...
SHE'S RIGHT. IF I EVEN LIKE A GIRL A LITTLE BIT, I ACT LIKE A SELF-CONSCIOUS IDIOT AROUND HER.
SKREEK
YOU'RE JUST LUCKY THAT GIRLS DON'T PLAY POKER!

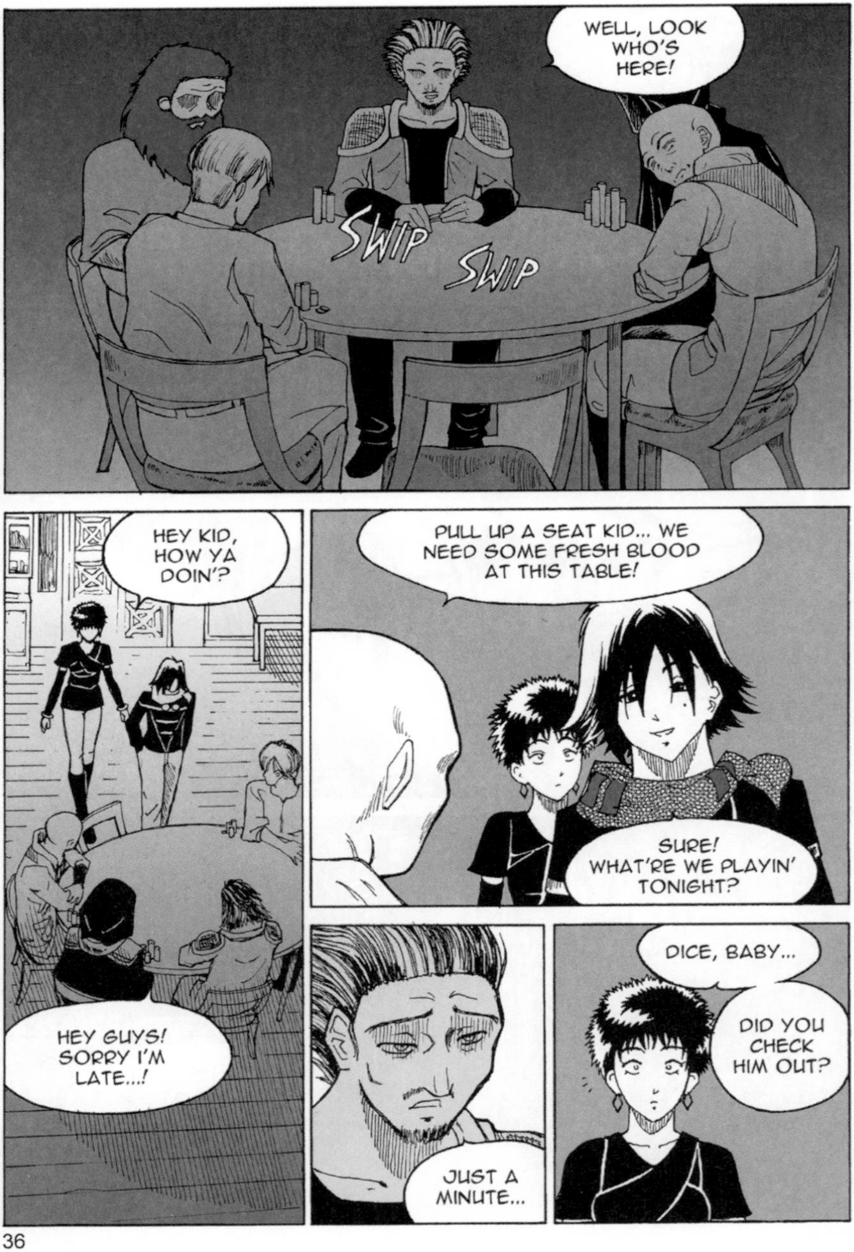
WELL, LOOK WHO'S HERE!
SWIP
SWIP
HEY KID, HOW YA DOIN'?
HEY GUYS! SORRY I'M LATE...!
PULL UP A SEAT KID... WE NEED SOME FRESH BLOOD AT THIS TABLE!
SURE! WHAT'RE WE PLAYIN' TONIGHT?
JUST A MINUTE...
DICE, BABY...
DID YOU CHECK HIM OUT?

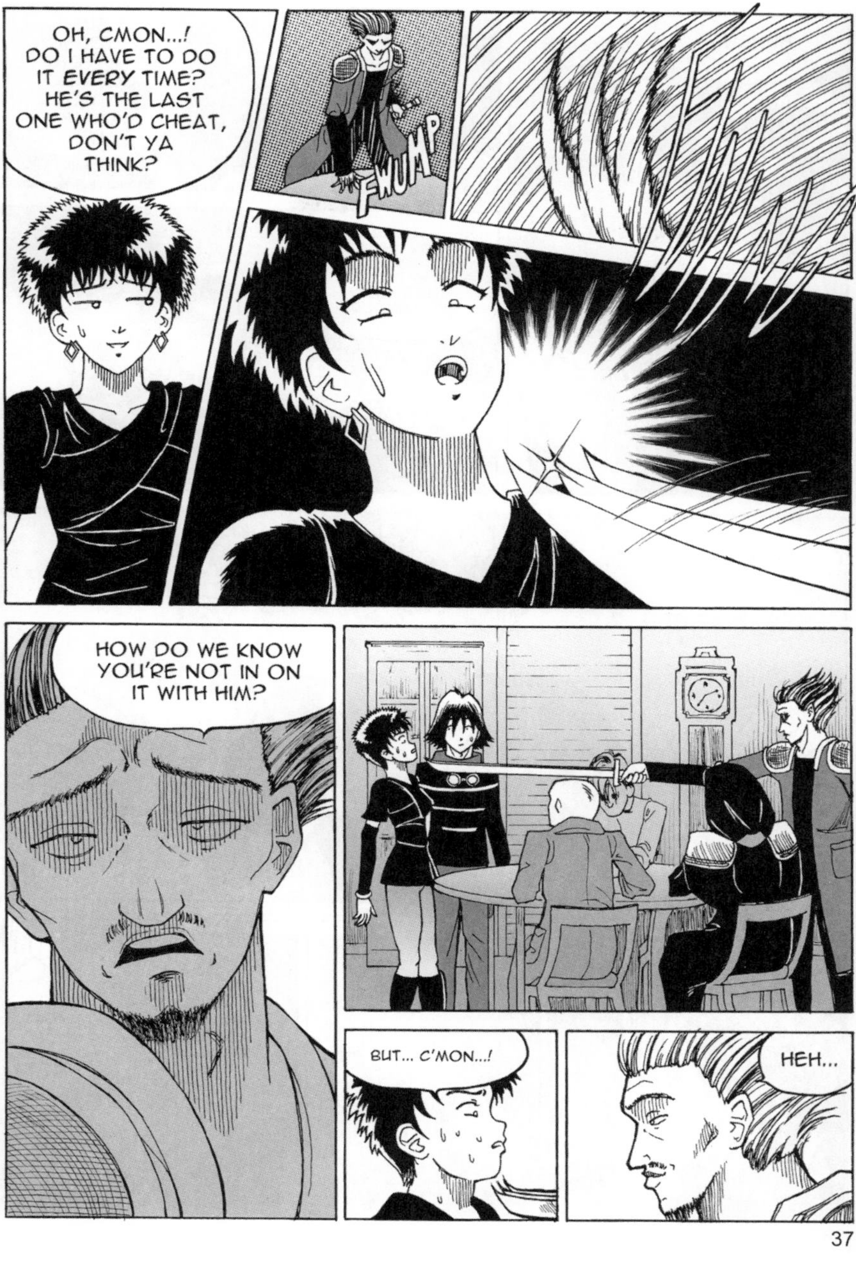
OH, CMON...! DO I HAVE TO DO IT EVERY TIME? HE'S THE LAST ONE WHO'D CHEAT, DON'T YA THINK?
FWUMP
FWWSSH
HOW DO WE KNOW YOU'RE NOT IN ON IT WITH HIM?
BUT... C'MON...!
HEH...

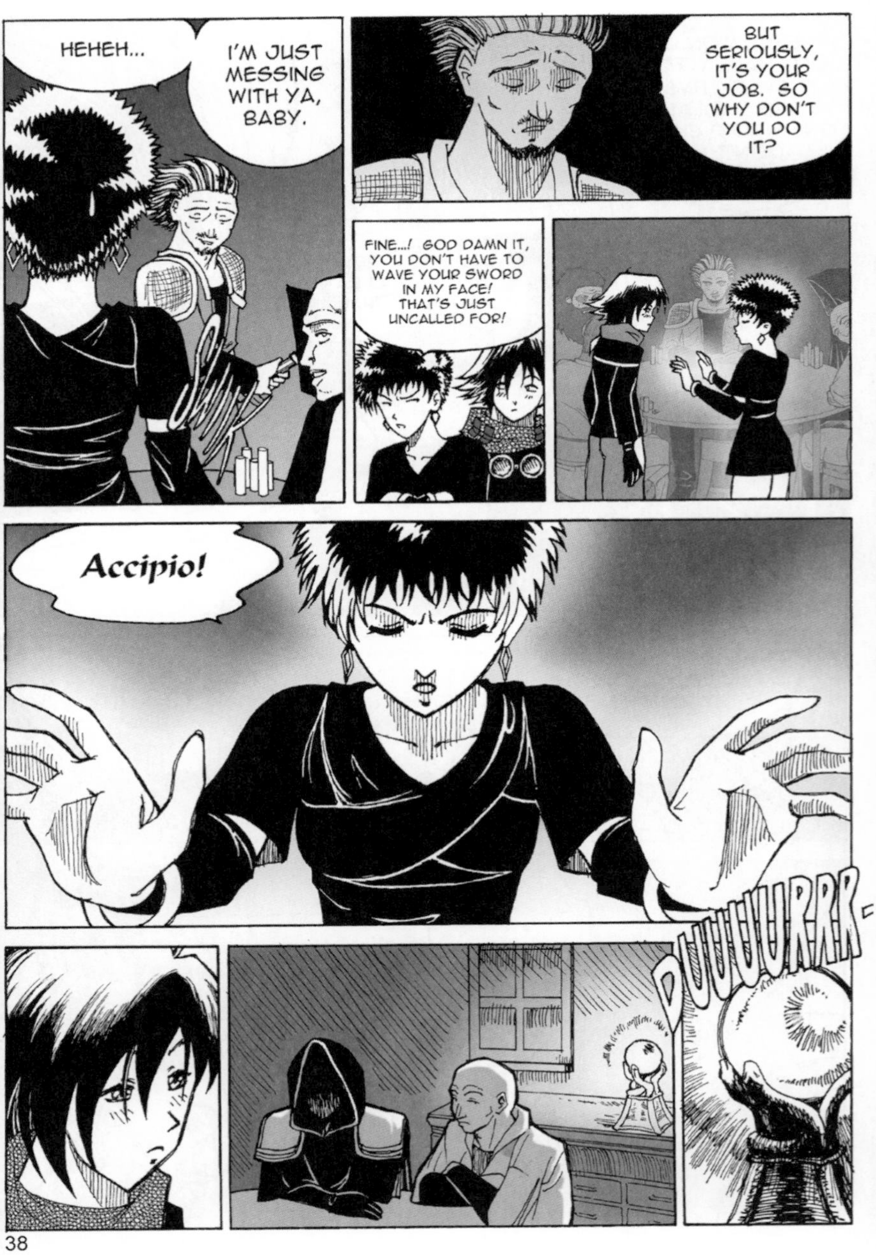

HEHEH...
I'M JUST MESSING WITH YA, BABY.
BUT SERIOUSLY, IT'S YOUR JOB. SO WHY DON'T YOU DO IT?
FINE...! GOD DAMN IT, YOU DON'T HAVE TO WAVE YOUR SWORD IN MY FACE! THAT'S JUST UNCALLED FOR!
Accipio!
DUUUURRR-

....

NOTHING SUSPICIOUS. JUST THE EVERYDAY ENCHANTMENTS.

AS IF THE *KID* WOULD CHEAT!

IF ANYONE'S CHEATING IT'S *YOU*, HELLMOUTH!

HEHEH. SHE'S GOT YOU THERE!

JUST TRYING TO MAKE A POINT, BABY!

DON'T TAKE IT SO PERSONALLY!

ENOUGH OF THIS BULLSHIT! LET'S GET STARTED!

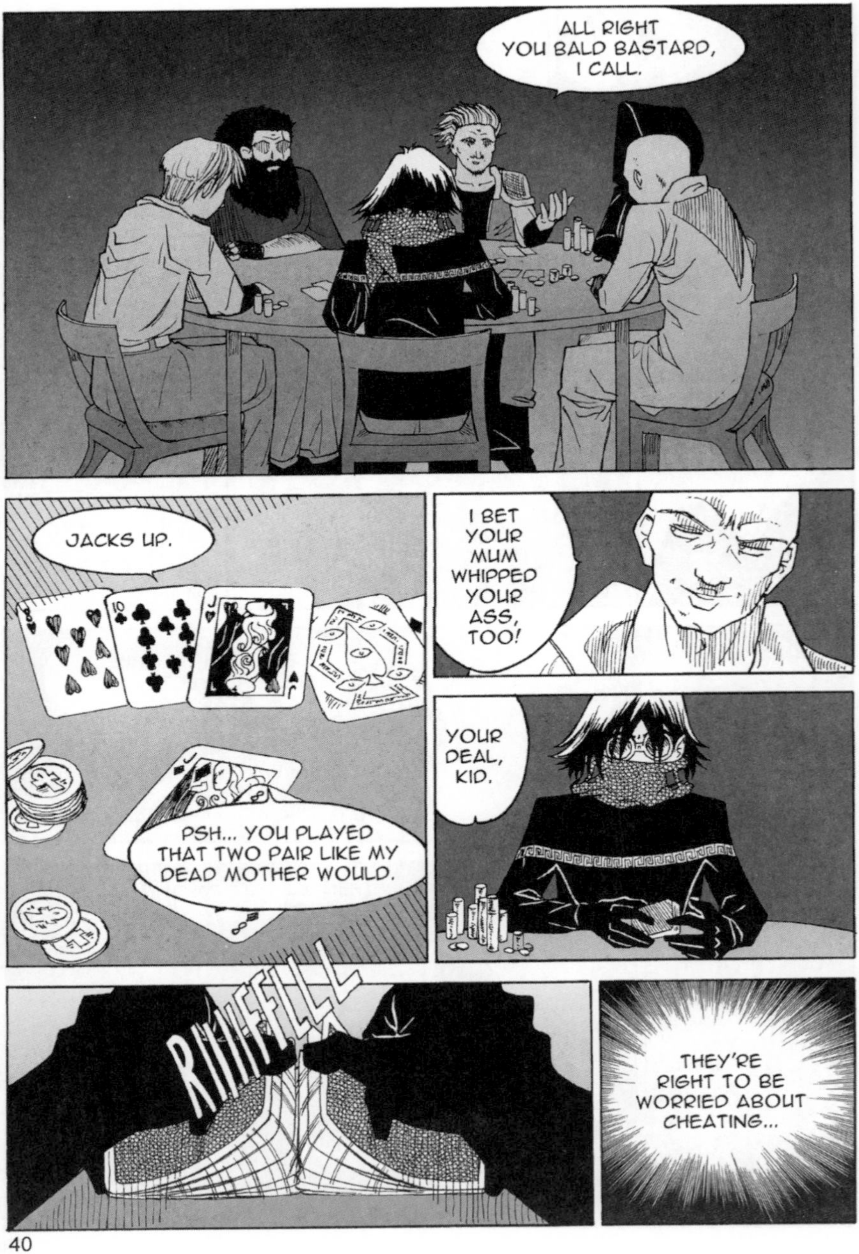
ALL RIGHT YOU BALD BASTARD, I CALL.
JACKS UP.
I BET YOUR MUM WHIPPED YOUR ASS, TOO!
PSH... YOU PLAYED THAT TWO PAIR LIKE MY DEAD MOTHER WOULD.
YOUR DEAL, KID.
RIIIIFFLLL
THEY'RE RIGHT TO BE WORRIED ABOUT CHEATING...

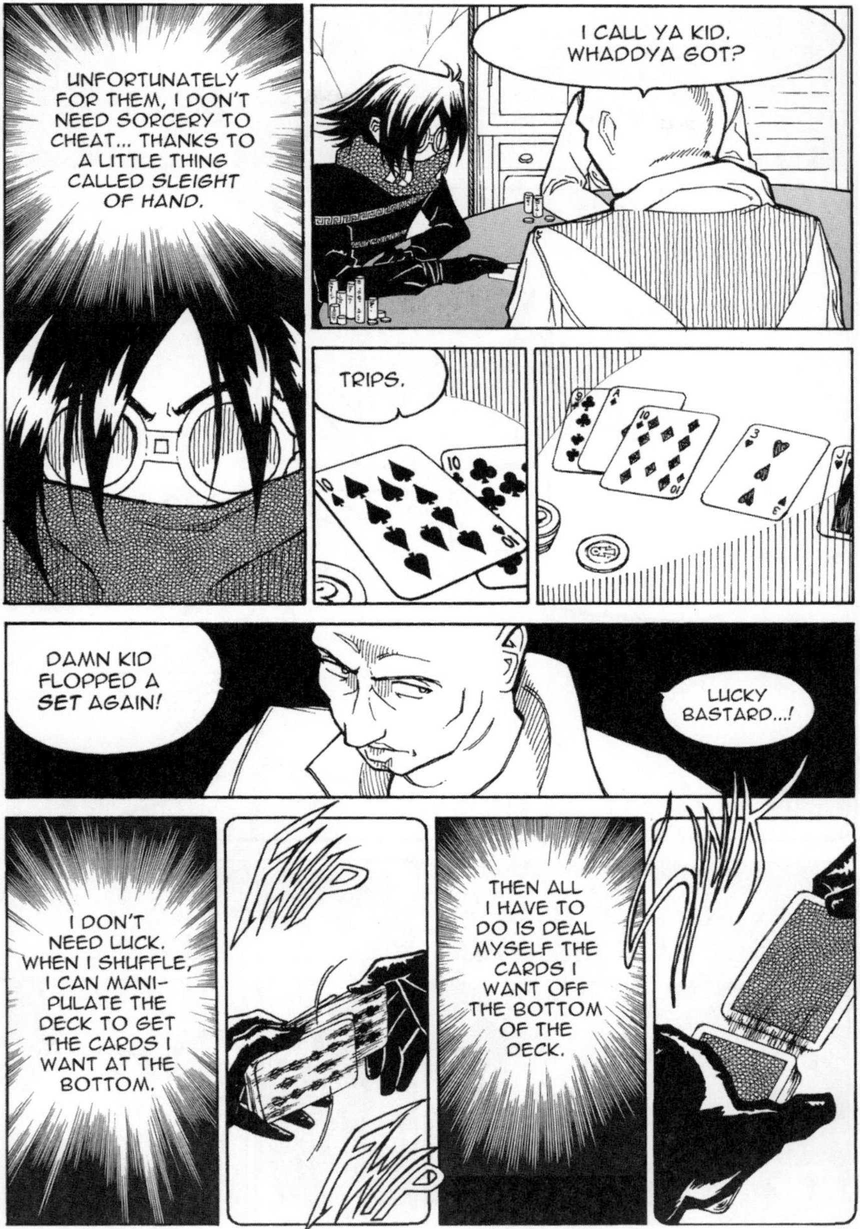
UNFORTUNATELY FOR THEM, I DON'T NEED SORCERY TO CHEAT... THANKS TO A LITTLE THING CALLED SLEIGHT OF HAND.
I CALL YA KID. WHADDYA GOT?
TRIPS.
DAMN KID FLOPPED A SET AGAIN!
LUCKY BASTARD...!
I DON'T NEED LUCK. WHEN I SHUFFLE, I CAN MANI-PULATE THE DECK TO GET THE CARDS I WANT AT THE BOTTOM.
THEN ALL I HAVE TO DO IS DEAL MYSELF THE CARDS I WANT OFF THE BOTTOM OF THE DECK.

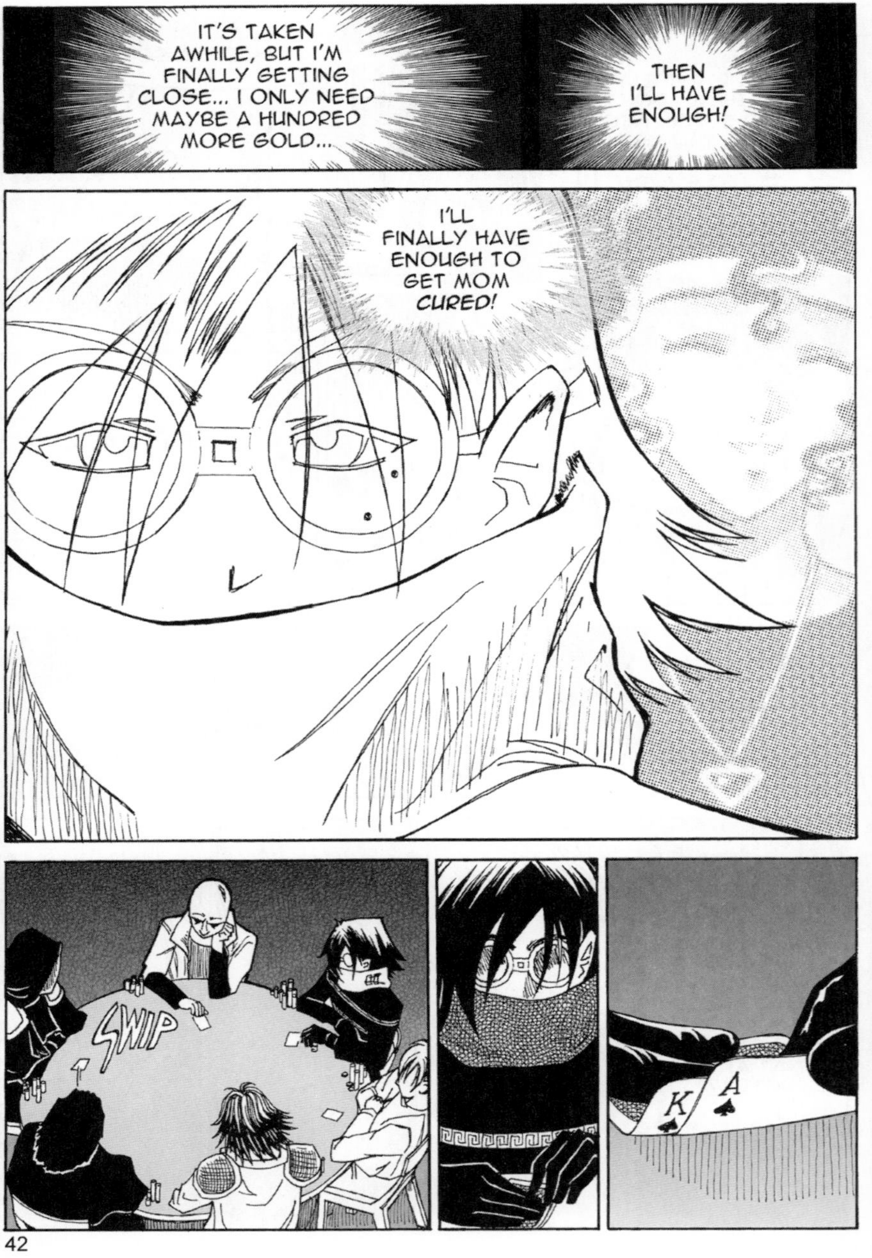
IT'S TAKEN AWHILE, BUT I'M FINALLY GETTING CLOSE... I ONLY NEED MAYBE A HUNDRED MORE GOLD...
THEN I'LL HAVE ENOUGH!
I'LL FINALLY HAVE ENOUGH TO GET MOM CURED!
SWIP
K
A

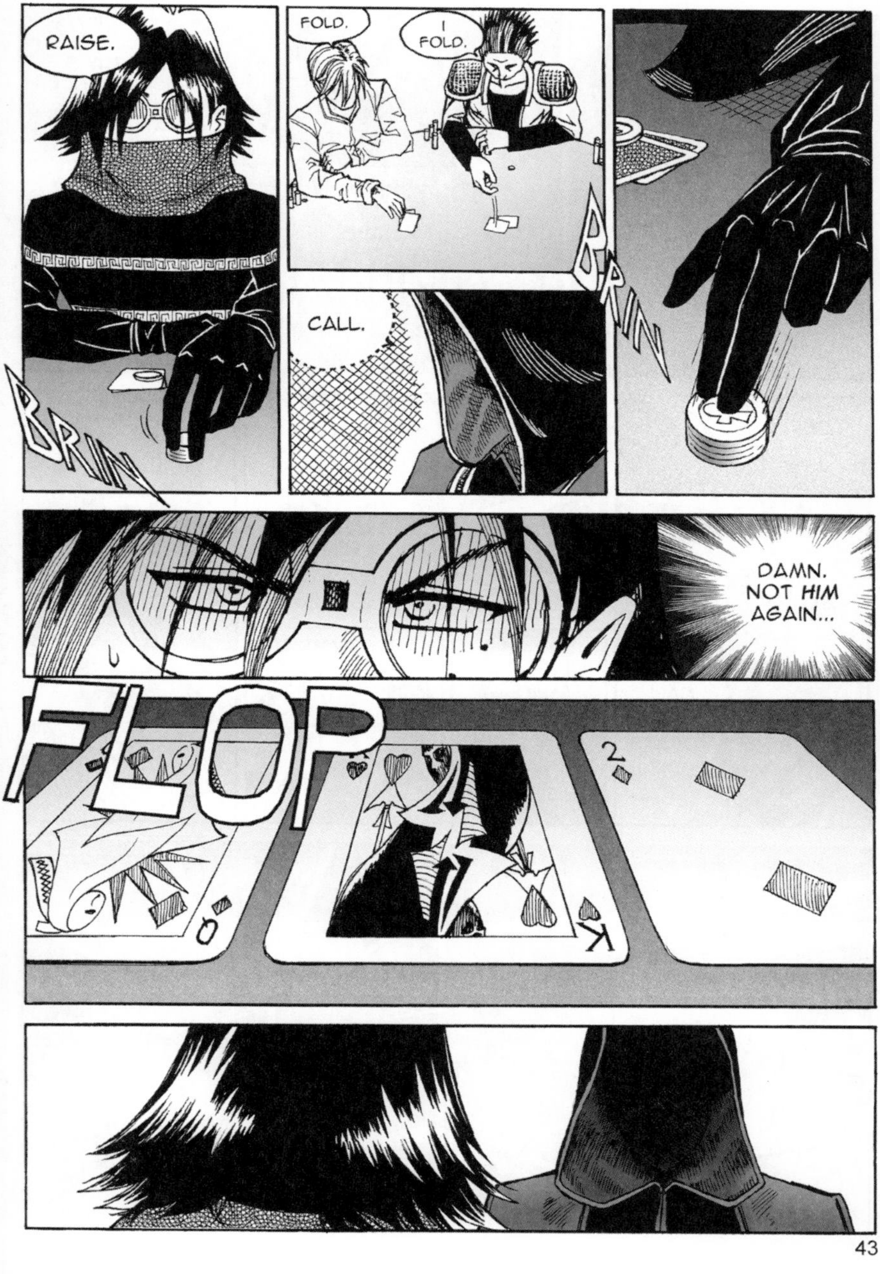
RAISE.
BRIN
FOLD.
I FOLD.
CALL.
BRIN
DAMN. NOT HIM AGAIN...
FLOP
2
Q
K

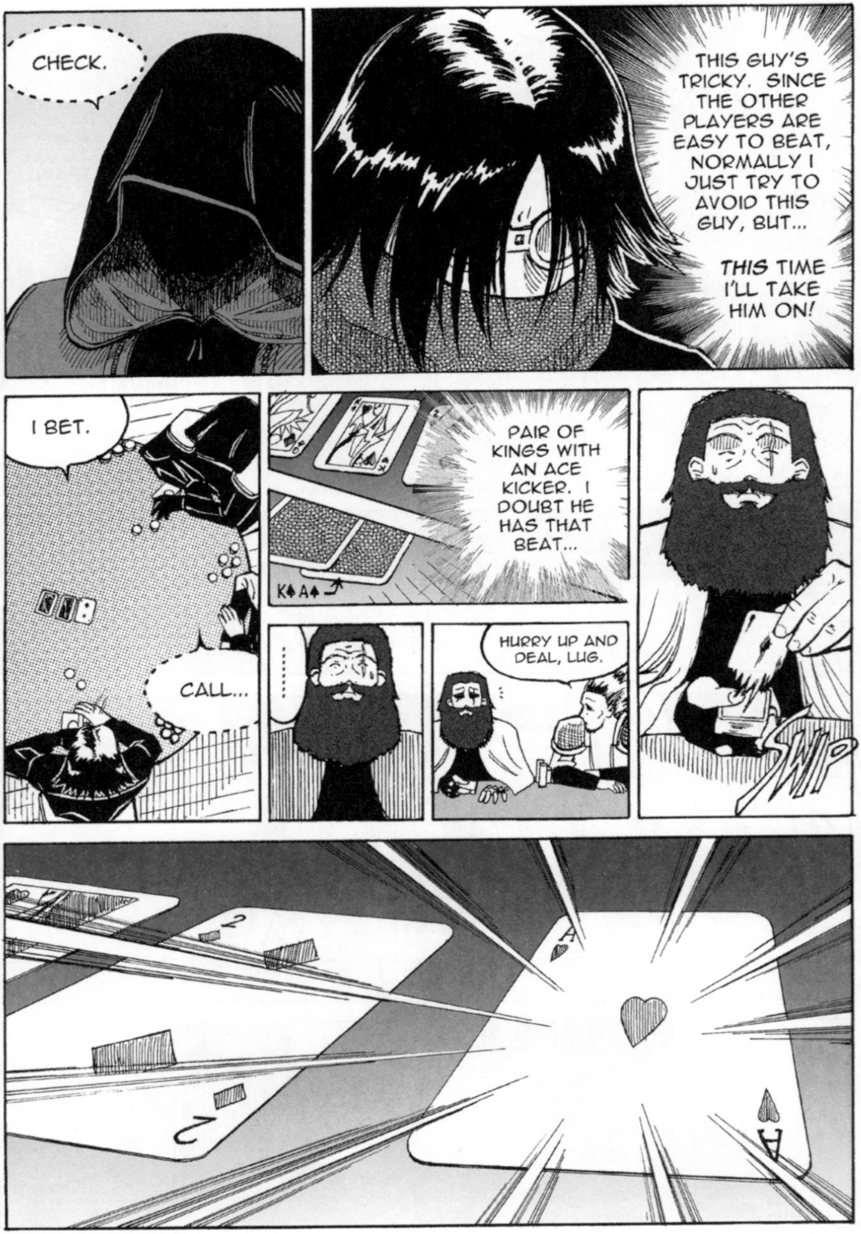
CHECK.
THIS GUY'S TRICKY. SINCE THE OTHER PLAYERS ARE EASY TO BEAT, NORMALLY I JUST TRY TO AVOID THIS GUY, BUT...
THIS TIME I'LL TAKE HIM ON!
I BET.
PAIR OF KINGS WITH AN ACE KICKER. I DOUBT HE HAS THAT BEAT...
K♠ A♠
CALL...
......
HURRY UP AND DEAL, LUG.
SWIP

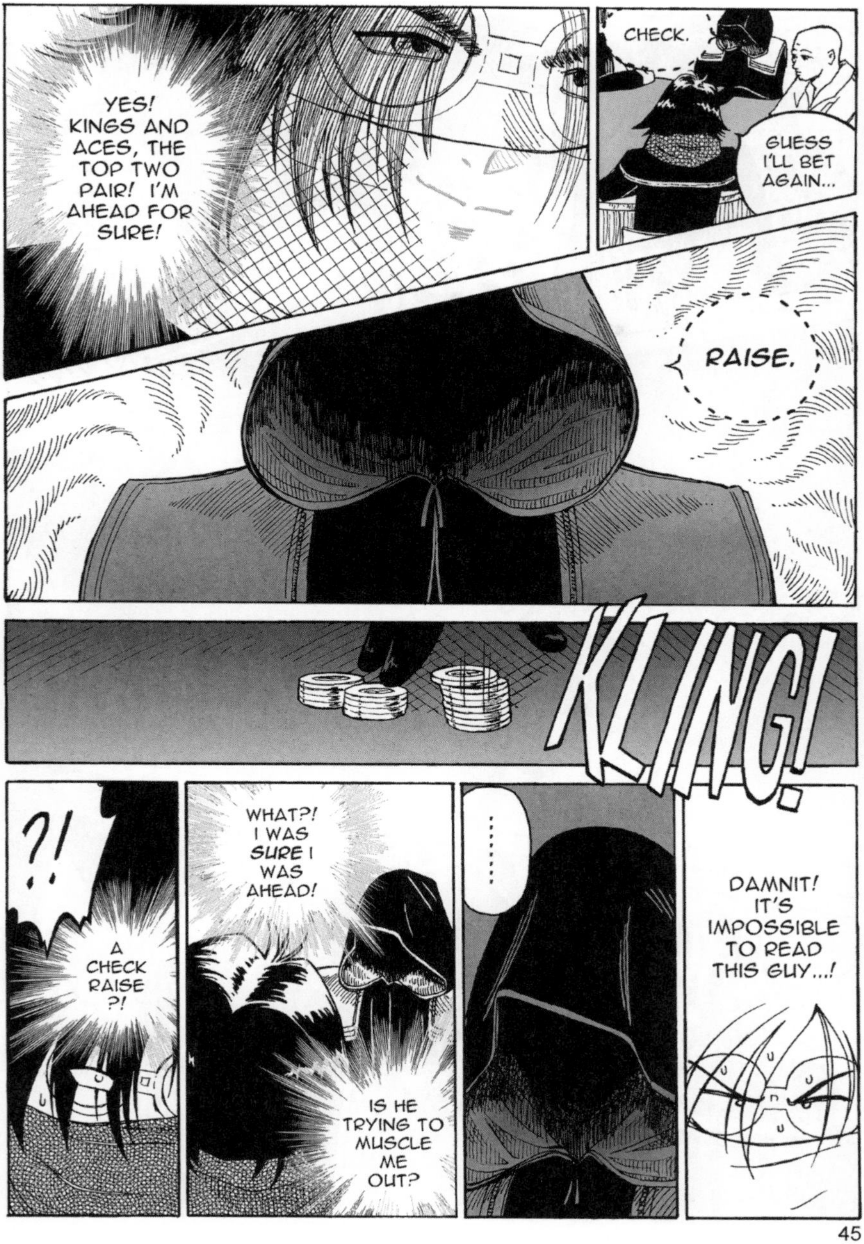

CHECK.
GUESS I'LL BET AGAIN...
YES! KINGS AND ACES, THE TOP TWO PAIR! I'M AHEAD FOR SURE!
RAISE.
KLING!
DAMNIT! IT'S IMPOSSIBLE TO READ THIS GUY...!
......
WHAT?! I WAS SURE I WAS AHEAD!
IS HE TRYING TO MUSCLE ME OUT?
?!
A CHECK RAISE ?!

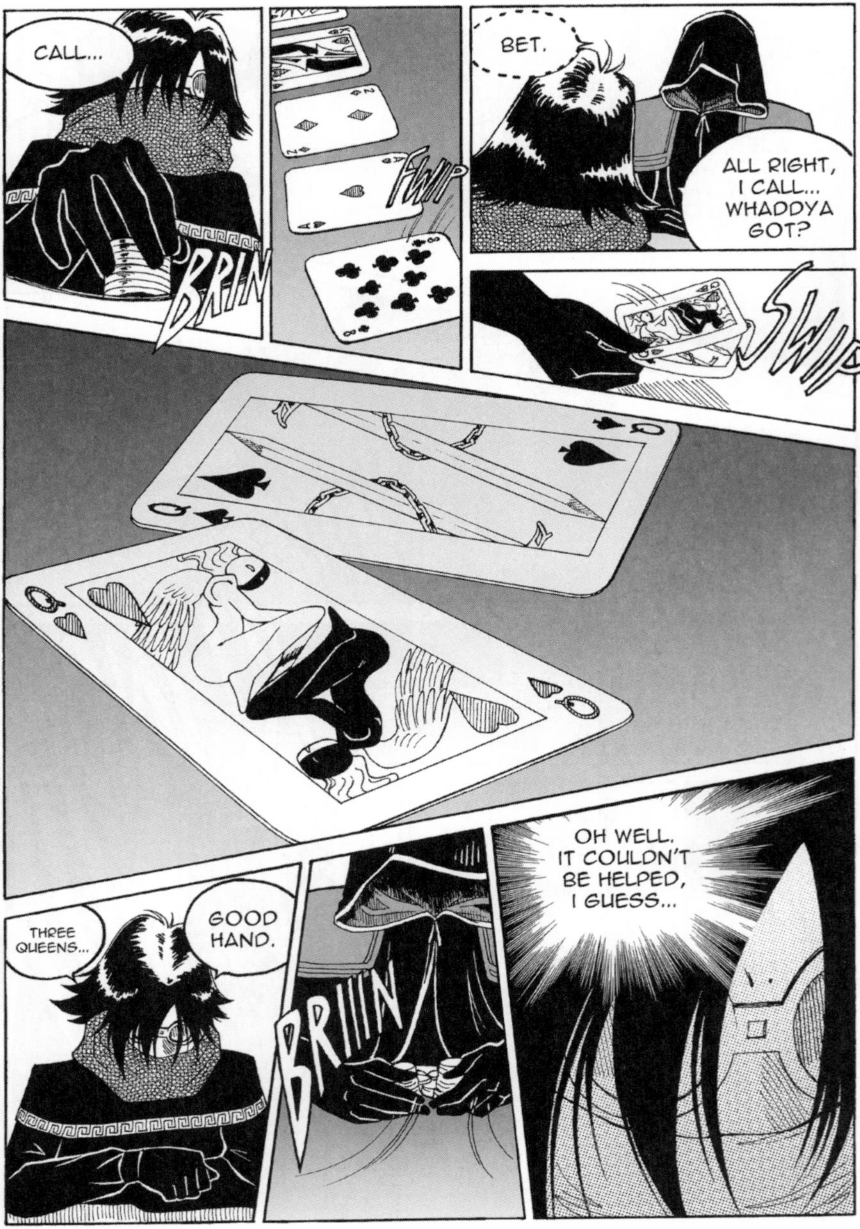
CALL...
BRIN
FWIP
BET.
ALL RIGHT, I CALL... WHADDYA GOT?
SWIP
THREE QUEENS...
GOOD HAND.
BRIIIN
OH WELL. IT COULDN'T BE HELPED, I GUESS...

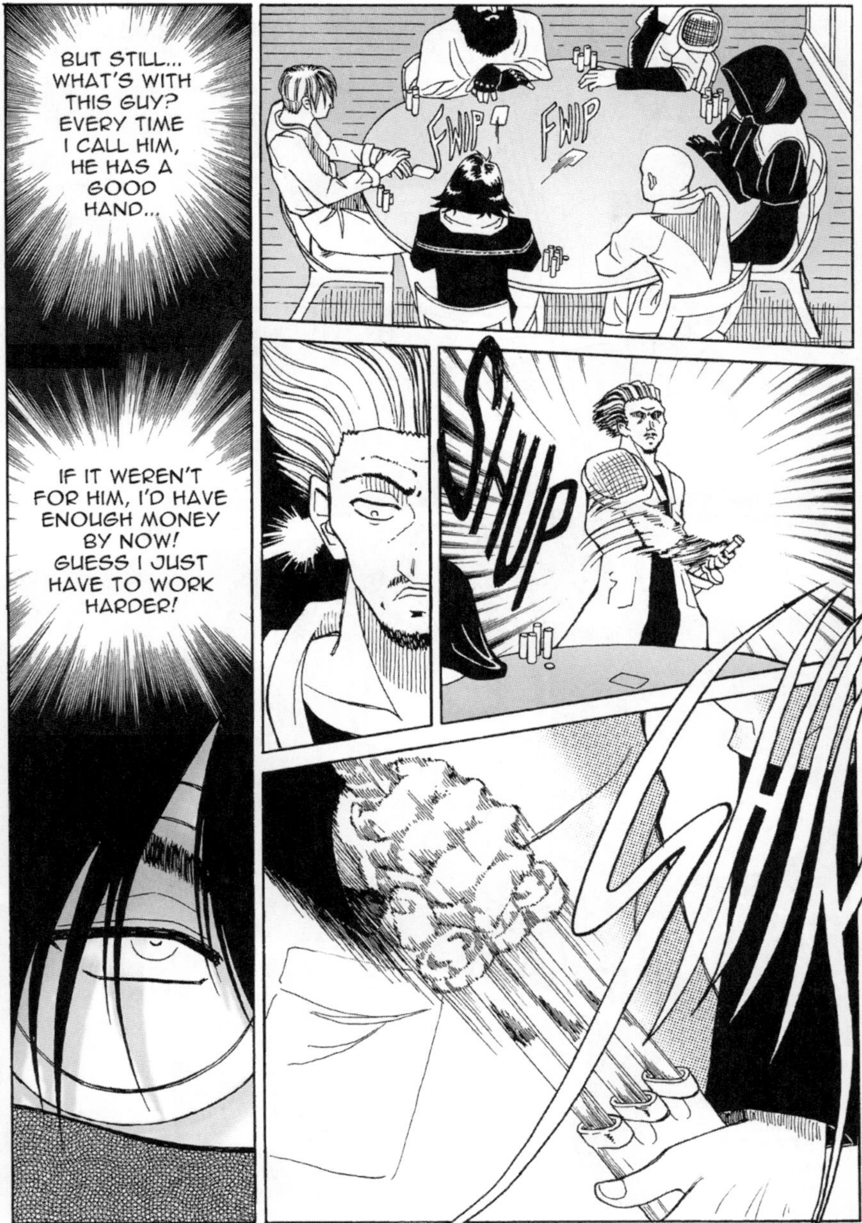
BUT STILL... WHAT'S WITH THIS GUY? EVERY TIME I CALL HIM, HE HAS A GOOD HAND...
FWIP
FWIP
IF IT WEREN'T FOR HIM, I'D HAVE ENOUGH MONEY BY NOW! GUESS I JUST HAVE TO WORK HARDER!
SHUP

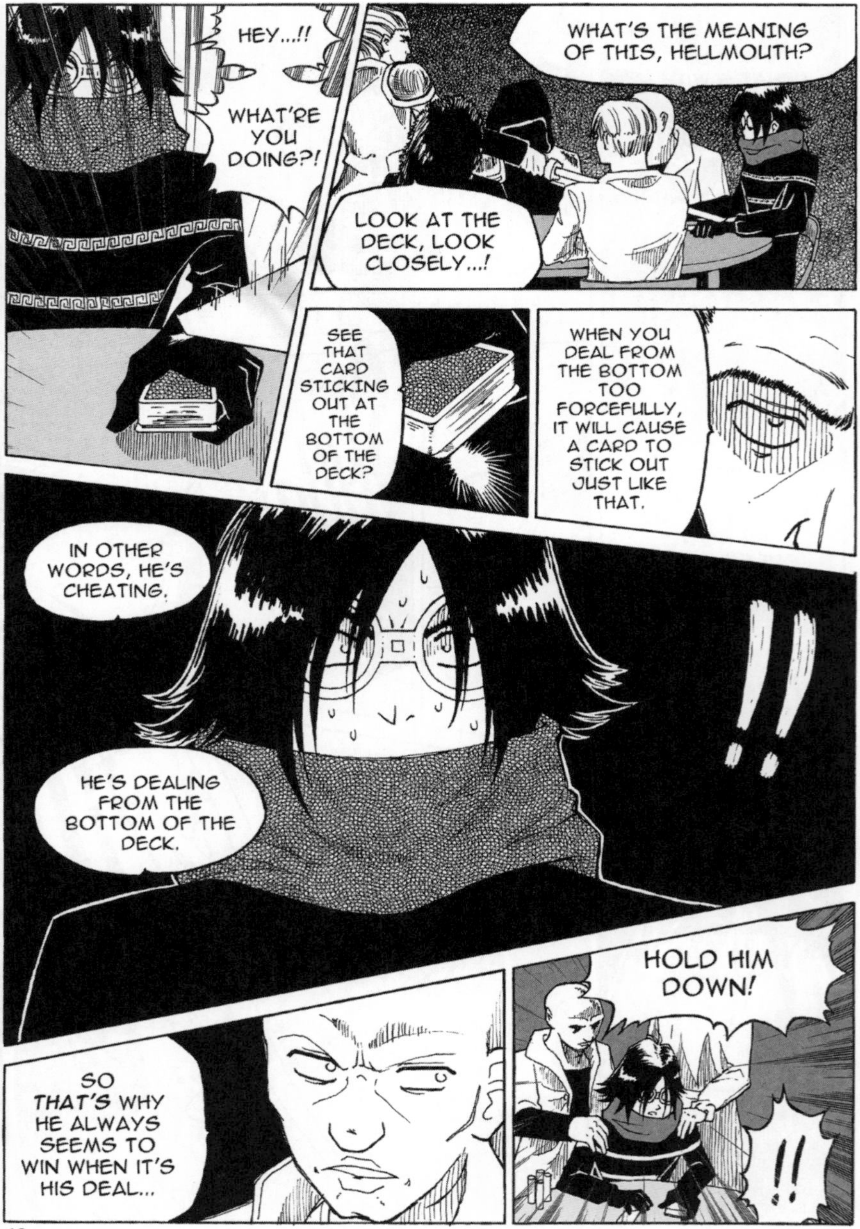
HEY...!!
WHAT'RE YOU DOING?!
WHAT'S THE MEANING OF THIS, HELLMOUTH?
LOOK AT THE DECK, LOOK CLOSELY...!
SEE THAT CARD STICKING OUT AT THE BOTTOM OF THE DECK?
WHEN YOU DEAL FROM THE BOTTOM TOO FORCEFULLY, IT WILL CAUSE A CARD TO STICK OUT JUST LIKE THAT.
IN OTHER WORDS, HE'S CHEATING.
HE'S DEALING FROM THE BOTTOM OF THE DECK.
!!
SO THAT'S WHY HE ALWAYS SEEMS TO WIN WHEN IT'S HIS DEAL...
HOLD HIM DOWN!
!!

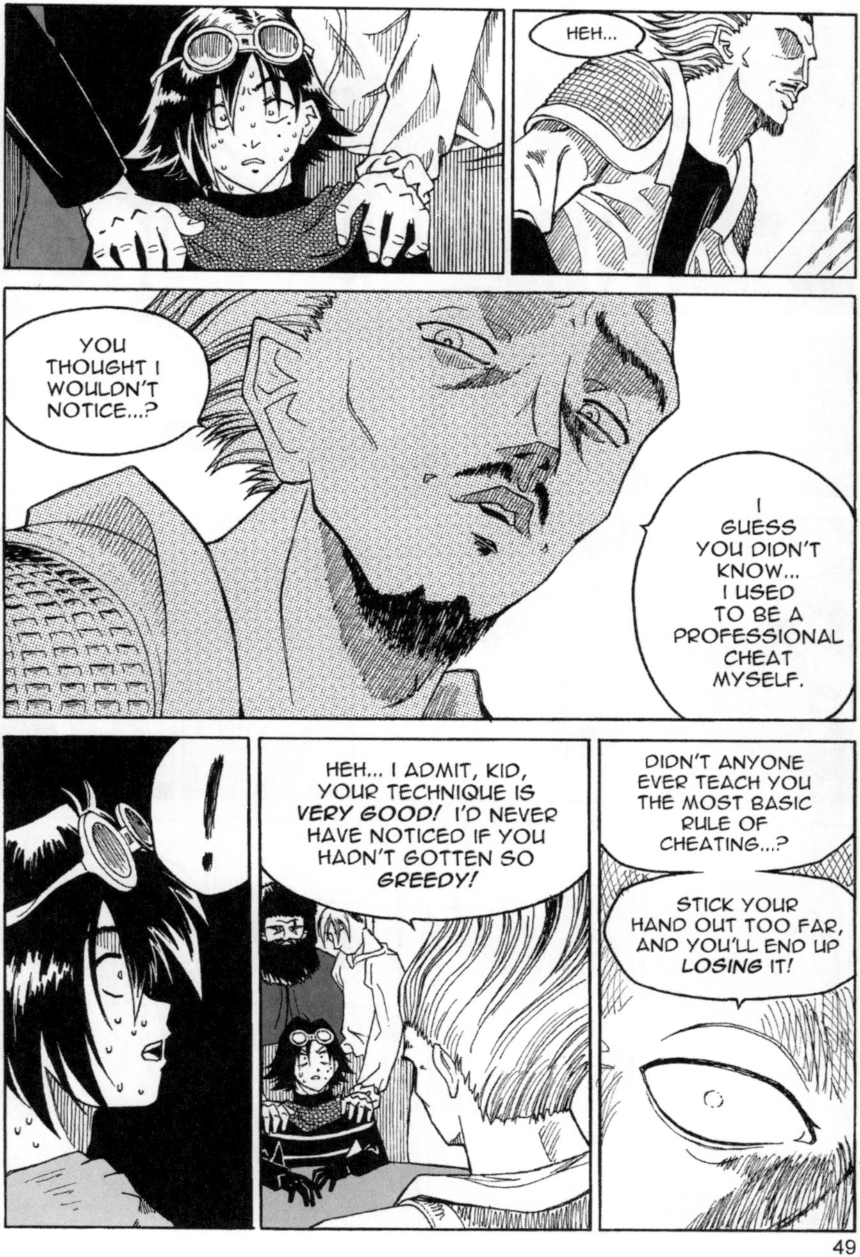
HEH...
YOU THOUGHT I WOULDN'T NOTICE...?
I GUESS YOU DIDN'T KNOW... I USED TO BE A PROFESSIONAL CHEAT MYSELF.
!
HEH... I ADMIT, KID, YOUR TECHNIQUE IS *VERY GOOD!* I'D NEVER HAVE NOTICED IF YOU HADN'T GOTTEN SO *GREEDY!*
DIDN'T ANYONE EVER TEACH YOU THE MOST BASIC RULE OF CHEATING...?
STICK YOUR HAND OUT TOO FAR, AND YOU'LL END UP *LOSING* IT!

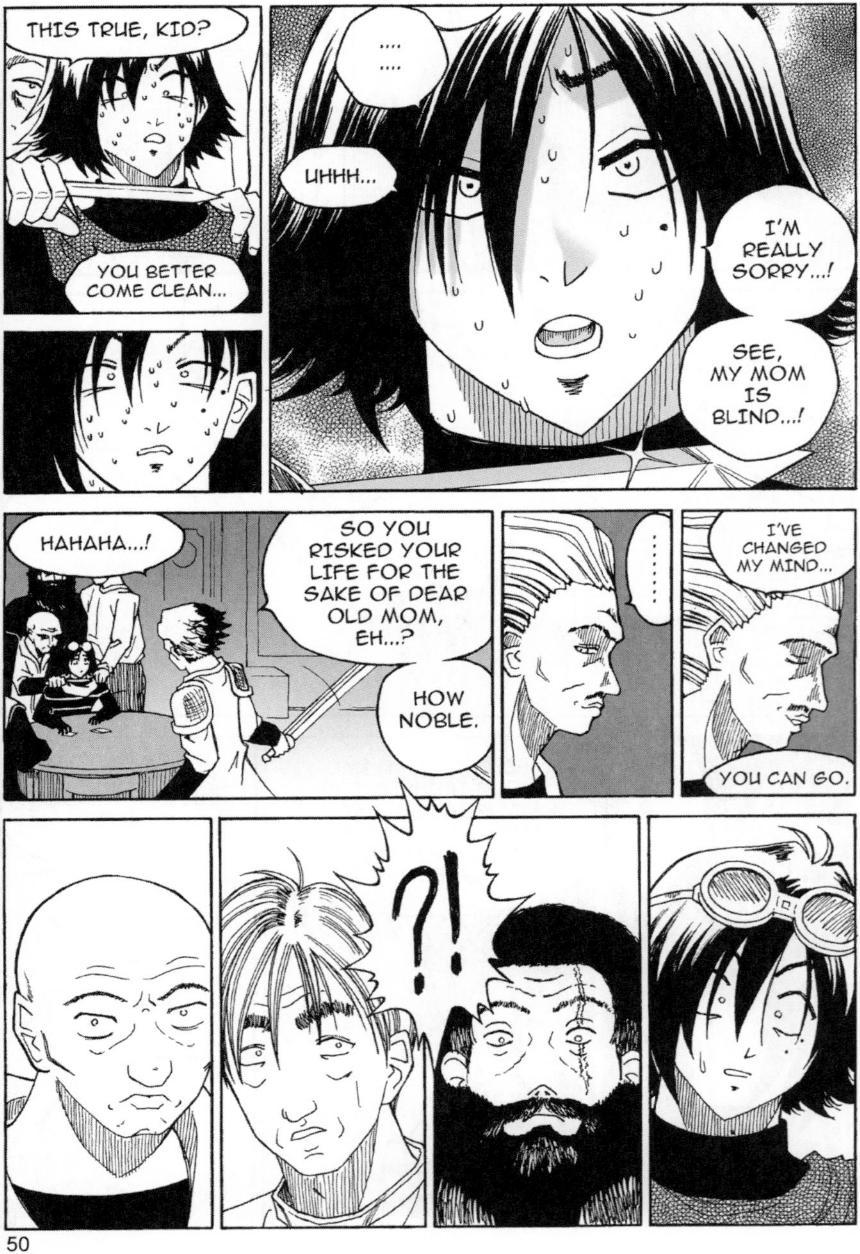

THIS TRUE, KID?
YOU BETTER COME CLEAN...
....
....
UHHH...
I'M REALLY SORRY...!
SEE, MY MOM IS BLIND...!
HAHAHA...!
SO YOU RISKED YOUR LIFE FOR THE SAKE OF DEAR OLD MOM, EH...?
HOW NOBLE.
....
I'VE CHANGED MY MIND...
YOU CAN GO.
?!

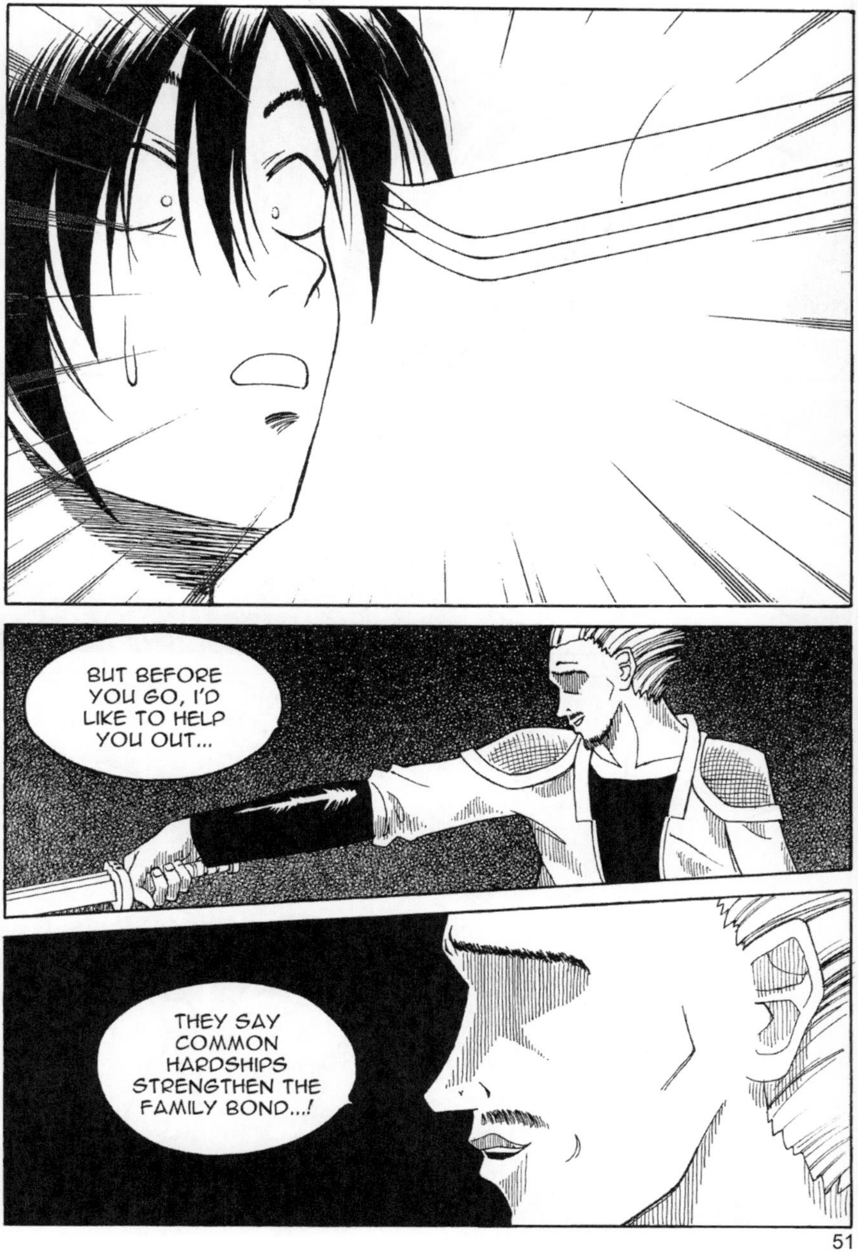
BUT BEFORE YOU GO, I'D LIKE TO HELP YOU OUT...
THEY SAY COMMON HARDSHIPS STRENGTHEN THE FAMILY BOND...!

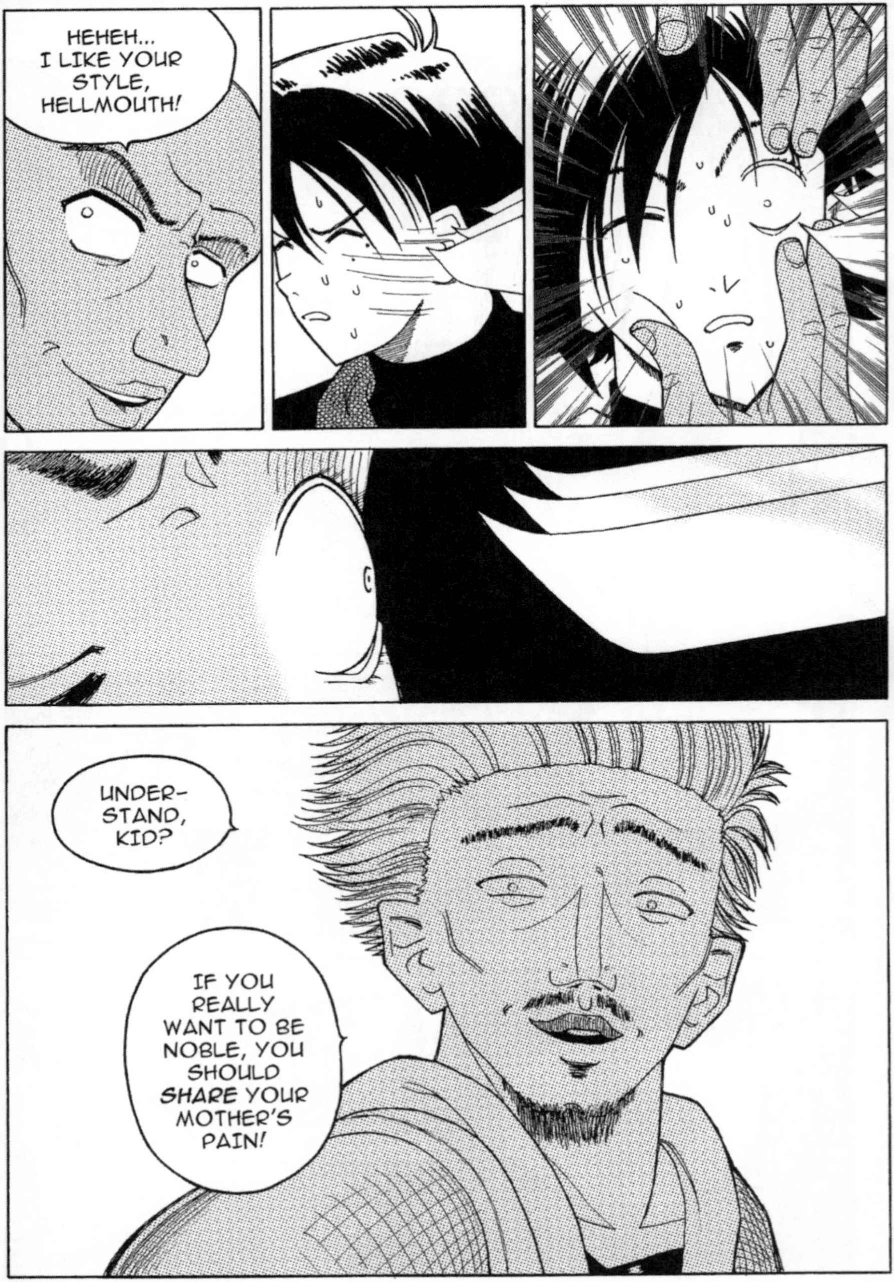
HEHEH... I LIKE YOUR STYLE, HELLMOUTH!
UNDER-STAND, KID?
IF YOU REALLY WANT TO BE NOBLE, YOU SHOULD SHARE YOUR MOTHER'S PAIN!

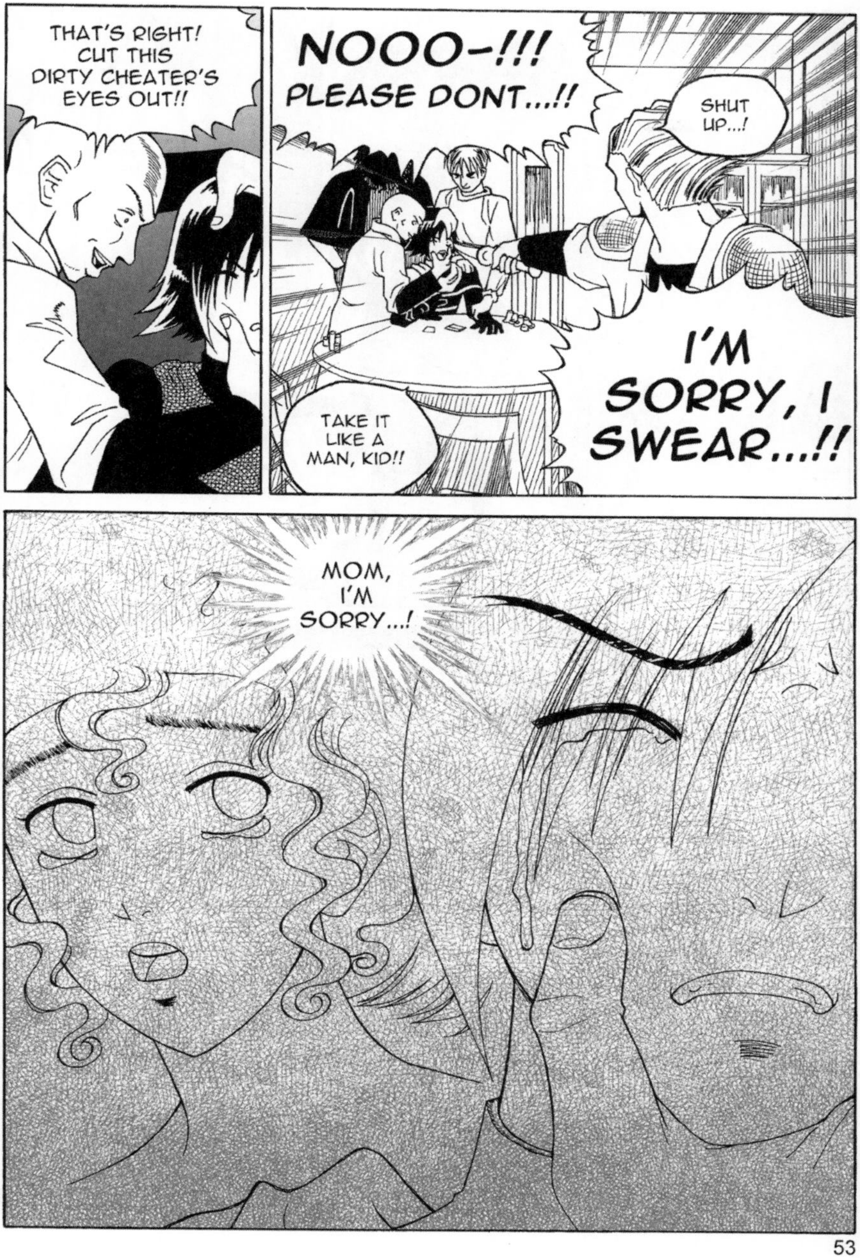
THAT'S RIGHT! CUT THIS DIRTY CHEATER'S EYES OUT!!
NOOO-!!! PLEASE DONT...!!
SHUT UP...!
TAKE IT LIKE A MAN, KID!!
I'M SORRY, I SWEAR...!!
MOM, I'M SORRY...!

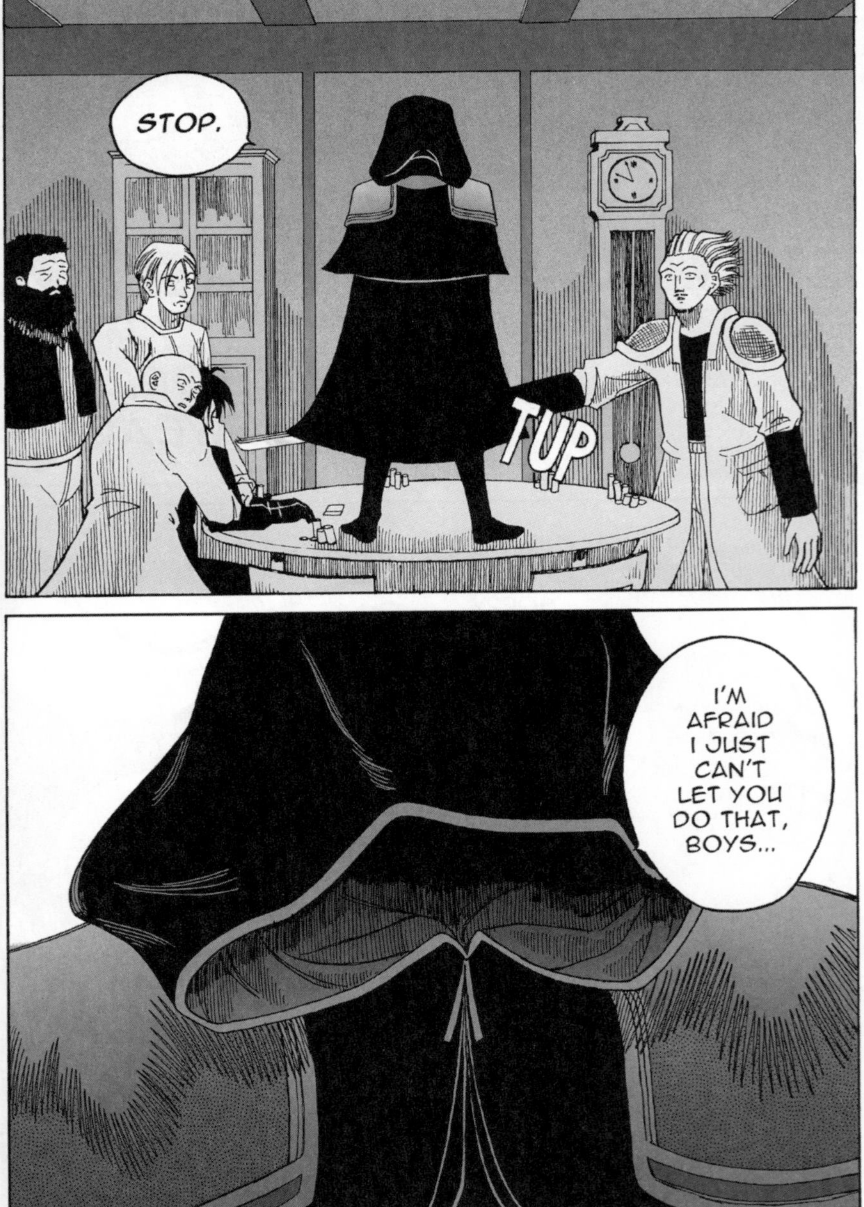
STOP.
TUP
I'M AFRAID I JUST CAN'T LET YOU DO THAT, BOYS...

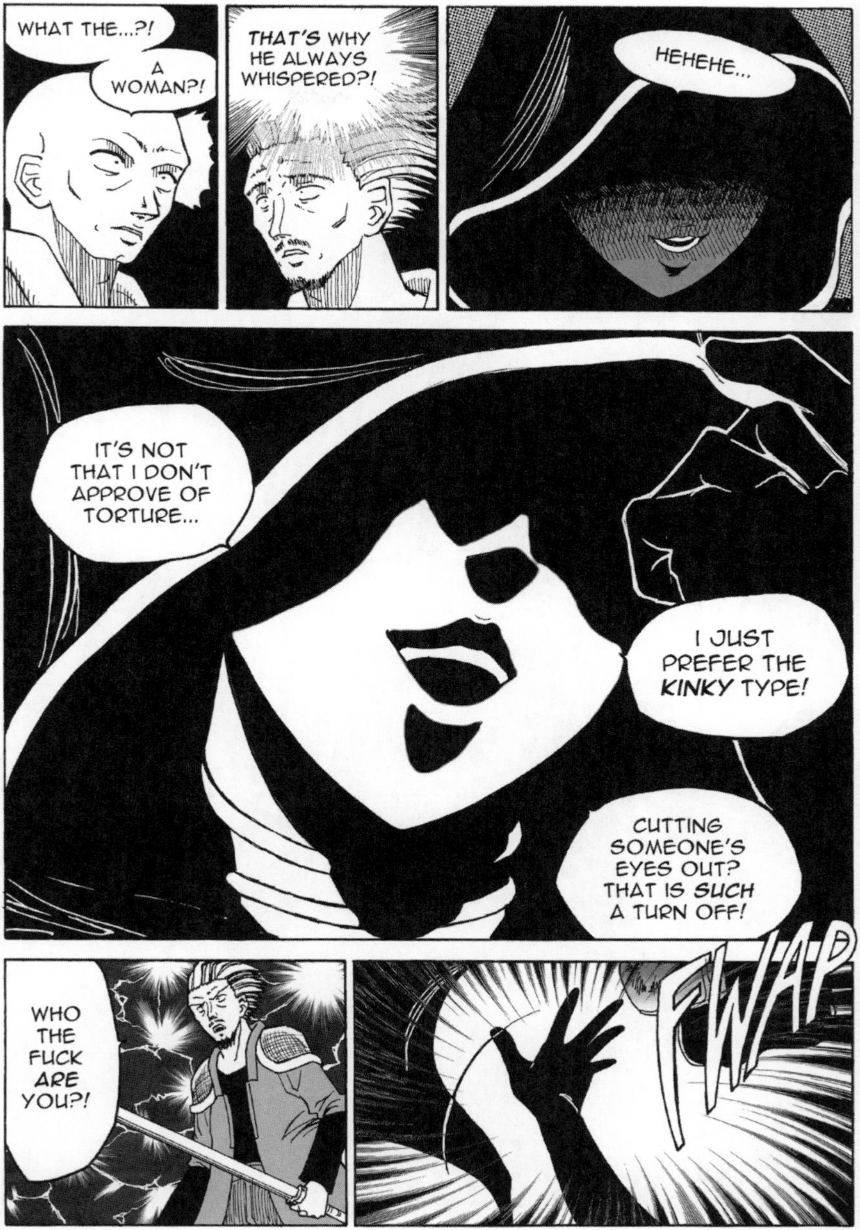

WHAT THE...?!
A WOMAN?!
THAT'S WHY HE ALWAYS WHISPERED?!
HEHEHE...
IT'S NOT THAT I DON'T APPROVE OF TORTURE...
I JUST PREFER THE KINKY TYPE!
CUTTING SOMEONE'S EYES OUT? THAT IS SUCH A TURN OFF!
WHO THE FUCK ARE YOU?!
FWAP

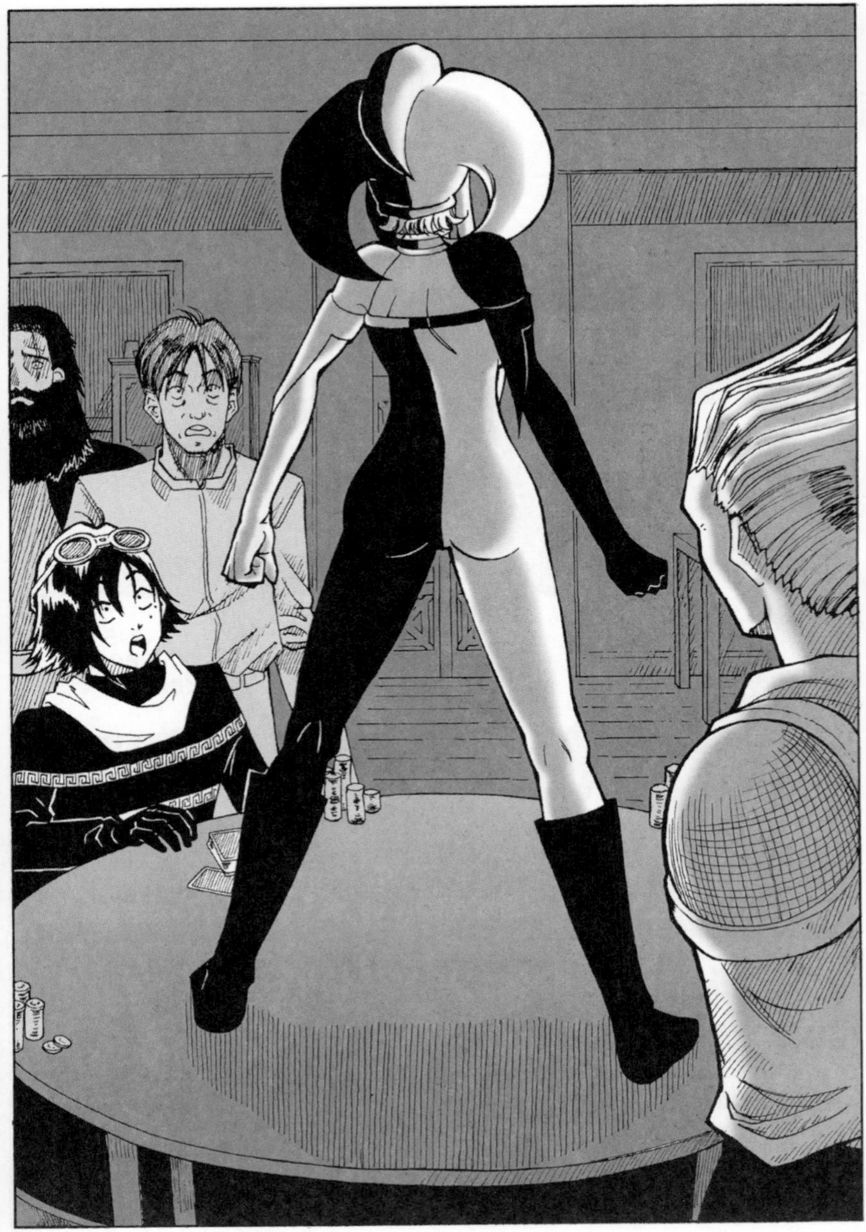

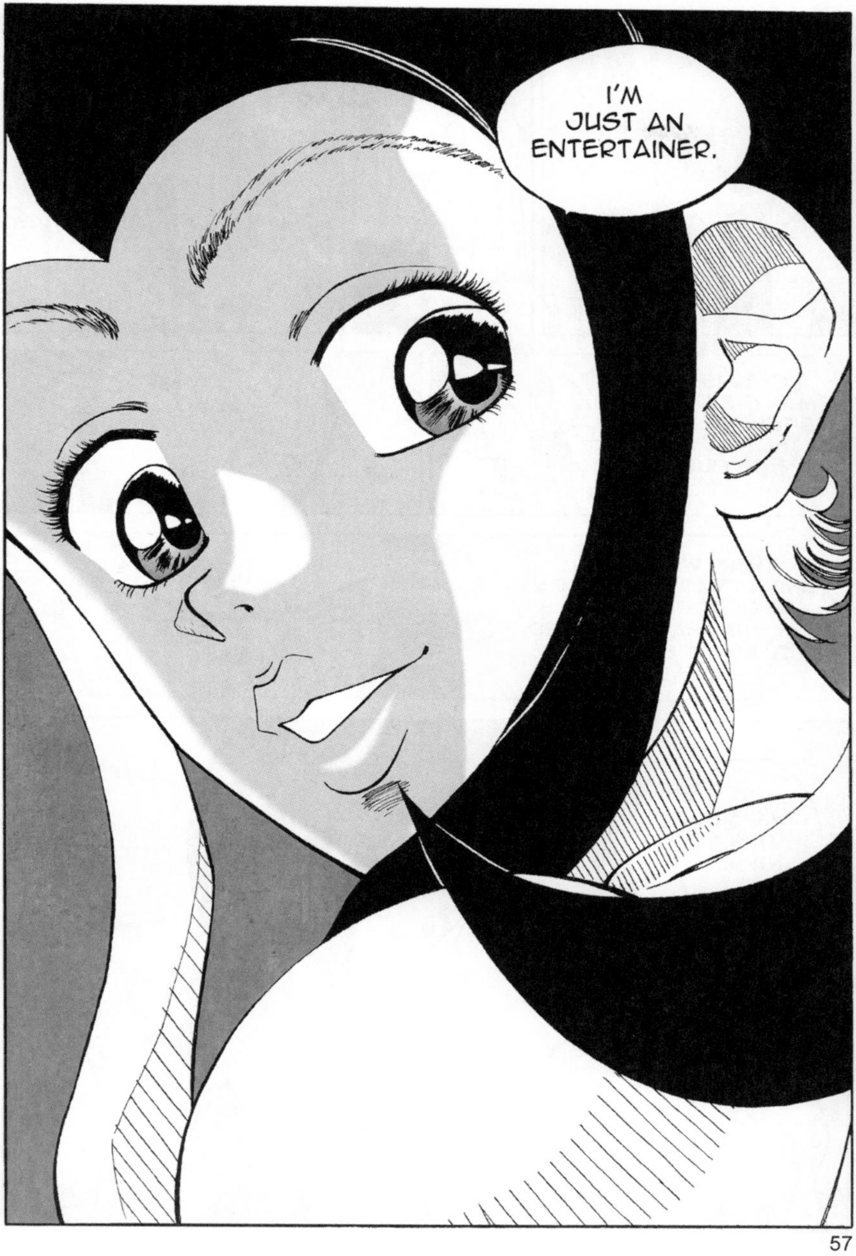
I'M JUST AN ENTERTAINER.

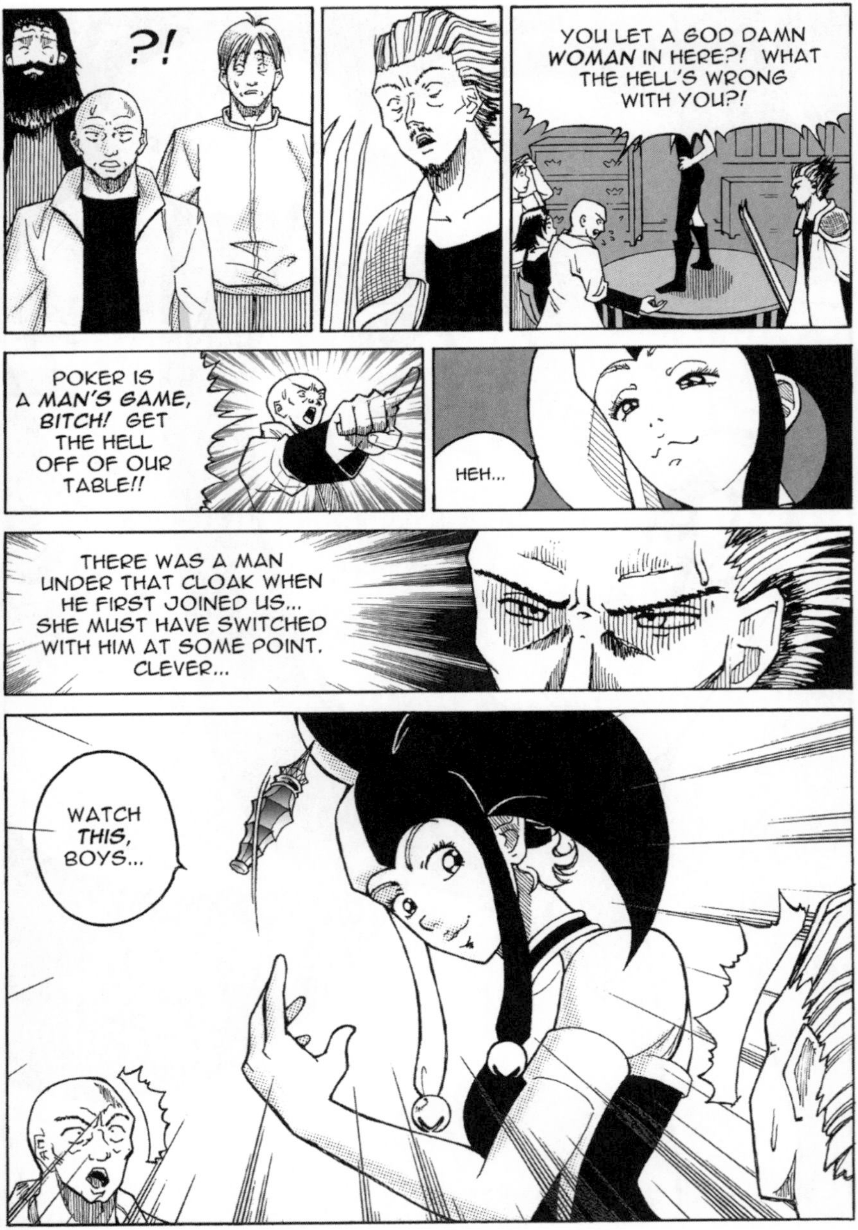
?!
YOU LET A GOD DAMN WOMAN IN HERE?! WHAT THE HELL'S WRONG WITH YOU?!
POKER IS A MAN'S GAME, BITCH! GET THE HELL OFF OF OUR TABLE!!
HEH...
THERE WAS A MAN UNDER THAT CLOAK WHEN HE FIRST JOINED US... SHE MUST HAVE SWITCHED WITH HIM AT SOME POINT. CLEVER...
WATCH THIS, BOYS...

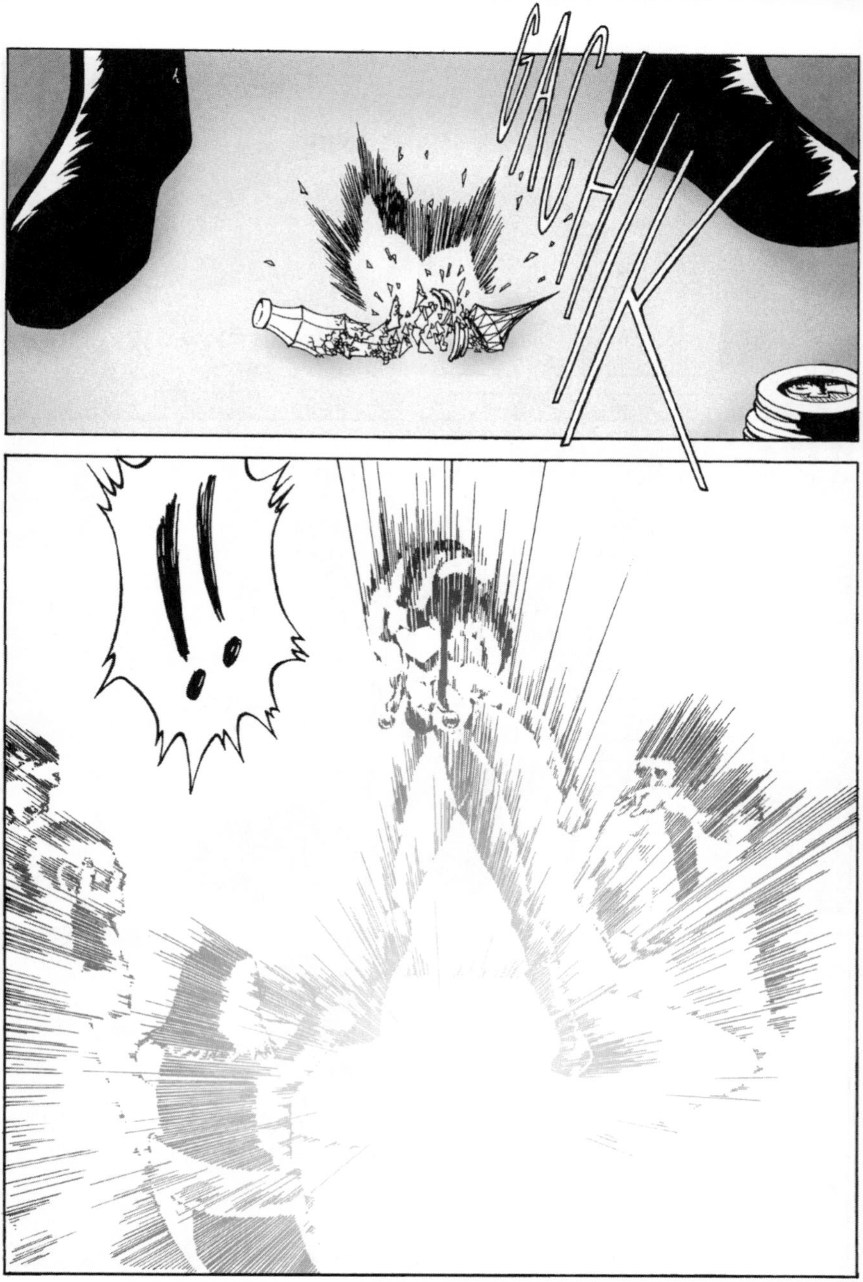
GACHIK
!!

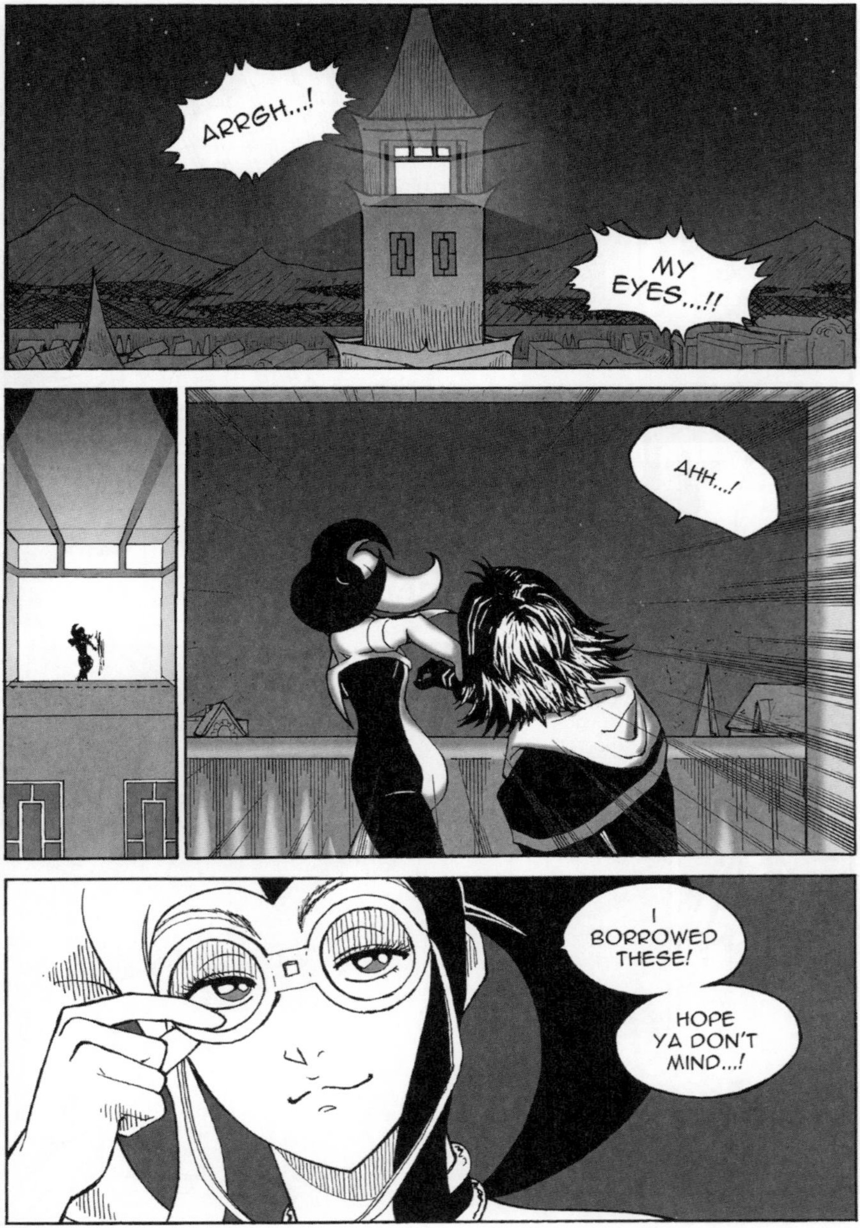
ARRGH...!
MY EYES...!!
AHH...!
I BORROWED THESE!
HOPE YA DON'T MIND...!

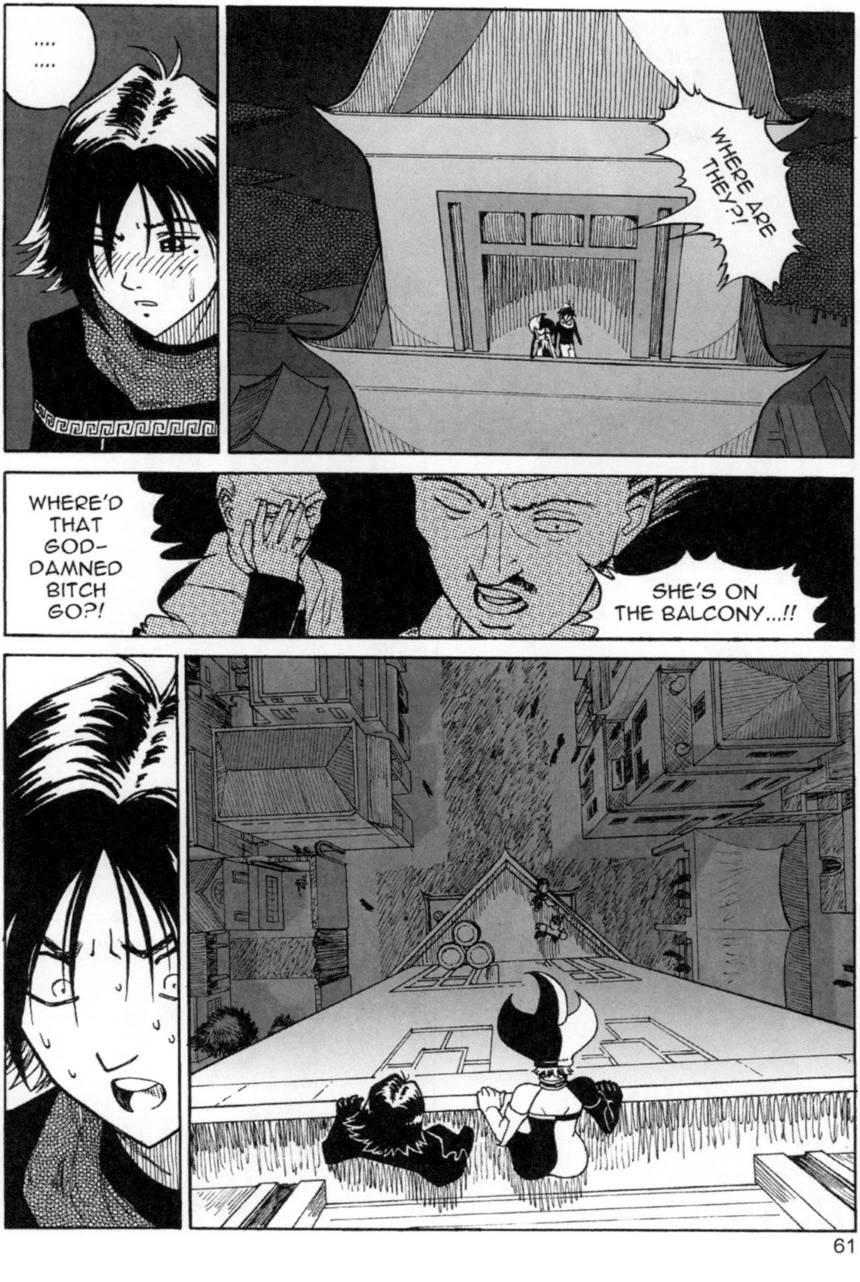
....
....
WHERE ARE THEY?!
WHERE'D THAT GOD-DAMNED BITCH GO?!
SHE'S ON THE BALCONY...!!

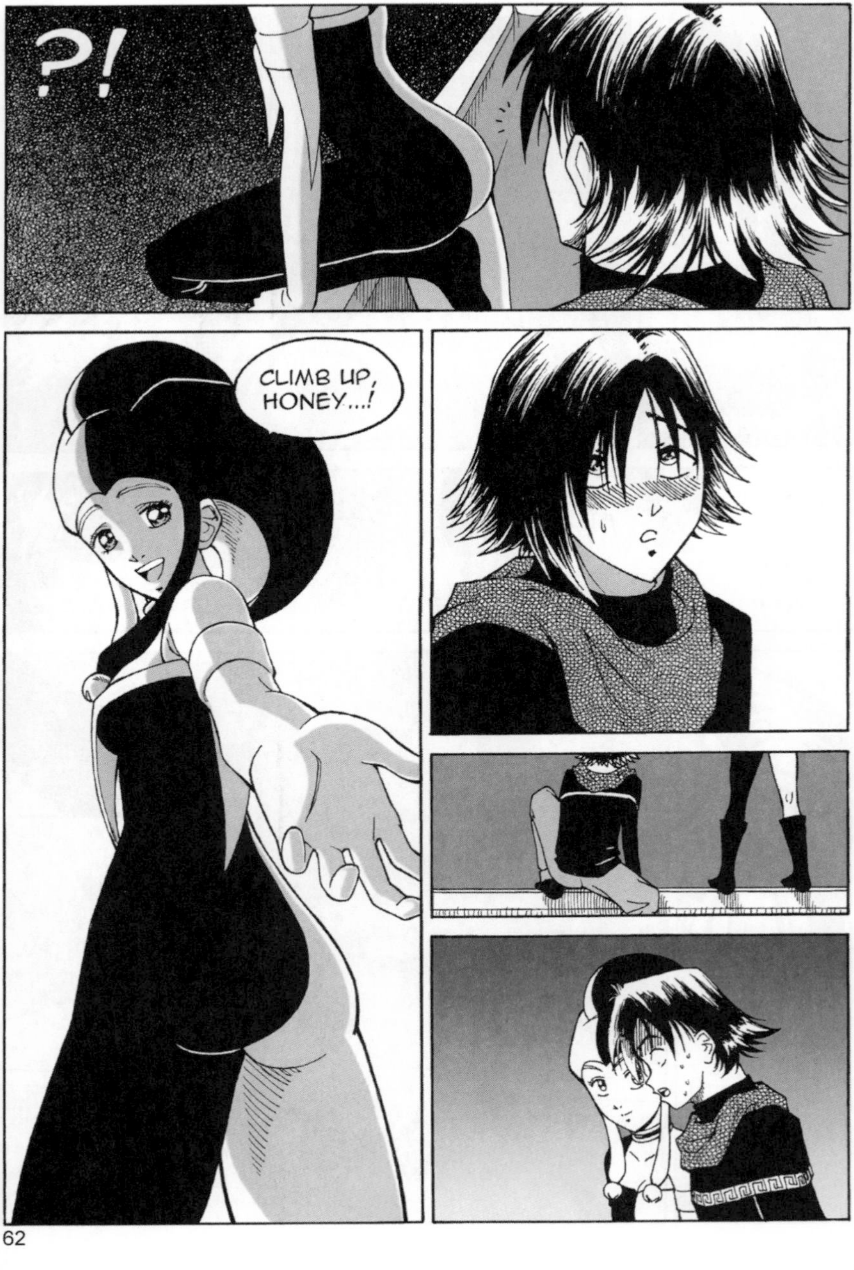
?!
CLIMB UP, HONEY...!

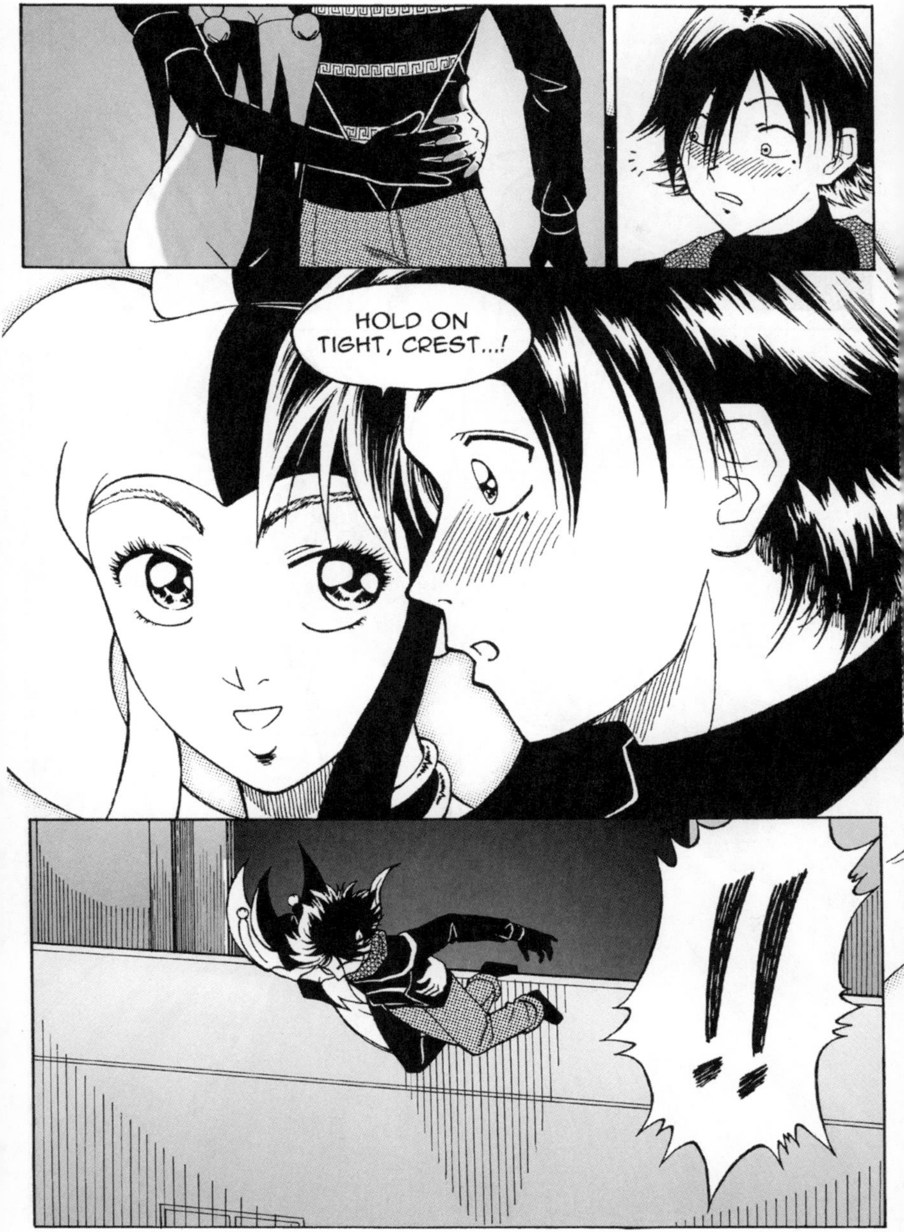
HOLD ON
TIGHT, CREST...!
!!

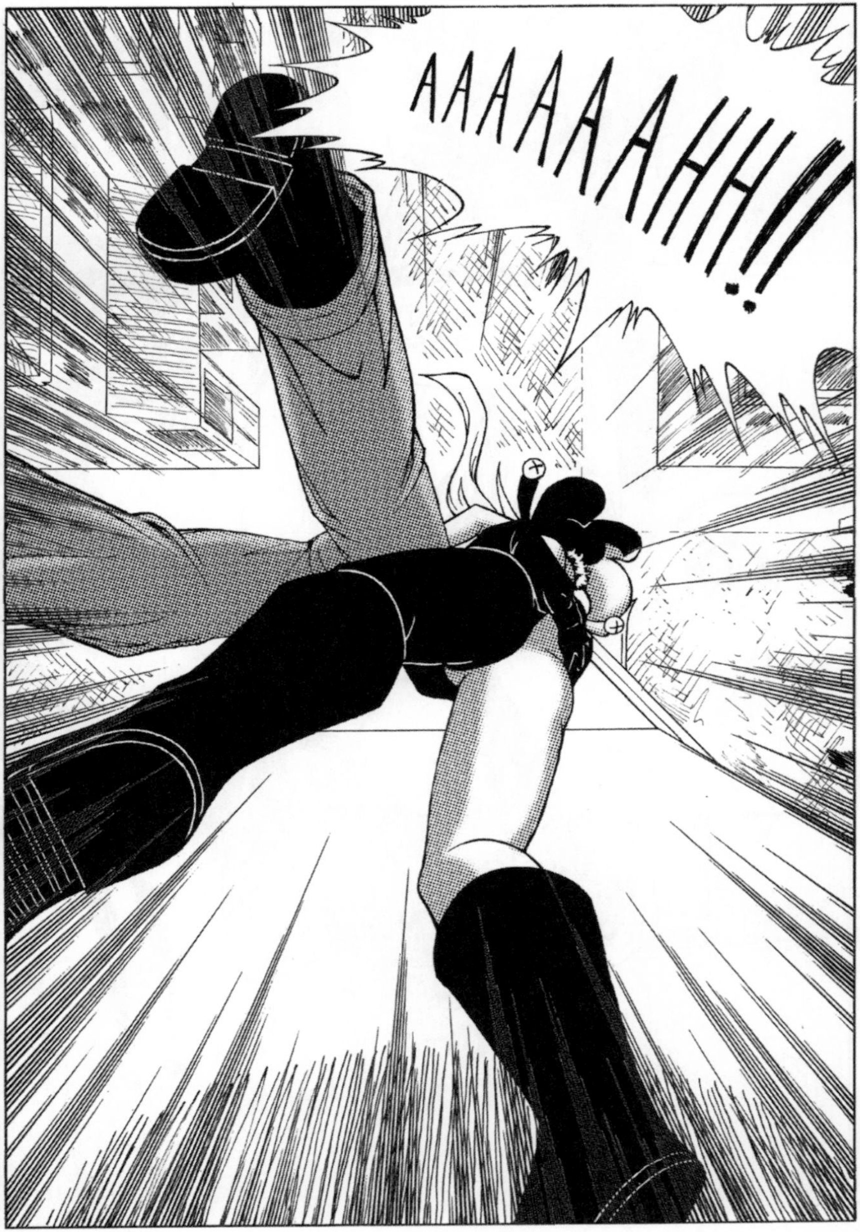
AAAAAAAHH!!

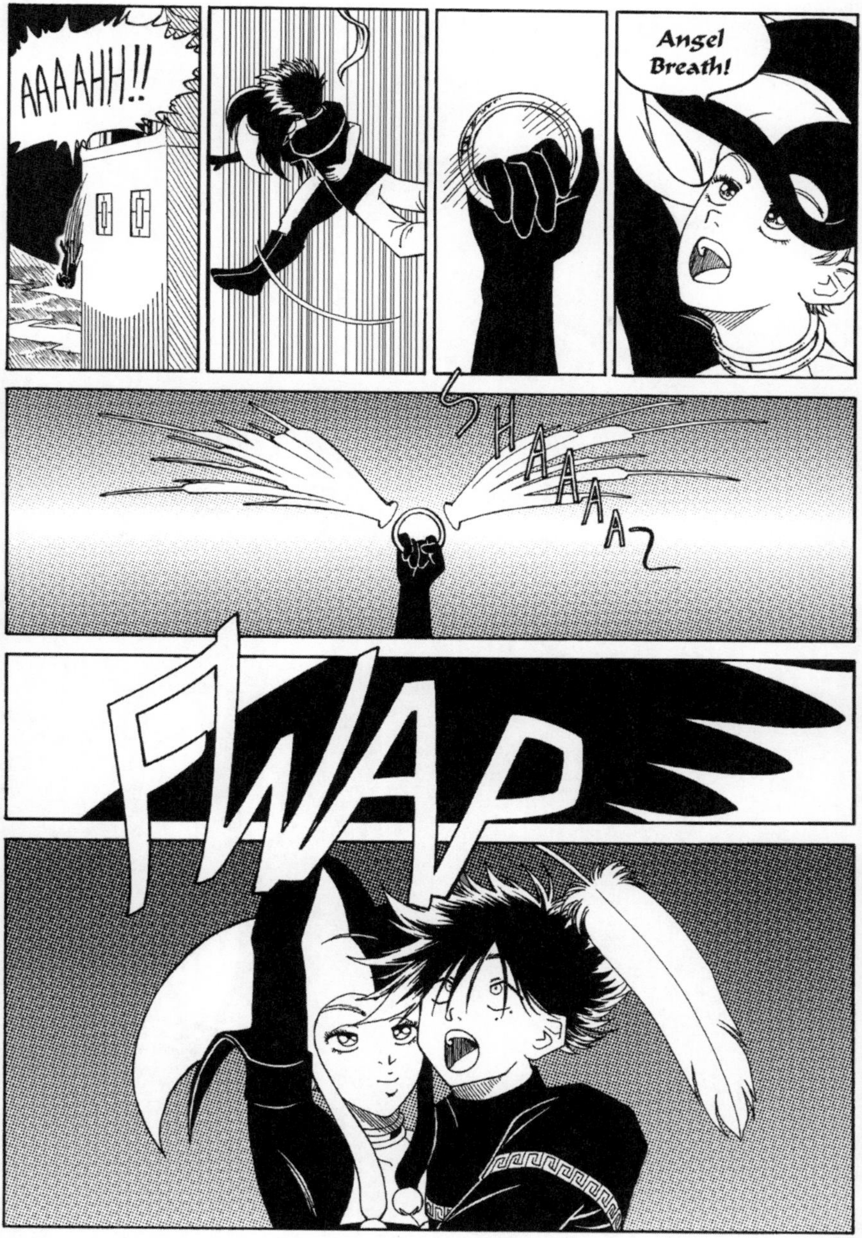
AAAAHH!!
Angel Breath!
SHAAAAAZ
FWAP

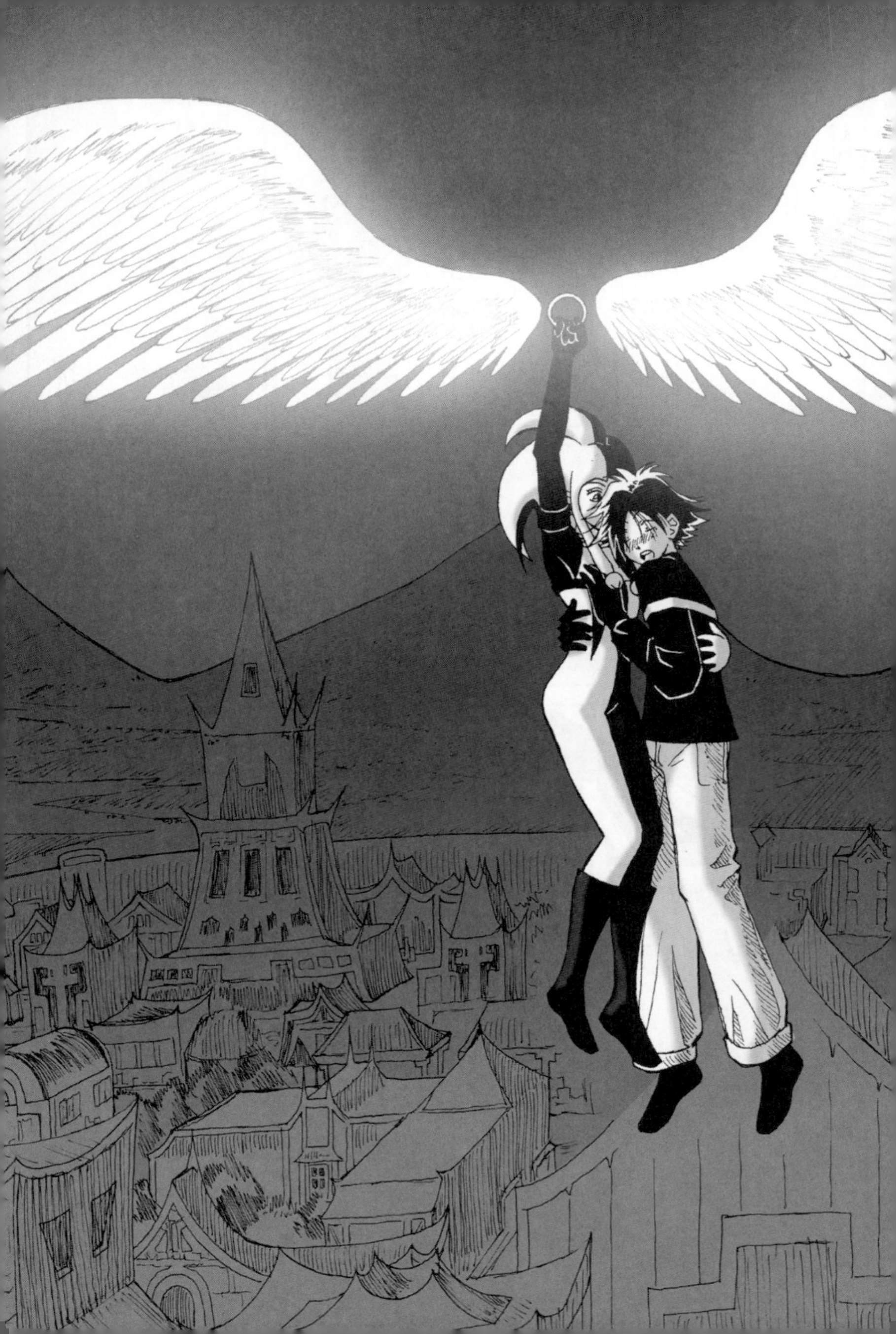

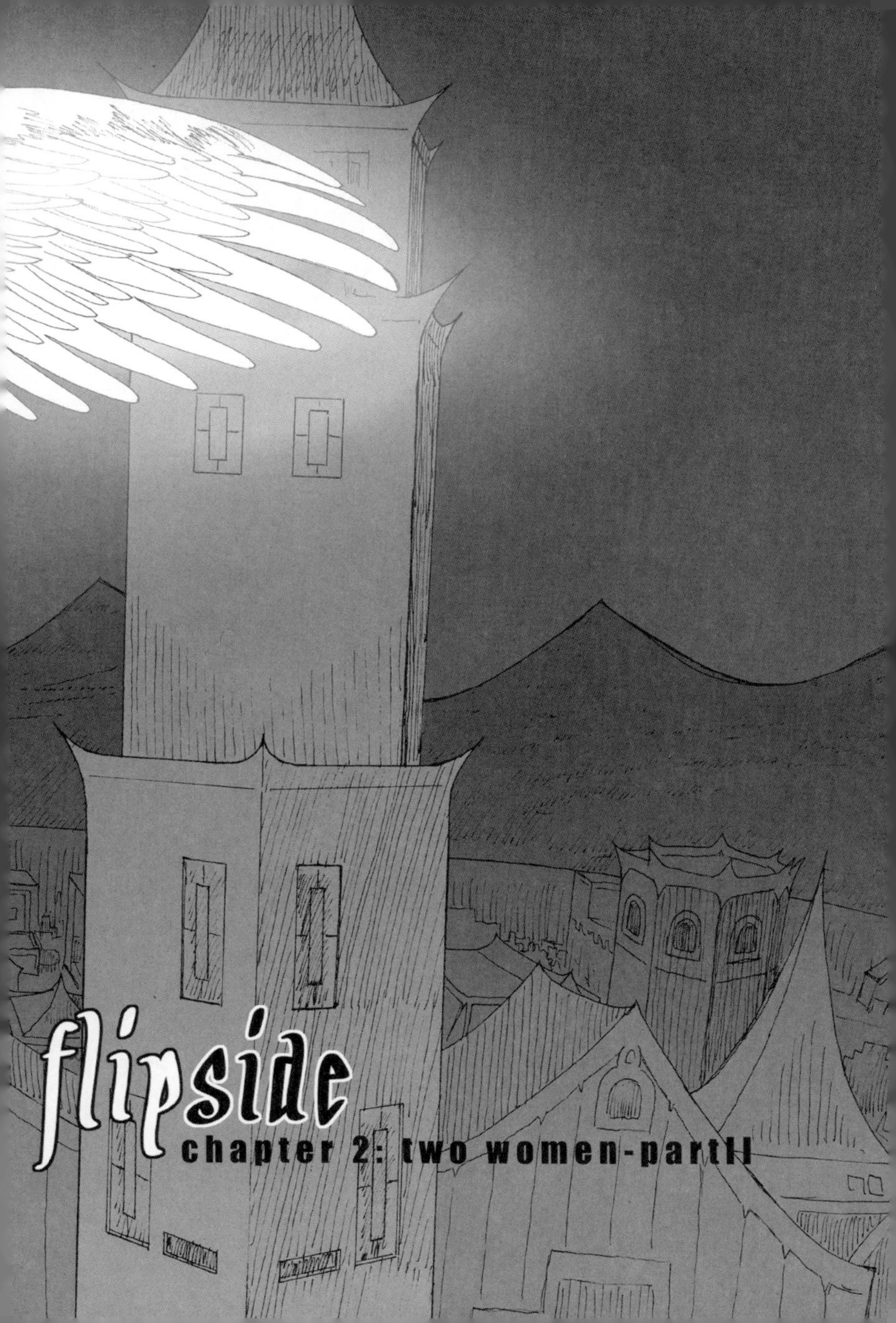
flipside
chapter 2: two women-partII

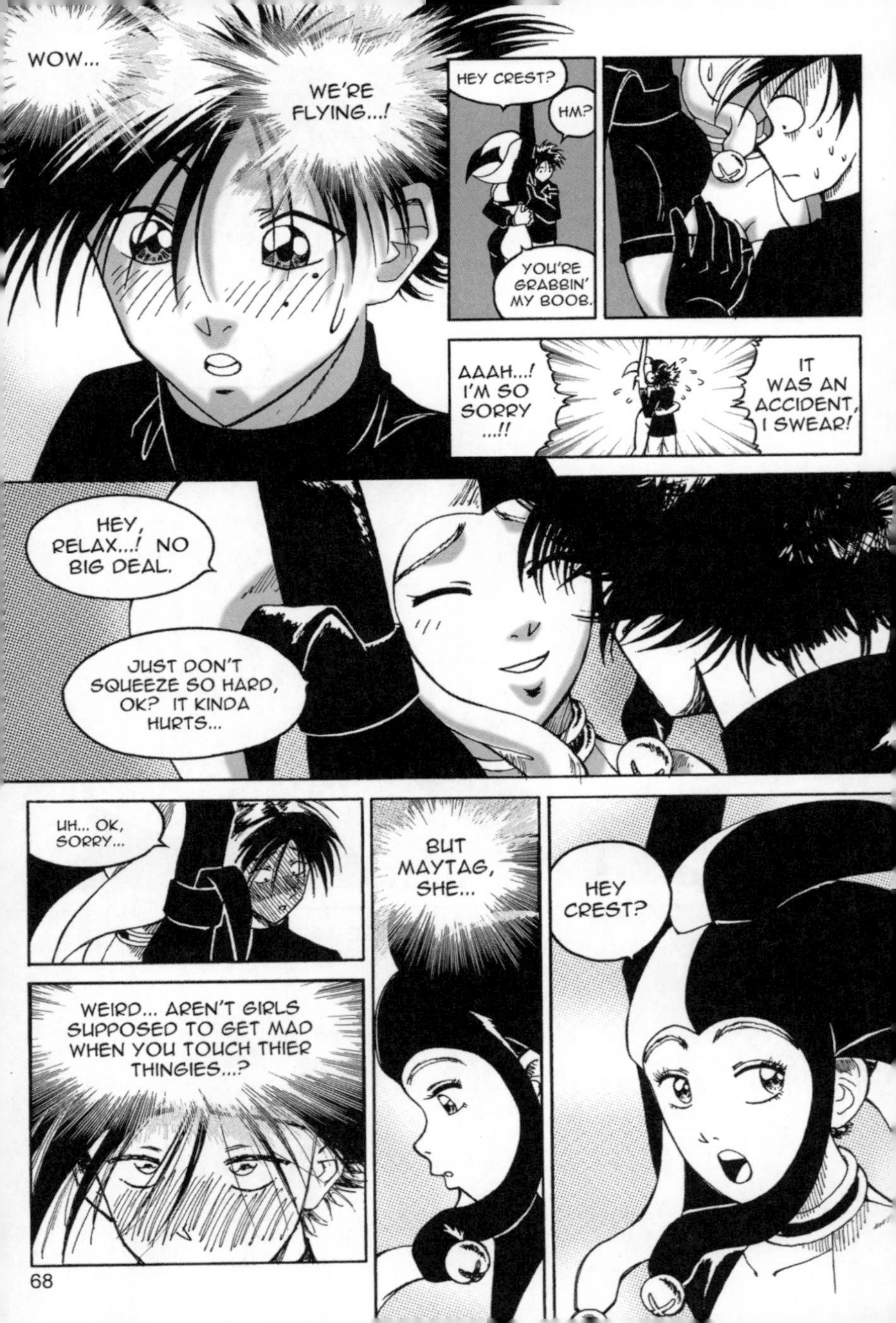
WOW...
WE'RE FLYING...!
HEY CREST?
HM?
YOU'RE GRABBIN' MY BOOB.
AAAH...! I'M SO SORRY ...!!
IT WAS AN ACCIDENT, I SWEAR!
HEY, RELAX...! NO BIG DEAL.
JUST DON'T SQUEEZE SO HARD, OK? IT KINDA HURTS...
UH... OK, SORRY...
BUT MAYTAG, SHE...
HEY CREST?
WEIRD... AREN'T GIRLS SUPPOSED TO GET MAD WHEN YOU TOUCH THIER THINGIES...?

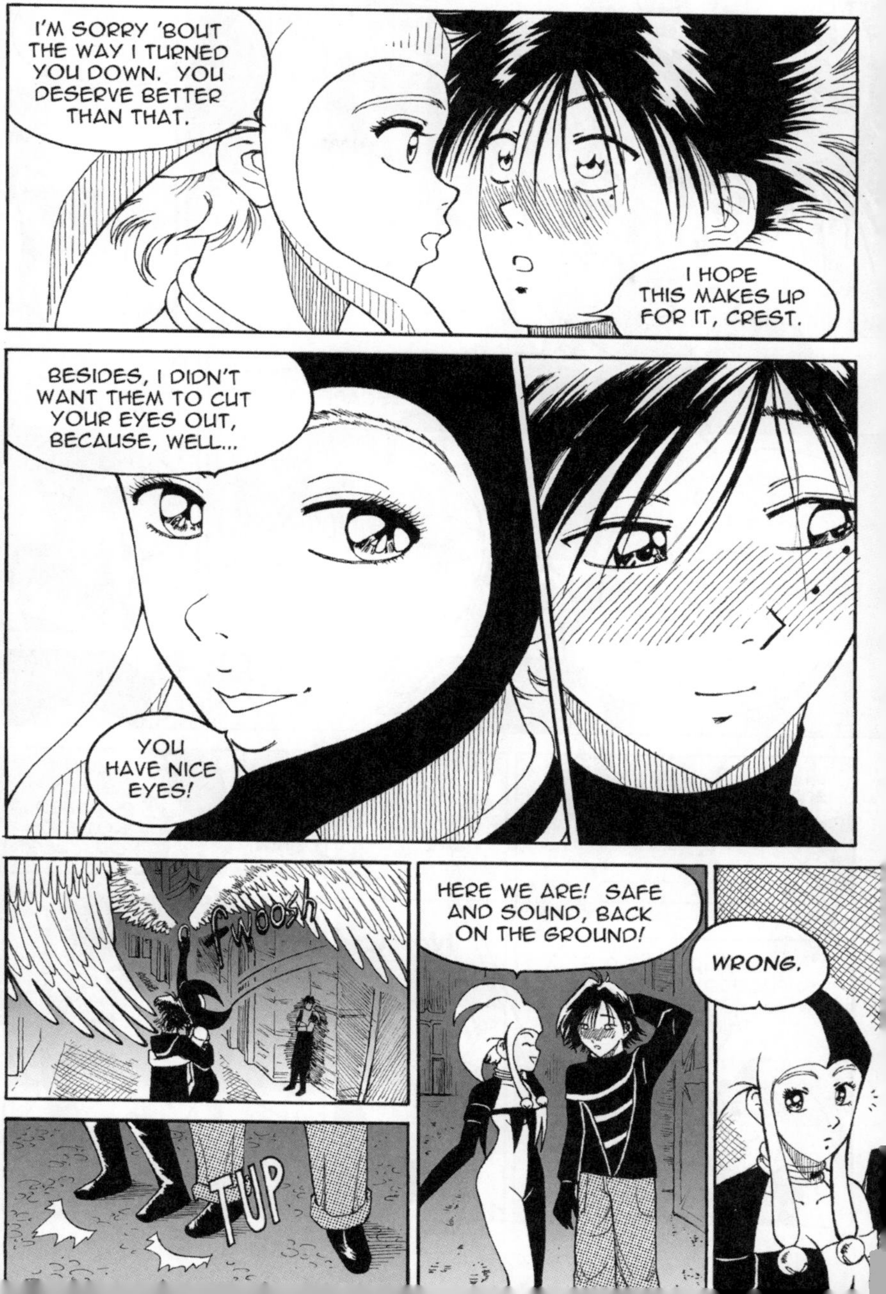
I'M SORRY 'BOUT THE WAY I TURNED YOU DOWN. YOU DESERVE BETTER THAN THAT.
I HOPE THIS MAKES UP FOR IT, CREST.
BESIDES, I DIDN'T WANT THEM TO CUT YOUR EYES OUT, BECAUSE, WELL...
YOU HAVE NICE EYES!
fwoosh
TUP
HERE WE ARE! SAFE AND SOUND, BACK ON THE GROUND!
WRONG.

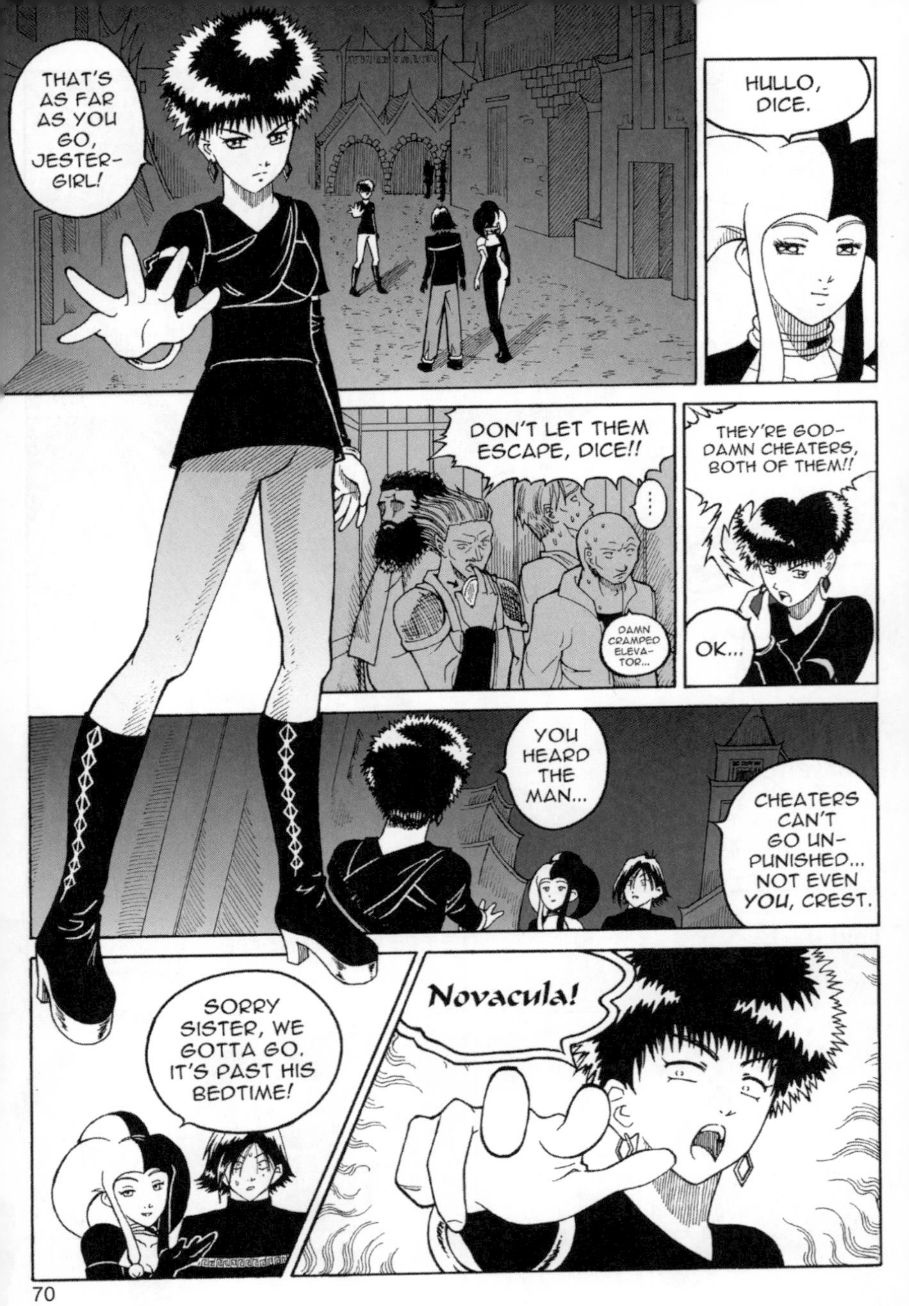
THAT'S AS FAR AS YOU GO, JESTER-GIRL!
HULLO, DICE.
DON'T LET THEM ESCAPE, DICE!!
...
DAMN CRAMPED ELEVATOR...
THEY'RE GOD-DAMN CHEATERS, BOTH OF THEM!!
OK...
YOU HEARD THE MAN...
CHEATERS CAN'T GO UN-PUNISHED... NOT EVEN YOU, CREST.
SORRY SISTER, WE GOTTA GO. IT'S PAST HIS BEDTIME!
Novacula!

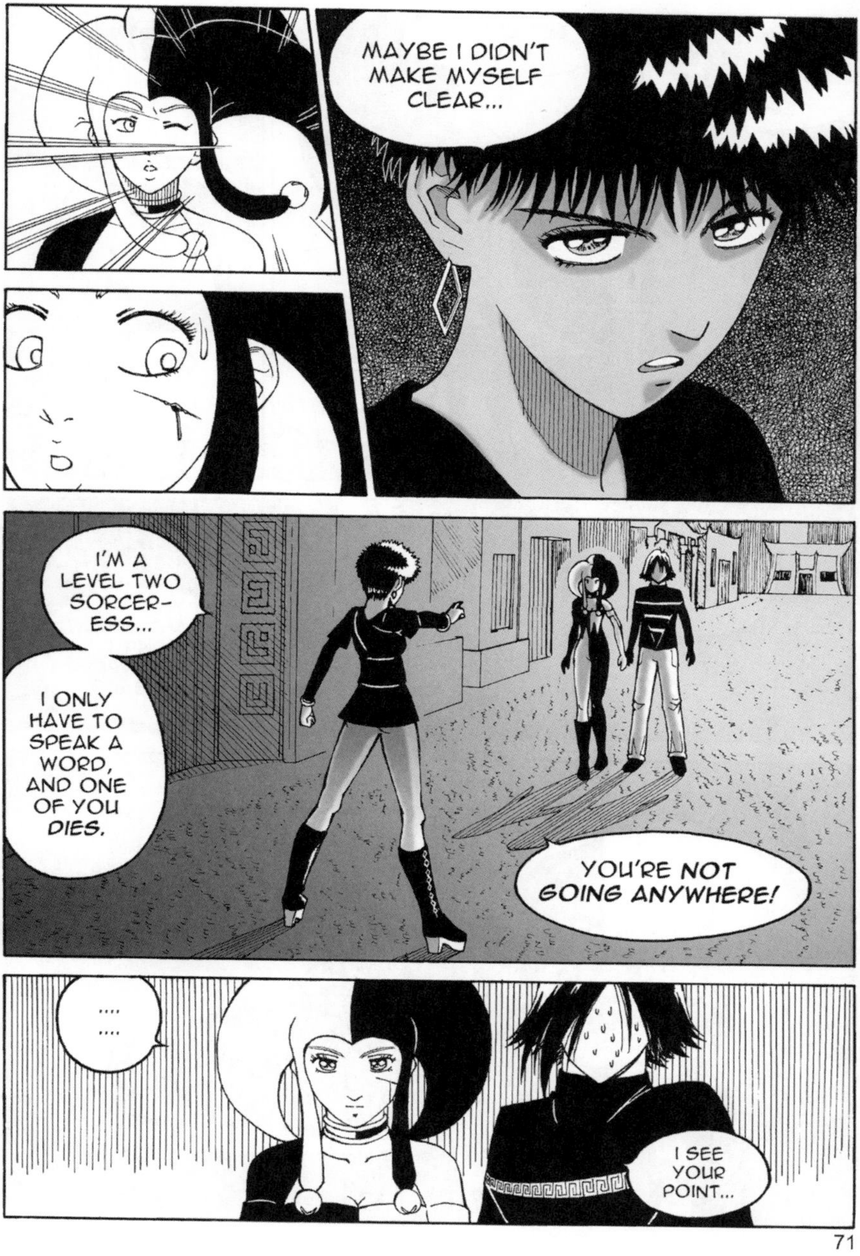
MAYBE I DIDN'T MAKE MYSELF CLEAR...
I'M A LEVEL TWO SORCERER-ESS...
I ONLY HAVE TO SPEAK A WORD, AND ONE OF YOU DIES.
YOU'RE NOT GOING ANYWHERE!
....
....
I SEE YOUR POINT...

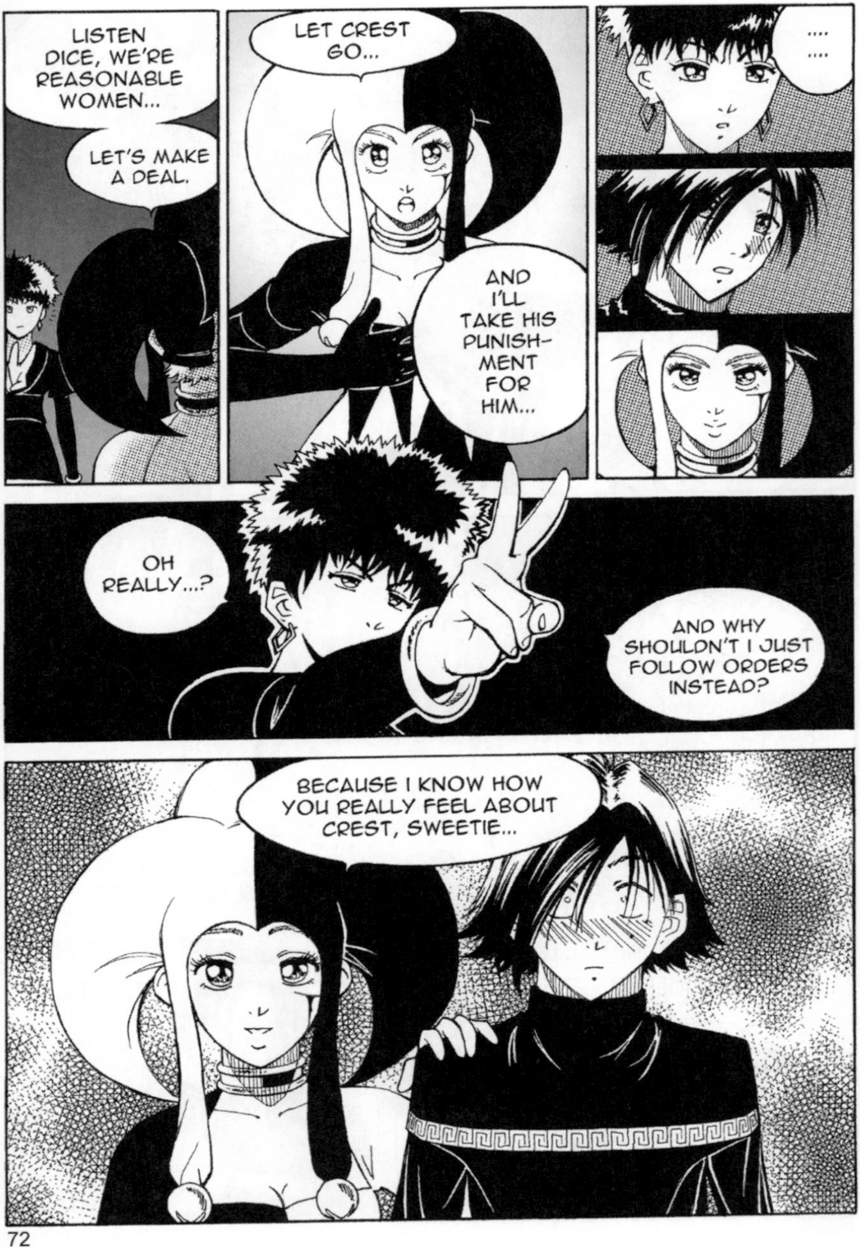
LISTEN DICE, WE'RE REASONABLE WOMEN...
LET'S MAKE A DEAL.
LET CREST GO...
AND I'LL TAKE HIS PUNISH-MENT FOR HIM...
....
....
OH REALLY...?
AND WHY SHOULDN'T I JUST FOLLOW ORDERS INSTEAD?
BECAUSE I KNOW HOW YOU REALLY FEEL ABOUT CREST, SWEETIE...

WHAT--??

THAT'S *RIDICULOUS!* I DON'T--!!

AREN'T YOU JUMPING TO CONCLUSIONS? I NEVER SAID YOU LOVE HIM...!

URK...!

GOTCHA. ♡

DICE, I'M A POKER PLAYER. YOU THINK THAT FLIMSY LITTLE TOUGH-GIRL ACT CAN FOOL ME?

IT'S IRONIC HOW YOU GIVE HIM A HARD TIME FOR BEING SHY...

YOU'RE PATHETIC, Y'KNOW THAT?

YOU'LL PROBABLY *NEVER* GET A GIRL-FRIEND.

...T, ...YA ...YS SO ...GUE-TIED AROUND ...LS?

UHHH...

....

BECAUSE *YOU'RE* THE ONE WHO'S TOO SCARED TO EXPRESS HER FEELINGS!

SHUT UP WITH YOUR *BULLSHIT!* I'M WITH *HELLMOUTH!* AND THAT'S THE WAY I LIKE MY MEN, TOUGH AND CONFIDENT!

THEN WHY ARE YOU BLUSHING?

YOU HATE THE WAY YOU'RE TREATED, DON'T YOU?

THAT'S WHY SECRETLY, YOU WISH YOU COULD BE WITH *CREST* INSTEAD.

73

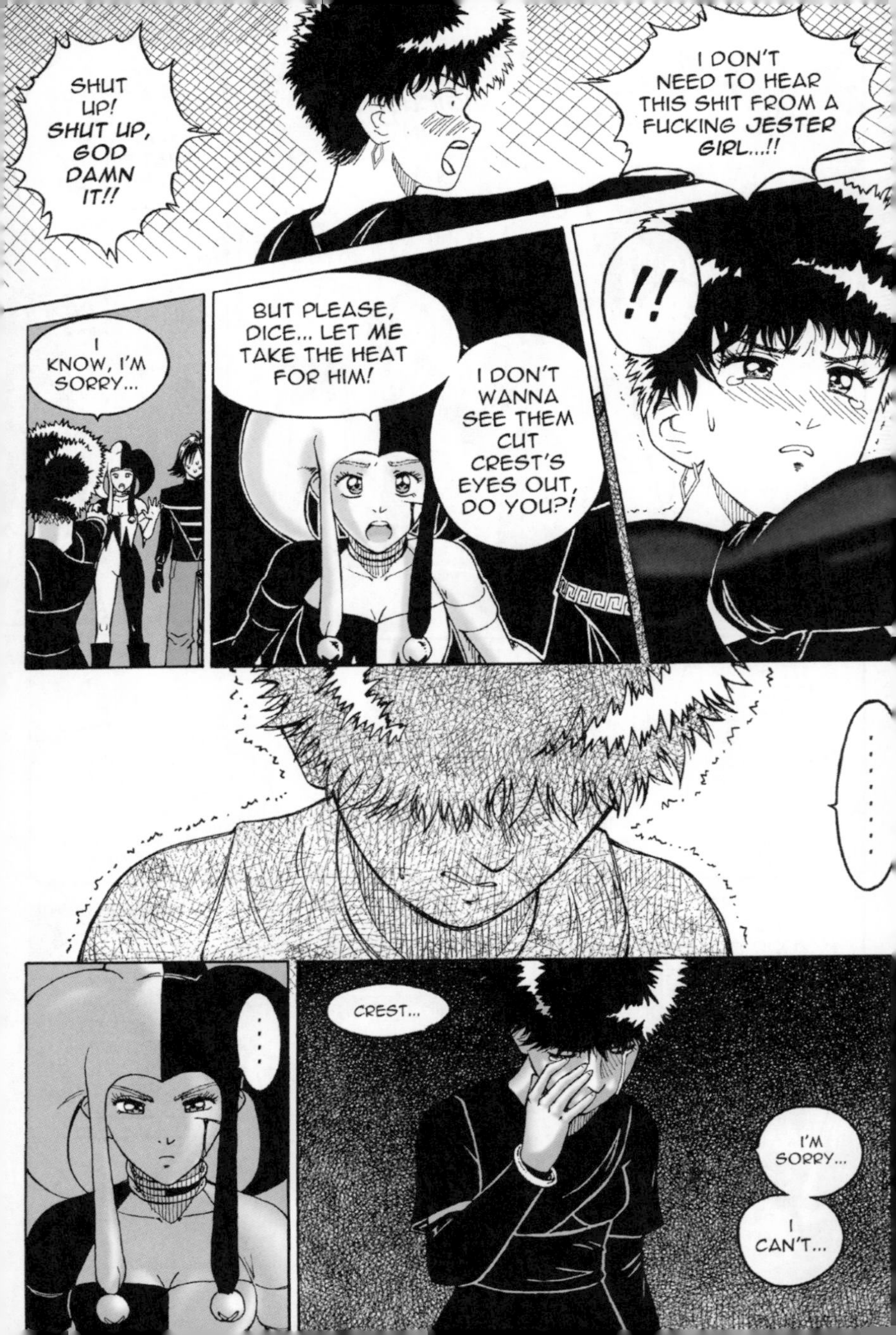
SHUT UP! SHUT UP, GOD DAMN IT!!
I DON'T NEED TO HEAR THIS SHIT FROM A FUCKING JESTER GIRL...!!
I KNOW, I'M SORRY...
BUT PLEASE, DICE... LET ME TAKE THE HEAT FOR HIM!
I DON'T WANNA SEE THEM CUT CREST'S EYES OUT, DO YOU?!
!!
....
...
CREST...
I'M SORRY...
I CAN'T...

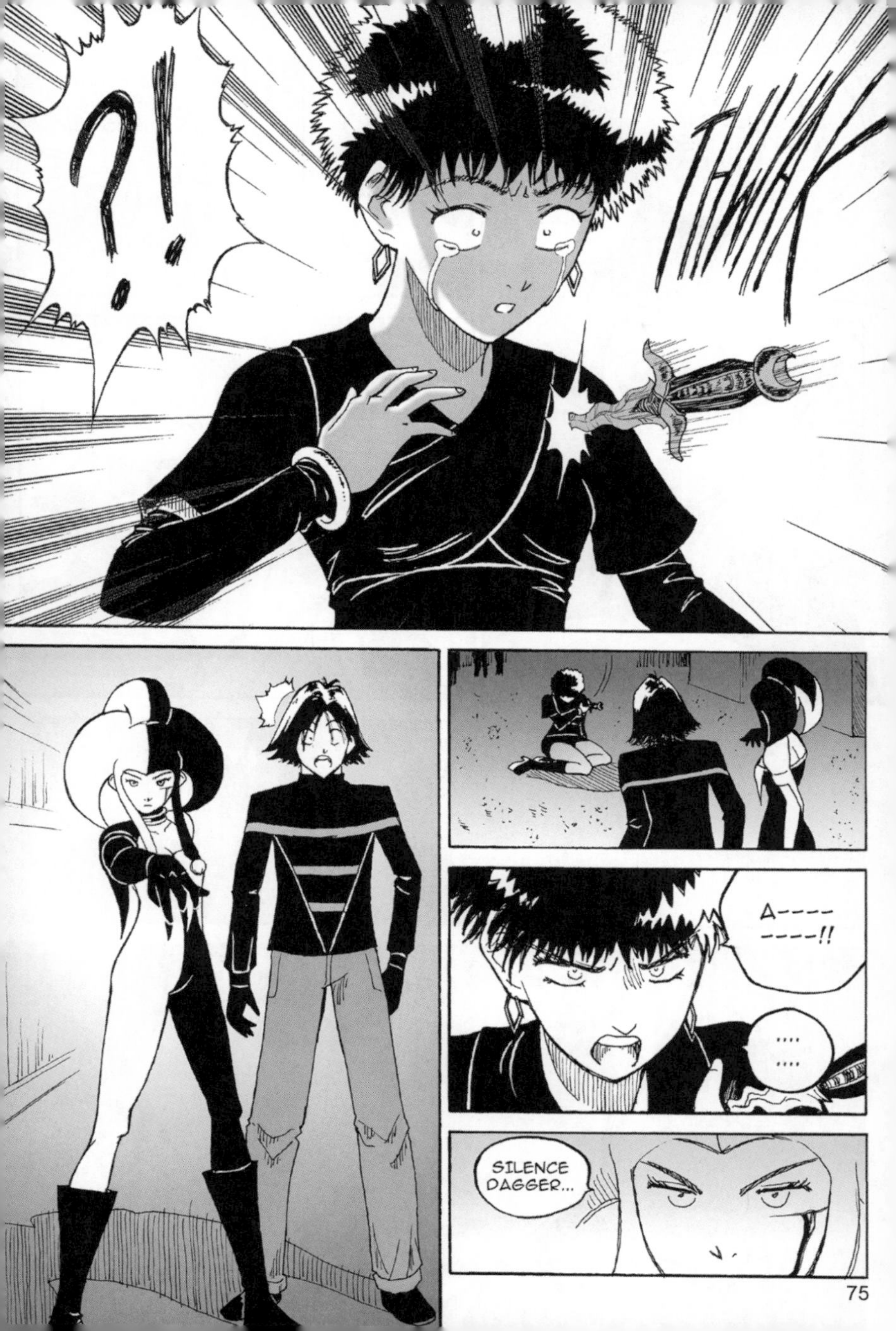
?!
THWAK
A----
----!!
....
....
SILENCE
DAGGER...

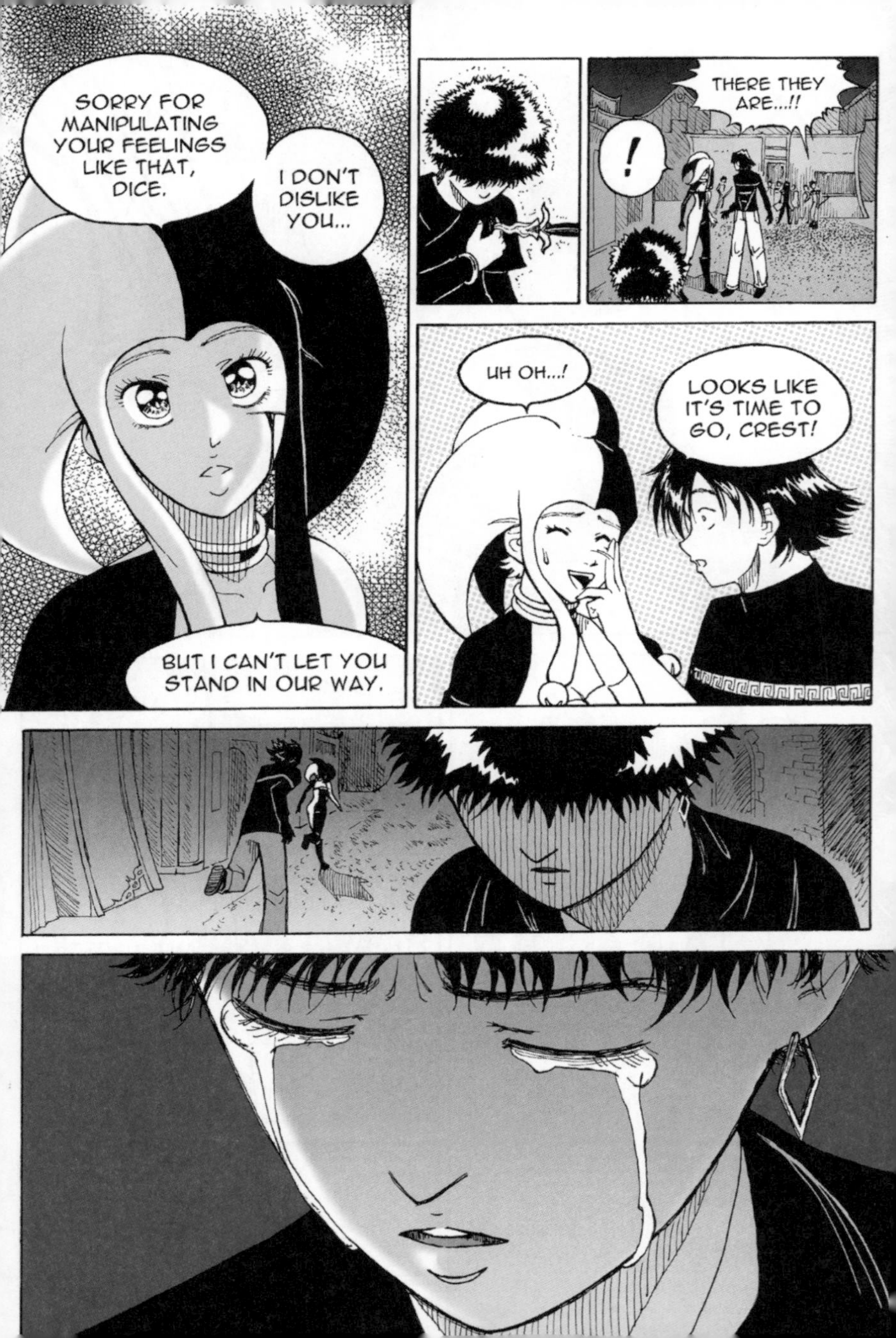
SORRY FOR MANIPULATING YOUR FEELINGS LIKE THAT, DICE.
I DON'T DISLIKE YOU...
BUT I CAN'T LET YOU STAND IN OUR WAY.
THERE THEY ARE...!!
!
UH OH...!
LOOKS LIKE IT'S TIME TO GO, CREST!

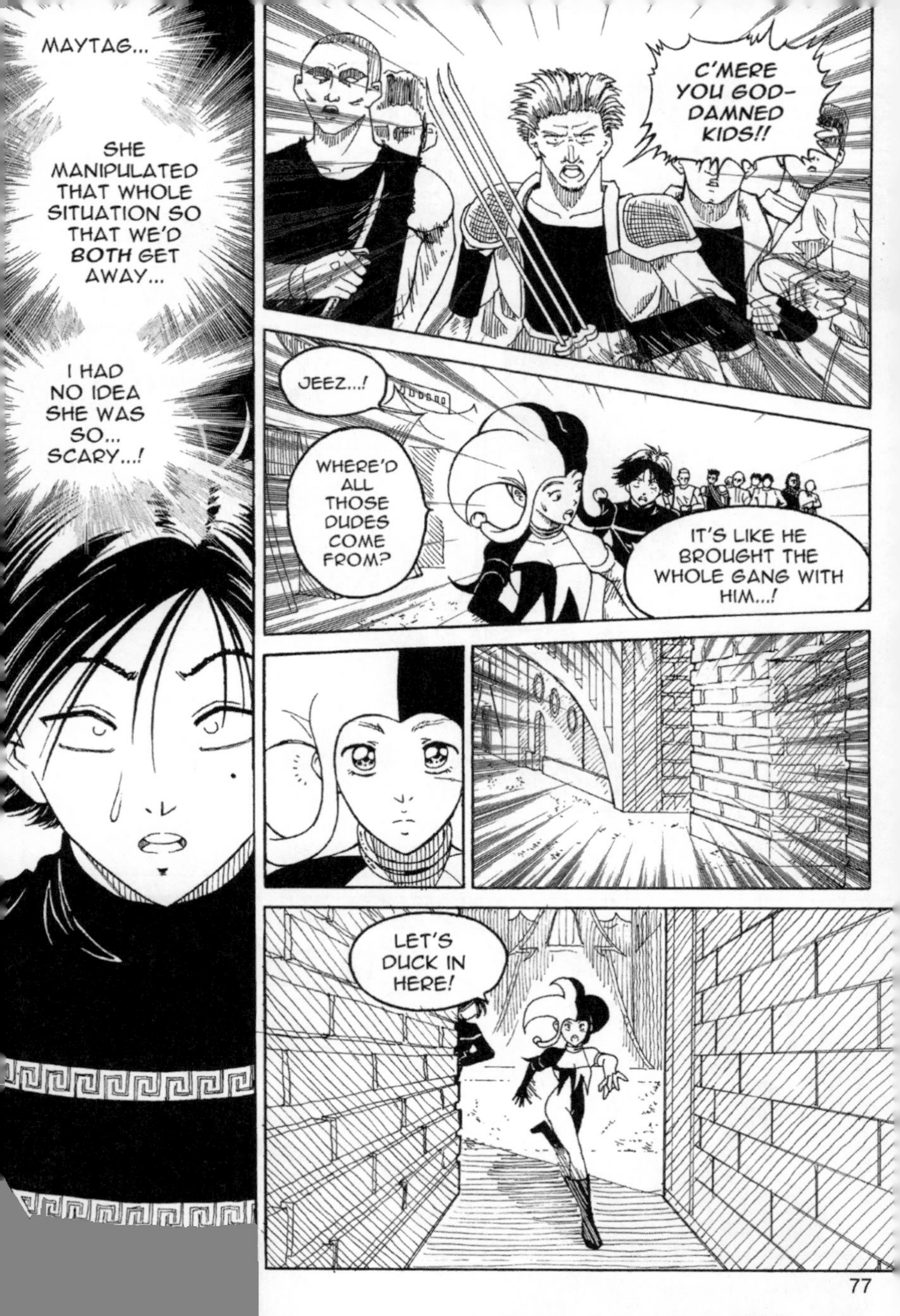
MAYTAG...
SHE MANIPULATED THAT WHOLE SITUATION SO THAT WE'D *BOTH* GET AWAY...
I HAD NO IDEA SHE WAS SO... SCARY...!
C'MERE YOU GOD-DAMNED KIDS!!
JEEZ...!
WHERE'D ALL THOSE DUDES COME FROM?
IT'S LIKE HE BROUGHT THE WHOLE GANG WITH HIM...!
LET'S DUCK IN HERE!

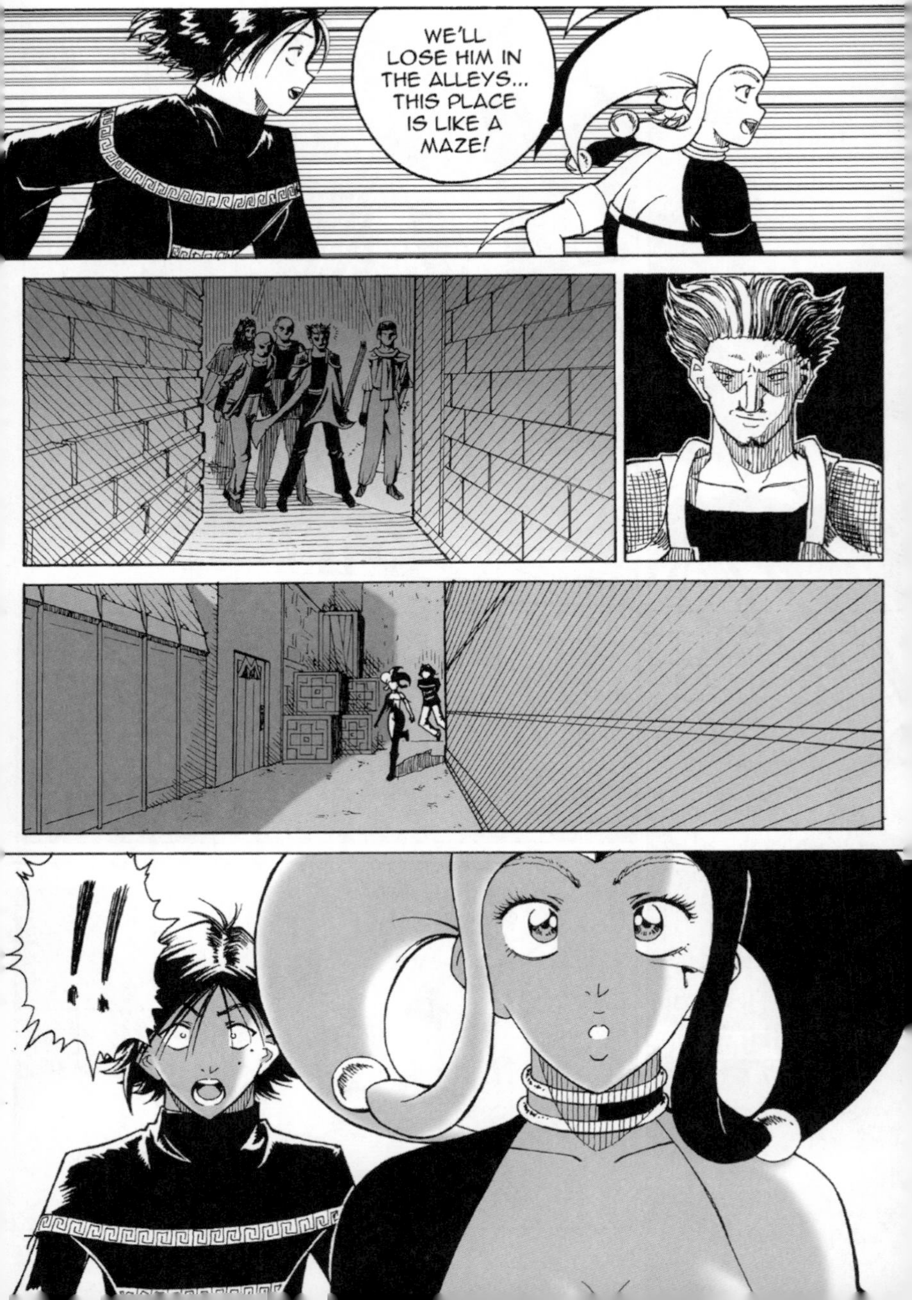
WE'LL LOSE HIM IN THE ALLEYS... THIS PLACE IS LIKE A MAZE!
!!

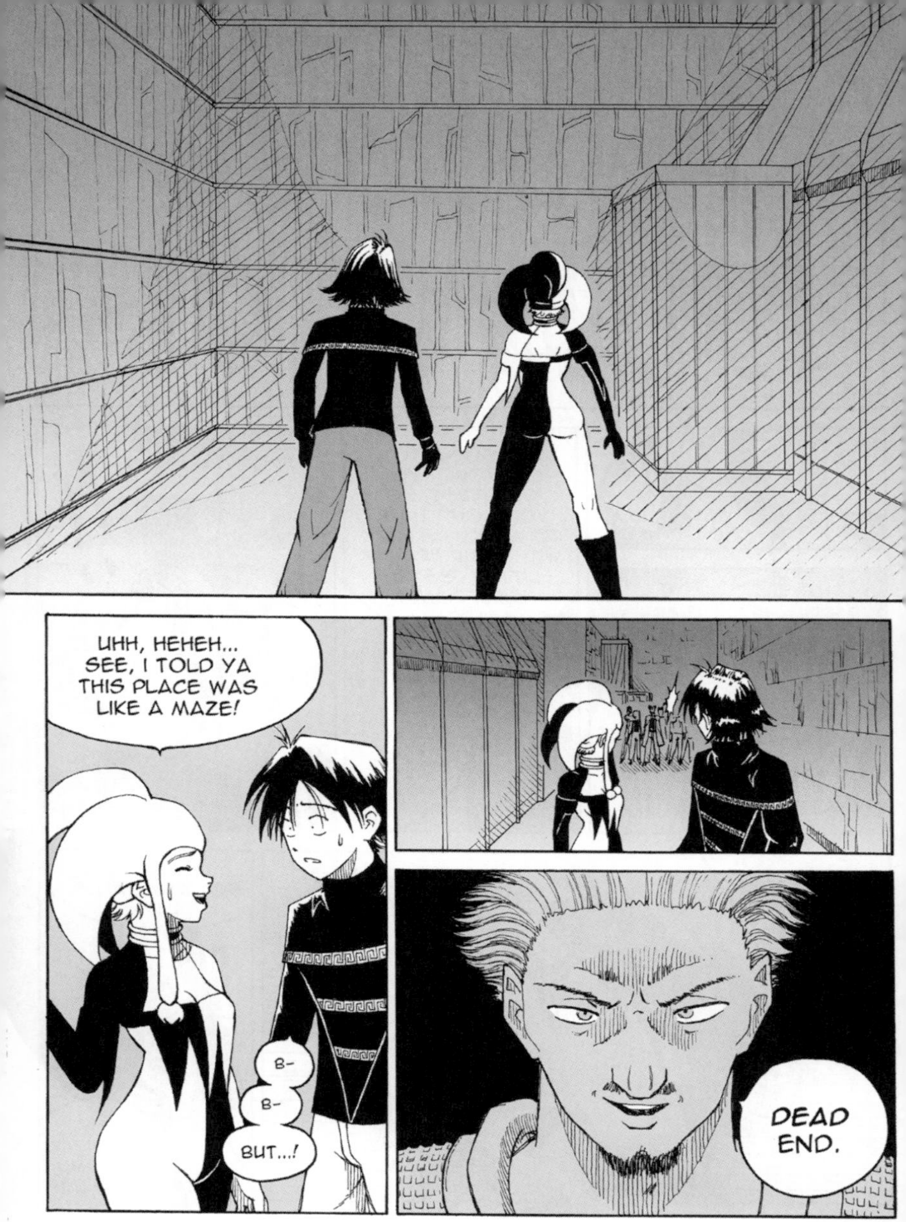
UHH, HEHEH... SEE, I TOLD YA THIS PLACE WAS LIKE A MAZE!
B-
B-
BUT...!
DEAD END.

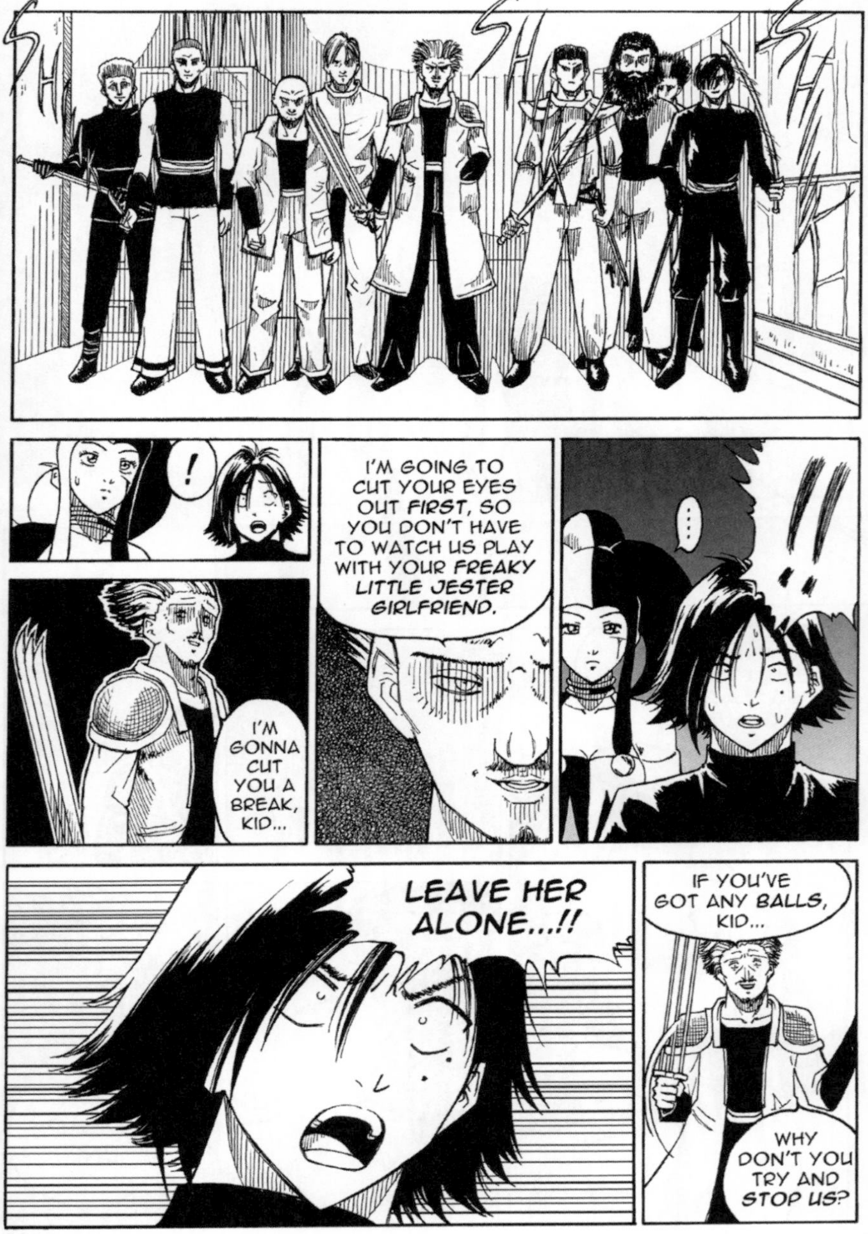
SHH
SHH
SHK
!
I'M GOING TO CUT YOUR EYES OUT FIRST, SO YOU DON'T HAVE TO WATCH US PLAY WITH YOUR FREAKY LITTLE JESTER GIRLFRIEND.
...
!!
I'M GONNA CUT YOU A BREAK, KID...
LEAVE HER ALONE...!!
IF YOU'VE GOT ANY BALLS, KID...
WHY DON'T YOU TRY AND STOP US?

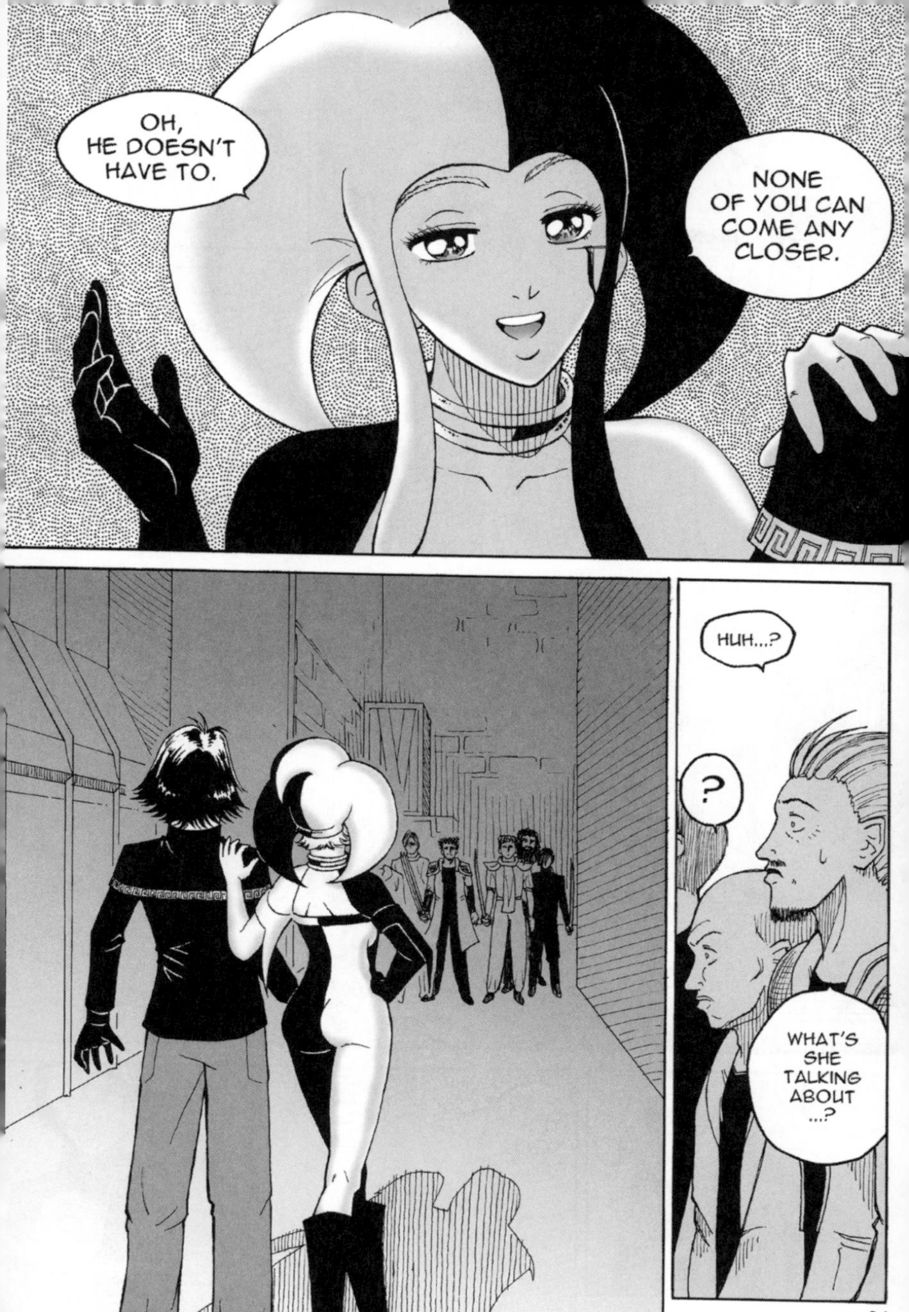
OH, HE DOESN'T HAVE TO.
NONE OF YOU CAN COME ANY CLOSER.
HUH...?
?
WHAT'S SHE TALKING ABOUT ...?

DISTANCE...

"DISTANCE?"

LOOK AT THE DISTANCE BETWEEN US.

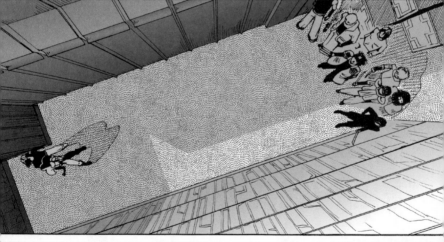

SO WHAT?

...

IT'S TOO FAR...

?

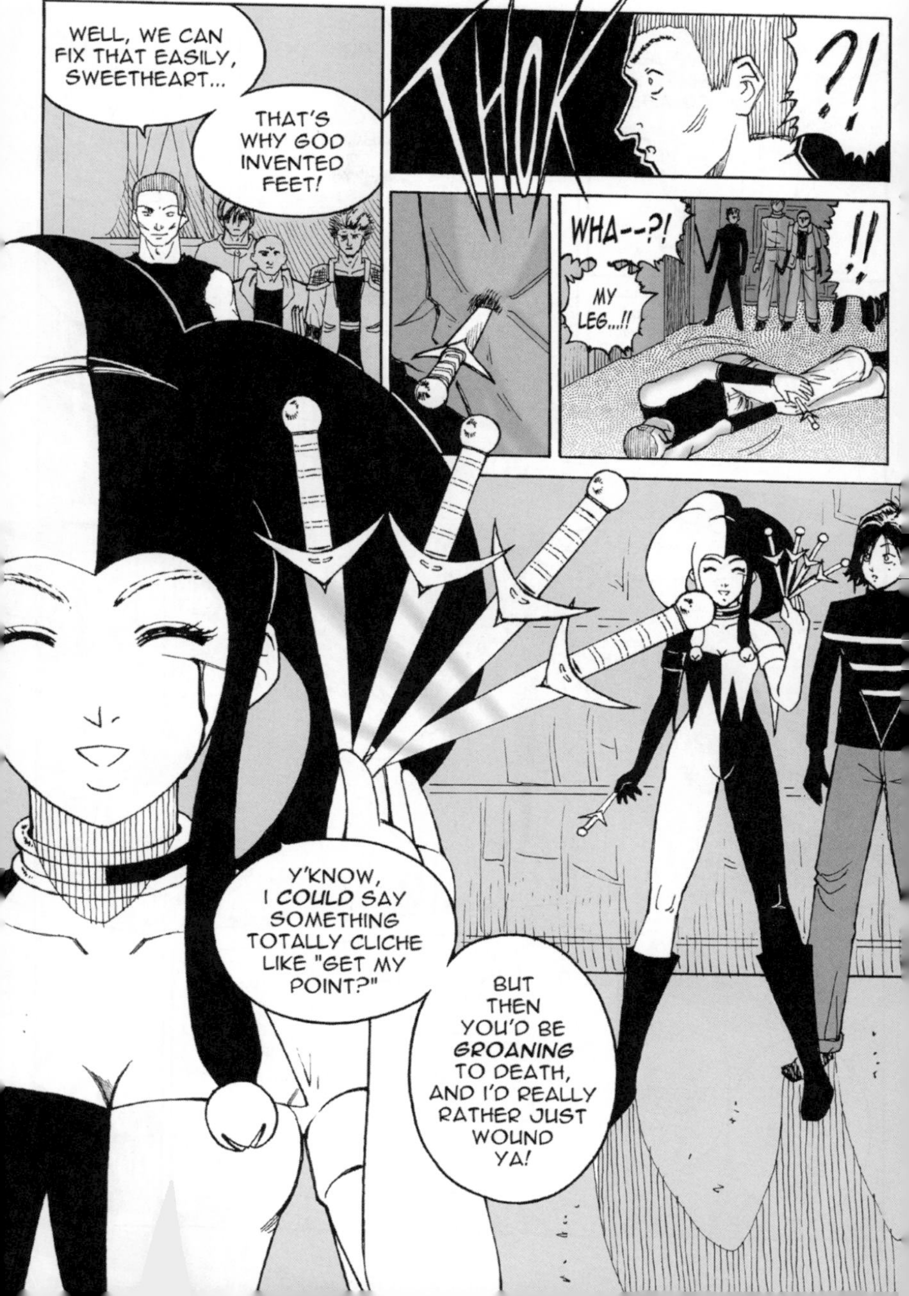
WELL, WE CAN FIX THAT EASILY, SWEETHEART...
THAT'S WHY GOD INVENTED FEET!
THOK
?!
WHA--?!
MY LEG...!!
!!
Y'KNOW, I **COULD** SAY SOMETHING TOTALLY CLICHE LIKE "GET MY POINT?"
BUT THEN YOU'D BE **GROANING** TO DEATH, AND I'D REALLY RATHER JUST WOUND YA!

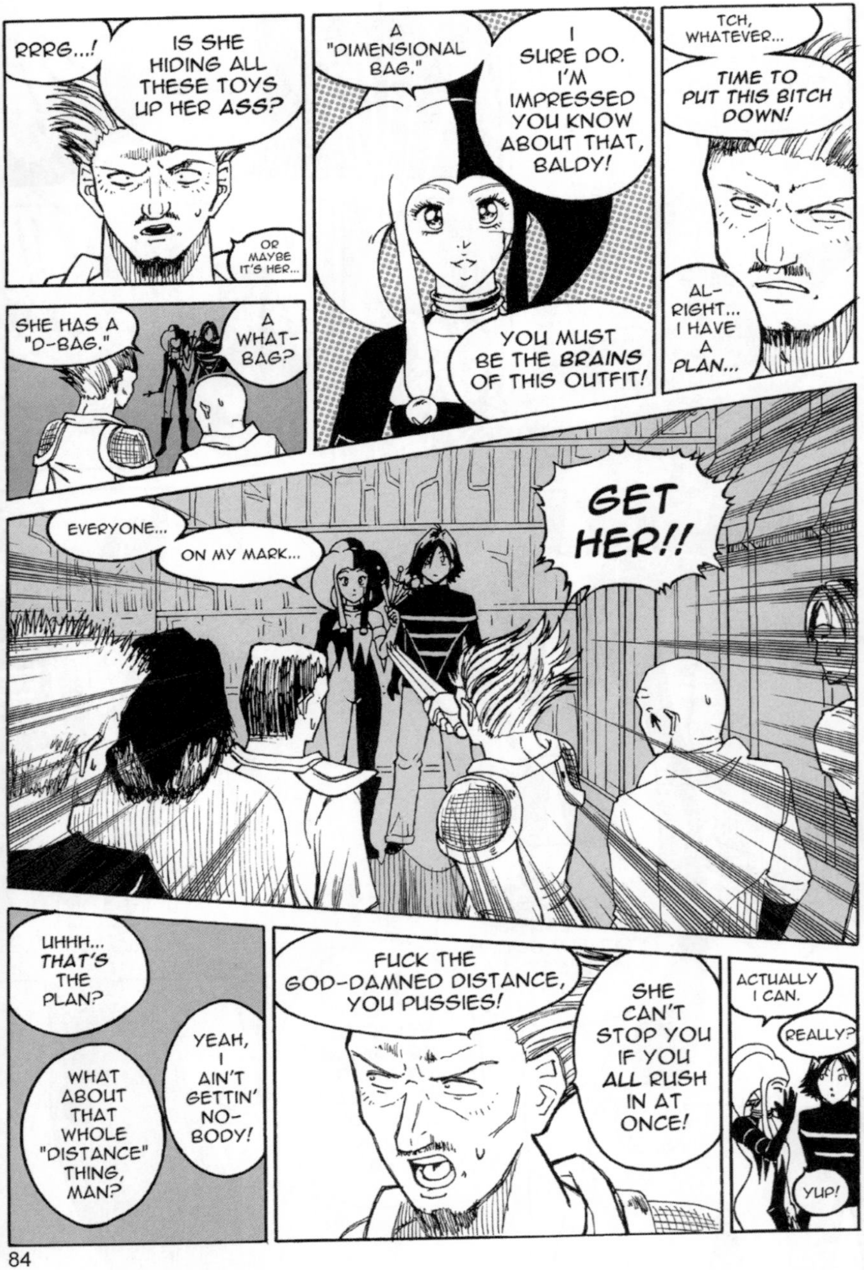
RRRG...!
IS SHE HIDING ALL THESE TOYS UP HER ASS?
OR MAYBE IT'S HER...
A "DIMENSIONAL BAG."
I SURE DO. I'M IMPRESSED YOU KNOW ABOUT THAT, BALDY!
TCH, WHATEVER...
TIME TO PUT THIS BITCH DOWN!
SHE HAS A "D-BAG."
A WHAT-BAG?
YOU MUST BE THE BRAINS OF THIS OUTFIT!
AL-RIGHT... I HAVE A PLAN...
EVERYONE...
ON MY MARK...
GET HER!!
UHHH... THAT'S THE PLAN?
WHAT ABOUT THAT WHOLE "DISTANCE" THING, MAN?
YEAH, I AIN'T GETTIN' NO-BODY!
FUCK THE GOD-DAMNED DISTANCE, YOU PUSSIES!
SHE CAN'T STOP YOU IF YOU ALL RUSH IN AT ONCE!
ACTUALLY I CAN.
REALLY?
YUP!

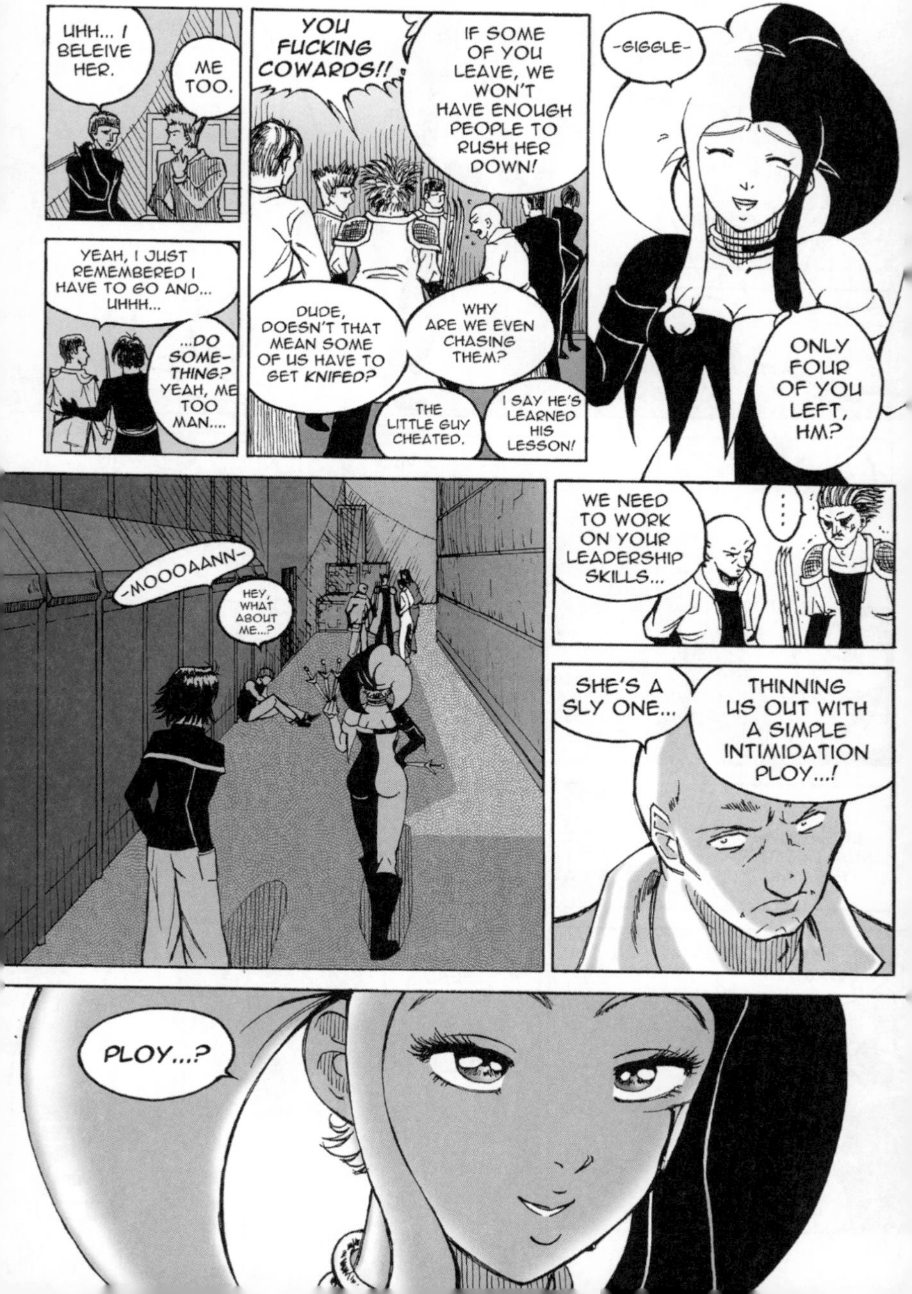
UHH... I BELEIVE HER.
ME TOO.
YOU FUCKING COWARDS!!
IF SOME OF YOU LEAVE, WE WON'T HAVE ENOUGH PEOPLE TO RUSH HER DOWN!
-GIGGLE-
YEAH, I JUST REMEMBERED I HAVE TO GO AND... UHHH...
...DO SOME-THING? YEAH, ME TOO MAN....
DUDE, DOESN'T THAT MEAN SOME OF US HAVE TO GET KNIFED?
WHY ARE WE EVEN CHASING THEM?
THE LITTLE GUY CHEATED.
I SAY HE'S LEARNED HIS LESSON!
ONLY FOUR OF YOU LEFT, HM?
-MOOOAANN-
HEY, WHAT ABOUT ME...?
WE NEED TO WORK ON YOUR LEADERSHIP SKILLS...
. . . .
SHE'S A SLY ONE...
THINNING US OUT WITH A SIMPLE INTIMIDATION PLOY...!
PLOY...?

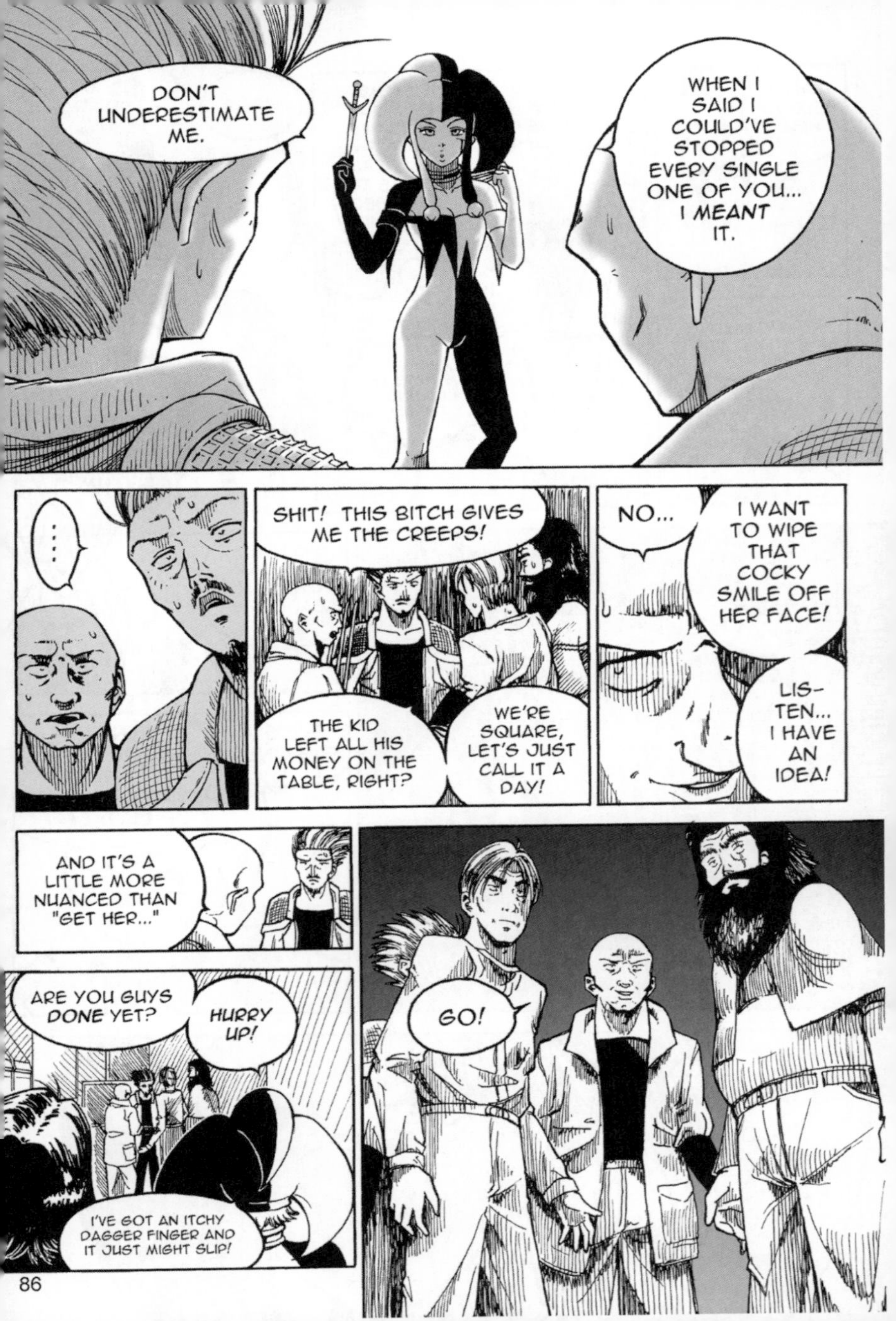
DON'T UNDERESTIMATE ME.
WHEN I SAID I COULD'VE STOPPED EVERY SINGLE ONE OF YOU... I MEANT IT.
...
SHIT! THIS BITCH GIVES ME THE CREEPS!
THE KID LEFT ALL HIS MONEY ON THE TABLE, RIGHT?
WE'RE SQUARE, LET'S JUST CALL IT A DAY!
NO...
I WANT TO WIPE THAT COCKY SMILE OFF HER FACE!
LIS-TEN... I HAVE AN IDEA!
AND IT'S A LITTLE MORE NUANCED THAN "GET HER..."
ARE YOU GUYS DONE YET?
HURRY UP!
I'VE GOT AN ITCHY DAGGER FINGER AND IT JUST MIGHT SLIP!
GO!

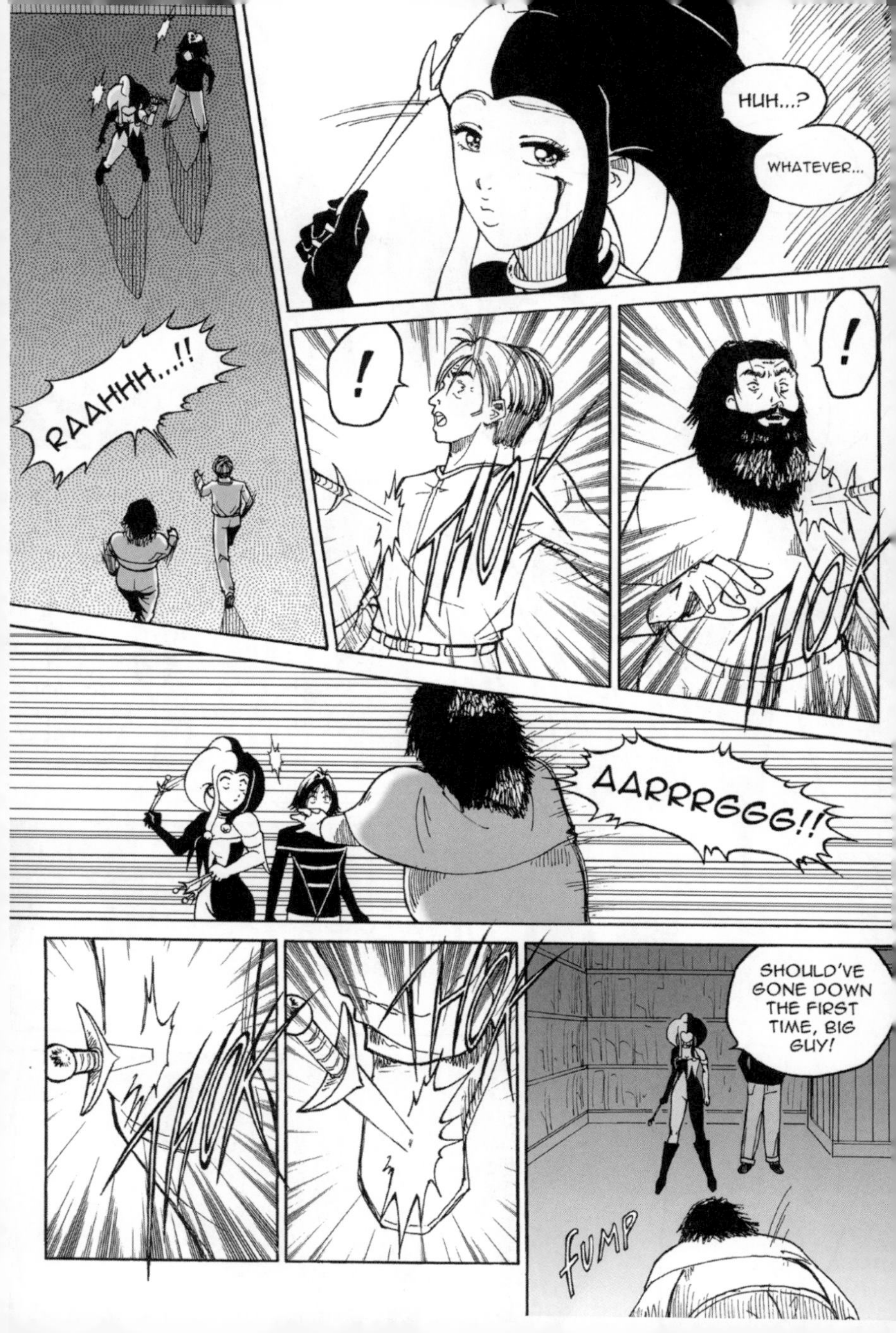
HUH...?
WHATEVER...
RAAHHH...!!
!
THOK
!
THOK
AARRRGGG!!
THOK
THOK
SHOULD'VE GONE DOWN THE FIRST TIME, BIG GUY!
FUMP

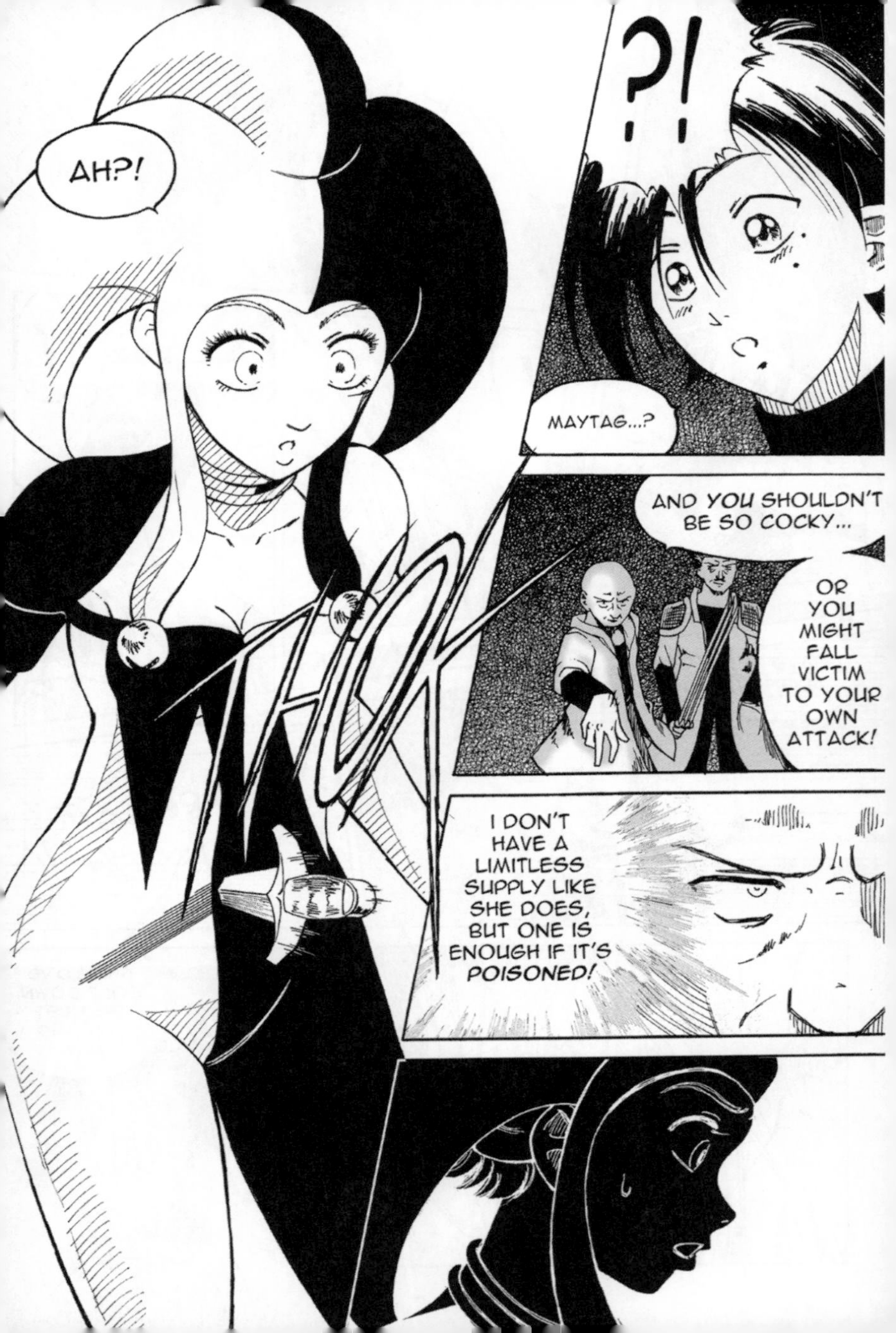
?!
MAYTAG...?
AH?!
THOK
AND YOU SHOULDN'T BE SO COCKY...
OR YOU MIGHT FALL VICTIM TO YOUR OWN ATTACK!
I DON'T HAVE A LIMITLESS SUPPLY LIKE SHE DOES, BUT ONE IS ENOUGH IF IT'S POISONED!

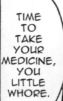

MAYTAG!!

TIME TO TAKE YOUR MEDICINE, YOU LITTLE WHORE.

LET'S FIND A GOOD USE FOR THAT DIRTY LITTLE MOUTH OF HERS...

NO...!

LEAVE HER ALONE!!

I'M THE ONE YOU WANT, RIGHT?

THIS DOESN'T INVOLVE HER!

SHE INVOLVED *HERSELF* WHEN SHE STARTED STABBING MY MEN!

SO YOU WANT ME TO GO THROUGH YOU, KID...?

FINE BY ME.

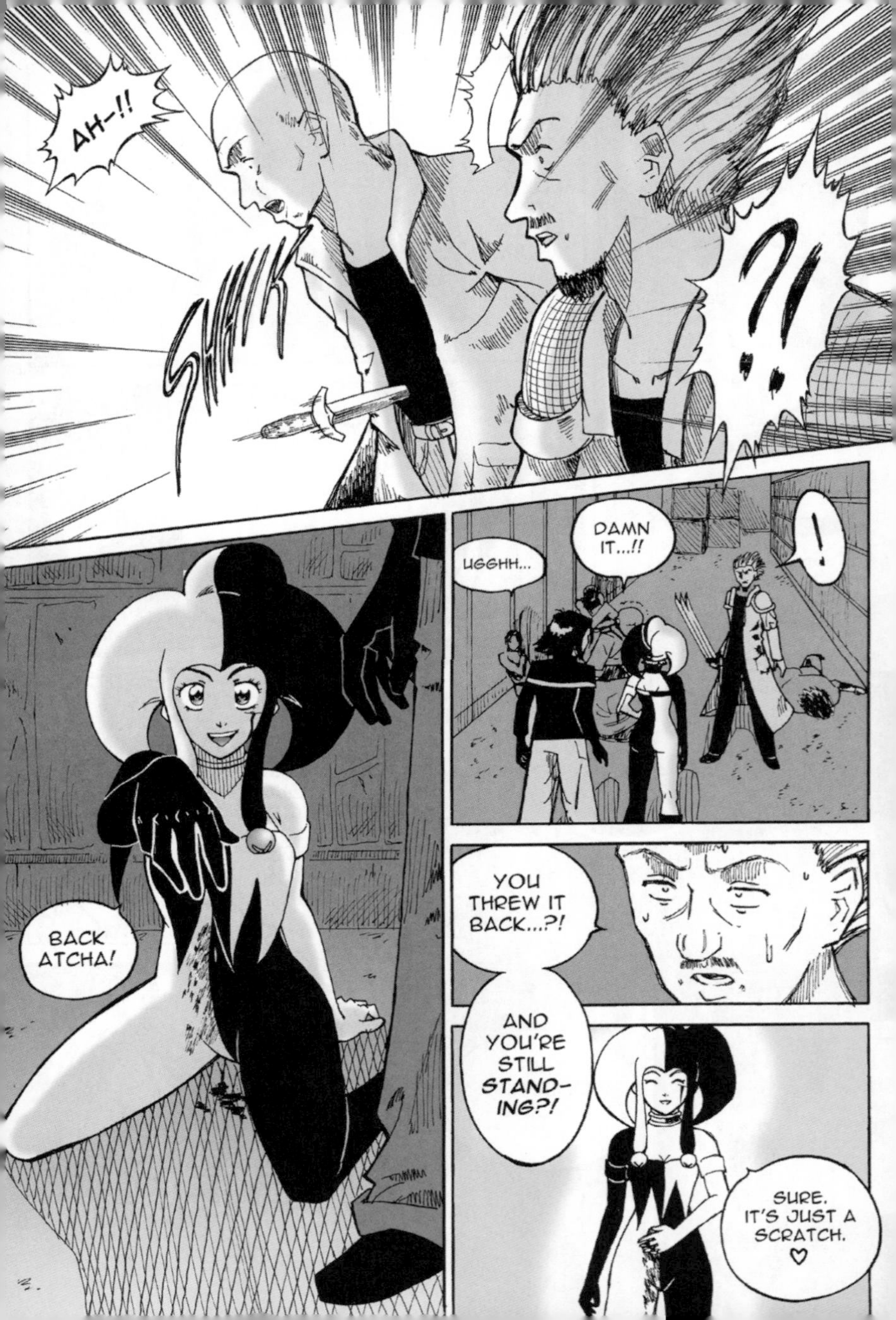

AH-!!
SHAK
?!
UGGHH...
DAMN IT...!!
!
BACK ATCHA!
YOU THREW IT BACK...?!
AND YOU'RE STILL STANDING?!
SURE. IT'S JUST A SCRATCH. ♡

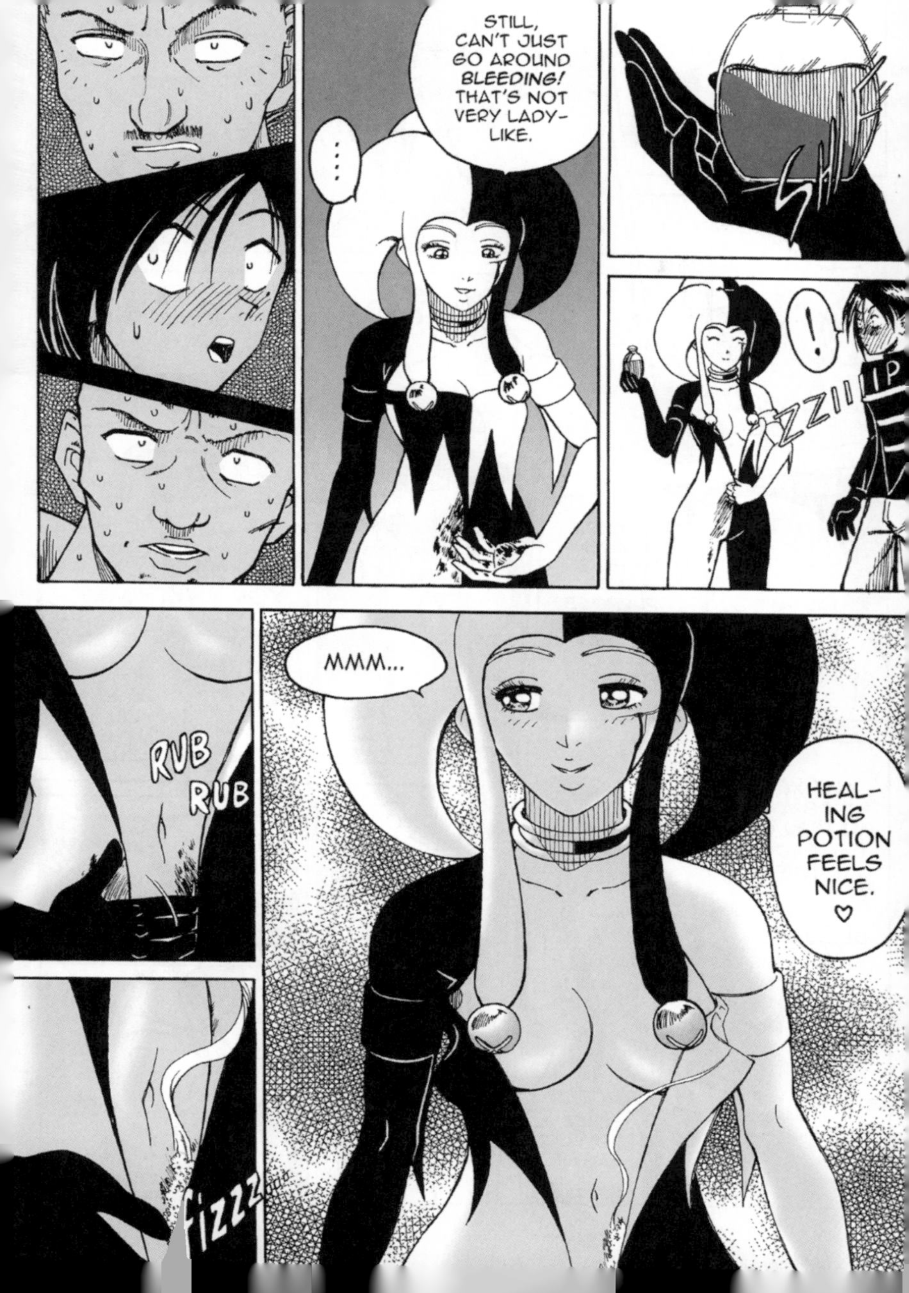
STILL, CAN'T JUST GO AROUND BLEEDING! THAT'S NOT VERY LADY-LIKE.
...
!
ZZIIIP
RUB RUB
MMM...
HEAL-ING POTION FEELS NICE. ♡
fizzz

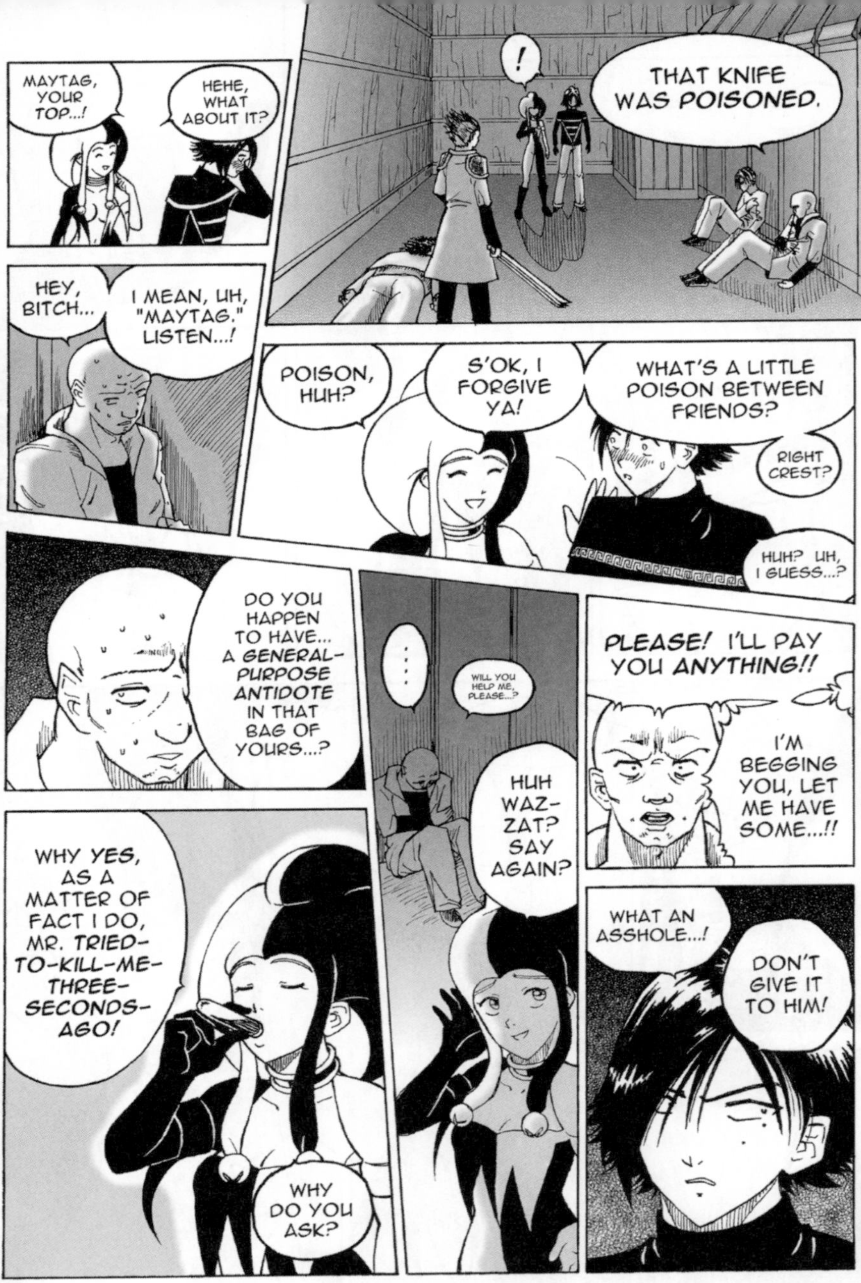

MAYTAG, YOUR TOP...!
HEHE, WHAT ABOUT IT?
!
THAT KNIFE WAS POISONED.
HEY, BITCH...
I MEAN, UH, "MAYTAG." LISTEN...!
POISON, HUH?
S'OK, I FORGIVE YA!
WHAT'S A LITTLE POISON BETWEEN FRIENDS?
RIGHT CREST?
HUH? UH, I GUESS...?
DO YOU HAPPEN TO HAVE... A GENERAL-PURPOSE ANTIDOTE IN THAT BAG OF YOURS...?
...
WILL YOU HELP ME, PLEASE...?
PLEASE! I'LL PAY YOU ANYTHING!!
I'M BEGGING YOU, LET ME HAVE SOME...!!
HUH WAZ-ZAT? SAY AGAIN?
WHY YES, AS A MATTER OF FACT I DO, MR. TRIED-TO-KILL-ME-THREE-SECONDS-AGO!
WHY DO YOU ASK?
WHAT AN ASSHOLE...!
DON'T GIVE IT TO HIM!

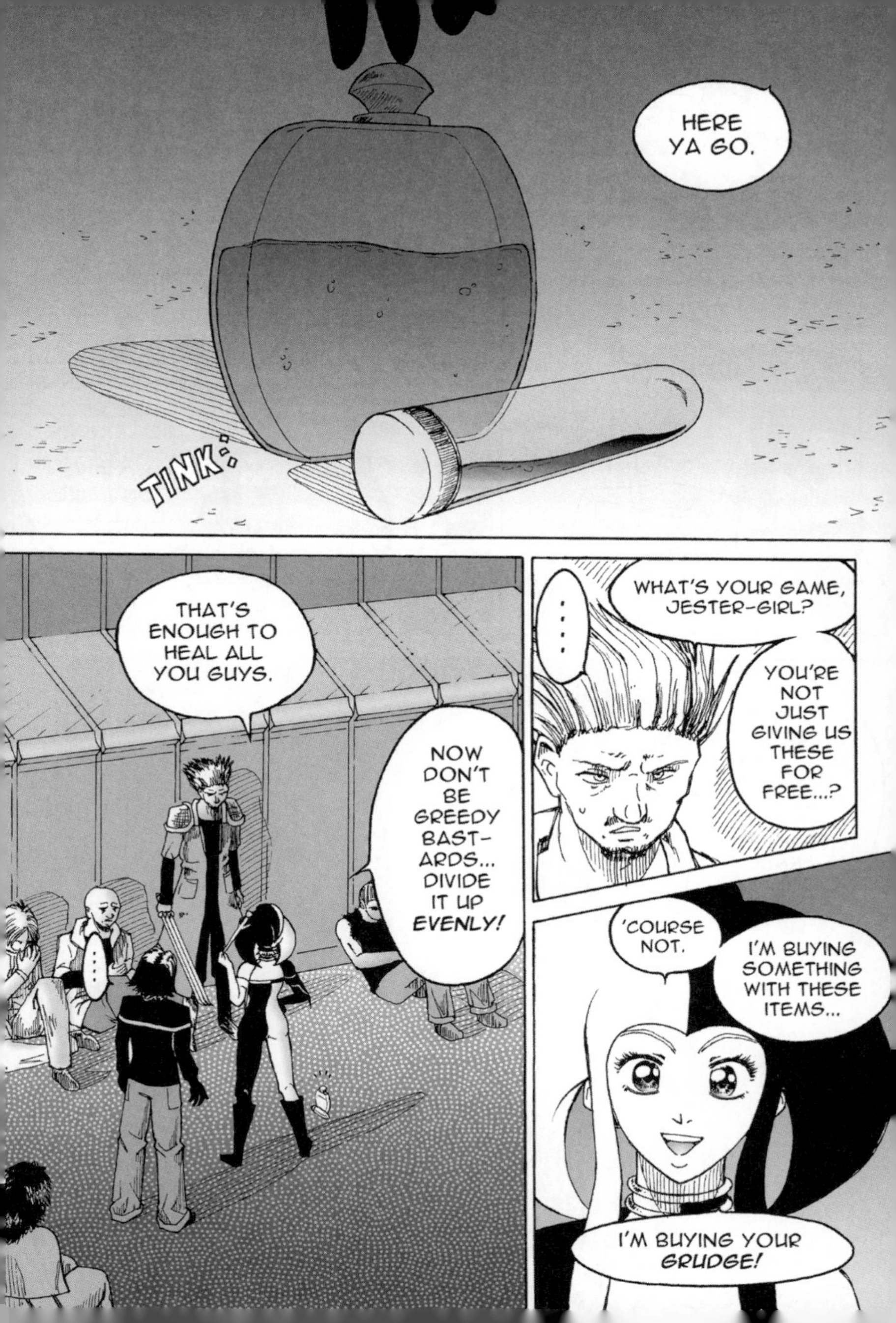

HERE YA GO.
TINK:
THAT'S ENOUGH TO HEAL ALL YOU GUYS.
NOW DON'T BE GREEDY BAST-ARDS... DIVIDE IT UP *EVENLY!*
. . . .
...
WHAT'S YOUR GAME, JESTER-GIRL?
YOU'RE NOT JUST GIVING US THESE FOR FREE...?
'COURSE NOT.
I'M BUYING SOMETHING WITH THESE ITEMS...
I'M BUYING YOUR *GRUDGE!*

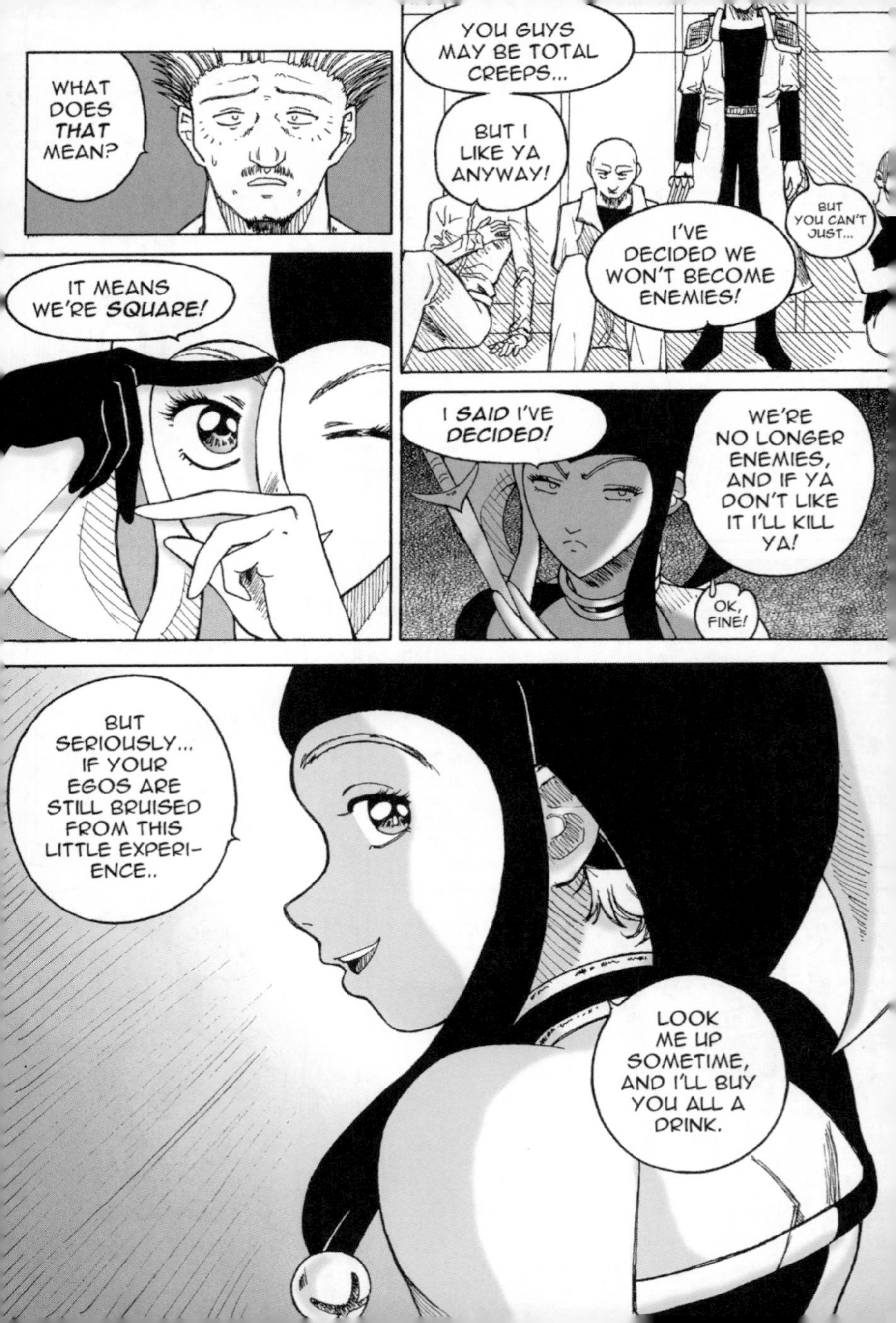

WHAT DOES THAT MEAN?
YOU GUYS MAY BE TOTAL CREEPS...
BUT I LIKE YA ANYWAY!
I'VE DECIDED WE WON'T BECOME ENEMIES!
BUT YOU CAN'T JUST...
IT MEANS WE'RE SQUARE!
I SAID I'VE DECIDED!
WE'RE NO LONGER ENEMIES, AND IF YA DON'T LIKE IT I'LL KILL YA!
OK, FINE!
BUT SERIOUSLY... IF YOUR EGOS ARE STILL BRUISED FROM THIS LITTLE EXPERI-ENCE..
LOOK ME UP SOMETIME, AND I'LL BUY YOU ALL A DRINK.

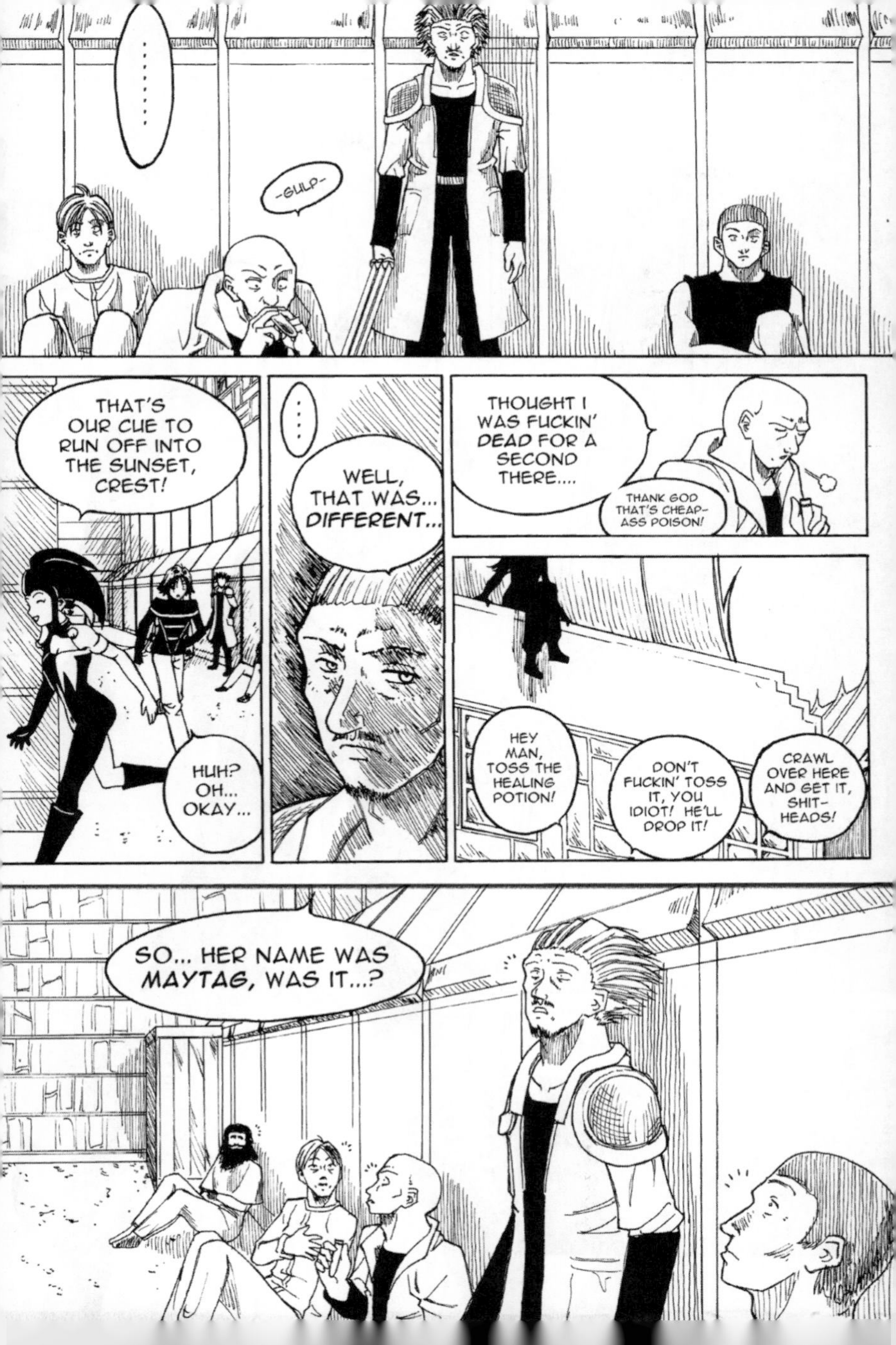
......
-GULP-
THAT'S OUR CUE TO RUN OFF INTO THE SUNSET, CREST!
HUH? OH... OKAY...
...
WELL, THAT WAS... DIFFERENT...
THOUGHT I WAS FUCKIN' DEAD FOR A SECOND THERE....
THANK GOD THAT'S CHEAP-ASS POISON!
HEY MAN, TOSS THE HEALING POTION!
DON'T FUCKIN' TOSS IT, YOU IDIOT! HE'LL DROP IT!
CRAWL OVER HERE AND GET IT, SHIT-HEADS!
SO... HER NAME WAS MAYTAG, WAS IT...?

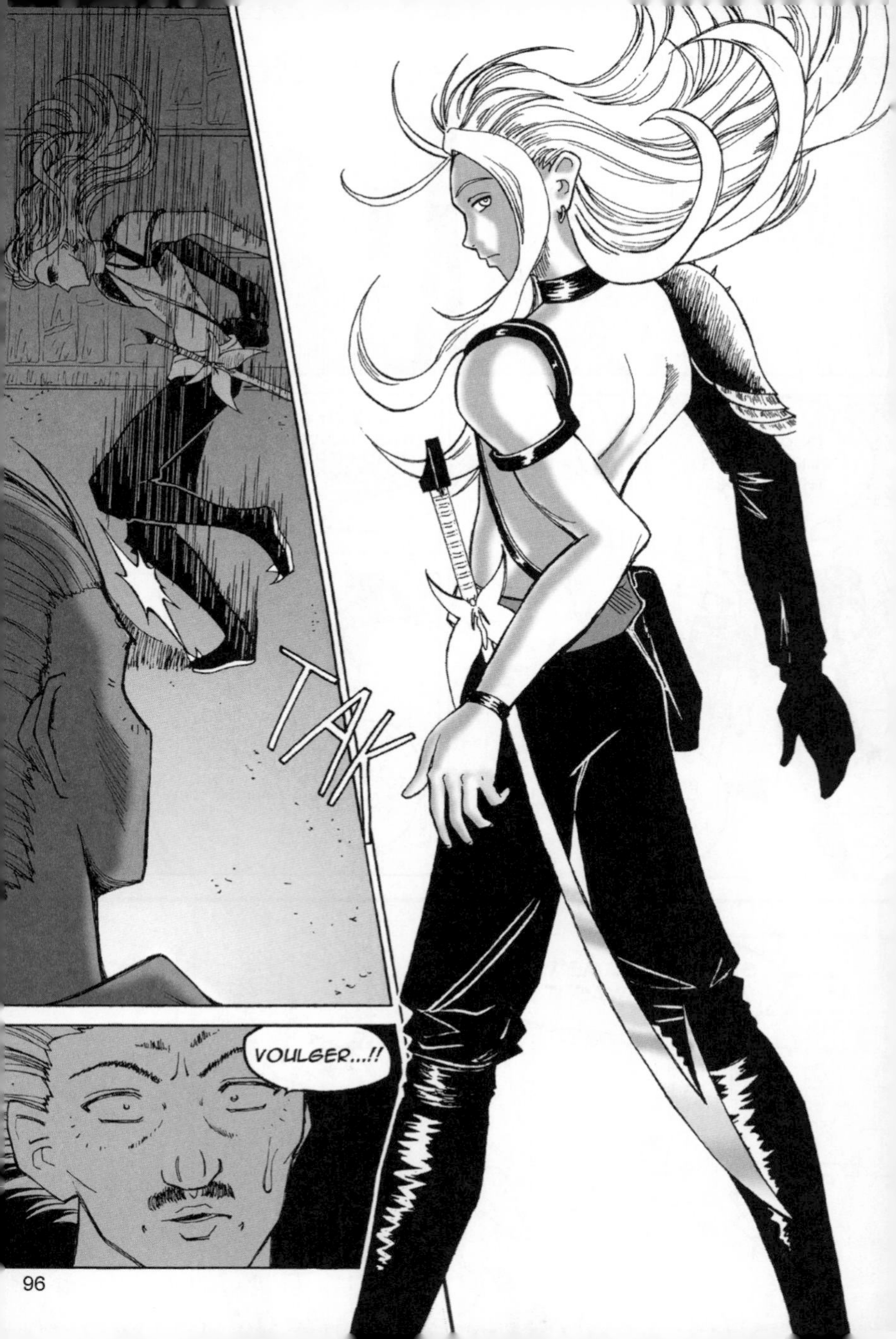
TAK
VOULGER...!!

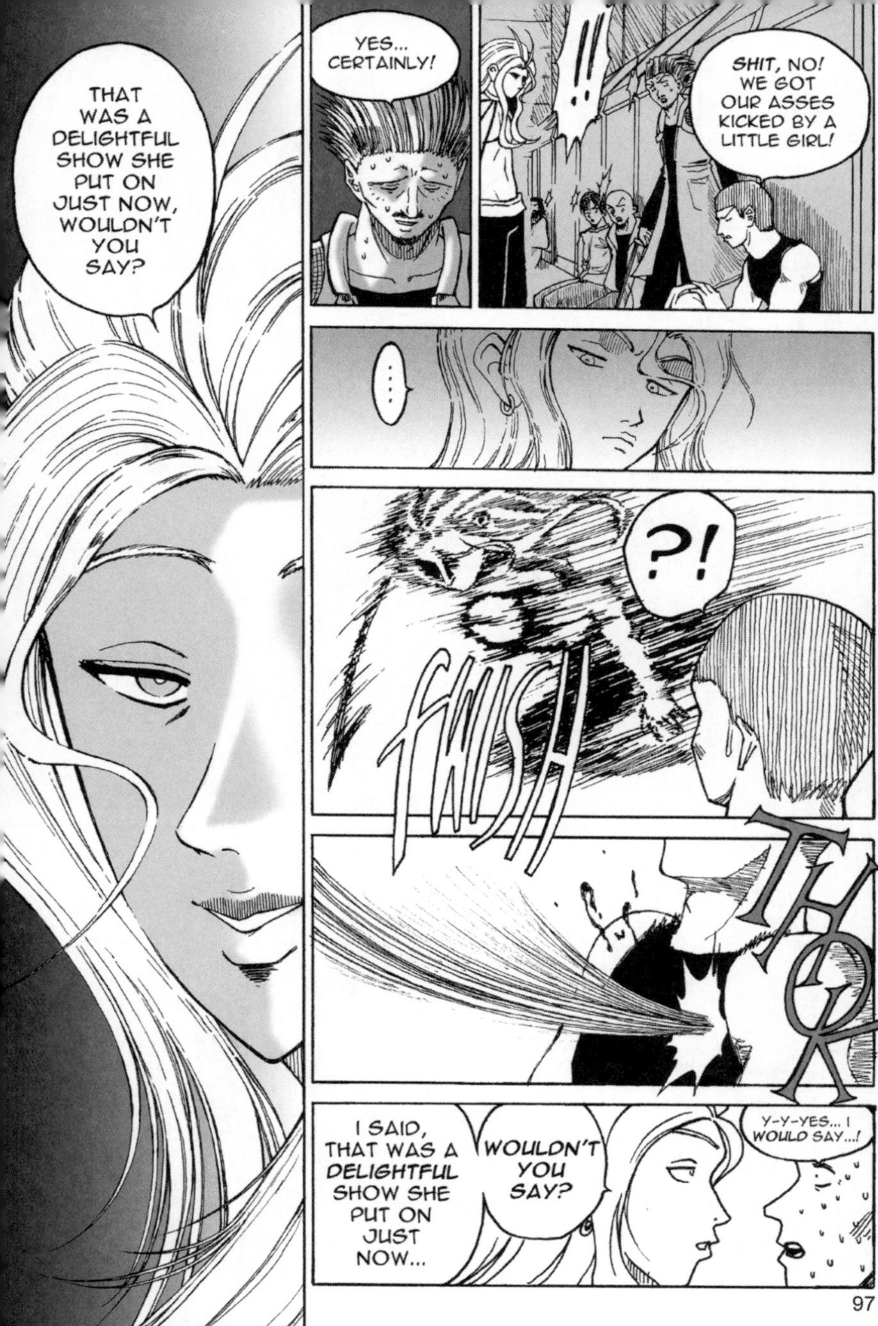
THAT WAS A DELIGHTFUL SHOW SHE PUT ON JUST NOW, WOULDN'T YOU SAY?
YES... CERTAINLY!
!!
SHIT, NO! WE GOT OUR ASSES KICKED BY A LITTLE GIRL!
....
?!
FWISH
THOK
I SAID, THAT WAS A DELIGHTFUL SHOW SHE PUT ON JUST NOW...
WOULDN'T YOU SAY?
Y-Y-YES... I WOULD SAY...!

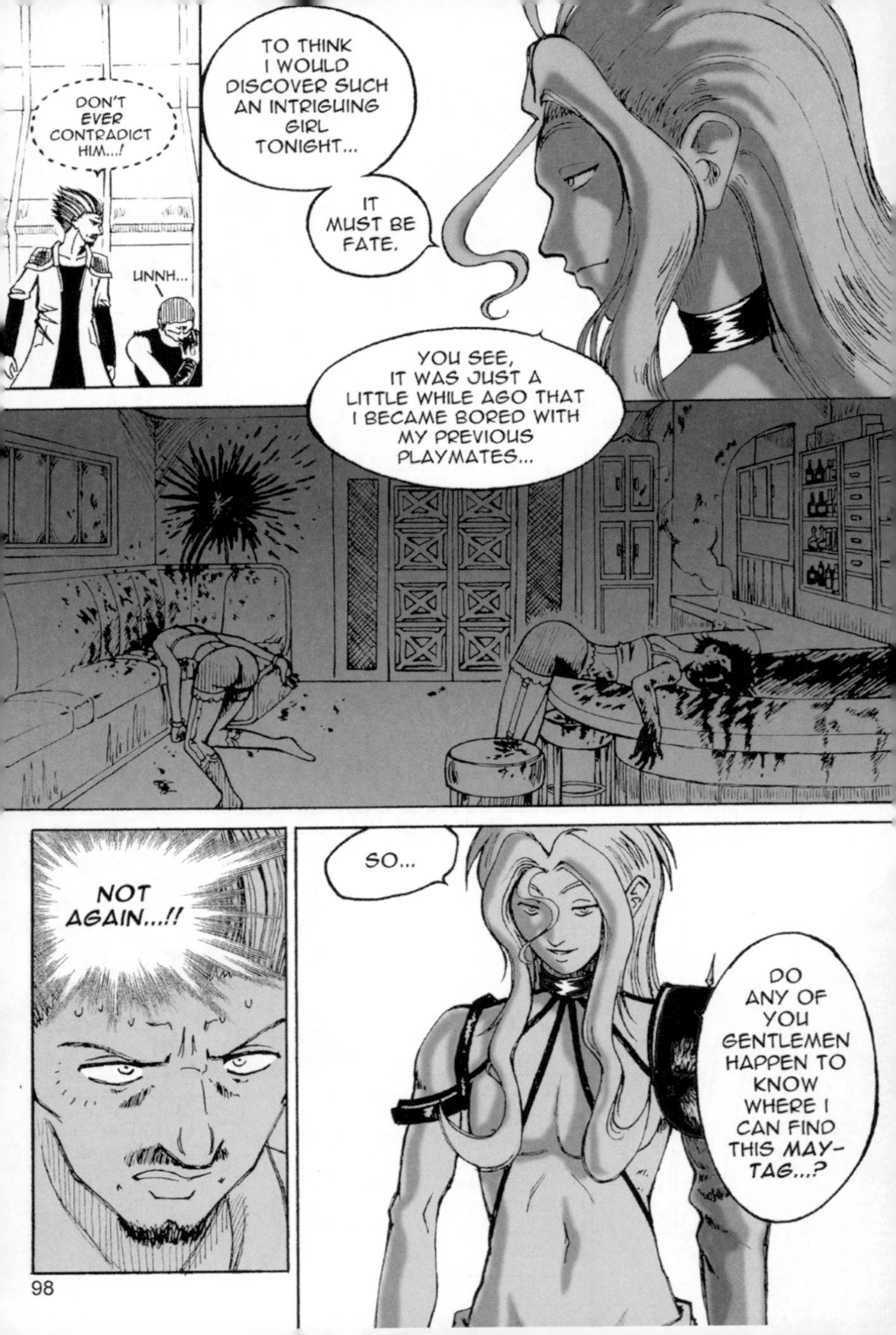
DON'T EVER CONTRADICT HIM...!
TO THINK I WOULD DISCOVER SUCH AN INTRIGUING GIRL TONIGHT...
IT MUST BE FATE.
UNNH...
YOU SEE, IT WAS JUST A LITTLE WHILE AGO THAT I BECAME BORED WITH MY PREVIOUS PLAYMATES...
SO...
NOT AGAIN...!!
DO ANY OF YOU GENTLEMEN HAPPEN TO KNOW WHERE I CAN FIND THIS MAY-TAG...?

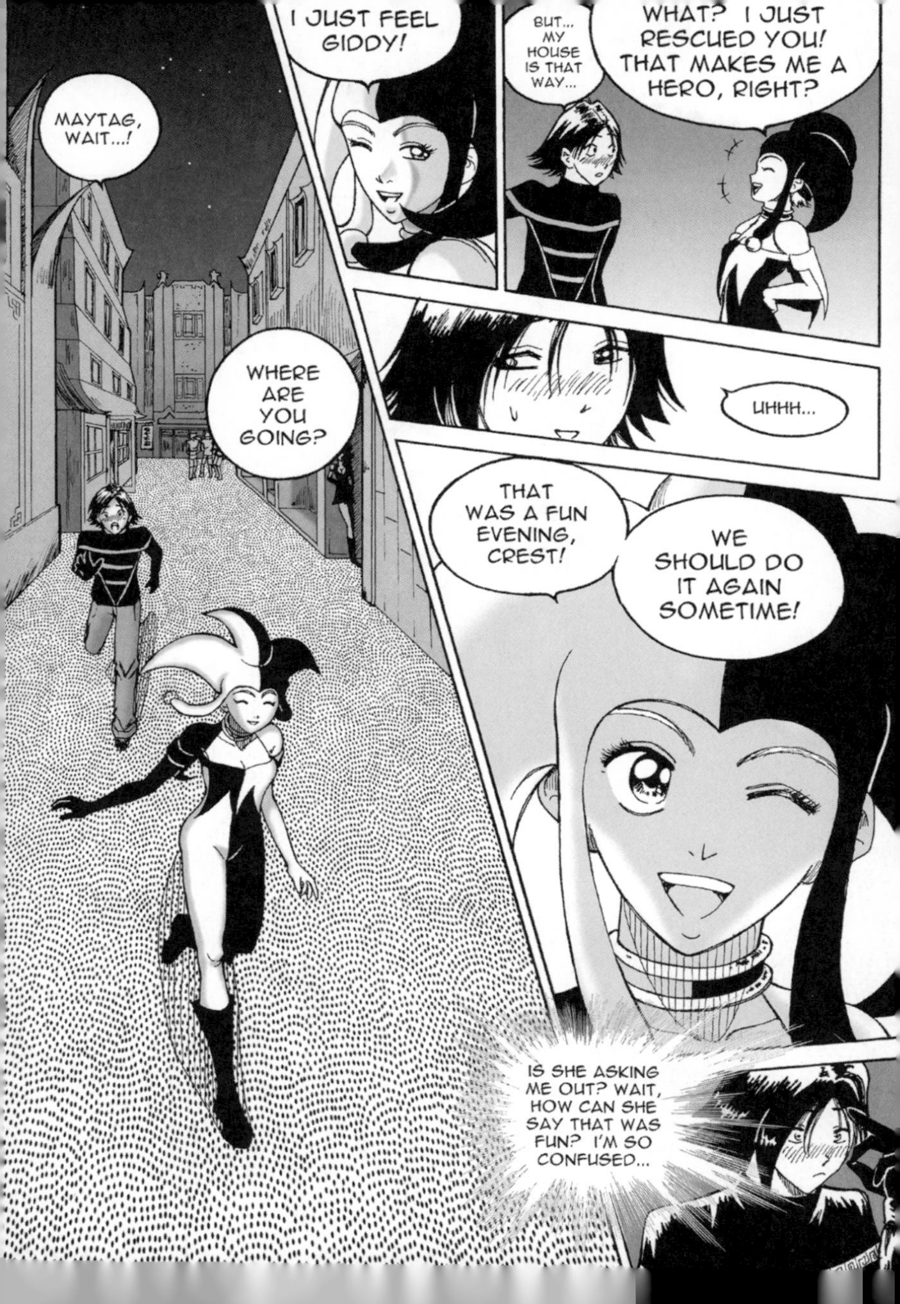
MAYTAG, WAIT...!
WHERE ARE YOU GOING?
I JUST FEEL GIDDY!
BUT... MY HOUSE IS THAT WAY...
WHAT? I JUST RESCUED YOU! THAT MAKES ME A HERO, RIGHT?
UHHH...
THAT WAS A FUN EVENING, CREST!
WE SHOULD DO IT AGAIN SOMETIME!
IS SHE ASKING ME OUT? WAIT, HOW CAN SHE SAY THAT WAS FUN? I'M SO CONFUSED...

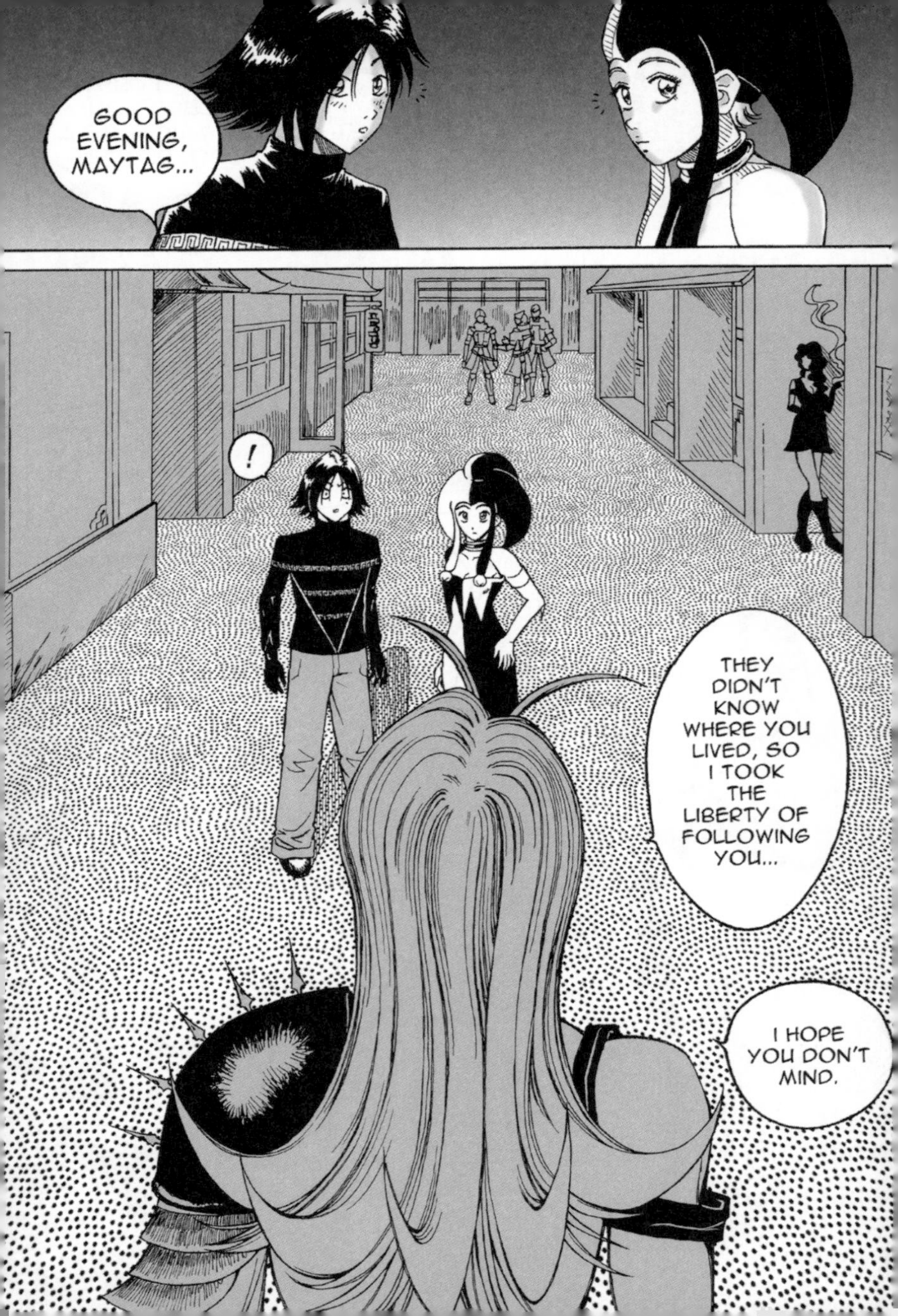

GOOD EVENING, MAYTAG...
!
THEY DIDN'T KNOW WHERE YOU LIVED, SO I TOOK THE LIBERTY OF FOLLOWING YOU...
I HOPE YOU DON'T MIND.

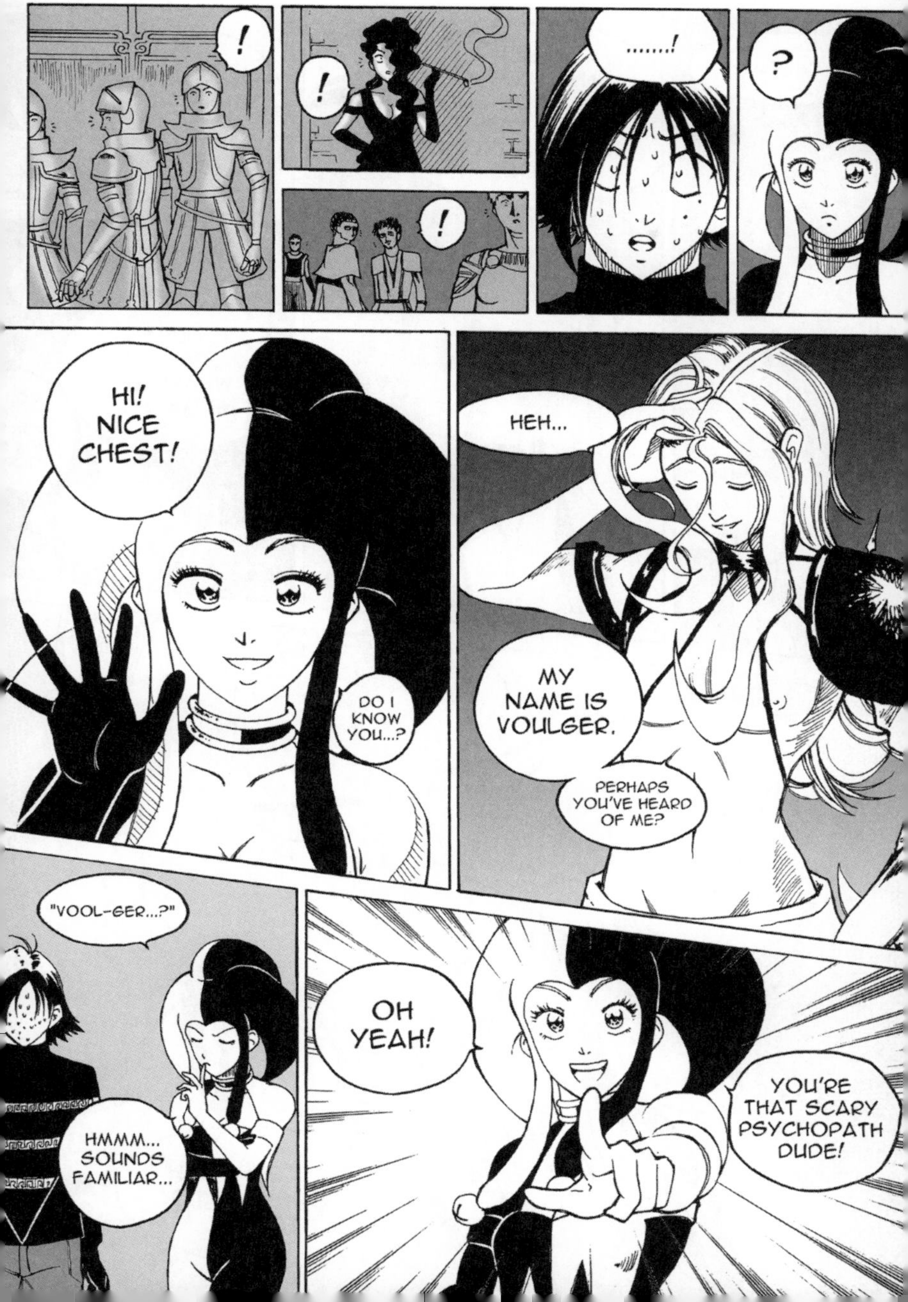
!
!
!
.......!
?
HI! NICE CHEST!
DO I KNOW YOU...?
HEH...
MY NAME IS VOULGER.
PERHAPS YOU'VE HEARD OF ME?
"VOOL-GER...?"
HMMM... SOUNDS FAMILIAR...
OH YEAH!
YOU'RE THAT SCARY PSYCHOPATH DUDE!

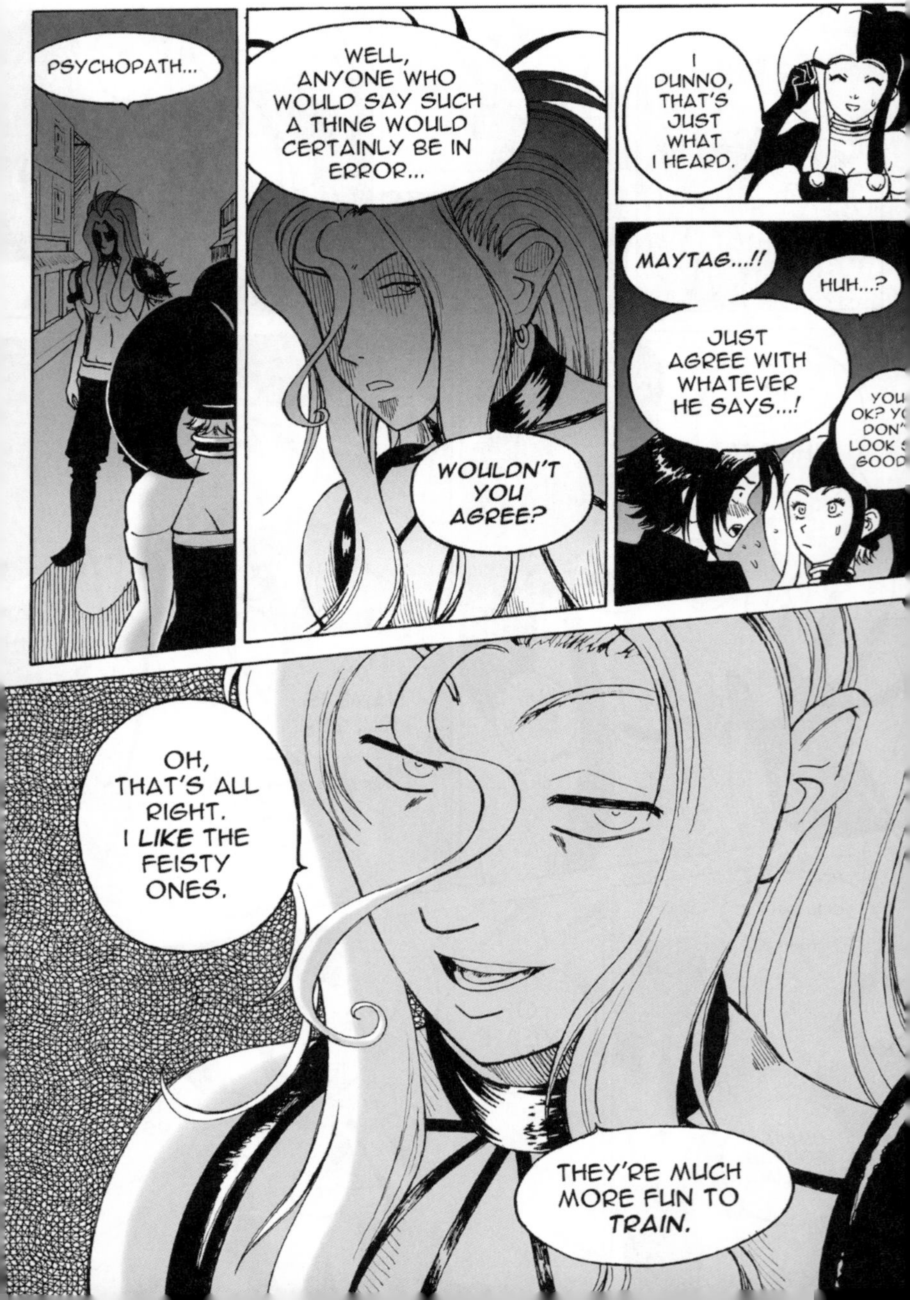
PSYCHOPATH...
WELL, ANYONE WHO WOULD SAY SUCH A THING WOULD CERTAINLY BE IN ERROR...
WOULDN'T YOU AGREE?
I DUNNO, THAT'S JUST WHAT I HEARD.
MAYTAG...!!
HUH...?
JUST AGREE WITH WHATEVER HE SAYS...!
OH, THAT'S ALL RIGHT. I LIKE THE FEISTY ONES.
THEY'RE MUCH MORE FUN TO TRAIN.

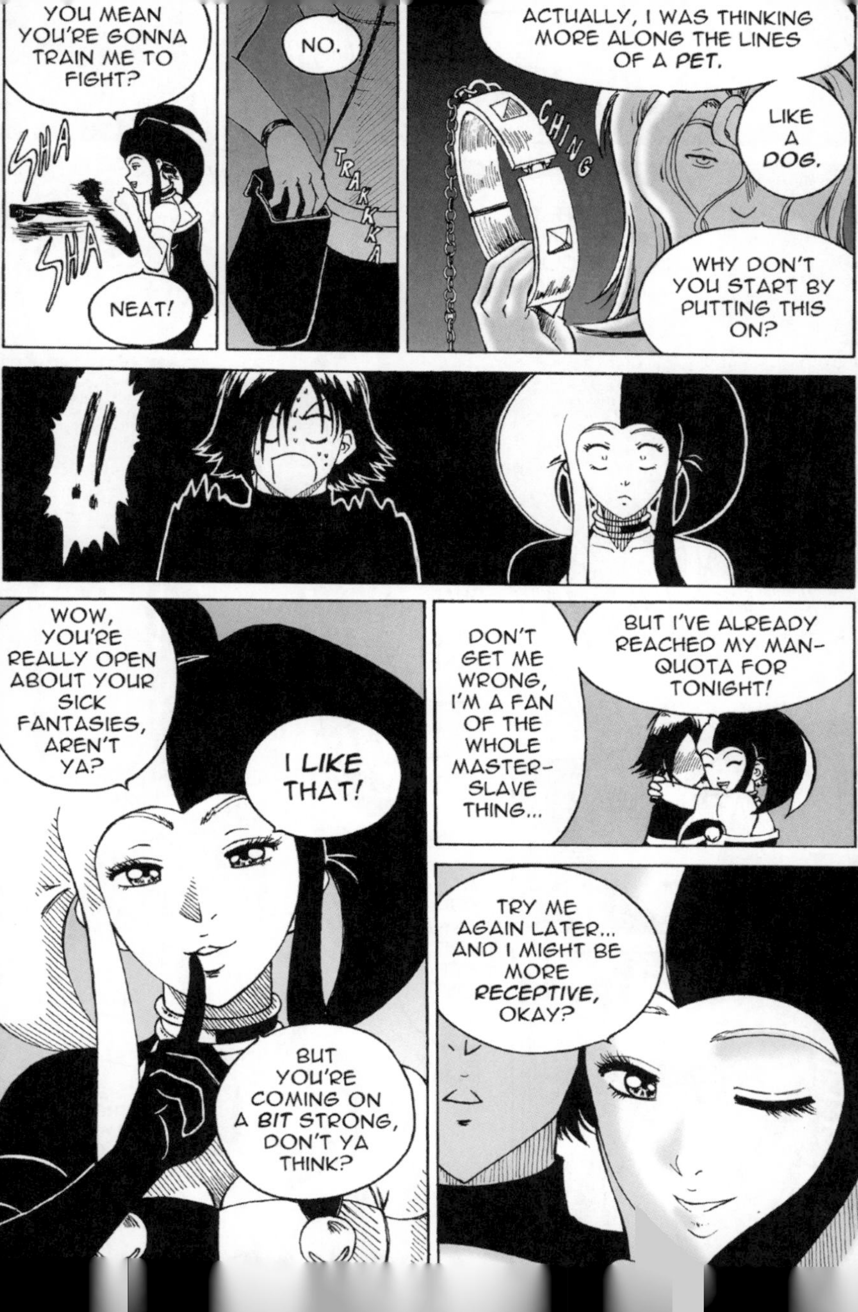
YOU MEAN YOU'RE GONNA TRAIN ME TO FIGHT?
SHA
SHA
NEAT!
NO.
TRAKKKA
ACTUALLY, I WAS THINKING MORE ALONG THE LINES OF A PET.
CHING
LIKE A DOG.
WHY DON'T YOU START BY PUTTING THIS ON?
!!
WOW, YOU'RE REALLY OPEN ABOUT YOUR SICK FANTASIES, AREN'T YA?
I LIKE THAT!
BUT YOU'RE COMING ON A BIT STRONG, DON'T YA THINK?
DON'T GET ME WRONG, I'M A FAN OF THE WHOLE MASTER-SLAVE THING...
BUT I'VE ALREADY REACHED MY MAN-QUOTA FOR TONIGHT!
TRY ME AGAIN LATER... AND I MIGHT BE MORE RECEPTIVE, OKAY?

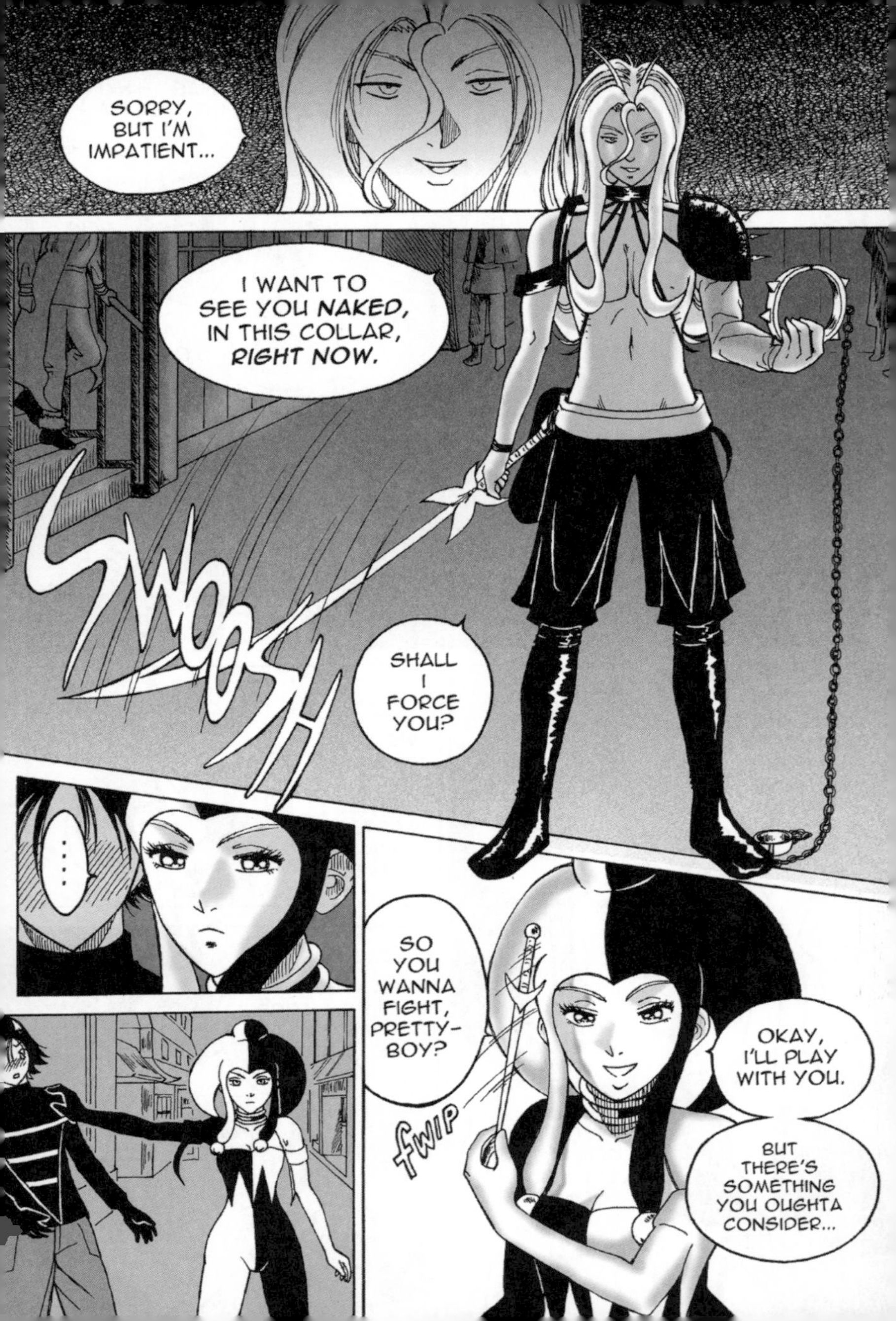
SORRY, BUT I'M IMPATIENT...
I WANT TO SEE YOU NAKED, IN THIS COLLAR, RIGHT NOW.
SWOOSH
SHALL I FORCE YOU?
....
SO YOU WANNA FIGHT, PRETTY-BOY?
fwip
OKAY, I'LL PLAY WITH YOU.
BUT THERE'S SOMETHING YOU OUGHTA CONSIDER...

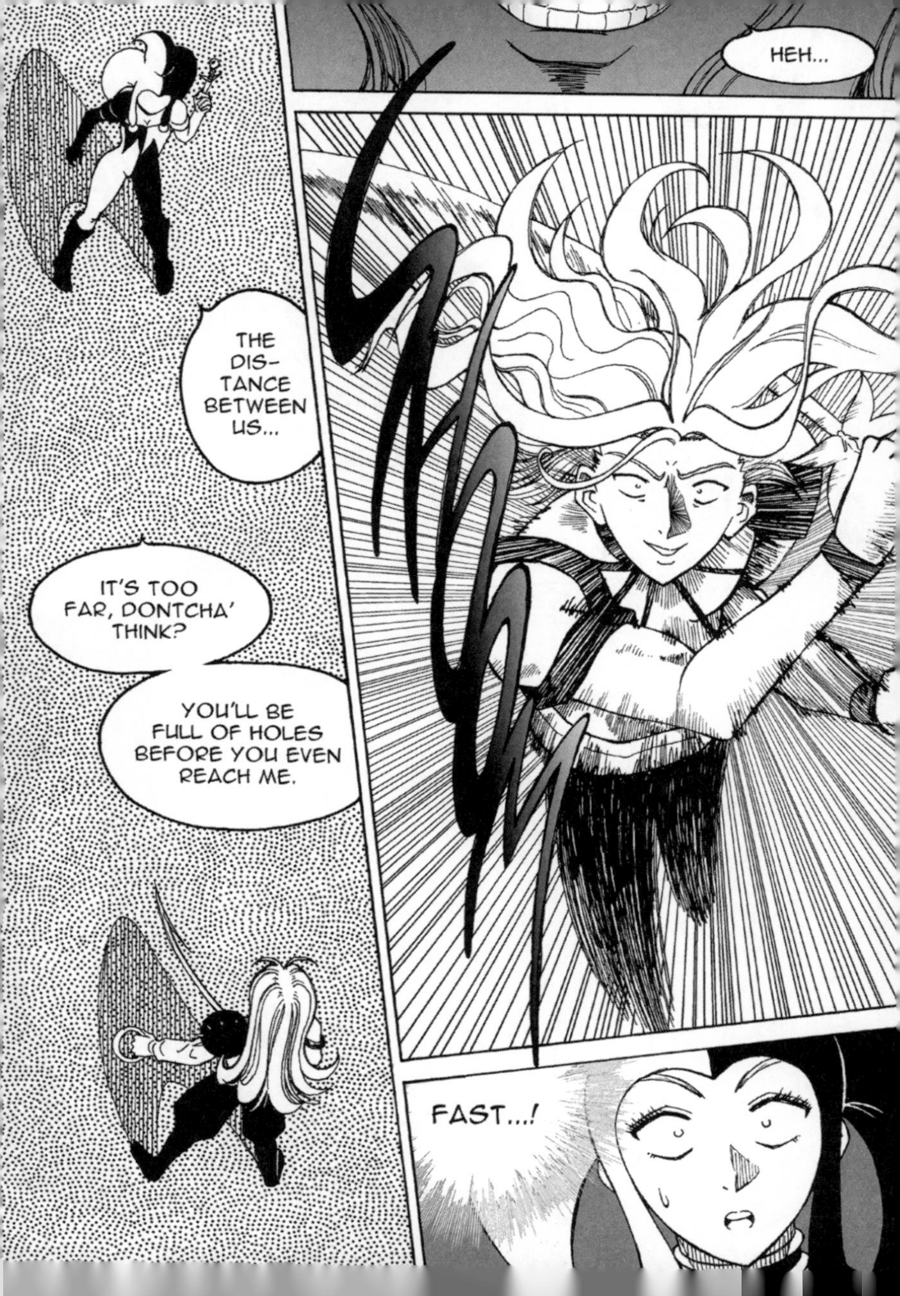
HEH...
THE DIS- TANCE BETWEEN US...
IT'S TOO FAR, DONTCHA' THINK?
YOU'LL BE FULL OF HOLES BEFORE YOU EVEN REACH ME.
FAST...!

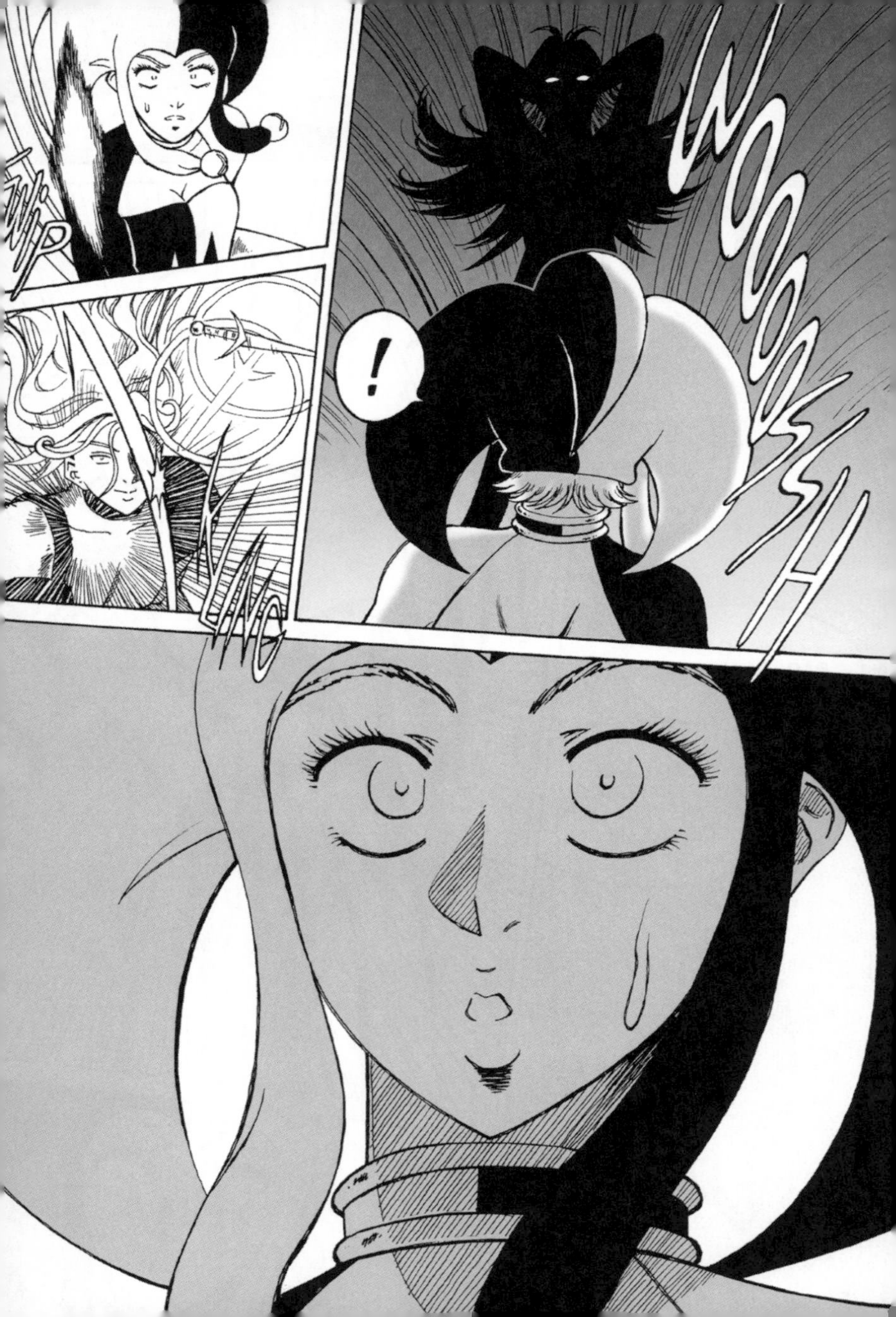

!

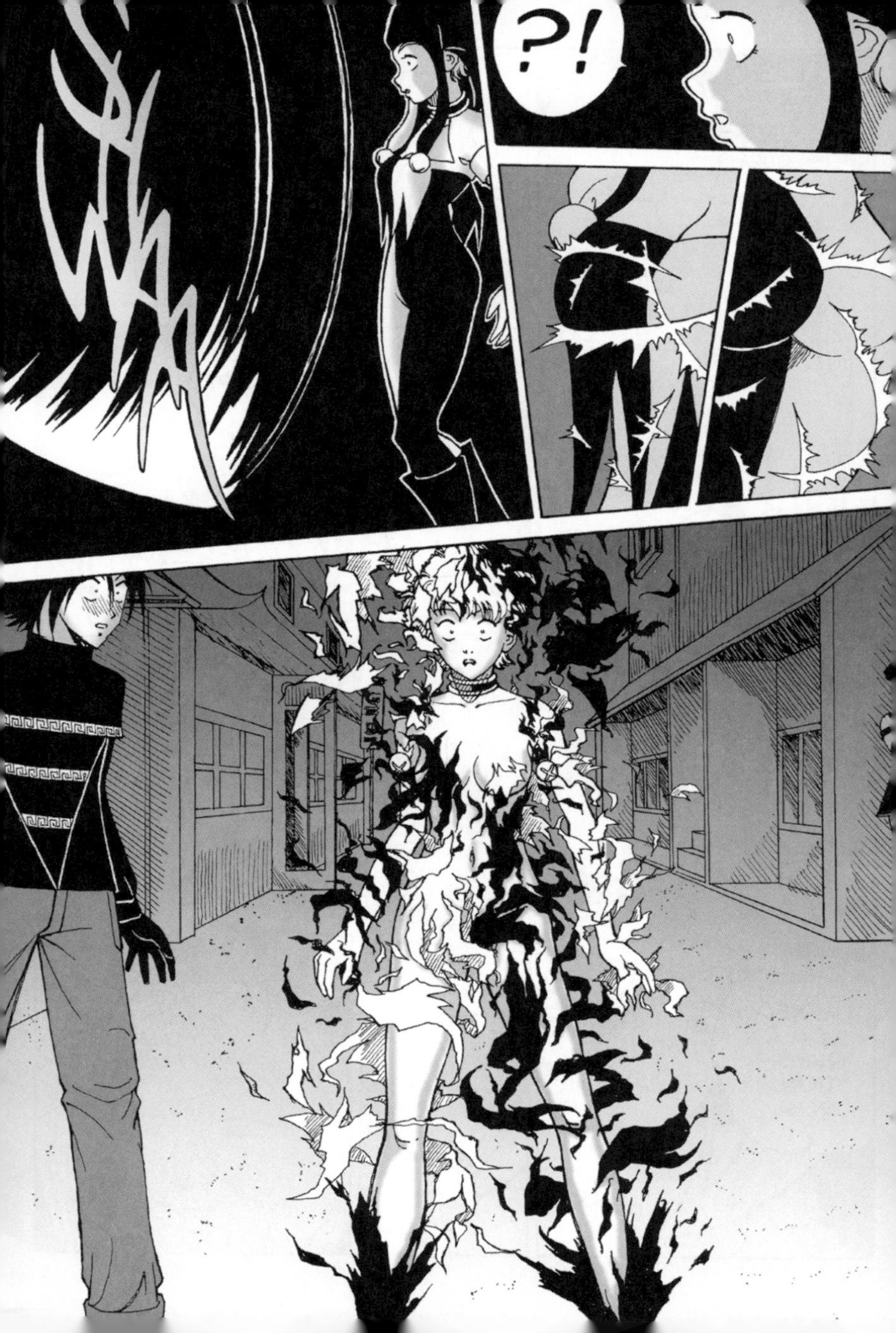
?!
SHWAP

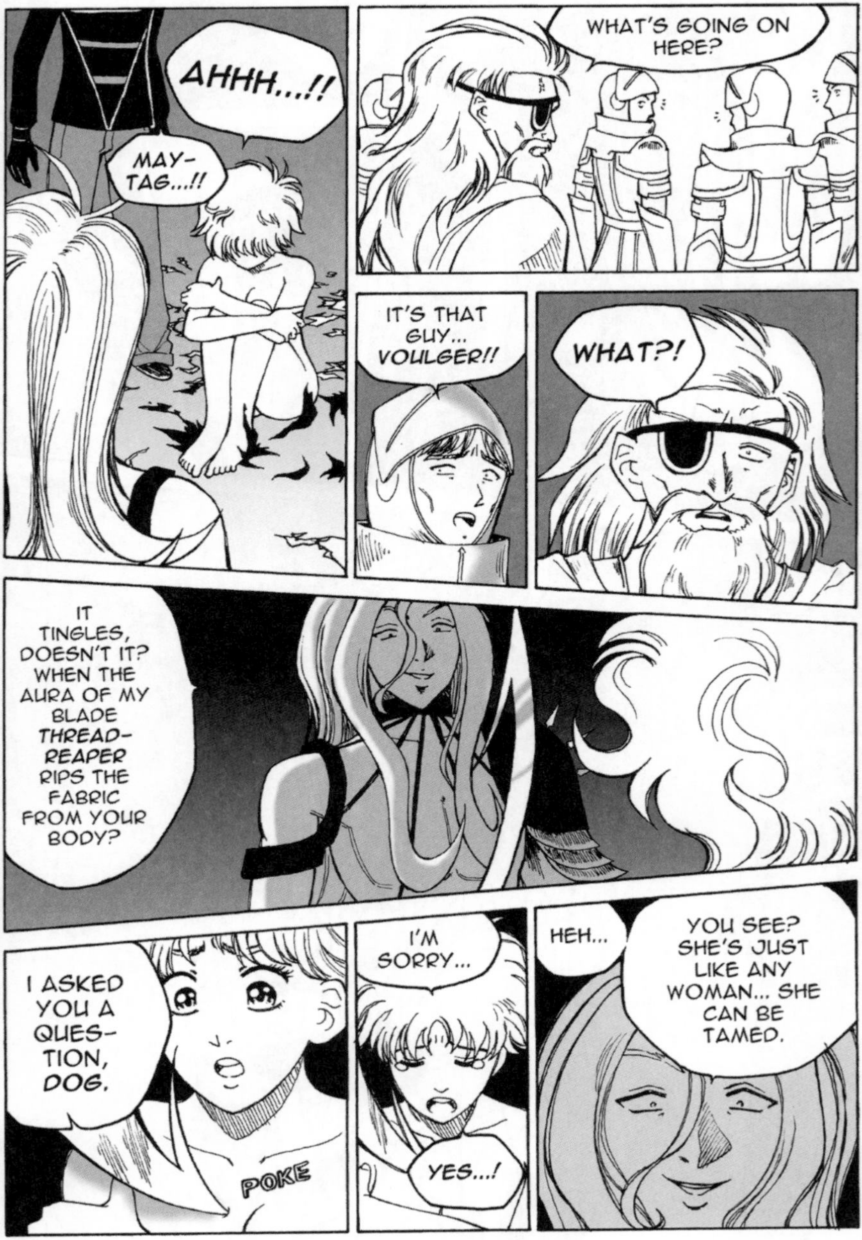
AHHH...!!
MAY-TAG...!!
WHAT'S GOING ON HERE?
IT'S THAT GUY... VOULGER!!
WHAT?!
IT TINGLES, DOESN'T IT? WHEN THE AURA OF MY BLADE THREAD-REAPER RIPS THE FABRIC FROM YOUR BODY?
I ASKED YOU A QUES-TION, DOG.
POKE
I'M SORRY...
YES...!
HEH...
YOU SEE? SHE'S JUST LIKE ANY WOMAN... SHE CAN BE TAMED.

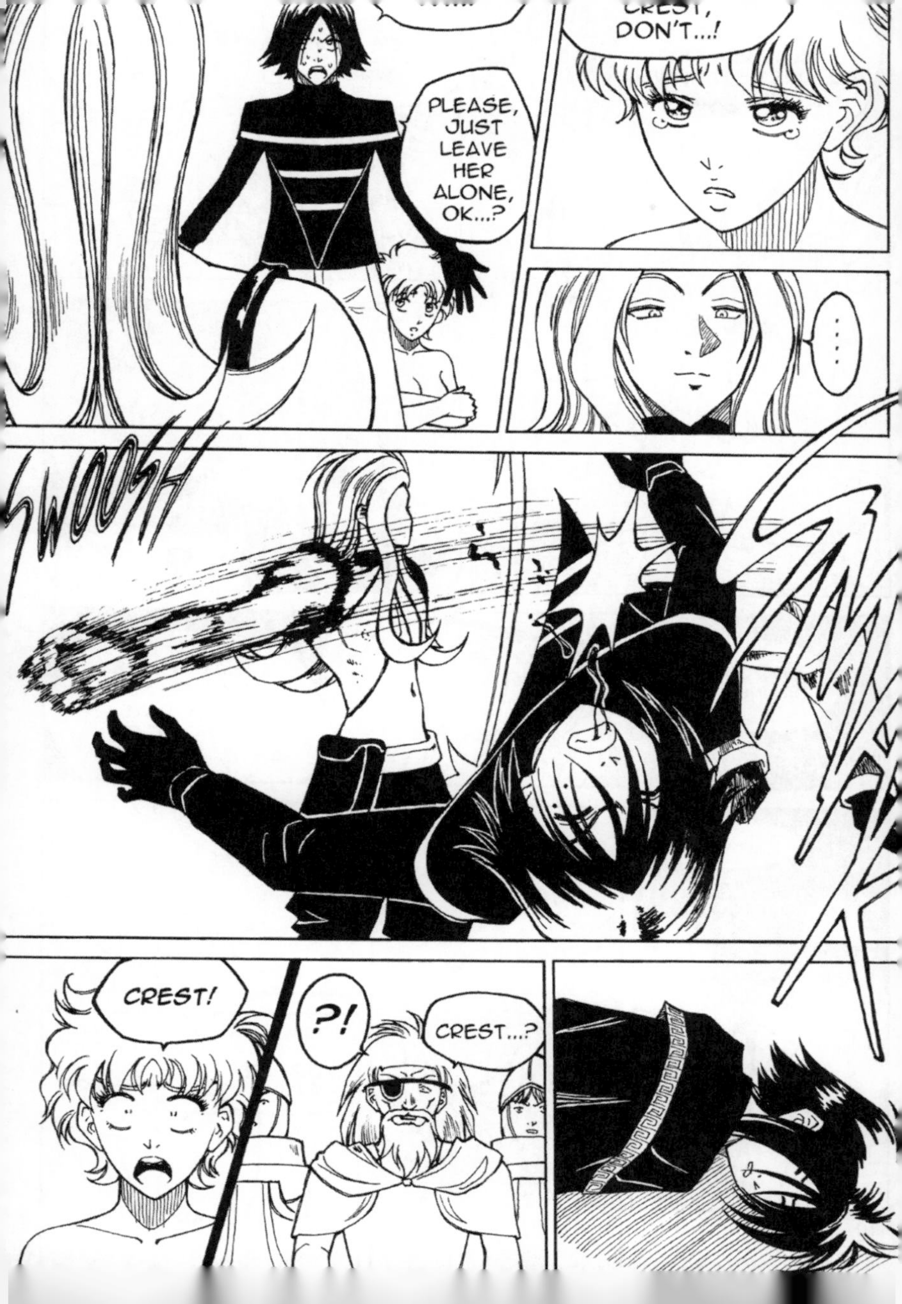
PLEASE, JUST LEAVE HER ALONE, OK...?
CREST, DON'T...!
....
SWOOSH
CREST!
?!
CREST...?

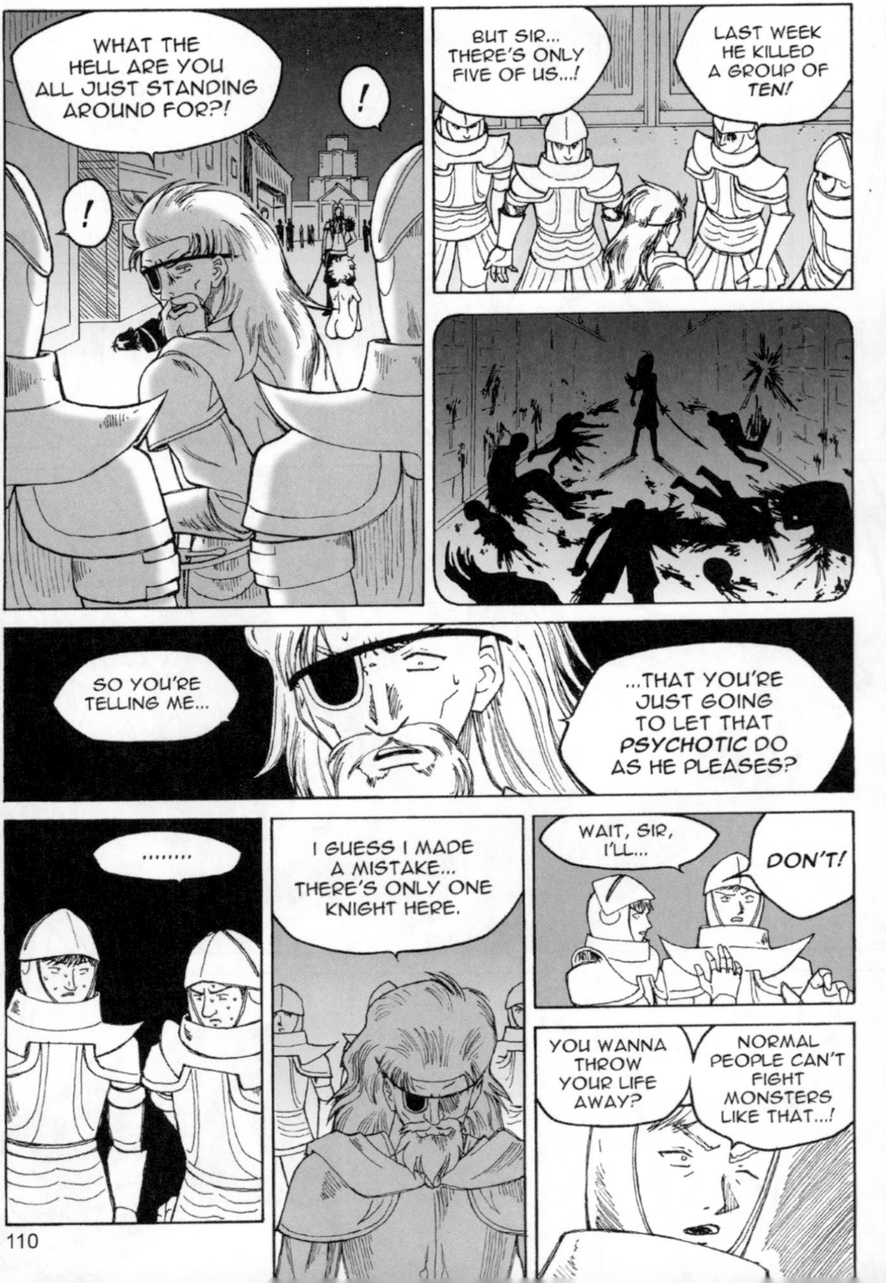
WHAT THE HELL ARE YOU ALL JUST STANDING AROUND FOR?!
!
!
BUT SIR... THERE'S ONLY FIVE OF US...!
LAST WEEK HE KILLED A GROUP OF TEN!
SO YOU'RE TELLING ME...
...THAT YOU'RE JUST GOING TO LET THAT PSYCHOTIC DO AS HE PLEASES?
....
I GUESS I MADE A MISTAKE... THERE'S ONLY ONE KNIGHT HERE.
WAIT, SIR, I'LL...
DON'T!
YOU WANNA THROW YOUR LIFE AWAY?
NORMAL PEOPLE CAN'T FIGHT MONSTERS LIKE THAT...!

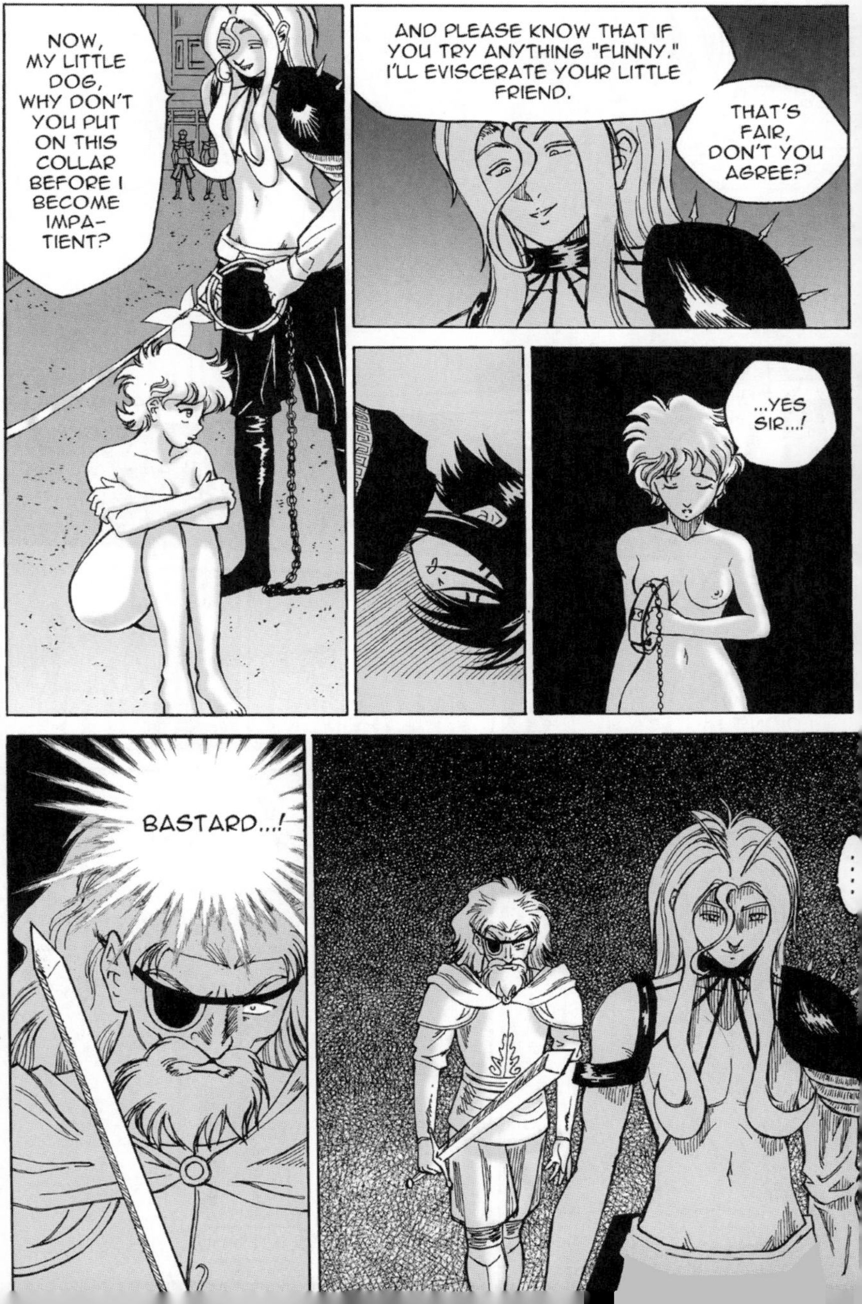

NOW, MY LITTLE DOG, WHY DON'T YOU PUT ON THIS COLLAR BEFORE I BECOME IMPA-TIENT?
AND PLEASE KNOW THAT IF YOU TRY ANYTHING "FUNNY." I'LL EVISCERATE YOUR LITTLE FRIEND.
THAT'S FAIR, DON'T YOU AGREE?
...YES SIR...!
BASTARD...!

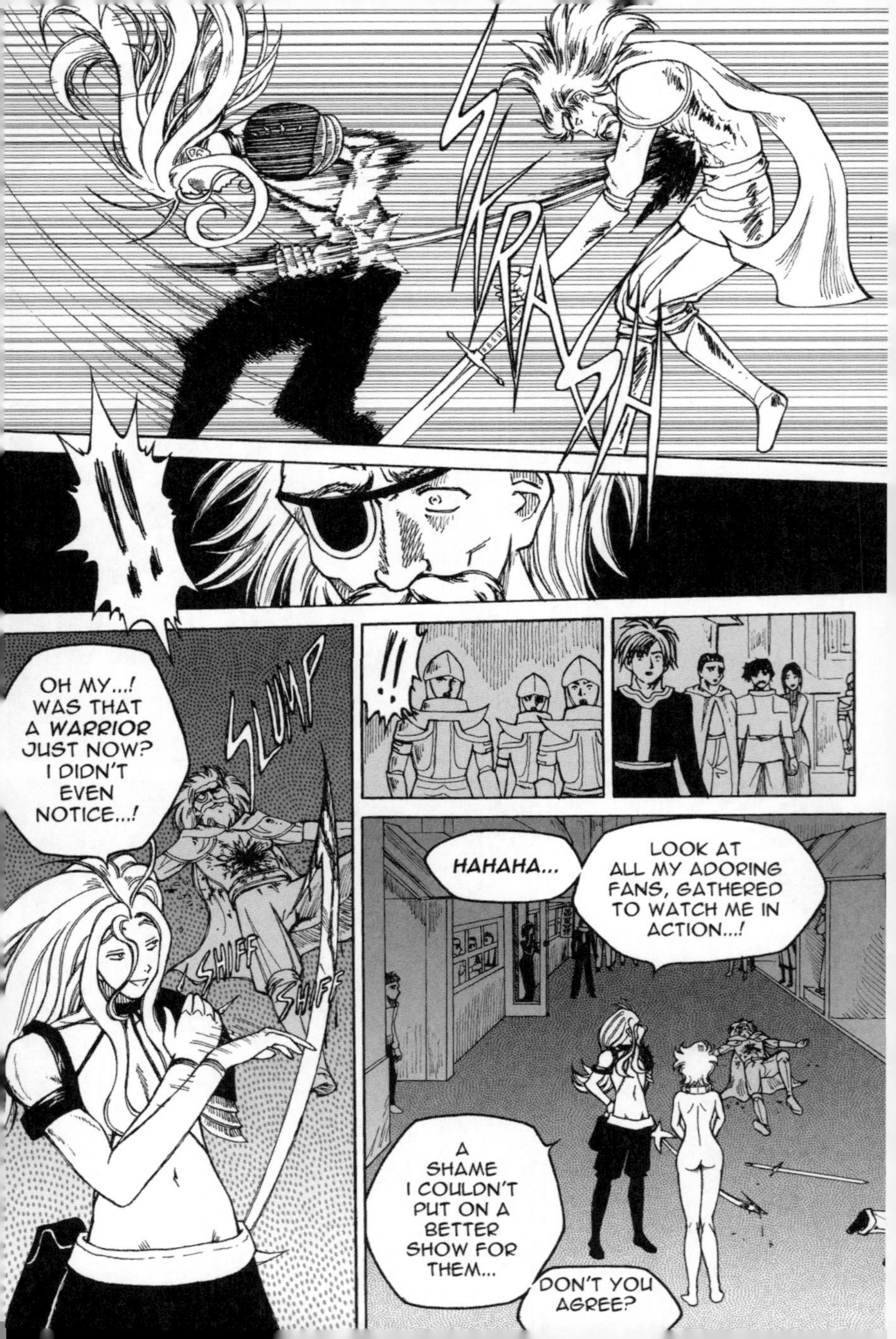
SKRASSH
!!
OH MY...! WAS THAT A WARRIOR JUST NOW? I DIDN'T EVEN NOTICE...!
SLUMP
SHIFF
SHIFF
!!
HAHAHA...
LOOK AT ALL MY ADORING FANS, GATHERED TO WATCH ME IN ACTION...!
A SHAME I COULDN'T PUT ON A BETTER SHOW FOR THEM...
DON'T YOU AGREE?

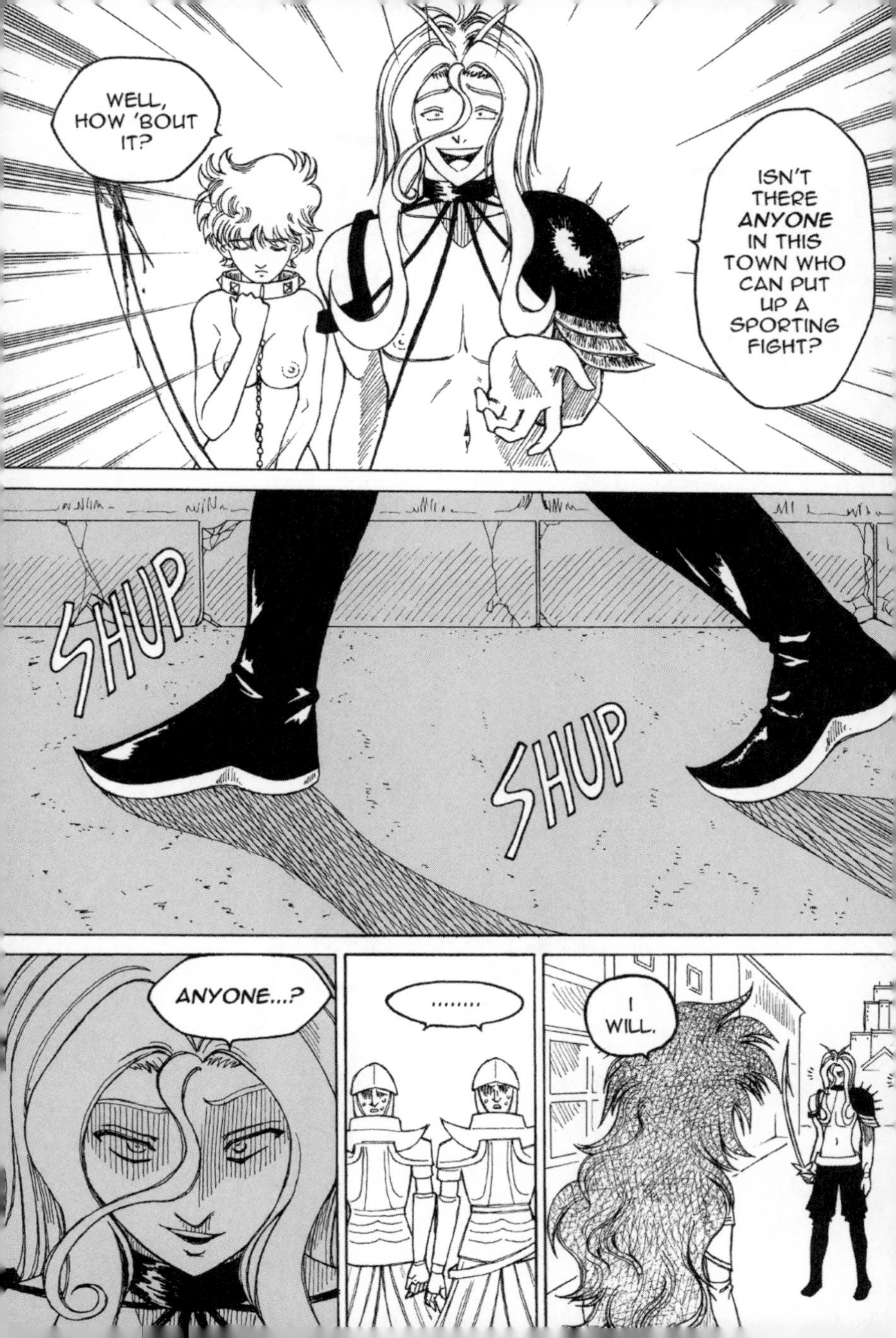
WELL, HOW 'BOUT IT?
ISN'T THERE ANYONE IN THIS TOWN WHO CAN PUT UP A SPORTING FIGHT?
SHUP
SHUP
ANYONE...?
....
I WILL.

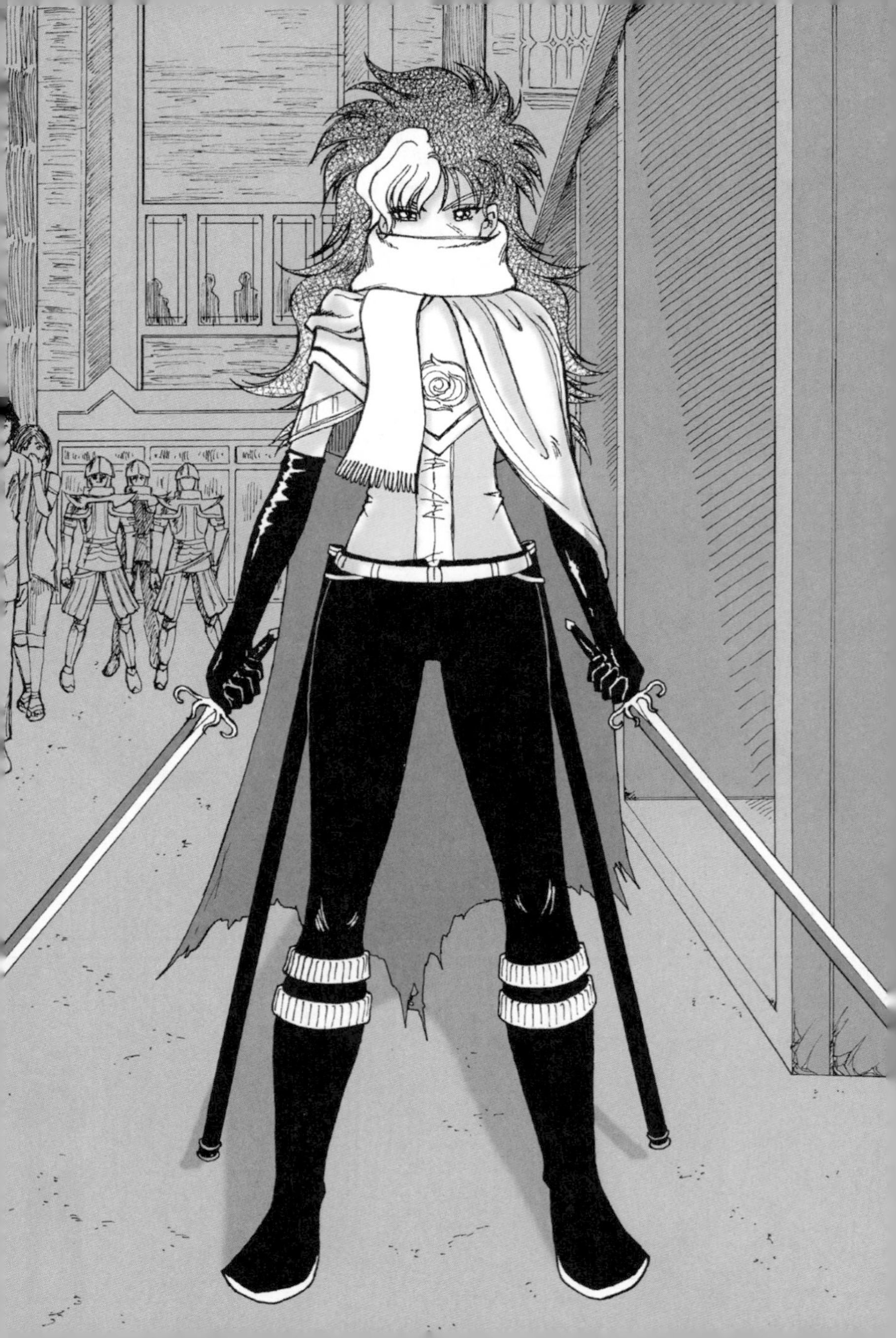

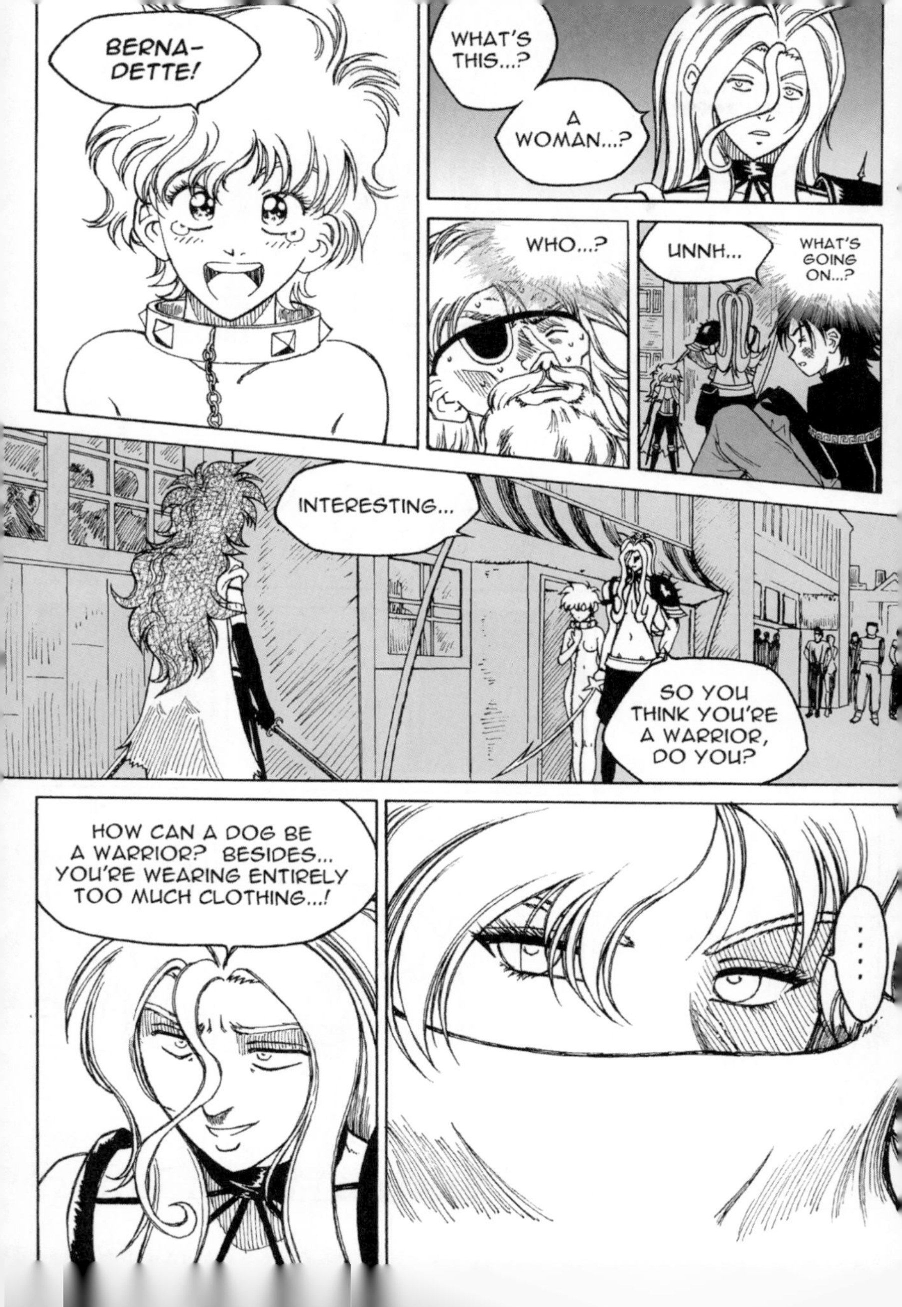
BERNA-DETTE!
WHAT'S THIS...?
A WOMAN...?
WHO...?
UNNH...
WHAT'S GOING ON...?
INTERESTING...
SO YOU THINK YOU'RE A WARRIOR, DO YOU?
HOW CAN A DOG BE A WARRIOR? BESIDES... YOU'RE WEARING ENTIRELY TOO MUCH CLOTHING...!
....

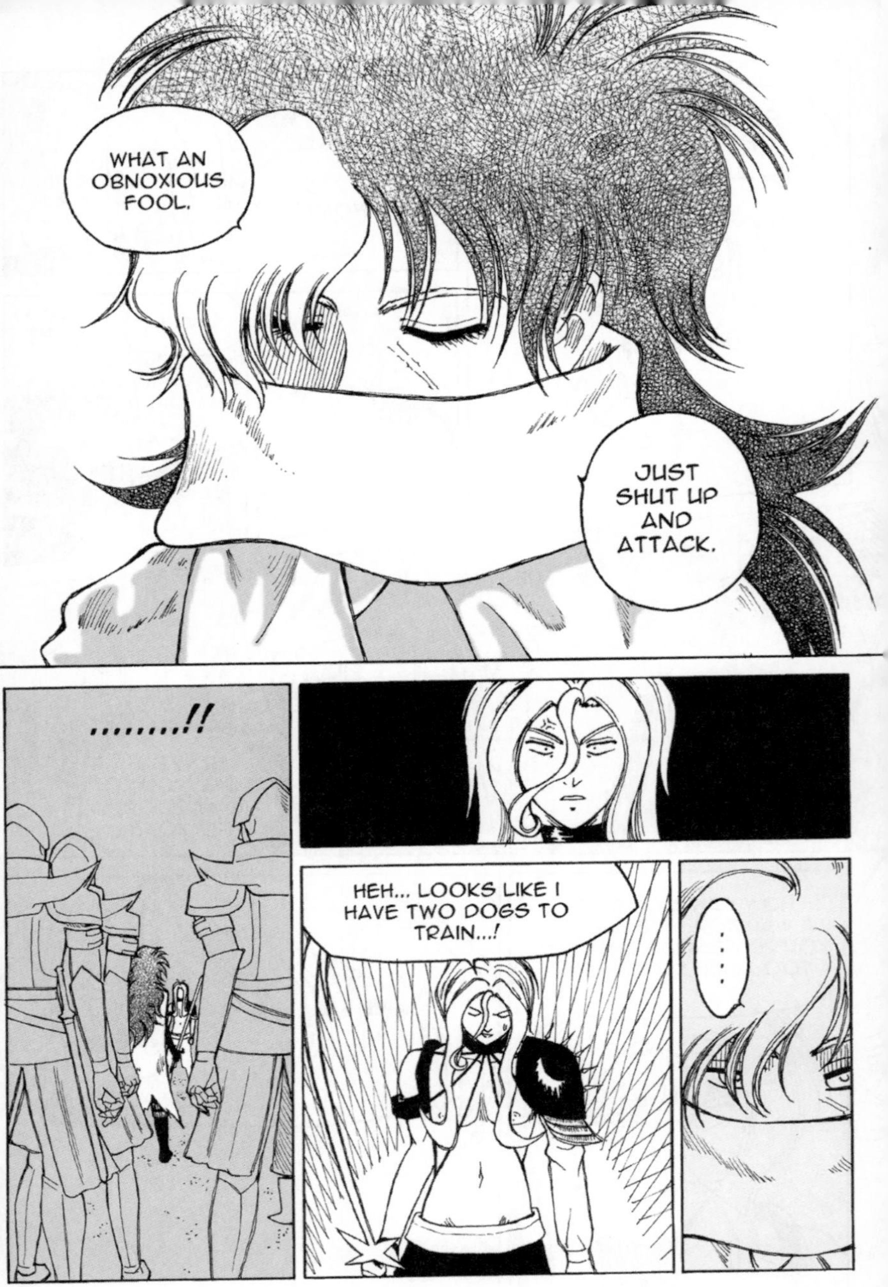
WHAT AN OBNOXIOUS FOOL.
JUST SHUT UP AND ATTACK.
.......!!
HEH... LOOKS LIKE I HAVE TWO DOGS TO TRAIN...!
....

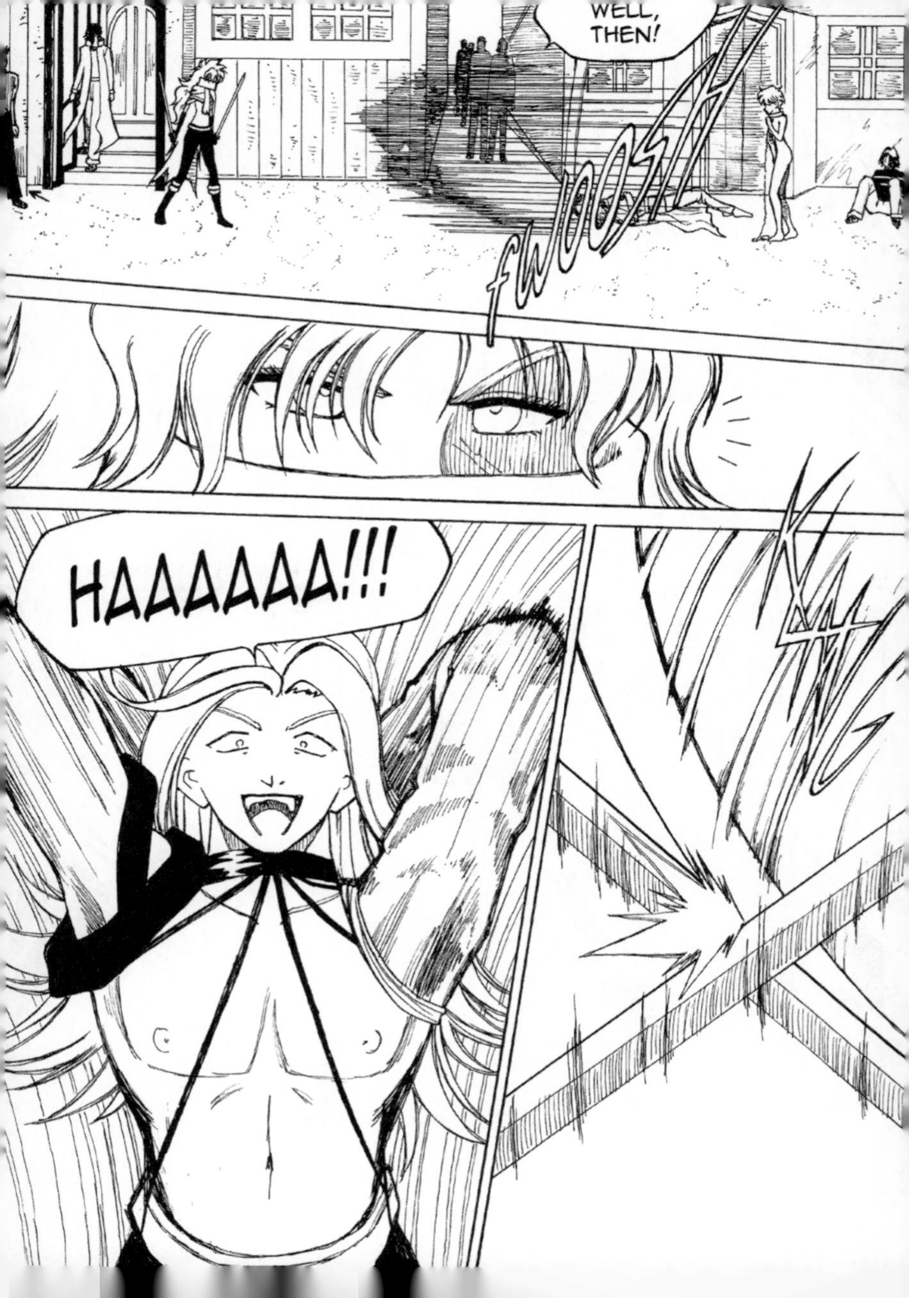
WELL, THEN!
fwoosh
HAAAAAA!!!

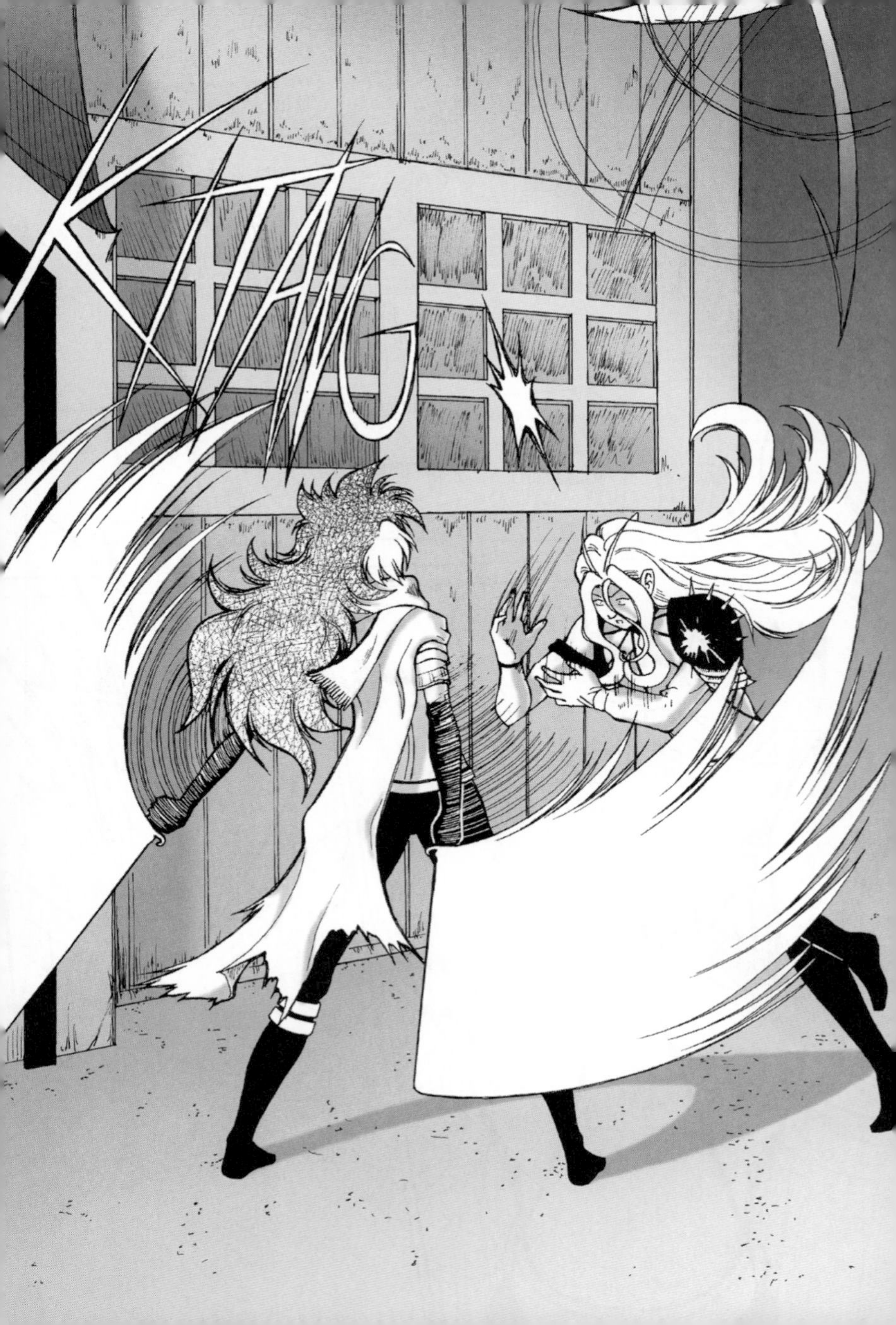
KTANG

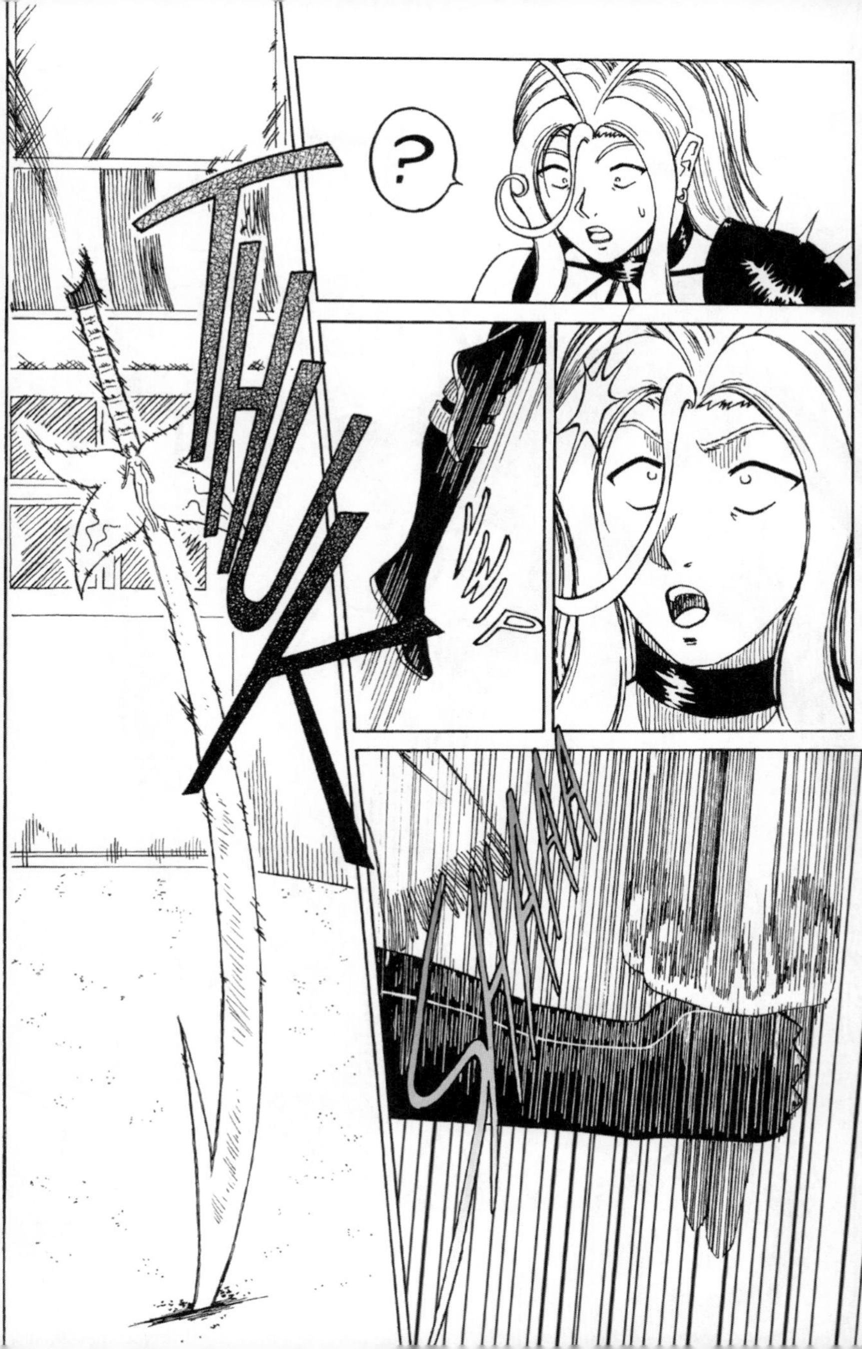
?
THUK
WIP
SHAAA

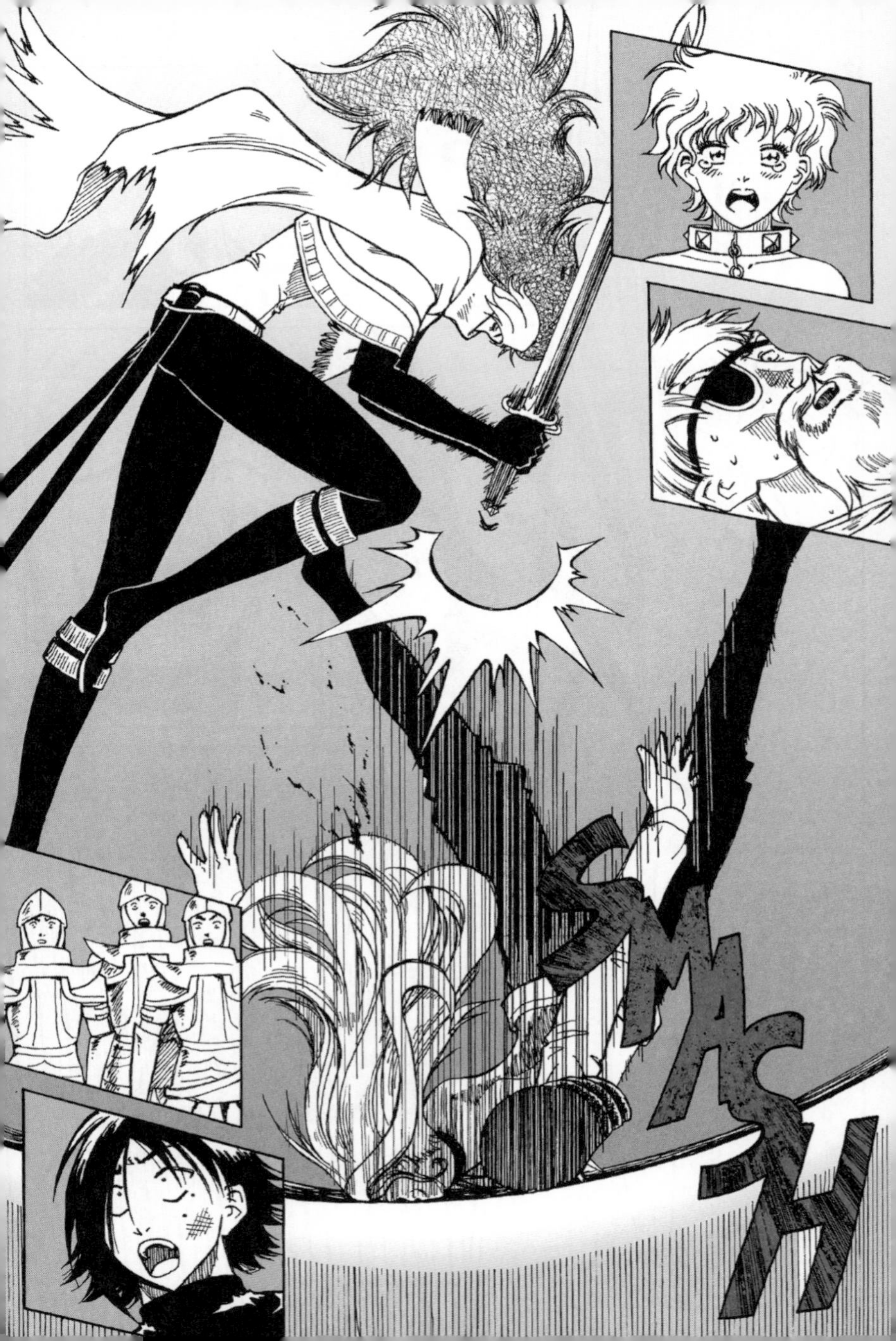
SMASH

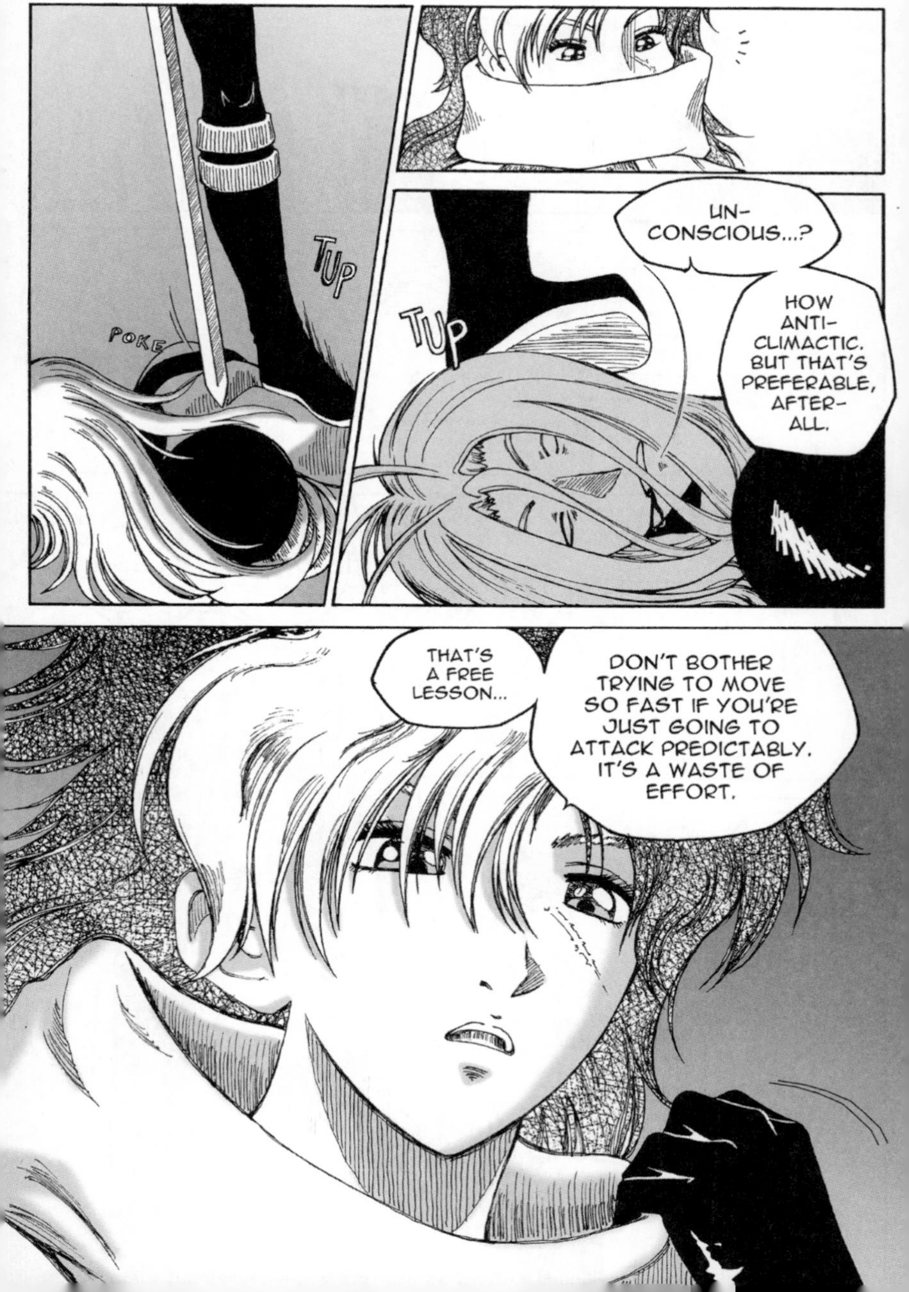
TUP
POKE
TUP
UN-CONSCIOUS...?
HOW ANTI-CLIMACTIC. BUT THAT'S PREFERABLE, AFTER-ALL.
THAT'S A FREE LESSON...
DON'T BOTHER TRYING TO MOVE SO FAST IF YOU'RE JUST GOING TO ATTACK PREDICTABLY. IT'S A WASTE OF EFFORT.

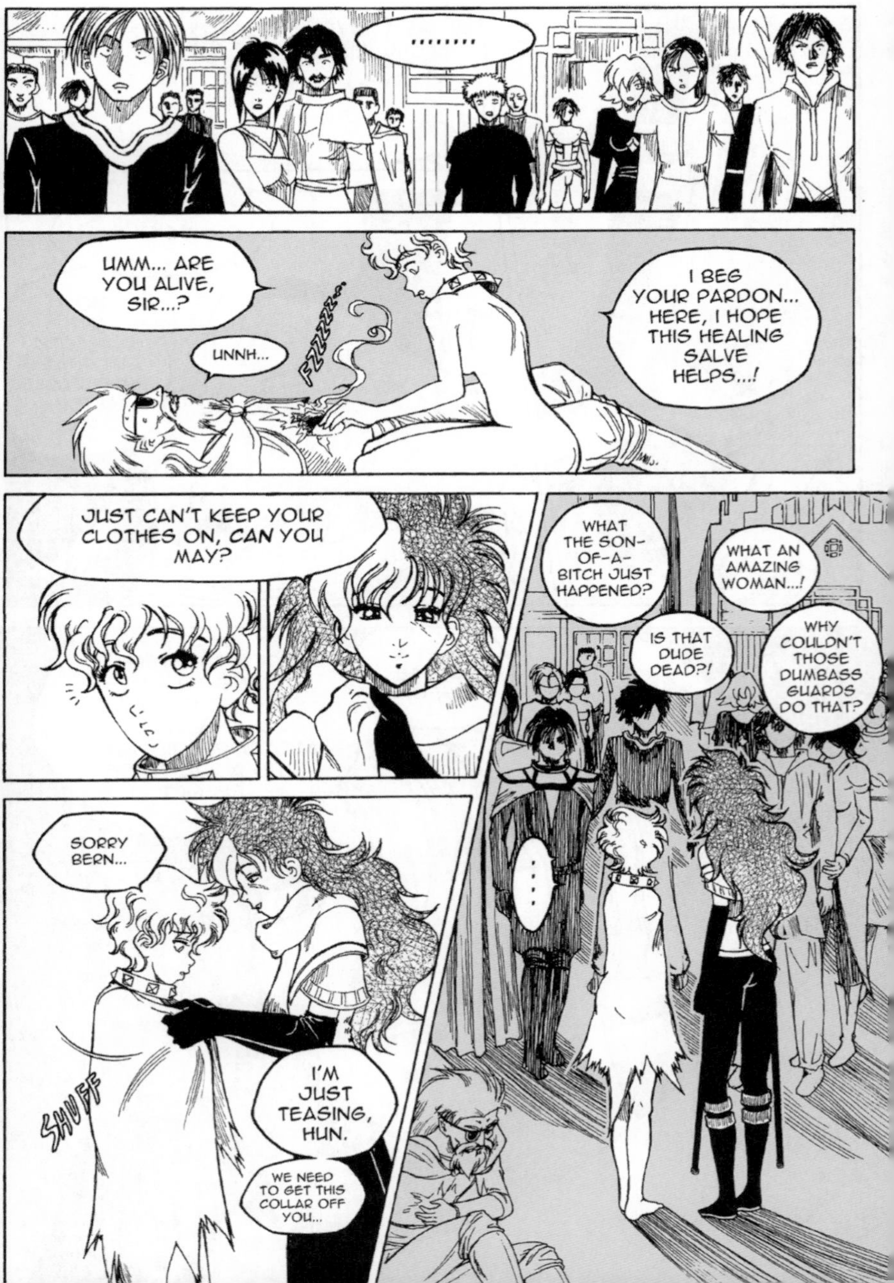
....
UMM... ARE YOU ALIVE, SIR...?
UNNH...
FZZZZZ...
I BEG YOUR PARDON... HERE, I HOPE THIS HEALING SALVE HELPS...!
JUST CAN'T KEEP YOUR CLOTHES ON, CAN YOU MAY?
SORRY BERN...
I'M JUST TEASING, HUN.
SHUFF
WE NEED TO GET THIS COLLAR OFF YOU...
WHAT THE SON-OF-A-BITCH JUST HAPPENED?
WHAT AN AMAZING WOMAN...!
IS THAT DUDE DEAD?!
WHY COULDN'T THOSE DUMBASS GUARDS DO THAT?
...

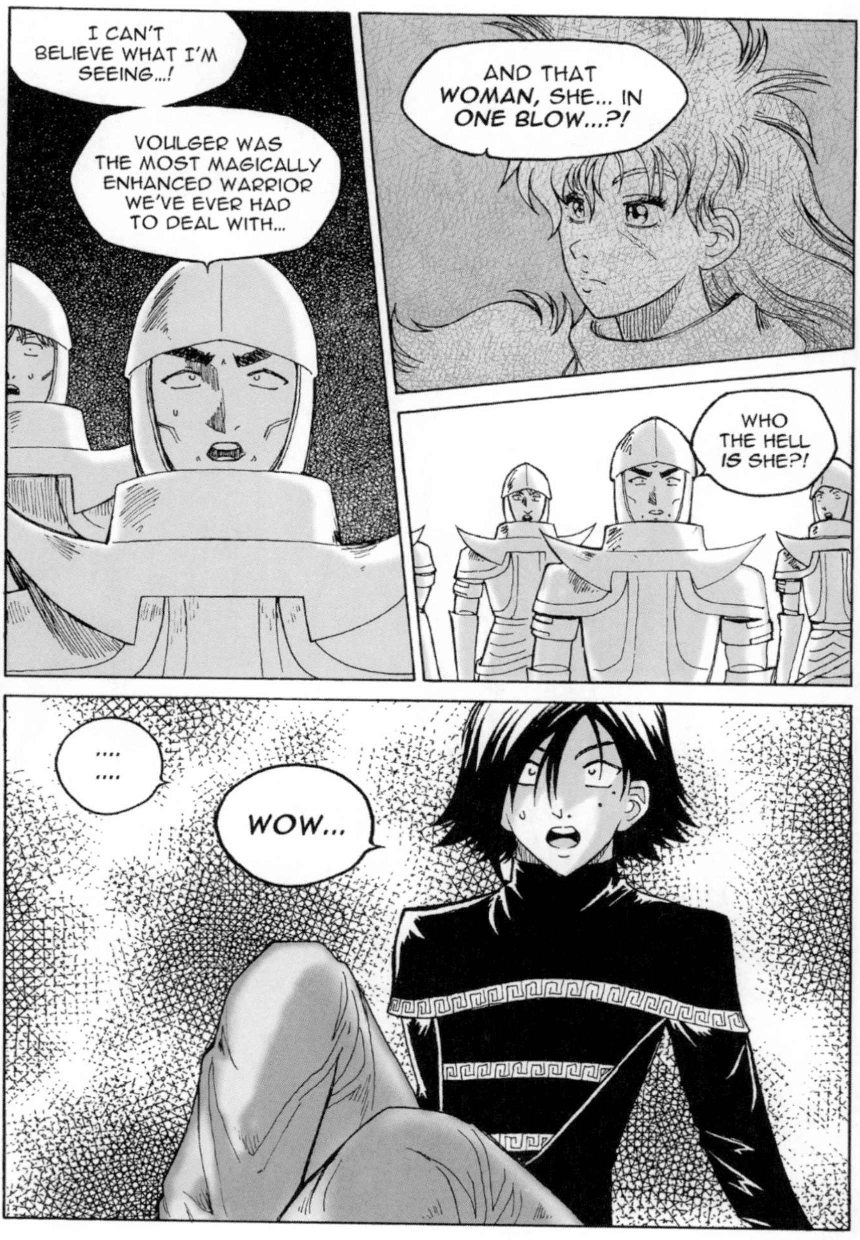
I CAN'T BELIEVE WHAT I'M SEEING...!
VOULGER WAS THE MOST MAGICALLY ENHANCED WARRIOR WE'VE EVER HAD TO DEAL WITH...
AND THAT WOMAN, SHE... IN ONE BLOW...?!
WHO THE HELL IS SHE?!
....
WOW...

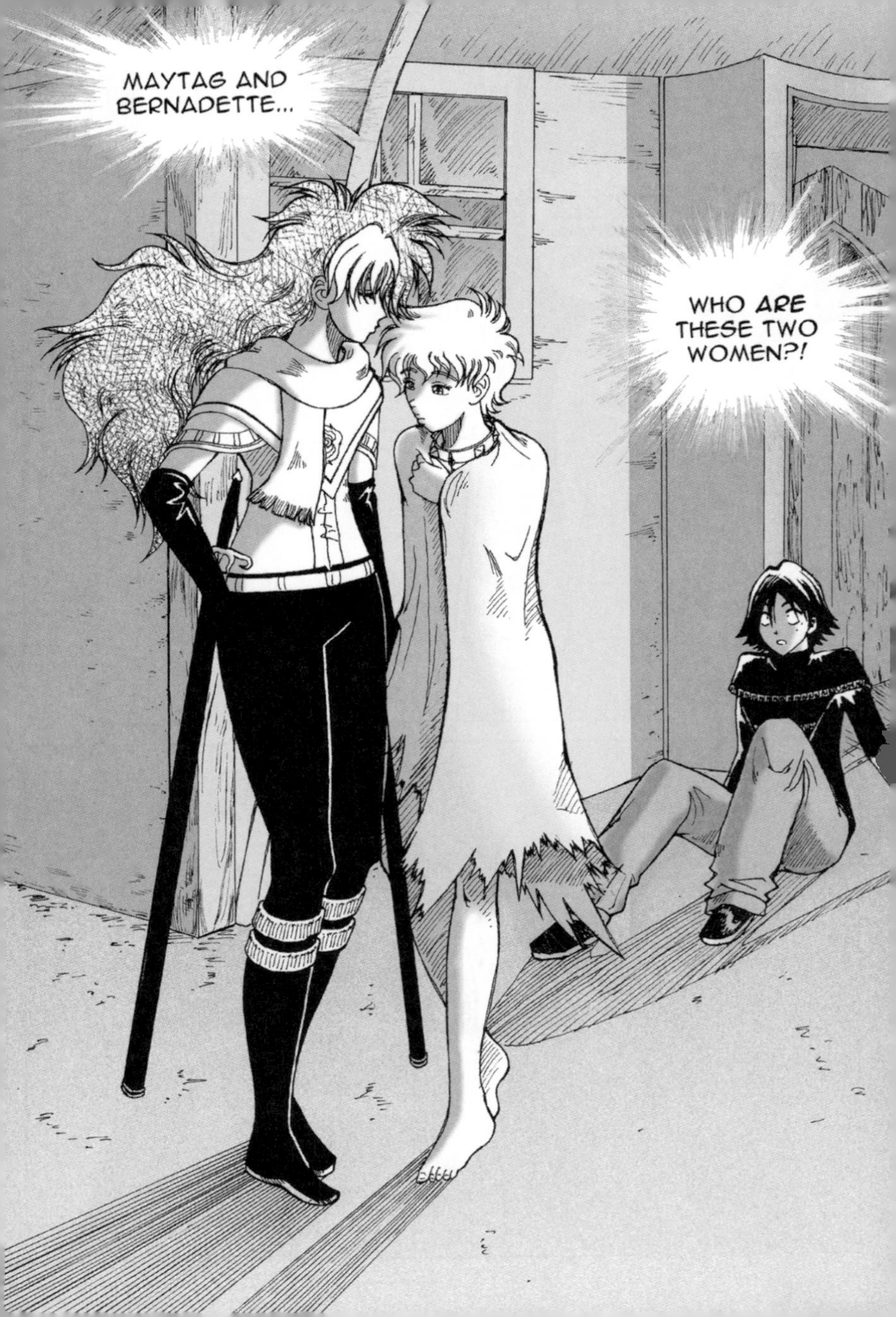
MAYTAG AND BERNADETTE...
WHO ARE THESE TWO WOMEN?!

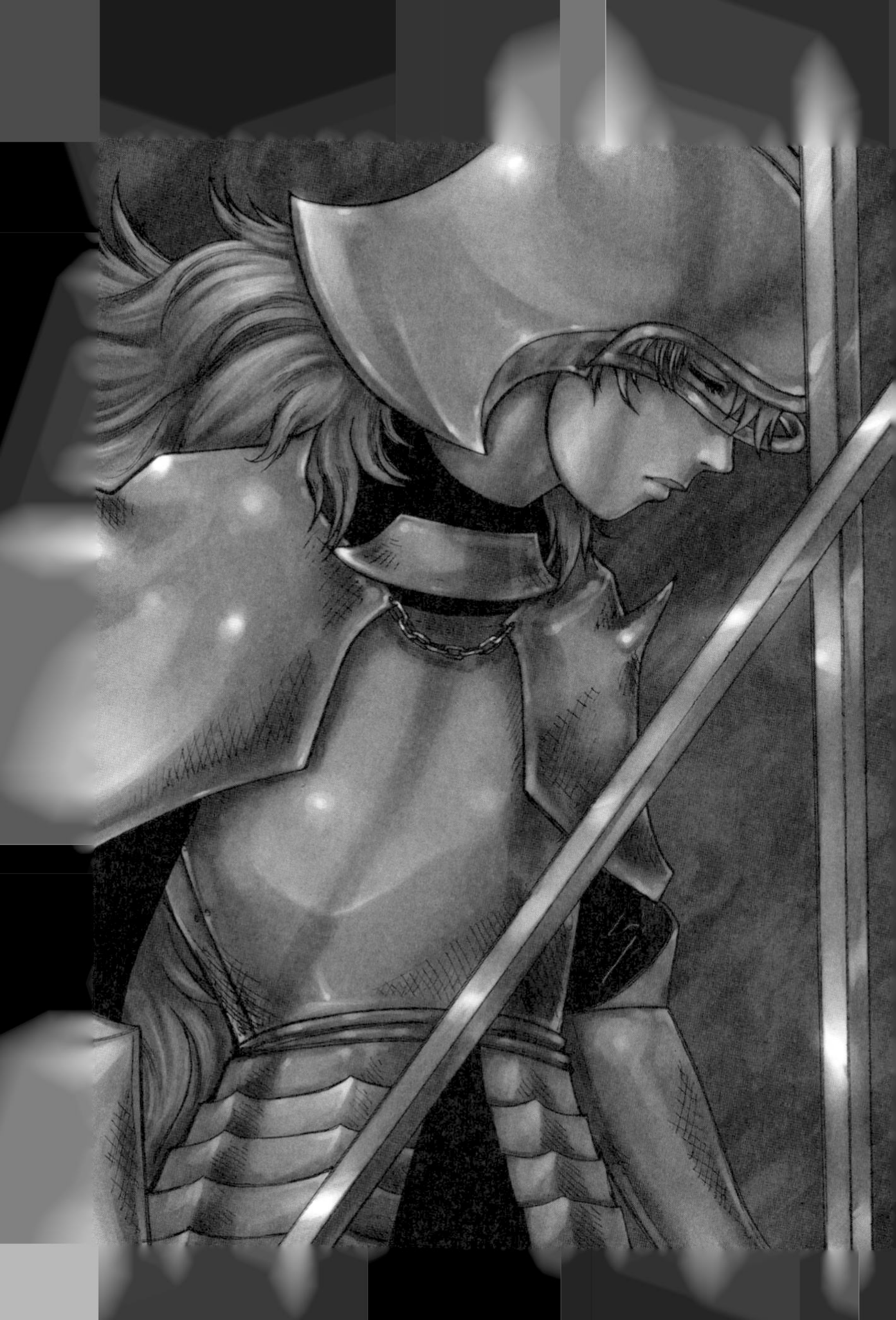

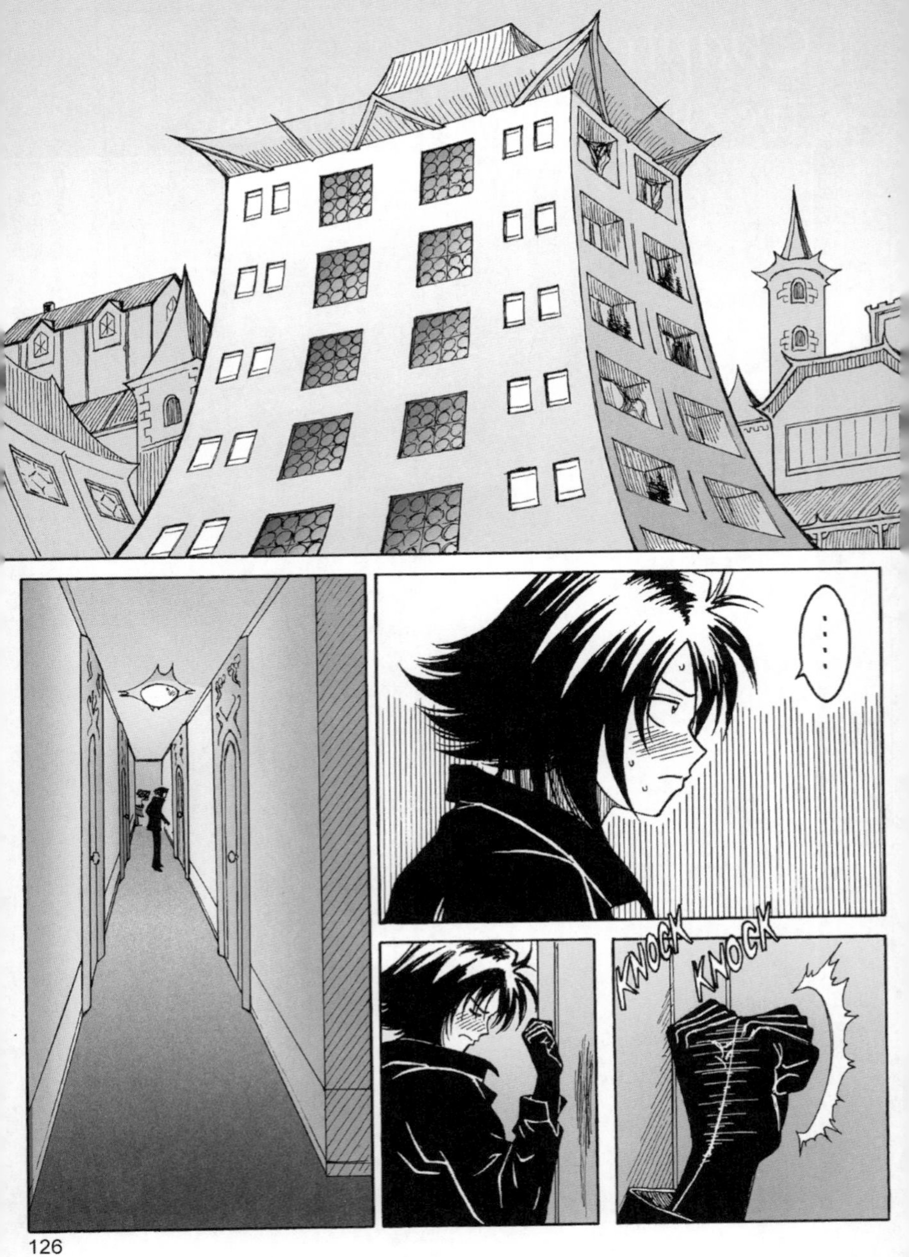
.....
KNOCK
KNOCK

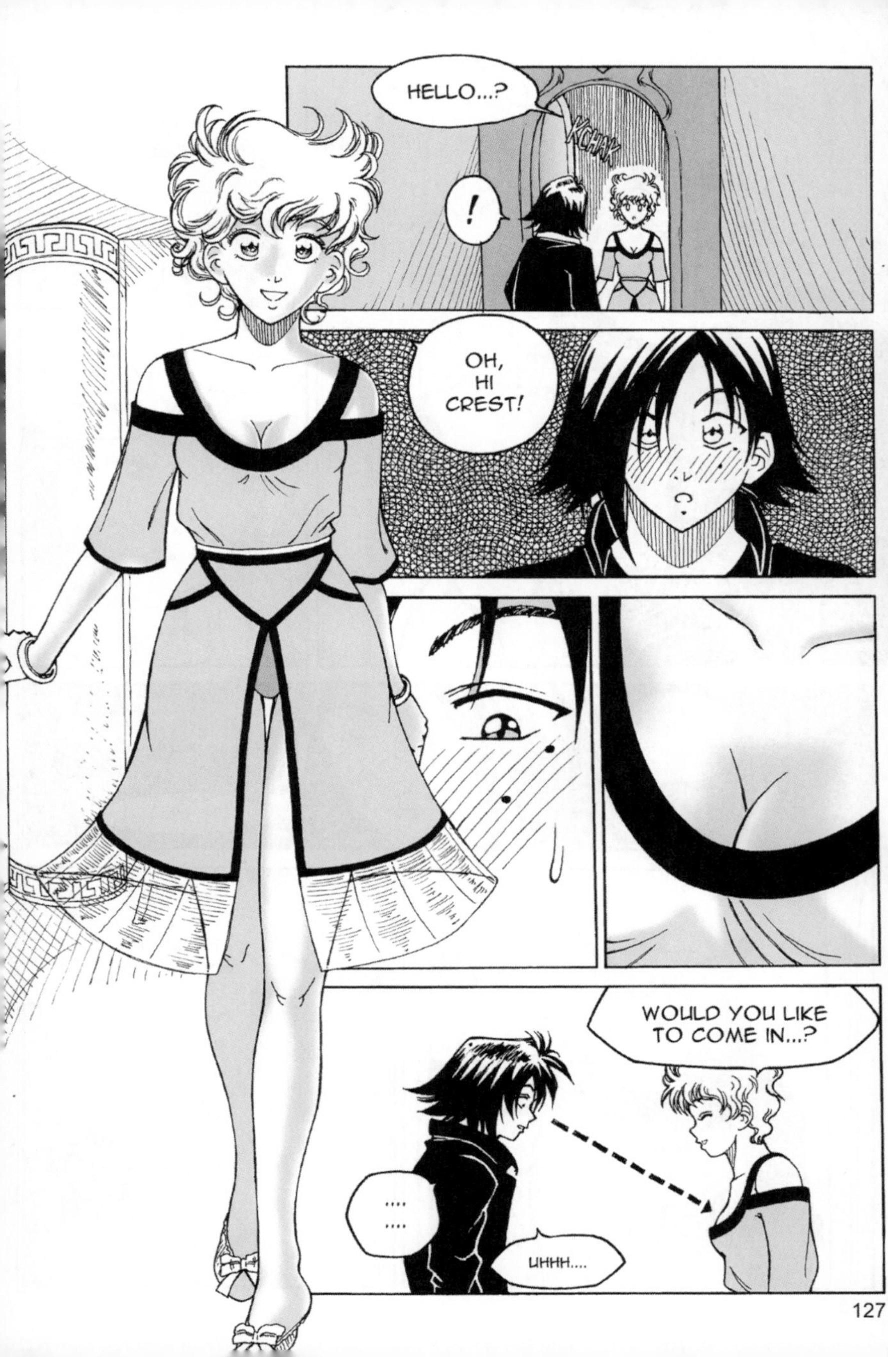
HELLO...?
KCHAK
!
OH, HI CREST!
WOULD YOU LIKE TO COME IN...?
....
....
UHHH....

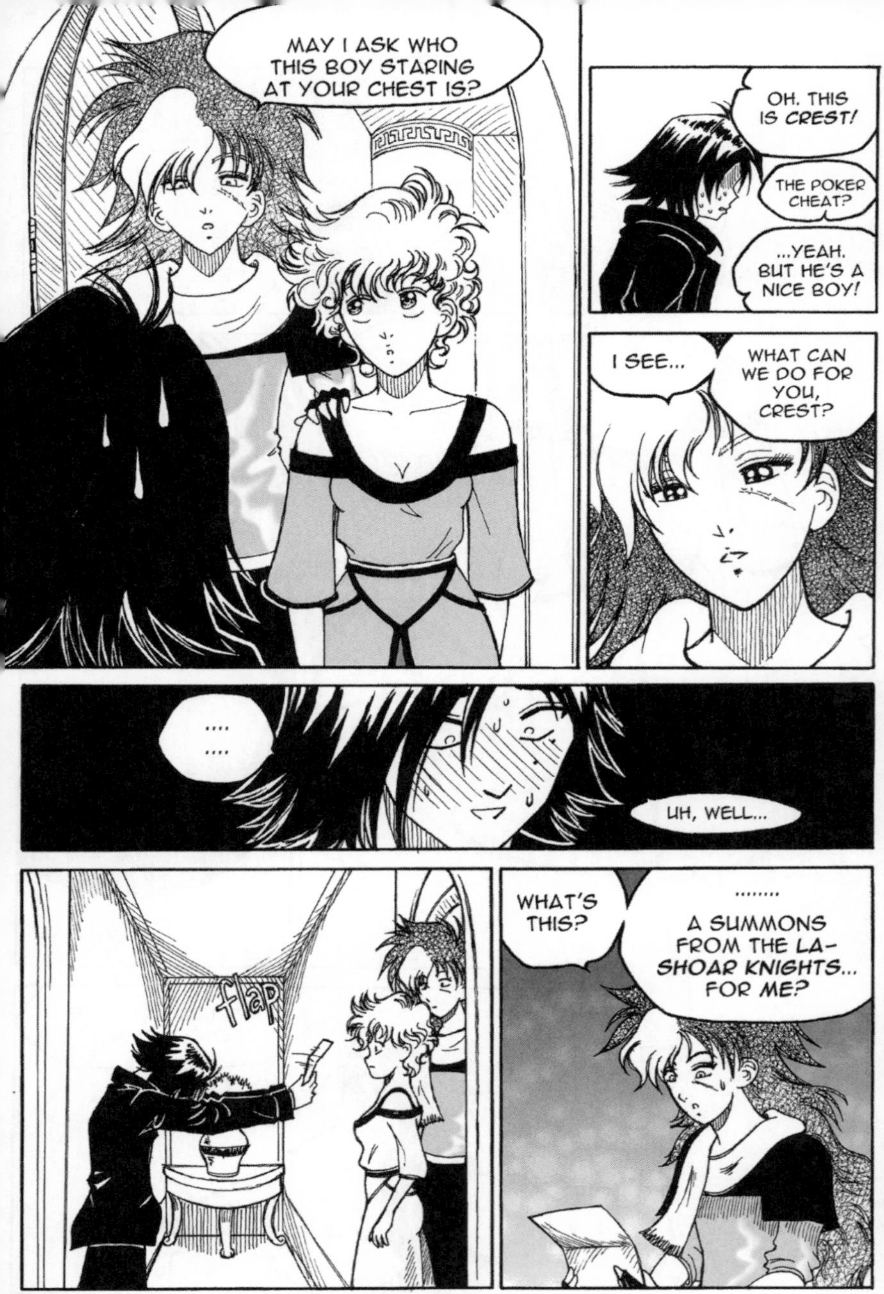
MAY I ASK WHO THIS BOY STARING AT YOUR CHEST IS?
OH. THIS IS CREST!
THE POKER CHEAT?
...YEAH. BUT HE'S A NICE BOY!
I SEE...
WHAT CAN WE DO FOR YOU, CREST?
....
....
UH, WELL...
flap
WHAT'S THIS?
....
A SUMMONS FROM THE LA-SHOAR KNIGHTS... FOR ME?

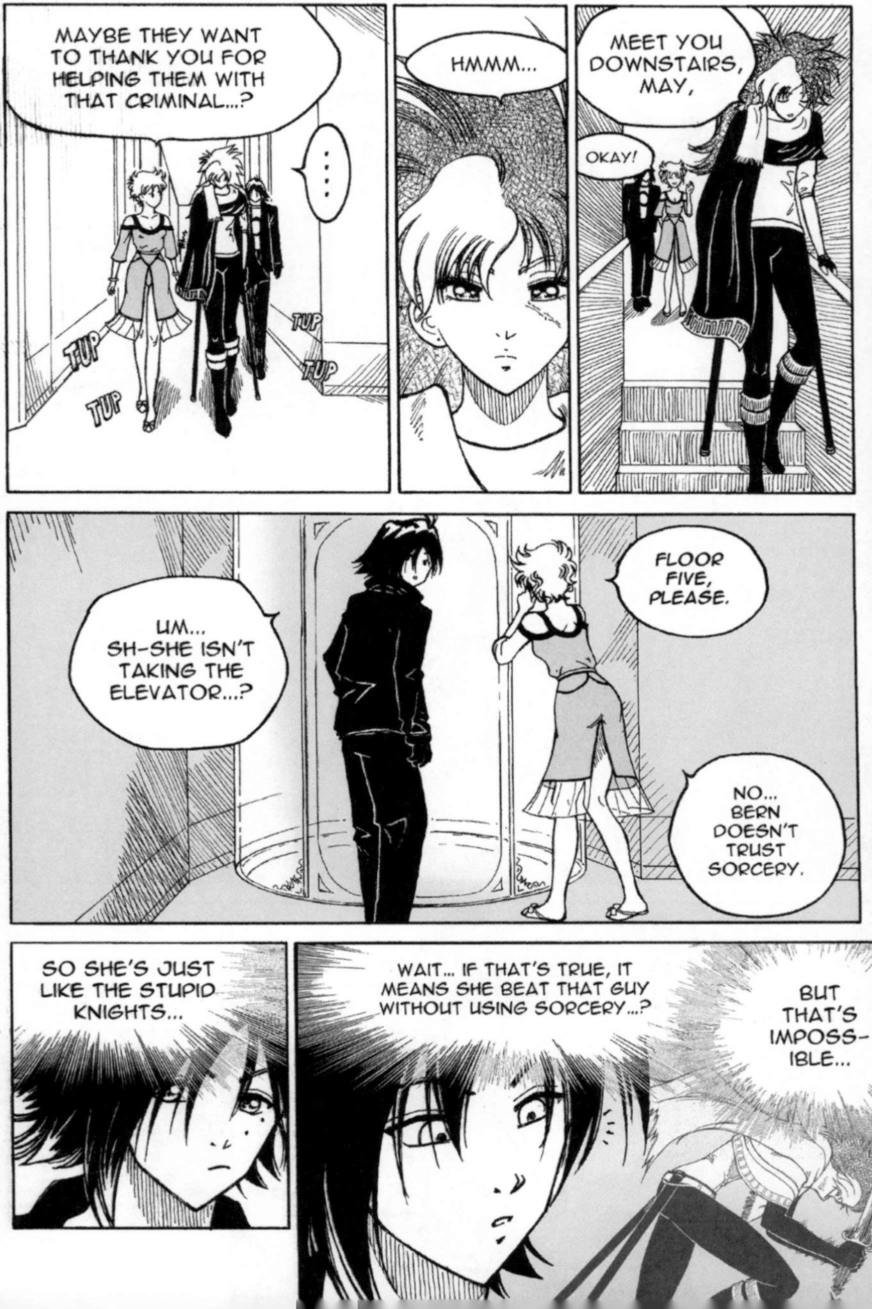
MAYBE THEY WANT TO THANK YOU FOR HELPING THEM WITH THAT CRIMINAL...?
....
TUP
TUP
TUP
TUP
HMMM...
MEET YOU DOWNSTAIRS, MAY,
OKAY!
UM... SH-SHE ISN'T TAKING THE ELEVATOR...?
FLOOR FIVE, PLEASE.
NO... BERN DOESN'T TRUST SORCERY.
SO SHE'S JUST LIKE THE STUPID KNIGHTS...
WAIT... IF THAT'S TRUE, IT MEANS SHE BEAT THAT GUY WITHOUT USING SORCERY...?
BUT THAT'S IMPOSS-IBLE...

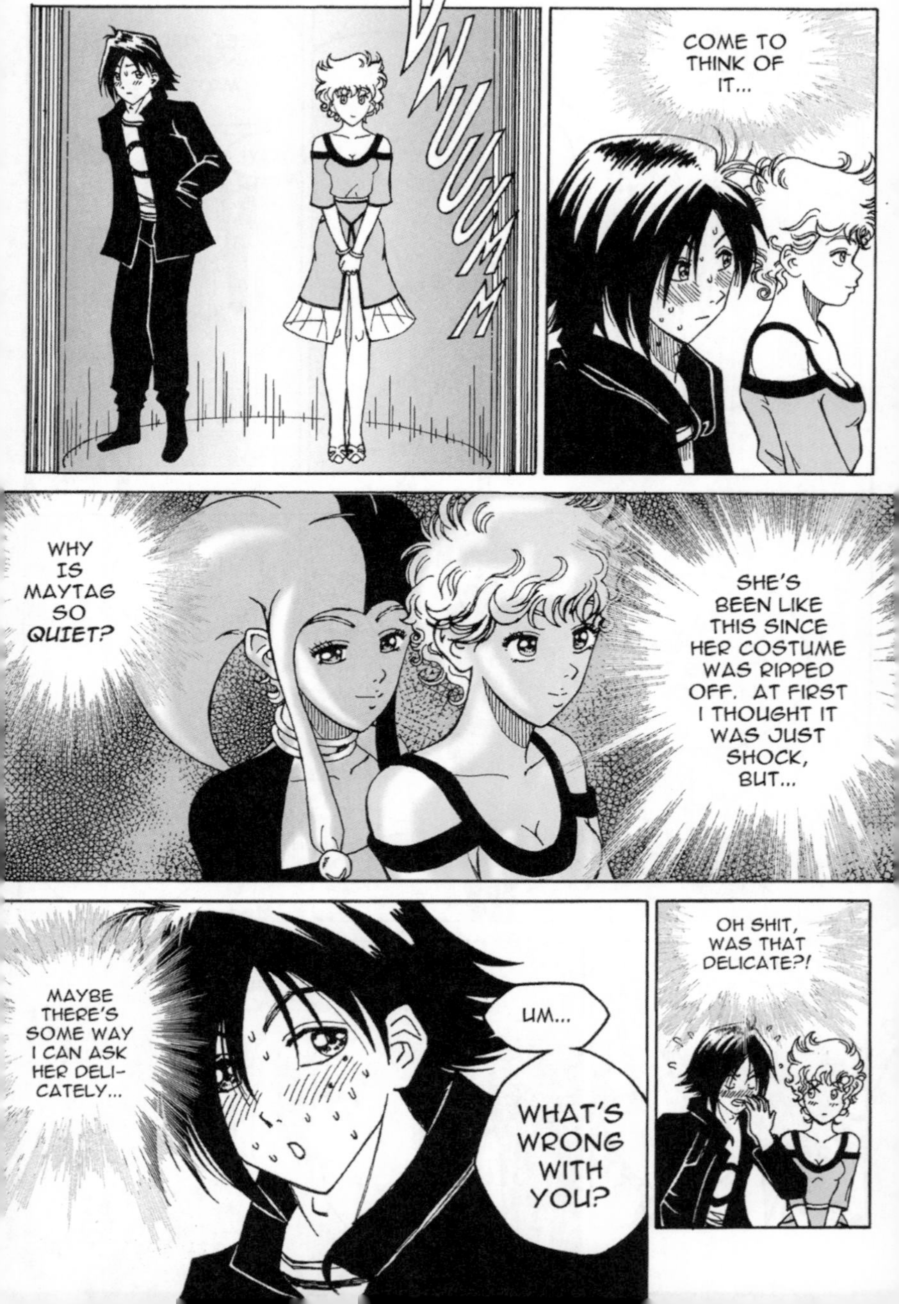
VWUUMM
COME TO THINK OF IT...
WHY IS MAYTAG SO QUIET?
SHE'S BEEN LIKE THIS SINCE HER COSTUME WAS RIPPED OFF. AT FIRST I THOUGHT IT WAS JUST SHOCK, BUT...
MAYBE THERE'S SOME WAY I CAN ASK HER DELI-CATELY...
UM...
WHAT'S WRONG WITH YOU?
OH SHIT, WAS THAT DELICATE?!

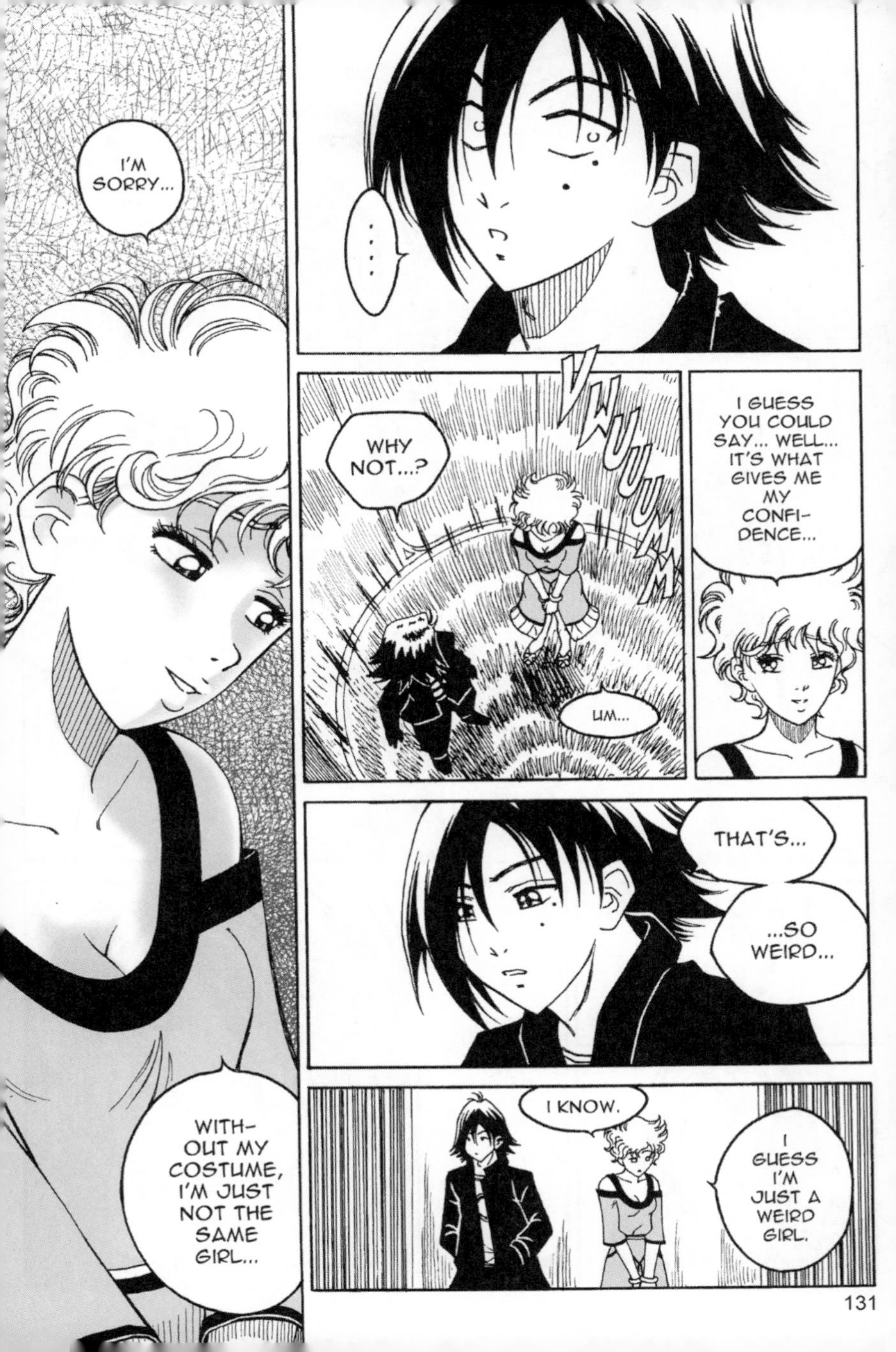
I'M SORRY...
...
WHY NOT...?
VWUUUUMM
UM...
I GUESS YOU COULD SAY... WELL... IT'S WHAT GIVES ME MY CONFI-DENCE...
WITH-OUT MY COSTUME, I'M JUST NOT THE SAME GIRL...
THAT'S...
...SO WEIRD...
I KNOW.
I GUESS I'M JUST A WEIRD GIRL.

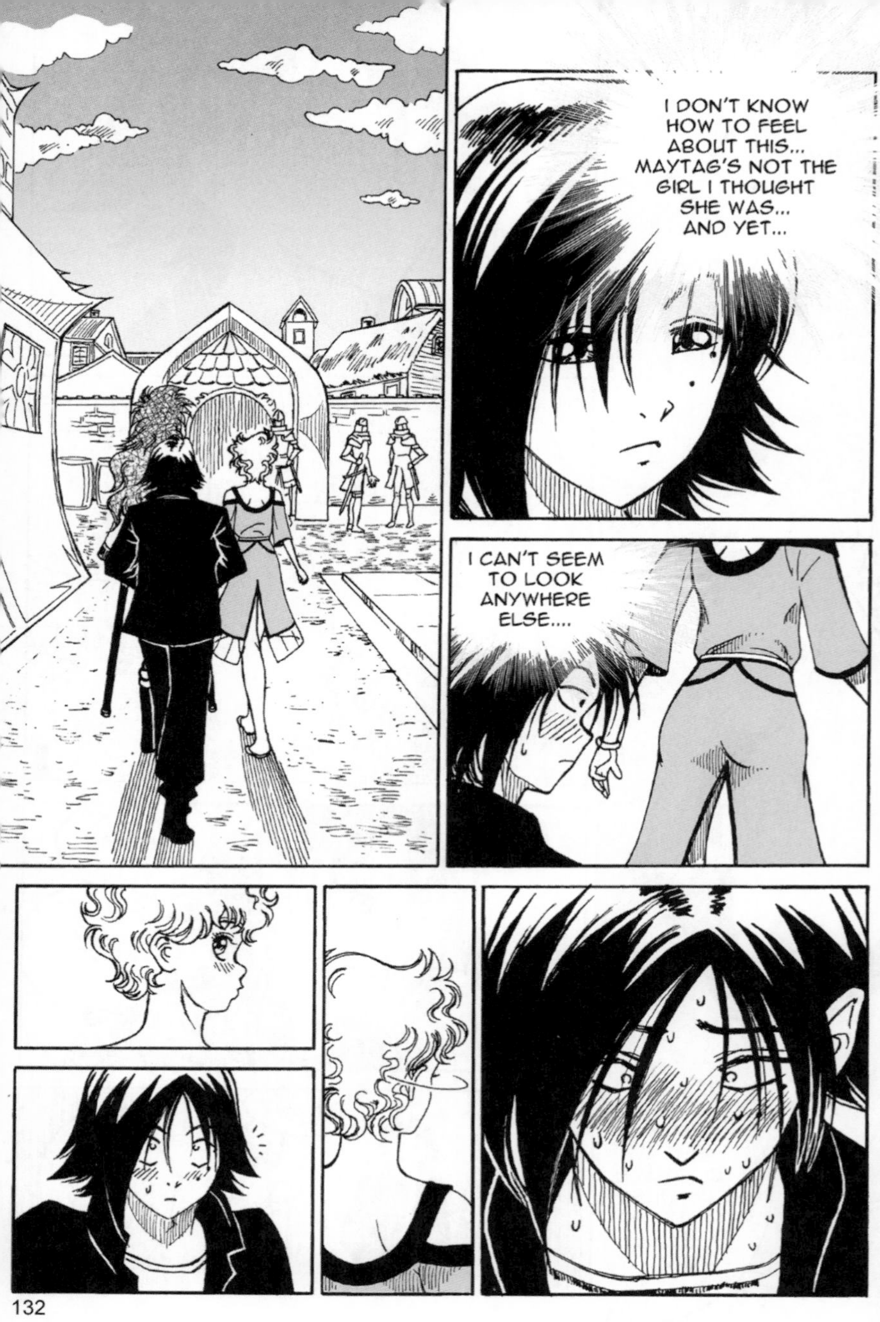
I DON'T KNOW HOW TO FEEL ABOUT THIS... MAYTAG'S NOT THE GIRL I THOUGHT SHE WAS... AND YET...
I CAN'T SEEM TO LOOK ANYWHERE ELSE....

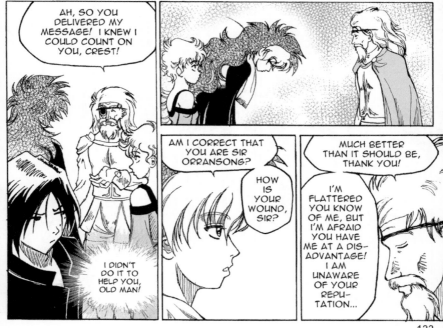

AH, SO YOU DELIVERED MY MESSAGE! I KNEW I COULD COUNT ON YOU, CREST!

I DIDN'T DO IT TO HELP YOU, OLD MAN!

AM I CORRECT THAT YOU ARE SIR ORRANSONG?

HOW IS YOUR WOUND, SIR?

MUCH BETTER THAN IT SHOULD BE, THANK YOU!

I'M FLATTERED YOU KNOW OF ME, BUT I'M AFRAID YOU HAVE ME AT A DIS-ADVANTAGE! I AM UNAWARE OF YOUR REPU-TATION...

133

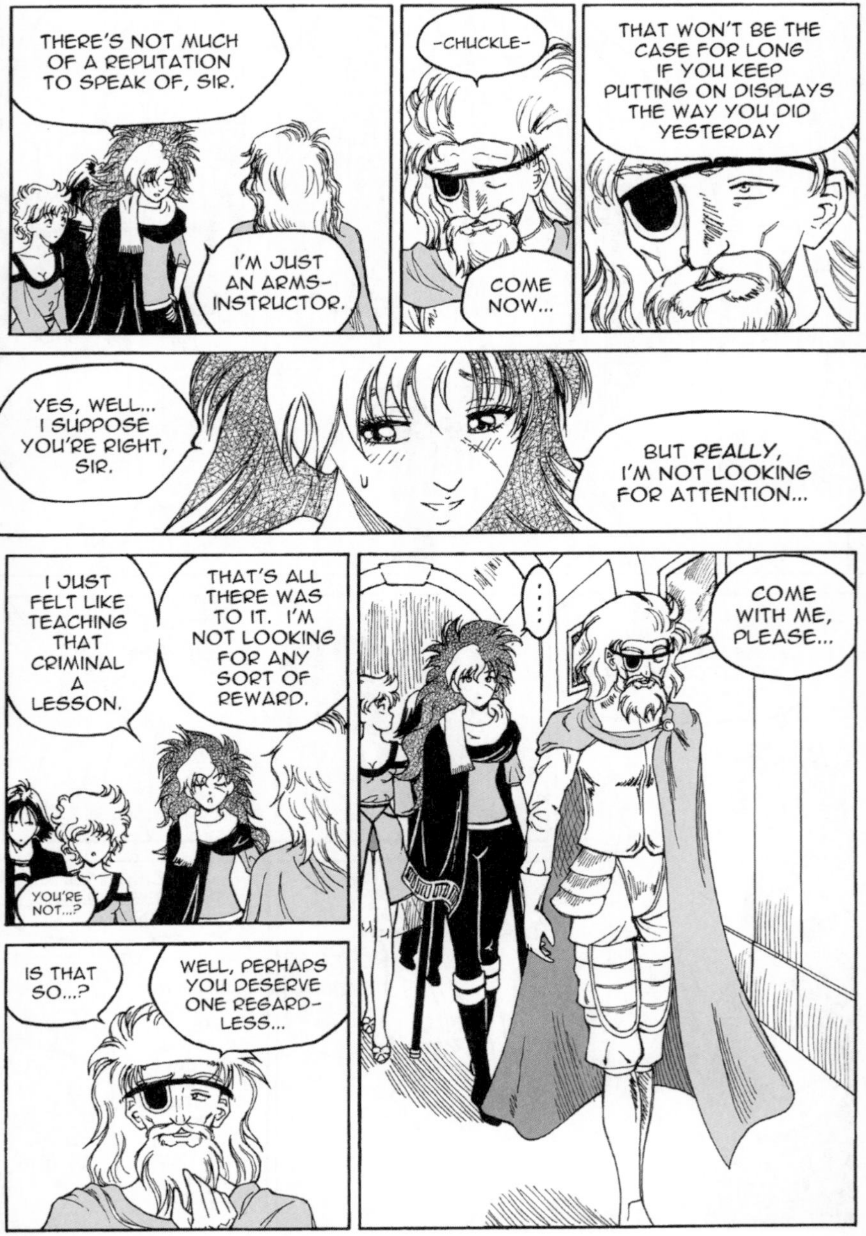
THERE'S NOT MUCH OF A REPUTATION TO SPEAK OF, SIR.
I'M JUST AN ARMS-INSTRUCTOR.
-CHUCKLE-
COME NOW...
THAT WON'T BE THE CASE FOR LONG IF YOU KEEP PUTTING ON DISPLAYS THE WAY YOU DID YESTERDAY
YES, WELL... I SUPPOSE YOU'RE RIGHT, SIR.
BUT *REALLY*, I'M NOT LOOKING FOR ATTENTION...
I JUST FELT LIKE TEACHING THAT CRIMINAL A LESSON.
THAT'S ALL THERE WAS TO IT. I'M NOT LOOKING FOR ANY SORT OF REWARD.
YOU'RE NOT...?
IS THAT SO...?
WELL, PERHAPS YOU DESERVE ONE REGARDLESS...
...
COME WITH ME, PLEASE...

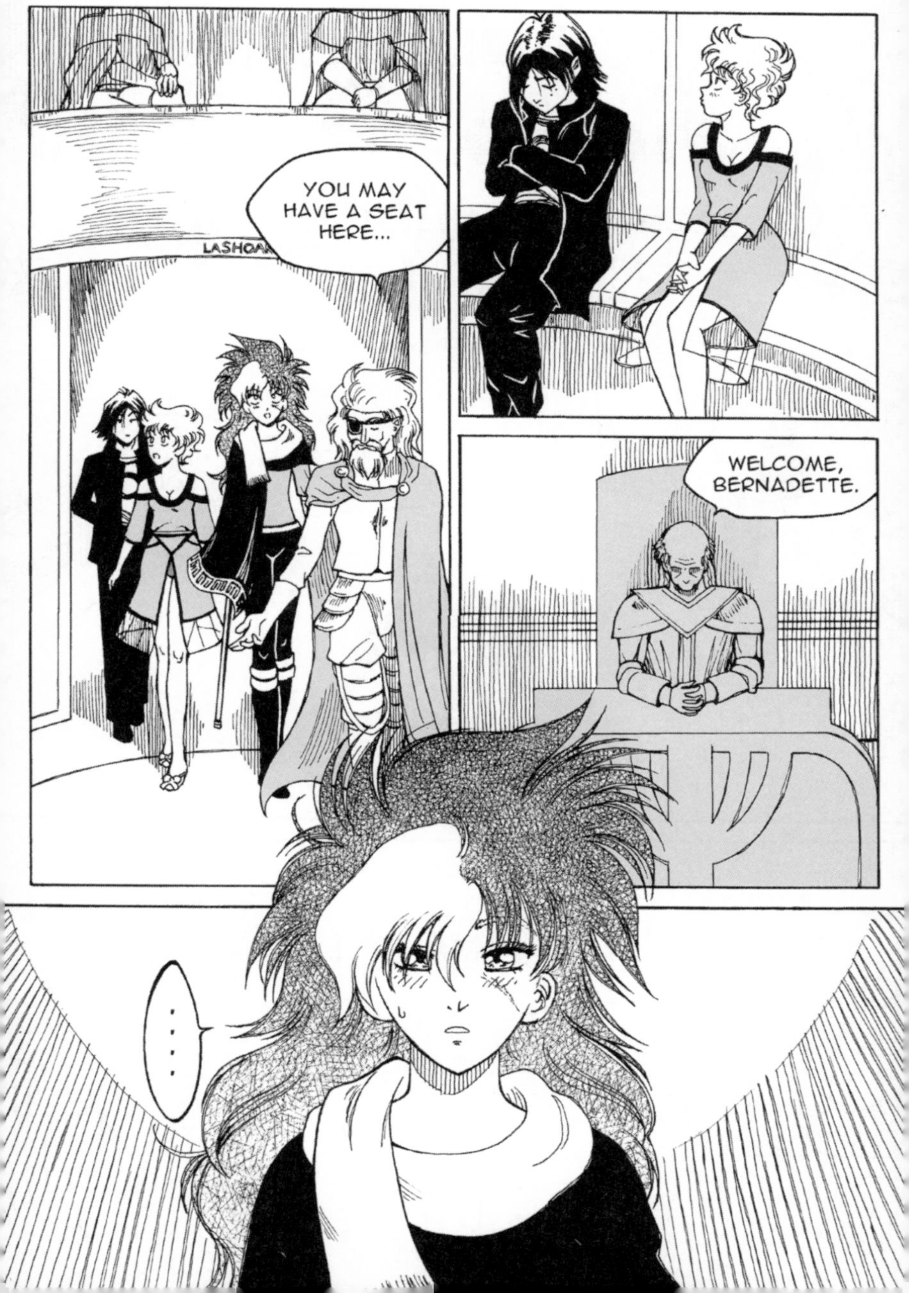
YOU MAY HAVE A SEAT HERE...
WELCOME, BERNADETTE.
....

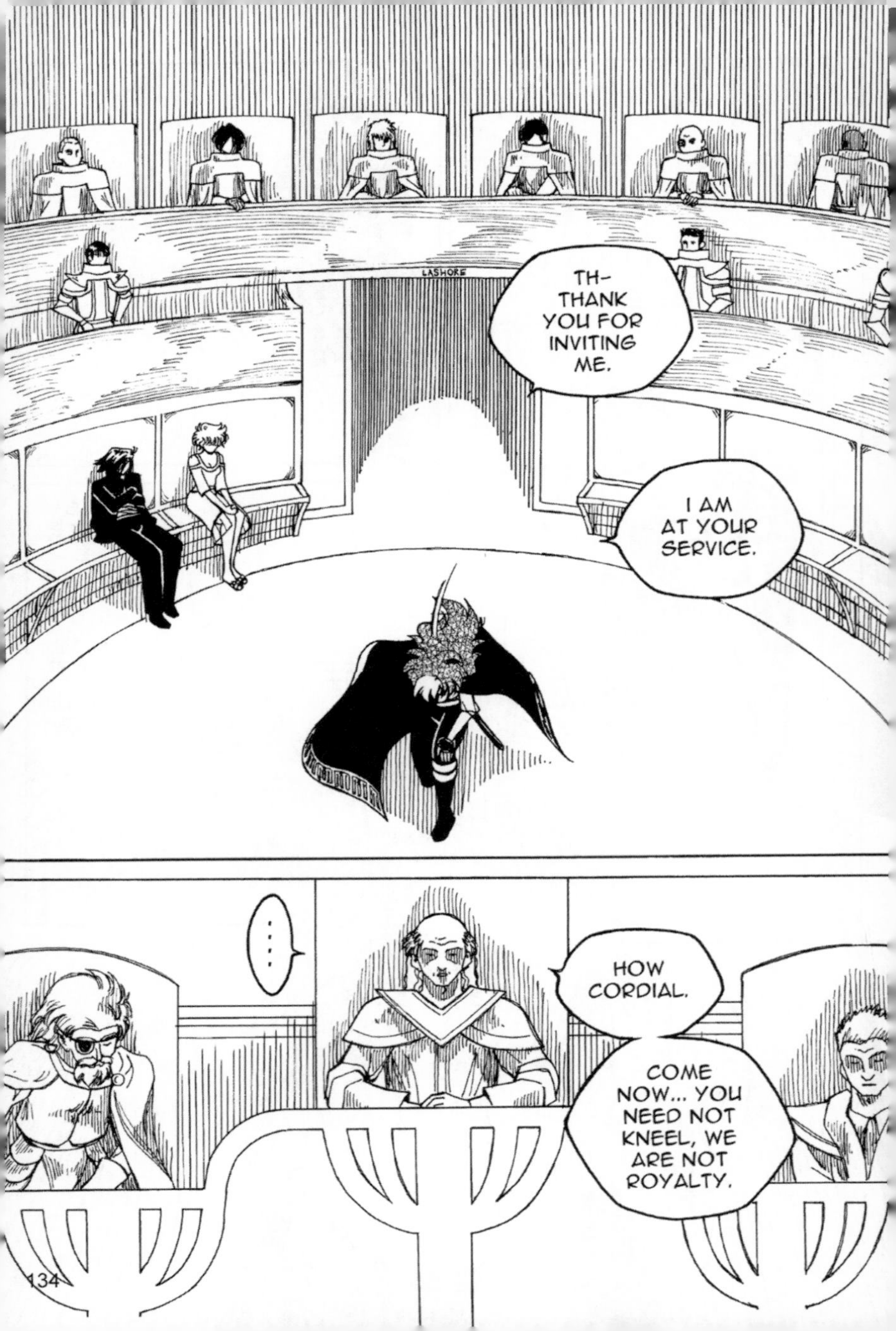
LASHORE
TH- THANK YOU FOR INVITING ME.
I AM AT YOUR SERVICE.
...
HOW CORDIAL.
COME NOW... YOU NEED NOT KNEEL, WE ARE NOT ROYALTY.

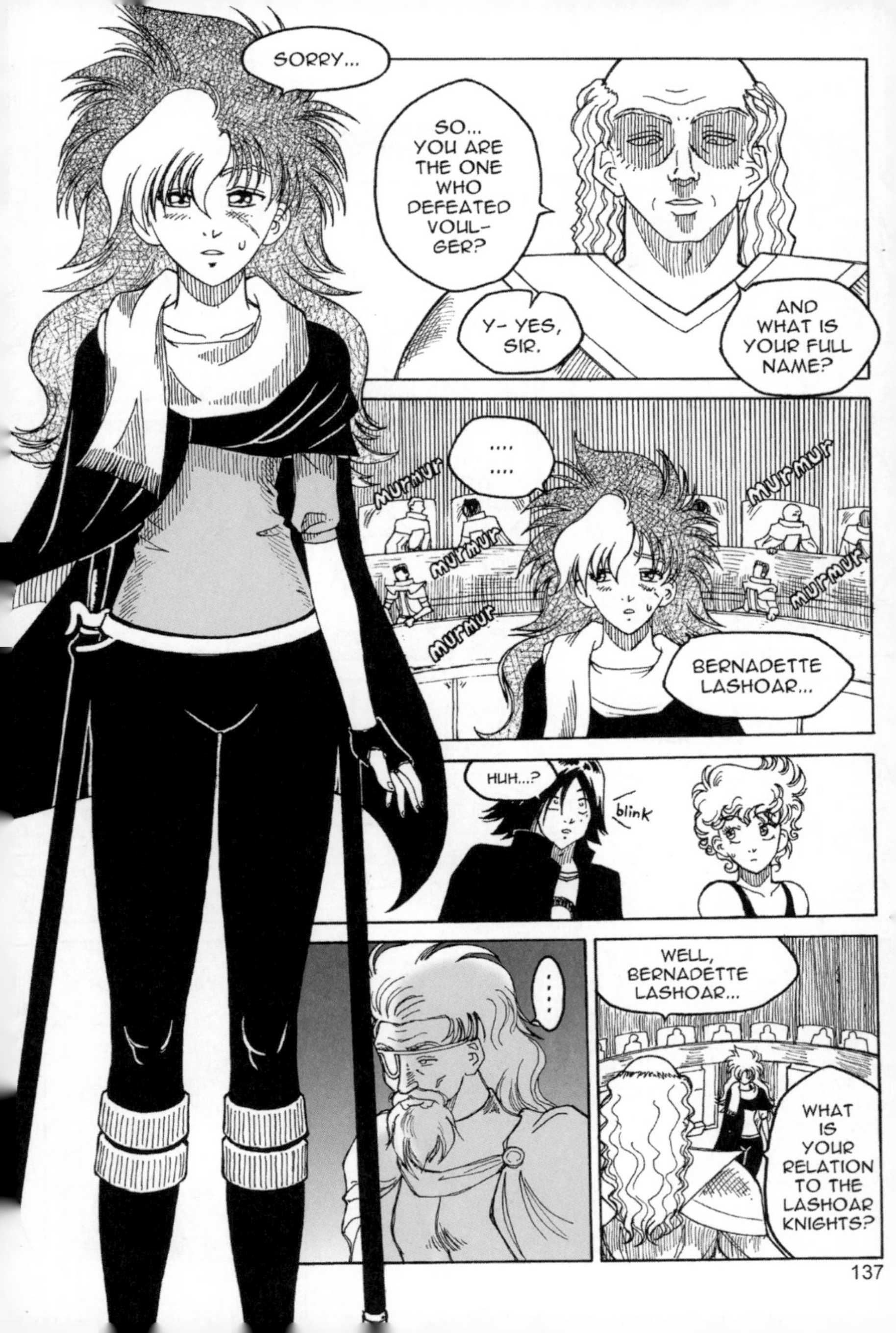
SORRY...
SO... YOU ARE THE ONE WHO DEFEATED VOUL-GER?
Y- YES, SIR.
AND WHAT IS YOUR FULL NAME?
....
....
murmur
murmur
murmur
murmur
murmur
BERNADETTE LASHOAR...
HUH...?
blink
....
WELL, BERNADETTE LASHOAR...
WHAT IS YOUR RELATION TO THE LASHOAR KNIGHTS?

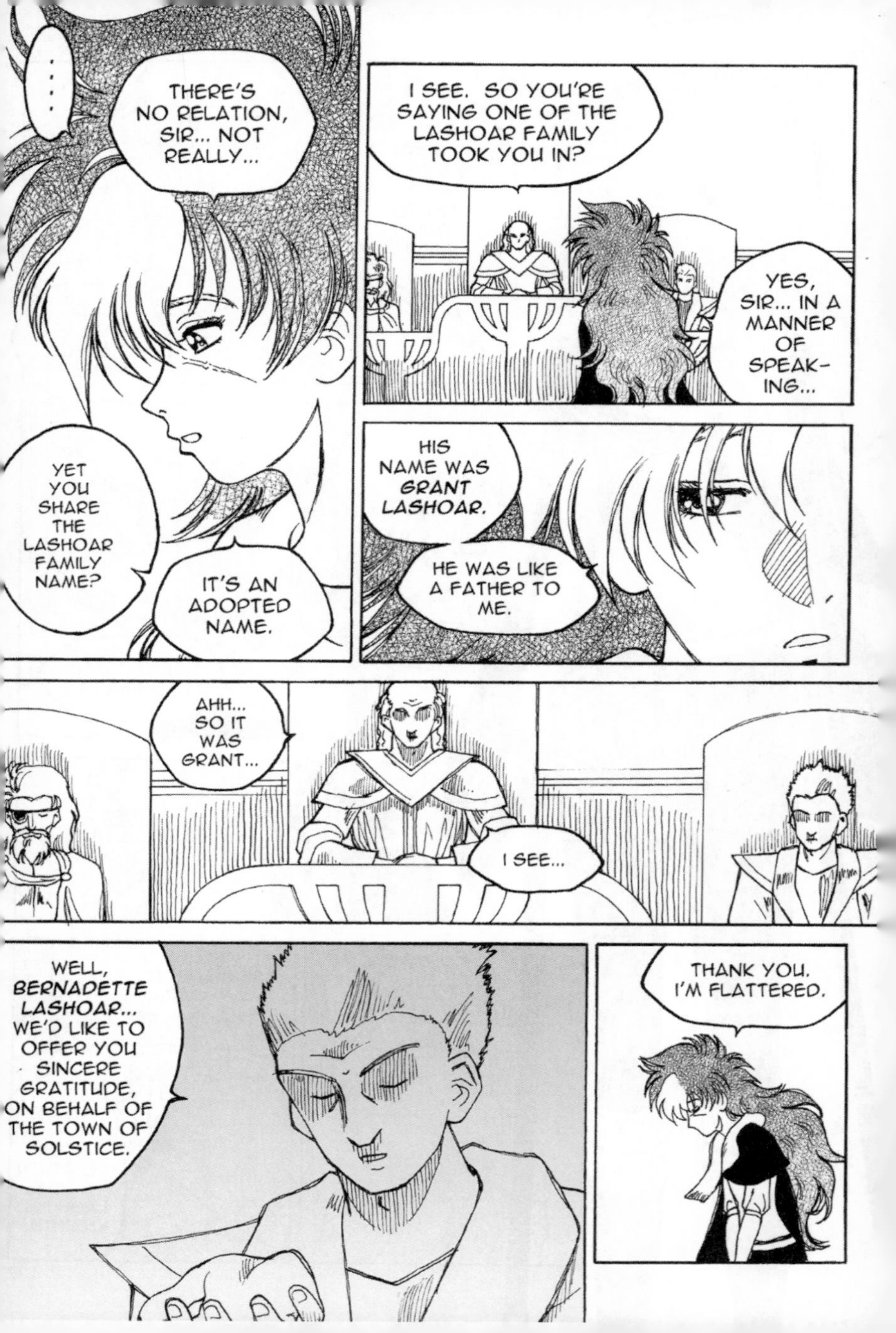
....
THERE'S NO RELATION, SIR... NOT REALLY...
I SEE. SO YOU'RE SAYING ONE OF THE LASHOAR FAMILY TOOK YOU IN?
YES, SIR... IN A MANNER OF SPEAKING...
YET YOU SHARE THE LASHOAR FAMILY NAME?
IT'S AN ADOPTED NAME.
HIS NAME WAS GRANT LASHOAR.
HE WAS LIKE A FATHER TO ME.
AHH... SO IT WAS GRANT...
I SEE...
WELL, BERNADETTE LASHOAR... WE'D LIKE TO OFFER YOU SINCERE GRATITUDE, ON BEHALF OF THE TOWN OF SOLSTICE.
THANK YOU. I'M FLATTERED.

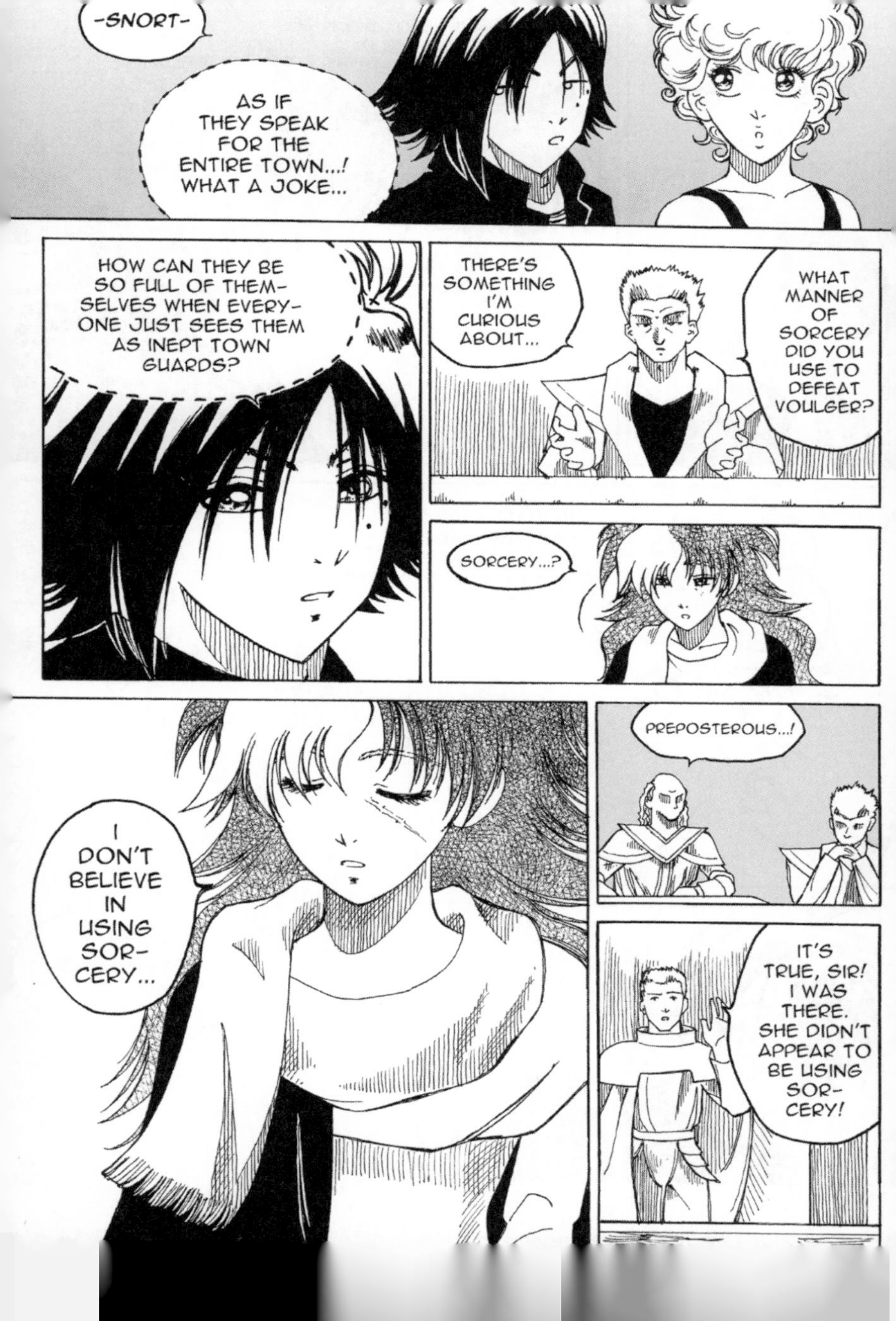
-SNORT-
AS IF THEY SPEAK FOR THE ENTIRE TOWN...! WHAT A JOKE...
HOW CAN THEY BE SO FULL OF THEM-SELVES WHEN EVERY-ONE JUST SEES THEM AS INEPT TOWN GUARDS?
THERE'S SOMETHING I'M CURIOUS ABOUT...
WHAT MANNER OF SORCERY DID YOU USE TO DEFEAT VOULGER?
SORCERY...?
I DON'T BELIEVE IN USING SOR-CERY...
PREPOSTEROUS...!
IT'S TRUE, SIR! I WAS THERE. SHE DIDN'T APPEAR TO BE USING SOR-CERY!

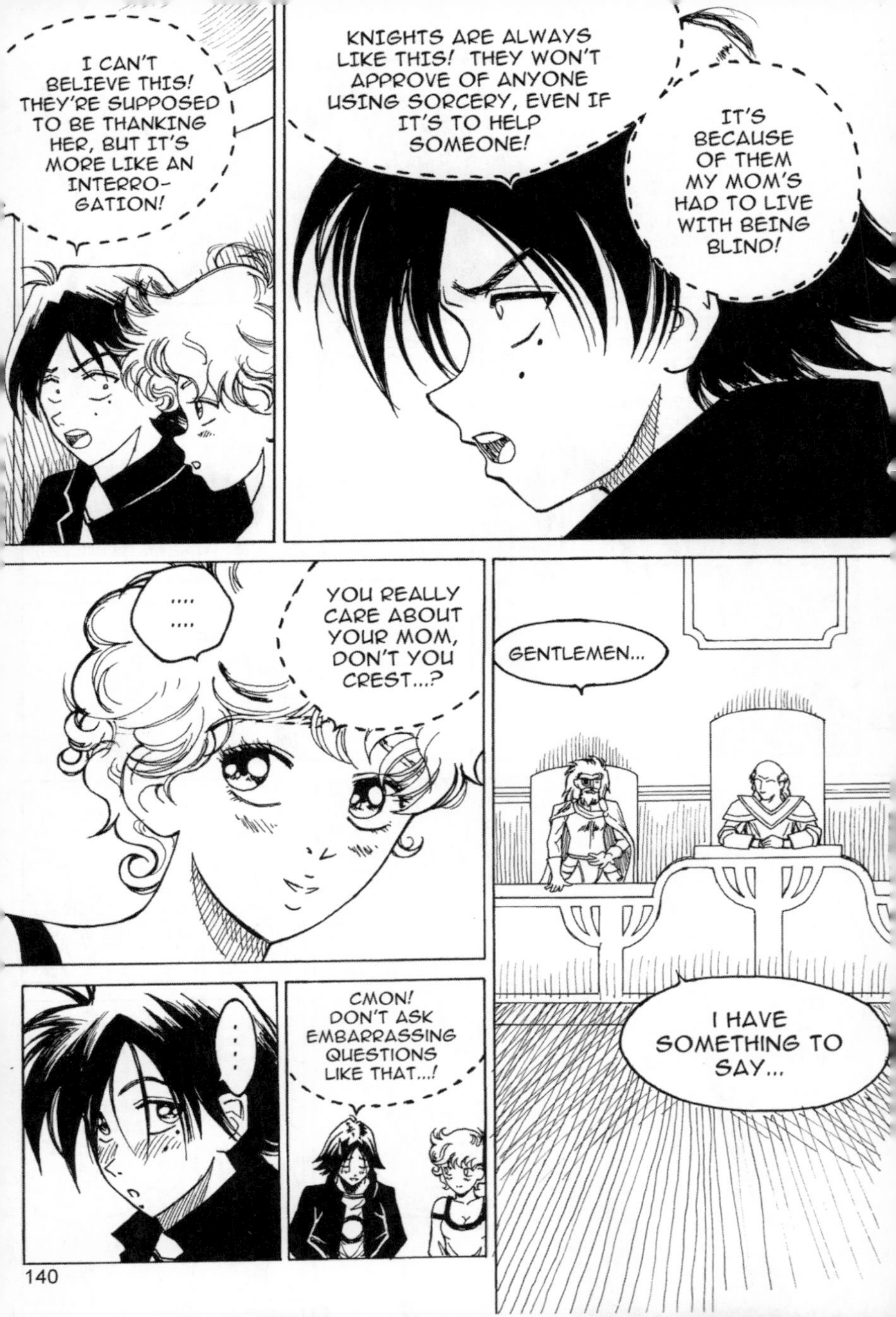
I CAN'T BELIEVE THIS! THEY'RE SUPPOSED TO BE THANKING HER, BUT IT'S MORE LIKE AN INTERRO-GATION!
KNIGHTS ARE ALWAYS LIKE THIS! THEY WON'T APPROVE OF ANYONE USING SORCERY, EVEN IF IT'S TO HELP SOMEONE!
IT'S BECAUSE OF THEM MY MOM'S HAD TO LIVE WITH BEING BLIND!
....
YOU REALLY CARE ABOUT YOUR MOM, DON'T YOU CREST...?
GENTLEMEN...
....
CMON! DON'T ASK EMBARRASSING QUESTIONS LIKE THAT...!
I HAVE SOMETHING TO SAY...

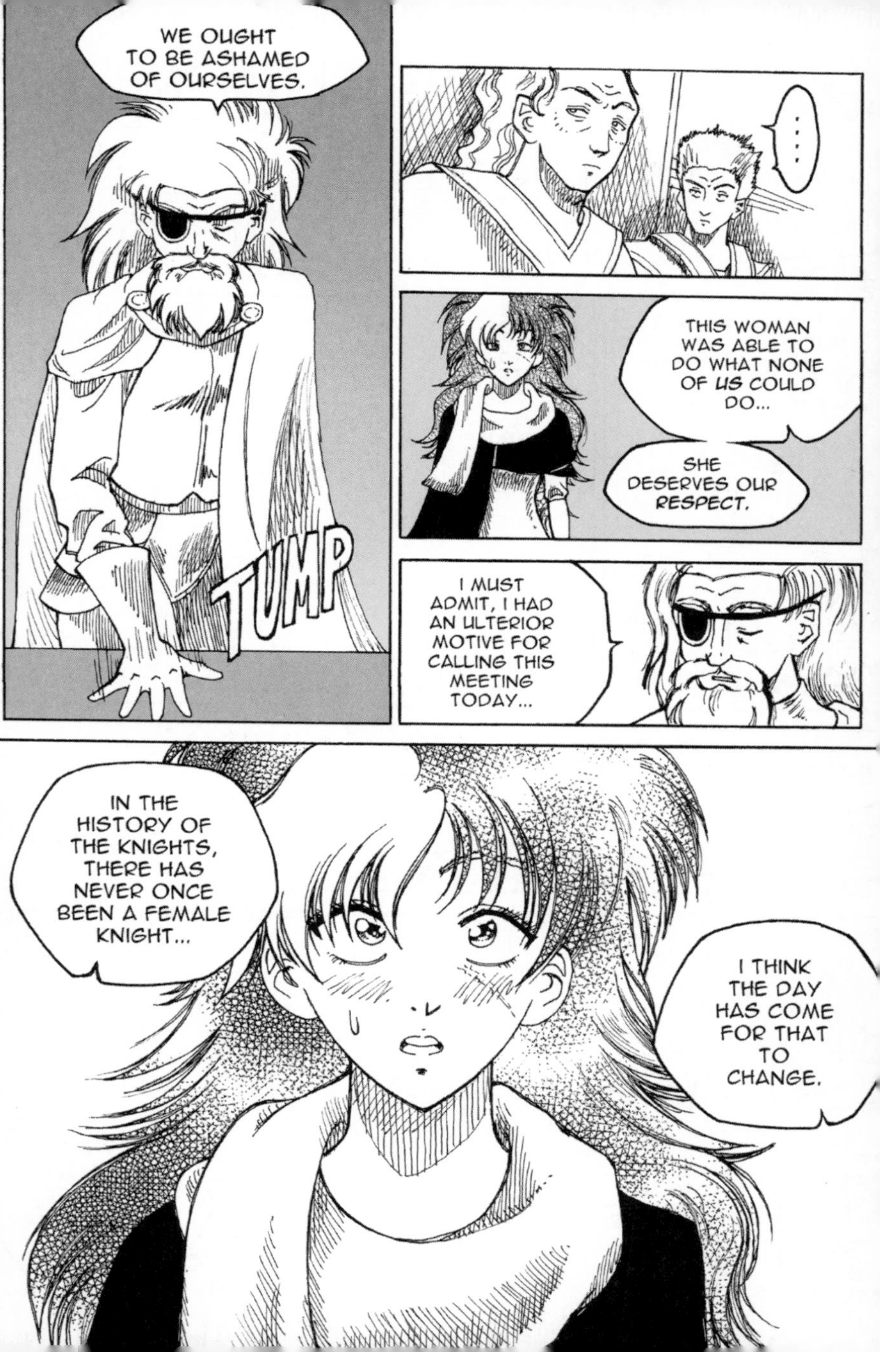
WE OUGHT TO BE ASHAMED OF OURSELVES.
...
TUMP
THIS WOMAN WAS ABLE TO DO WHAT NONE OF US COULD DO...
SHE DESERVES OUR RESPECT.
I MUST ADMIT, I HAD AN ULTERIOR MOTIVE FOR CALLING THIS MEETING TODAY...
IN THE HISTORY OF THE KNIGHTS, THERE HAS NEVER ONCE BEEN A FEMALE KNIGHT...
I THINK THE DAY HAS COME FOR THAT TO CHANGE.

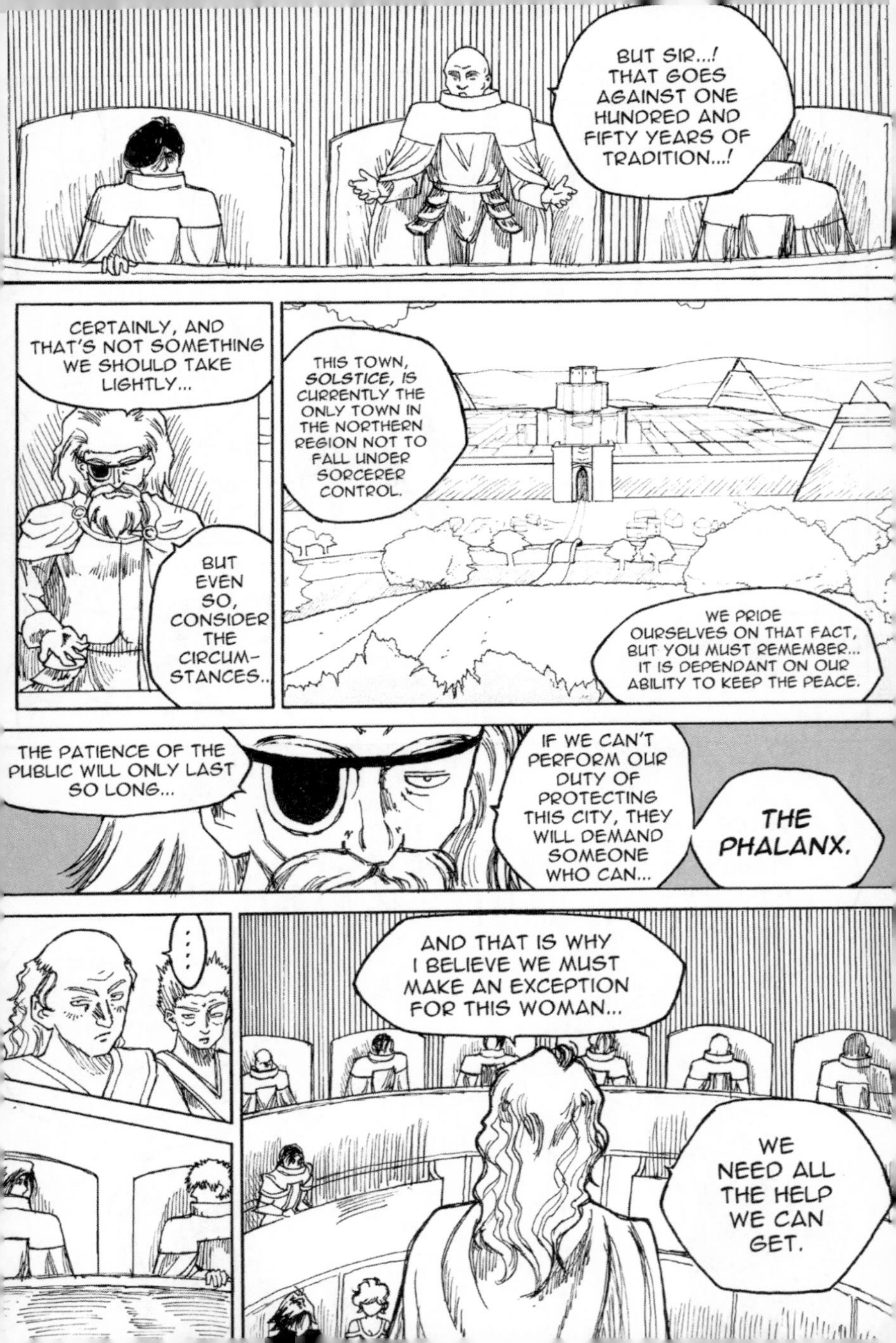
BUT SIR...! THAT GOES AGAINST ONE HUNDRED AND FIFTY YEARS OF TRADITION...!
CERTAINLY, AND THAT'S NOT SOMETHING WE SHOULD TAKE LIGHTLY...
BUT EVEN SO, CONSIDER THE CIRCUM-STANCES..
THIS TOWN, SOLSTICE, IS CURRENTLY THE ONLY TOWN IN THE NORTHERN REGION NOT TO FALL UNDER SORCERER CONTROL.
WE PRIDE OURSELVES ON THAT FACT, BUT YOU MUST REMEMBER... IT IS DEPENDANT ON OUR ABILITY TO KEEP THE PEACE.
THE PATIENCE OF THE PUBLIC WILL ONLY LAST SO LONG...
IF WE CAN'T PERFORM OUR DUTY OF PROTECTING THIS CITY, THEY WILL DEMAND SOMEONE WHO CAN...
THE PHALANX.
...
AND THAT IS WHY I BELIEVE WE MUST MAKE AN EXCEPTION FOR THIS WOMAN...
WE NEED ALL THE HELP WE CAN GET.

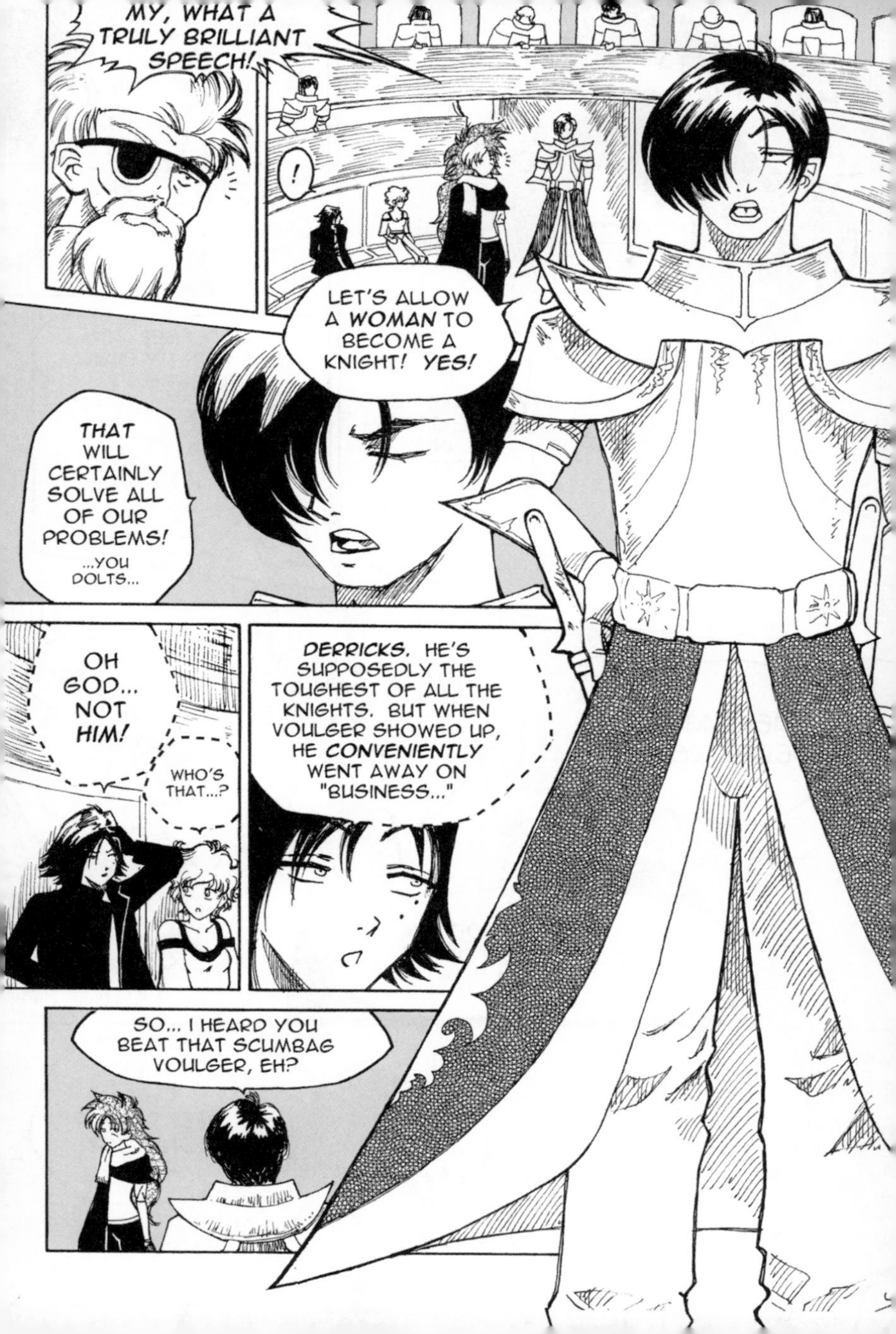

MY, WHAT A TRULY BRILLIANT SPEECH!
!
LET'S ALLOW A WOMAN TO BECOME A KNIGHT! YES!
THAT WILL CERTAINLY SOLVE ALL OF OUR PROBLEMS!
...YOU DOLTS...
OH GOD... NOT HIM!
WHO'S THAT...?
DERRICKS. HE'S SUPPOSEDLY THE TOUGHEST OF ALL THE KNIGHTS. BUT WHEN VOULGER SHOWED UP, HE CONVENIENTLY WENT AWAY ON "BUSINESS..."
SO... I HEARD YOU BEAT THAT SCUMBAG VOULGER, EH?

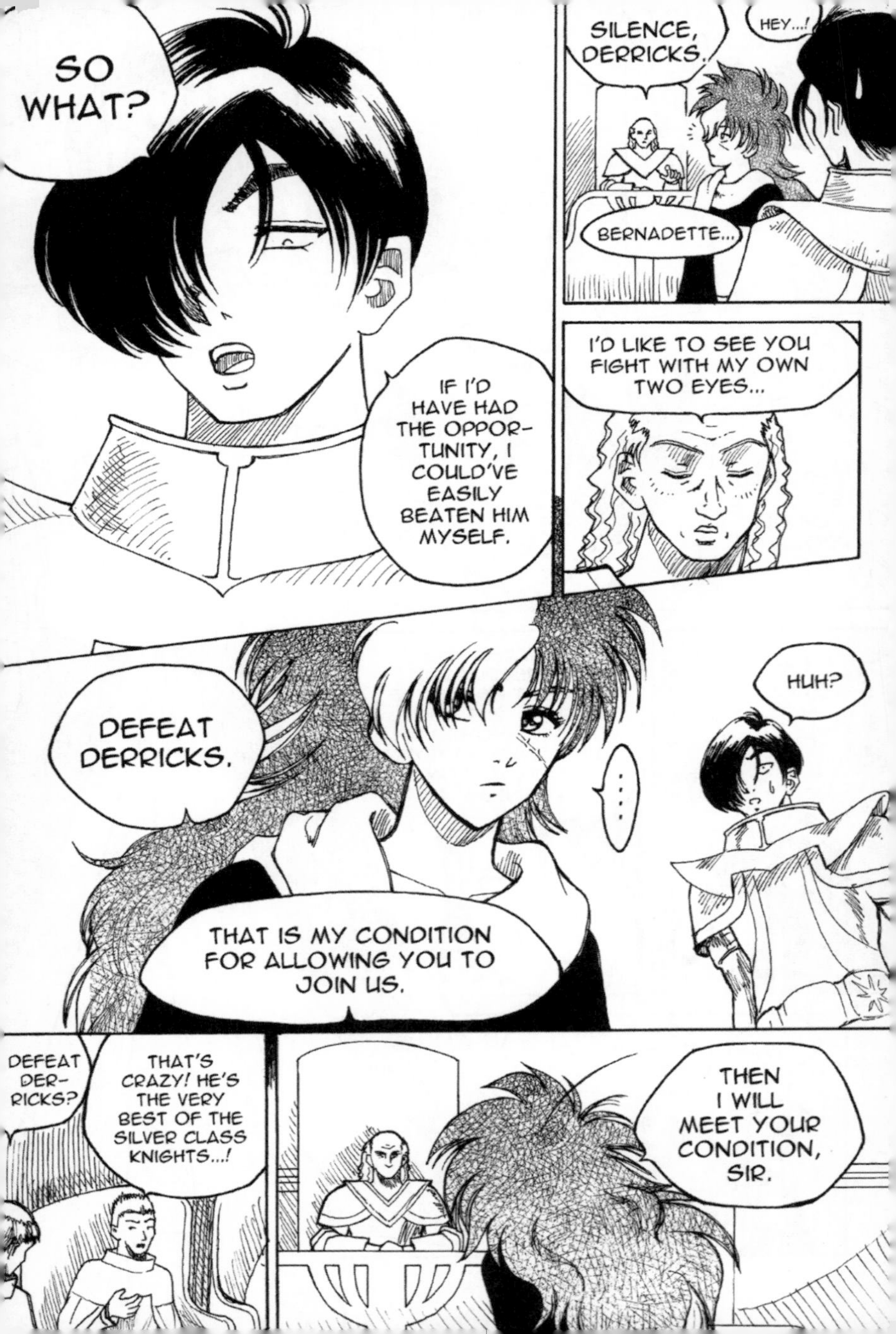
SO WHAT?
IF I'D HAVE HAD THE OPPOR-TUNITY, I COULD'VE EASILY BEATEN HIM MYSELF.
SILENCE, DERRICKS.
HEY...!
BERNADETTE...
I'D LIKE TO SEE YOU FIGHT WITH MY OWN TWO EYES...
DEFEAT DERRICKS.
...
HUH?
THAT IS MY CONDITION FOR ALLOWING YOU TO JOIN US.
DEFEAT DER-RICKS?
THAT'S CRAZY! HE'S THE VERY BEST OF THE SILVER CLASS KNIGHTS...!
THEN I WILL MEET YOUR CONDITION, SIR.

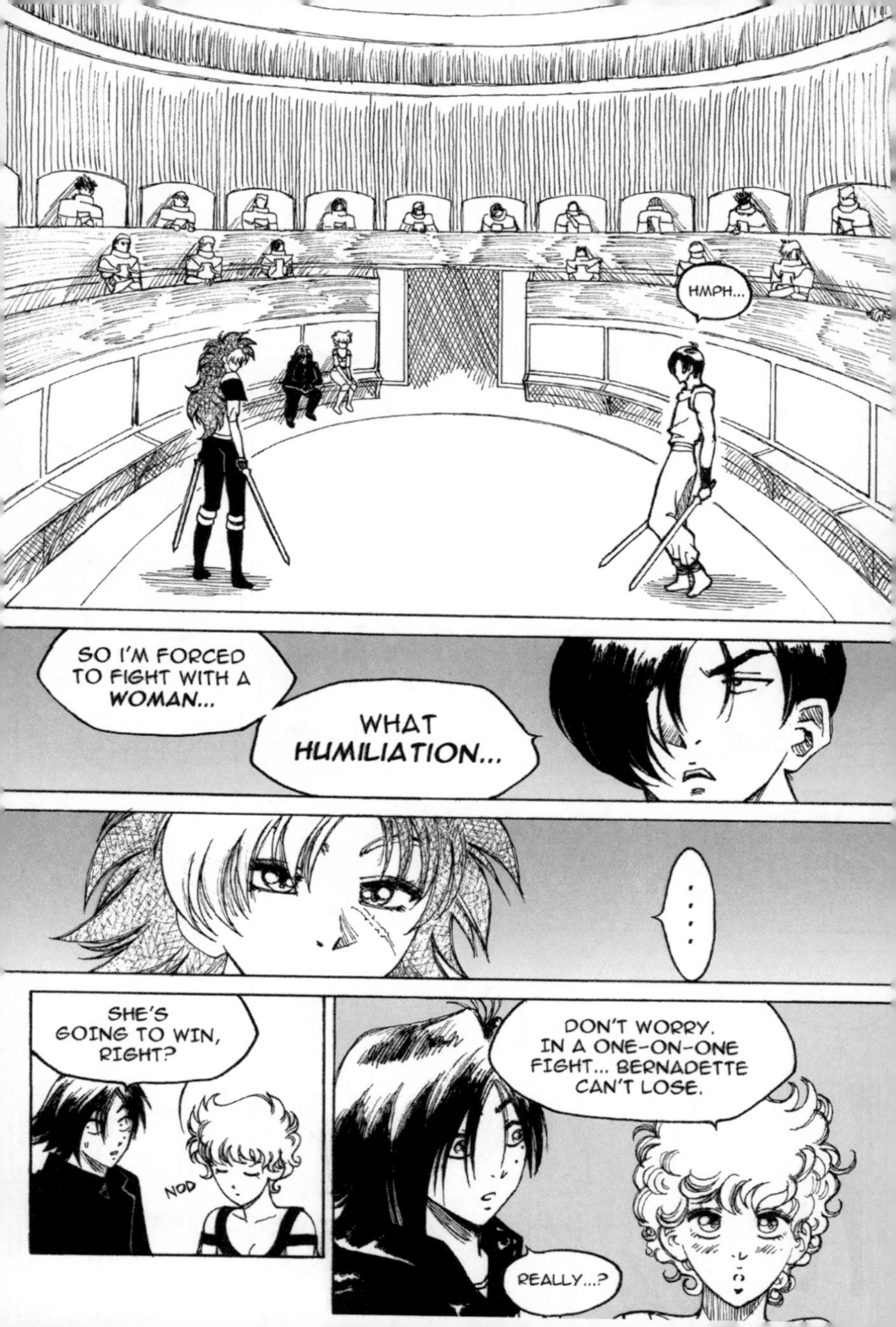
HMPH...
SO I'M FORCED TO FIGHT WITH A WOMAN...
WHAT HUMILIATION...
.....
SHE'S GOING TO WIN, RIGHT?
NOD
DON'T WORRY. IN A ONE-ON-ONE FIGHT... BERNADETTE CAN'T LOSE.
REALLY...?

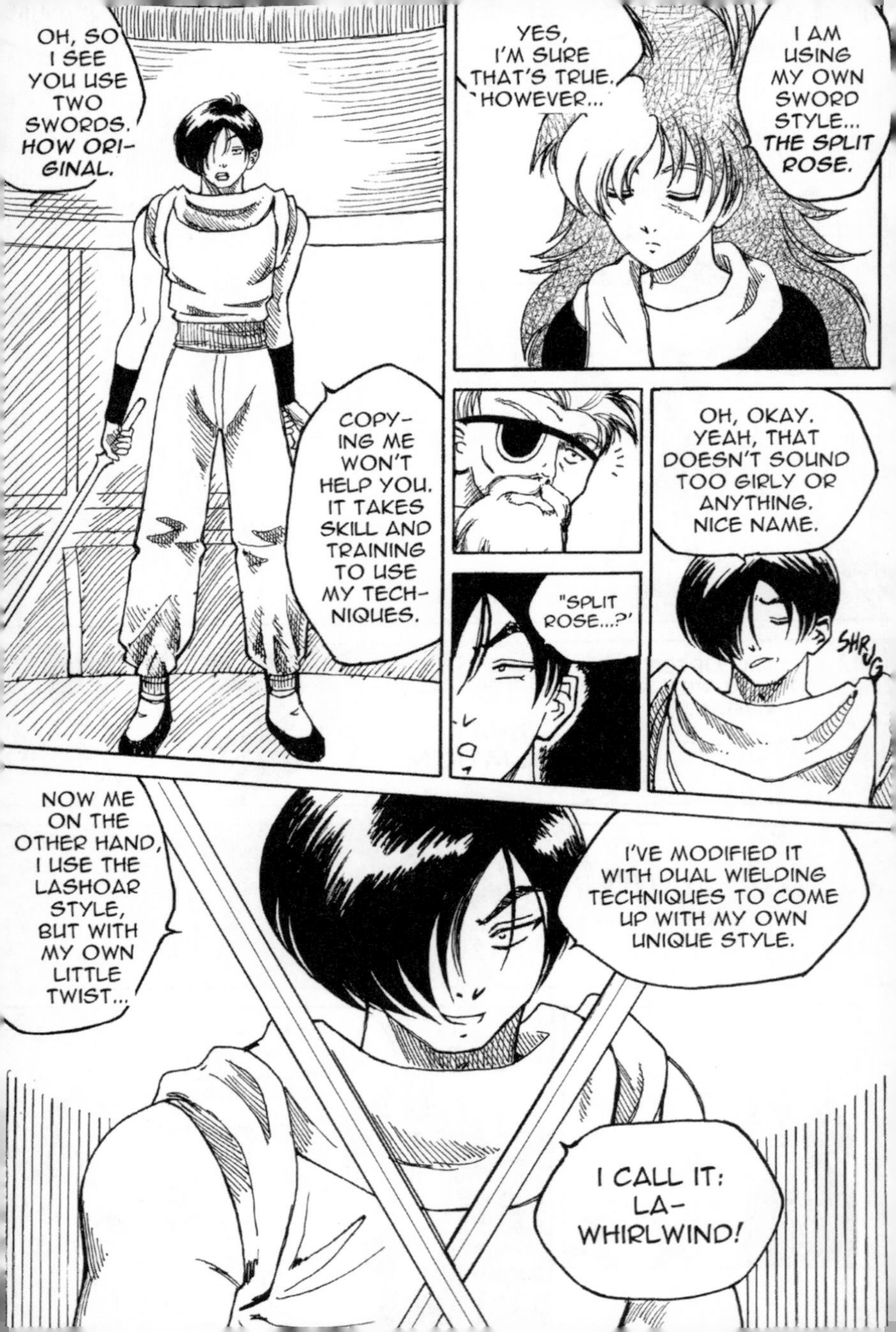

OH, SO I SEE YOU USE TWO SWORDS. HOW ORIGINAL.
YES, I'M SURE THAT'S TRUE. HOWEVER...
I AM USING MY OWN SWORD STYLE... THE SPLIT ROSE.
COPYING ME WON'T HELP YOU. IT TAKES SKILL AND TRAINING TO USE MY TECHNIQUES.
"SPLIT ROSE...?'
OH, OKAY. YEAH, THAT DOESN'T SOUND TOO GIRLY OR ANYTHING. NICE NAME.
SHRUG
NOW ME ON THE OTHER HAND, I USE THE LASHOAR STYLE, BUT WITH MY OWN LITTLE TWIST...
I'VE MODIFIED IT WITH DUAL WIELDING TECHNIQUES TO COME UP WITH MY OWN UNIQUE STYLE.
I CALL IT: LA-WHIRLWIND!

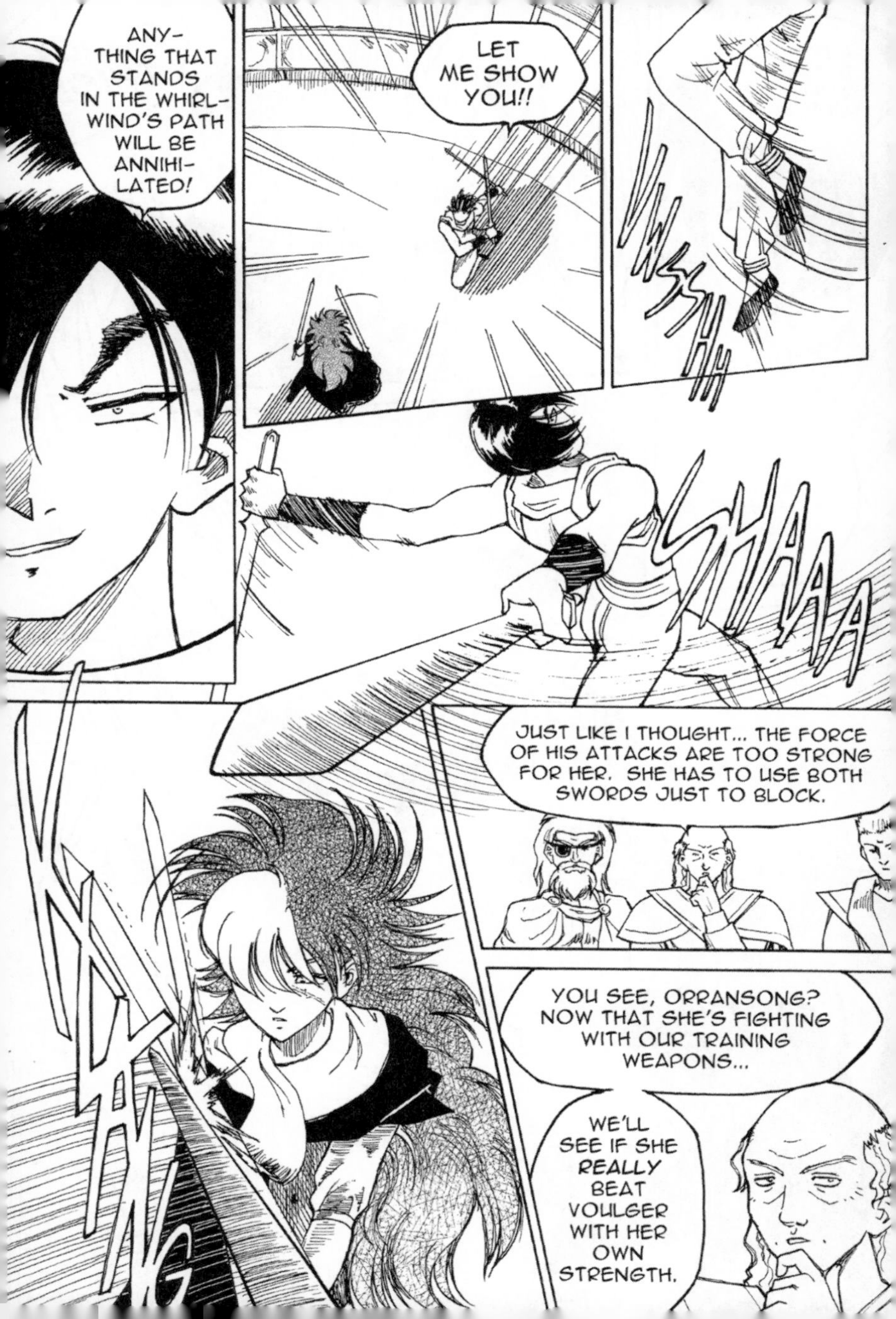
ANY-THING THAT STANDS IN THE WHIRL-WIND'S PATH WILL BE ANNIHI-LATED!
LET ME SHOW YOU!!
VWSSHHH
SHAAAA
JUST LIKE I THOUGHT... THE FORCE OF HIS ATTACKS ARE TOO STRONG FOR HER. SHE HAS TO USE BOTH SWORDS JUST TO BLOCK.
YOU SEE, ORRANSONG? NOW THAT SHE'S FIGHTING WITH OUR TRAINING WEAPONS...
WE'LL SEE IF SHE REALLY BEAT VOULGER WITH HER OWN STRENGTH.

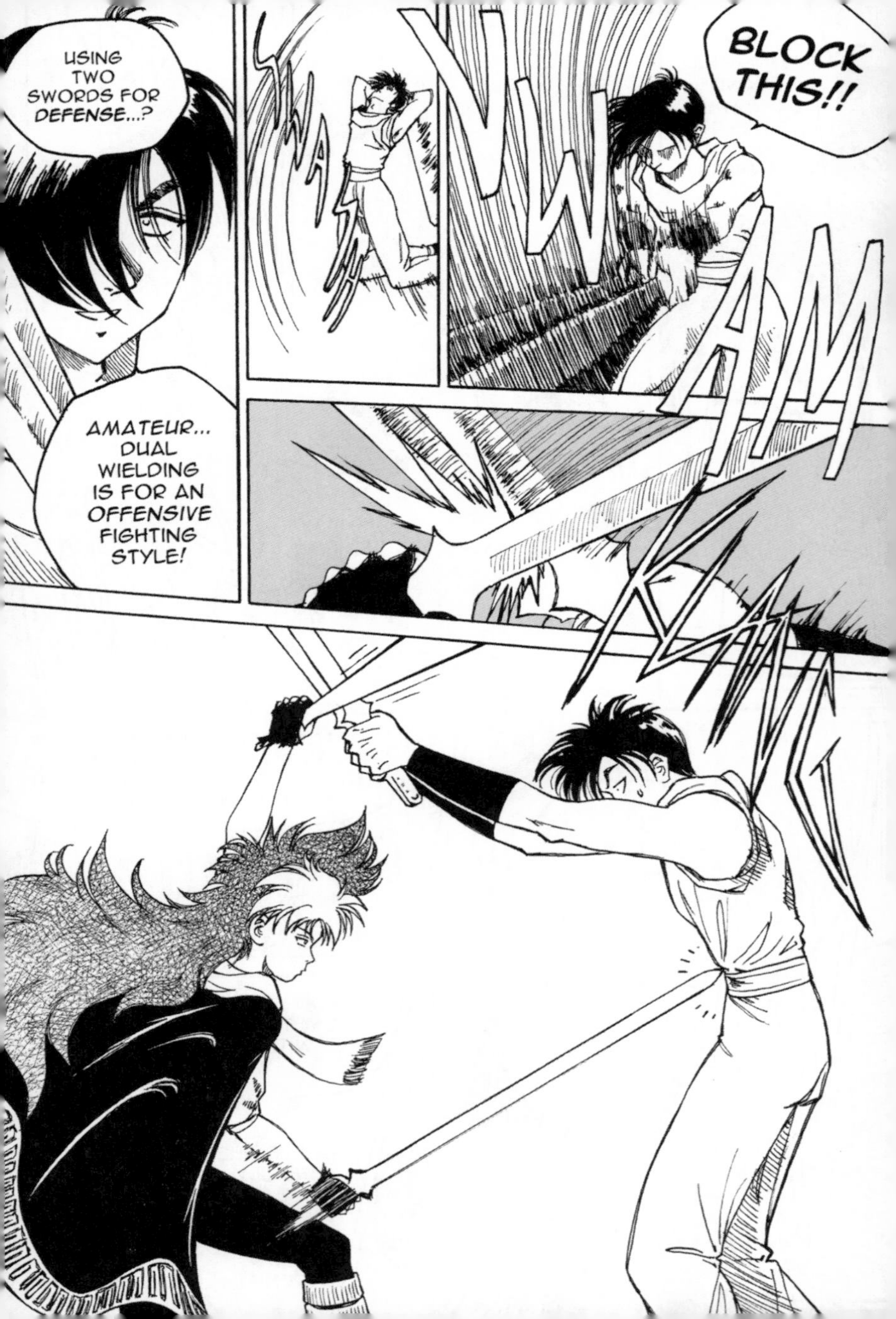
USING TWO SWORDS FOR DEFENSE...?
BLOCK THIS!!
AMATEUR... DUAL WIELDING IS FOR AN OFFENSIVE FIGHTING STYLE!

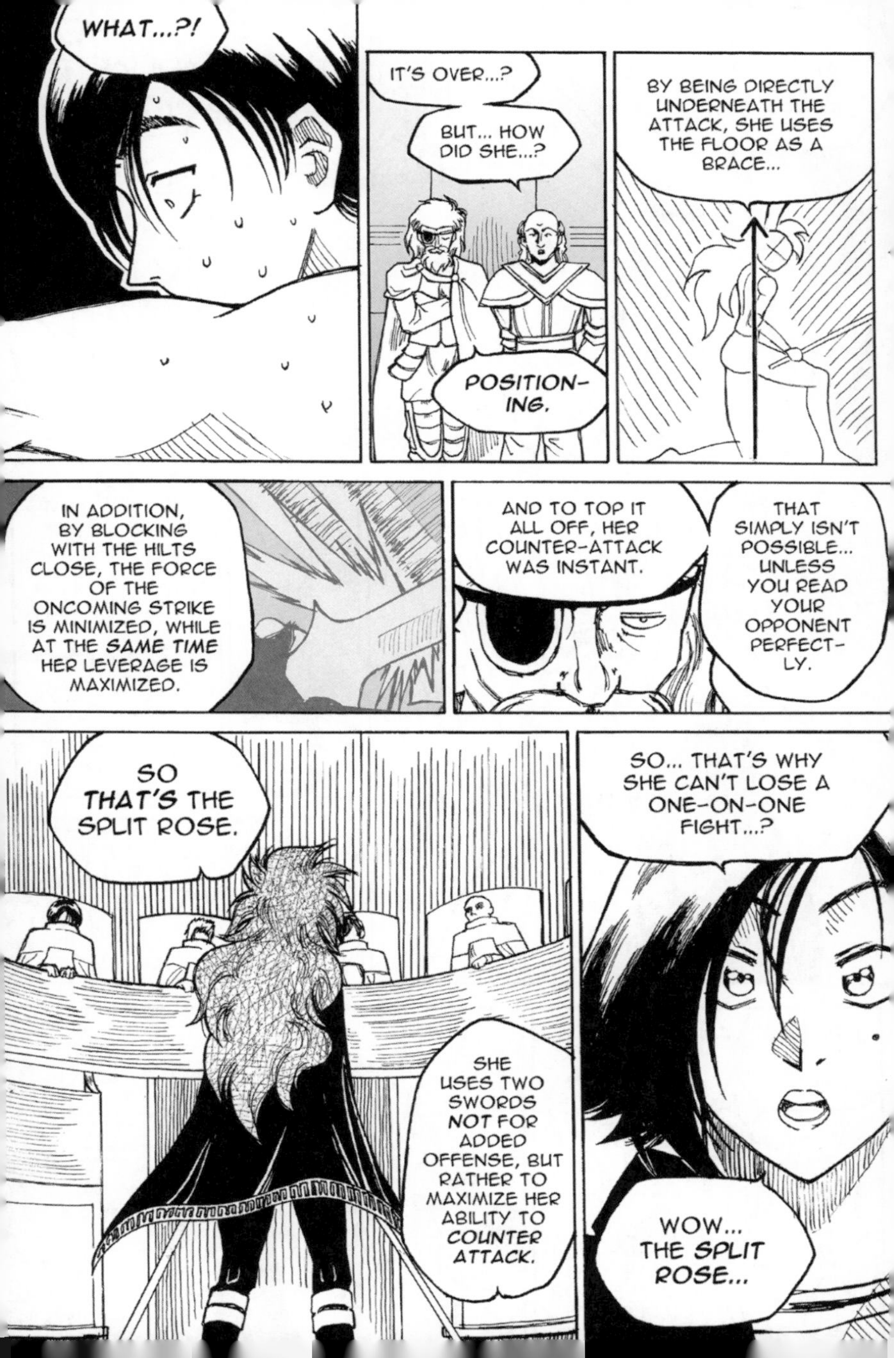
WHAT...?!
IT'S OVER...?
BUT... HOW DID SHE...?
POSITIONING.
BY BEING DIRECTLY UNDERNEATH THE ATTACK, SHE USES THE FLOOR AS A BRACE...
IN ADDITION, BY BLOCKING WITH THE HILTS CLOSE, THE FORCE OF THE ONCOMING STRIKE IS MINIMIZED, WHILE AT THE SAME TIME HER LEVERAGE IS MAXIMIZED.
AND TO TOP IT ALL OFF, HER COUNTER-ATTACK WAS INSTANT.
THAT SIMPLY ISN'T POSSIBLE... UNLESS YOU READ YOUR OPPONENT PERFECTLY.
SO THAT'S THE SPLIT ROSE.
SHE USES TWO SWORDS NOT FOR ADDED OFFENSE, BUT RATHER TO MAXIMIZE HER ABILITY TO COUNTER ATTACK.
SO... THAT'S WHY SHE CAN'T LOSE A ONE-ON-ONE FIGHT...?
WOW... THE SPLIT ROSE...

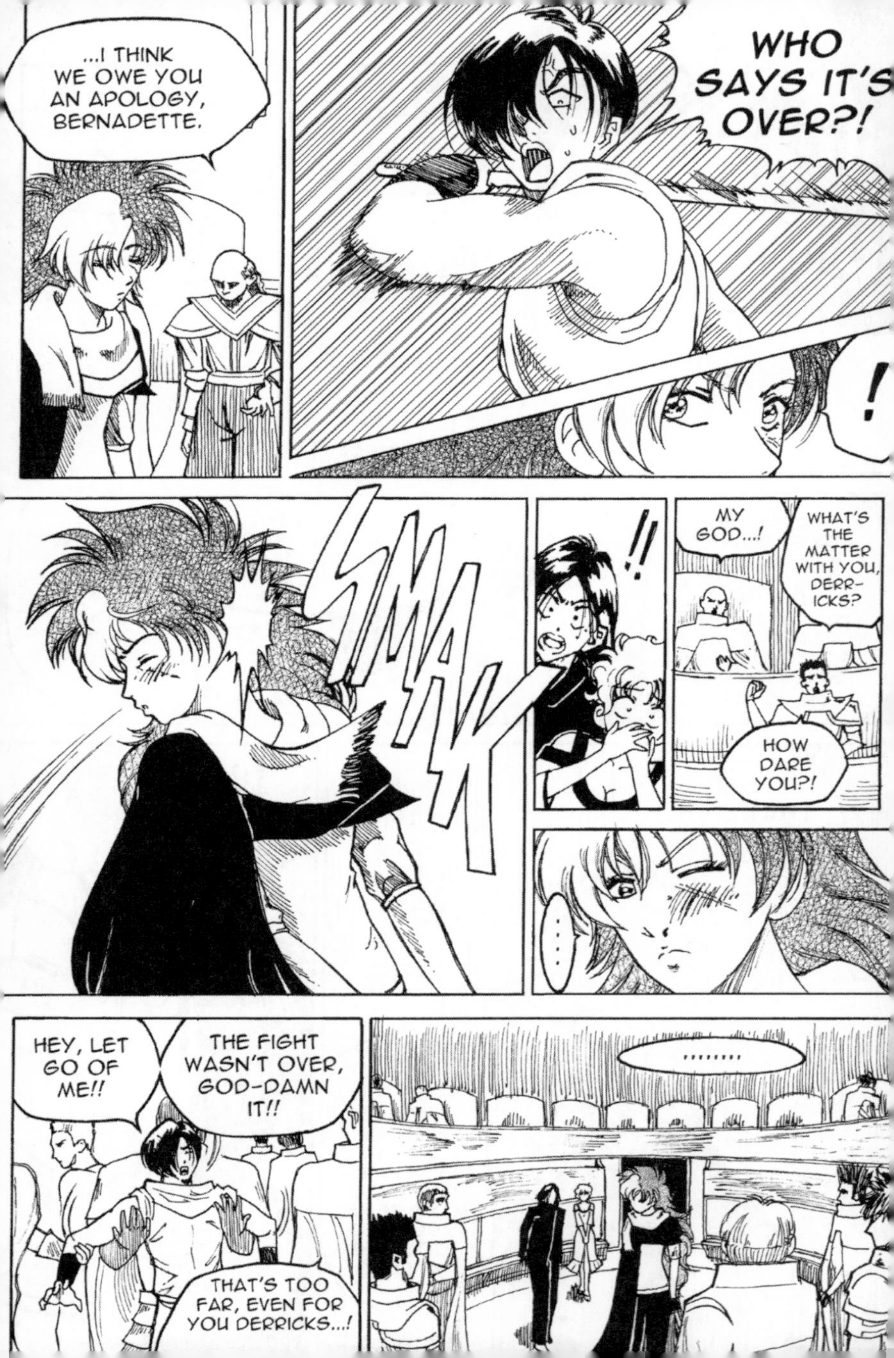
...I THINK WE OWE YOU AN APOLOGY, BERNADETTE.
WHO SAYS IT'S OVER?!
!
SMAK
!!
MY GOD...!
WHAT'S THE MATTER WITH YOU, DERR-ICKS?
HOW DARE YOU?!
...
HEY, LET GO OF ME!!
THE FIGHT WASN'T OVER, GOD-DAMN IT!!
THAT'S TOO FAR, EVEN FOR YOU DERRICKS...!
....

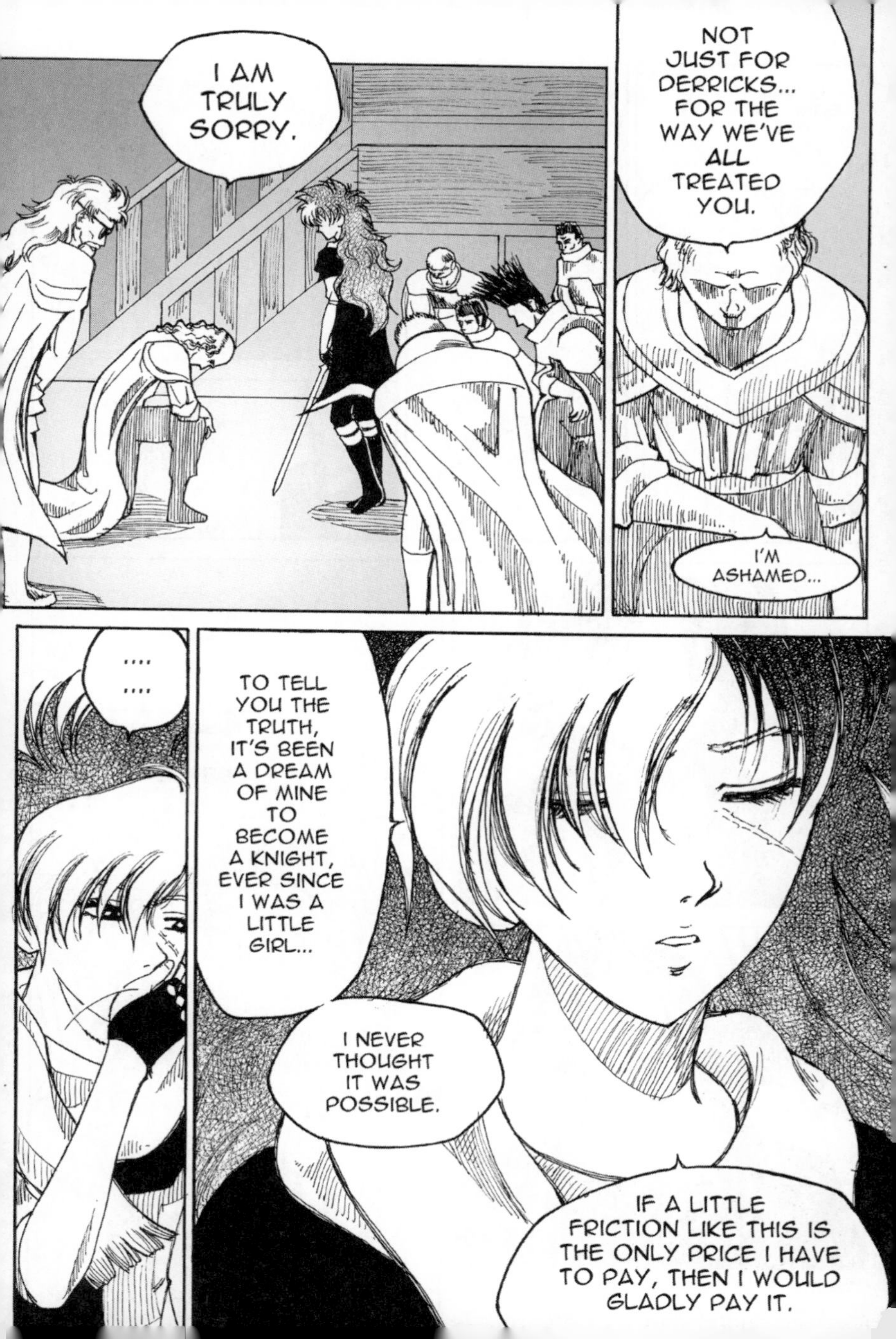
I AM TRULY SORRY.
NOT JUST FOR DERRICKS... FOR THE WAY WE'VE ALL TREATED YOU.
I'M ASHAMED...
....
....
TO TELL YOU THE TRUTH, IT'S BEEN A DREAM OF MINE TO BECOME A KNIGHT, EVER SINCE I WAS A LITTLE GIRL...
I NEVER THOUGHT IT WAS POSSIBLE.
IF A LITTLE FRICTION LIKE THIS IS THE ONLY PRICE I HAVE TO PAY, THEN I WOULD GLADLY PAY IT.

ORRAN- SONG, YOU WERE RIGHT...

YOU WERE RIGHT ABOUT HER.

LETS GIVE BOTH ORRANSONG AND MISS BERNADETTE A HAND.

CLAP
CLAP

CLAP CLAP CLAP

CLAP

CLAP

CLAP

YAAYY...!

CLAP
CLAP

CLAP

CLAP

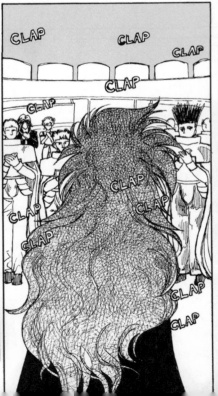

CLAP

CLAP

CLAP

CLAP

CLAP

CLAP

CLAP

CLAP

CLAP

CLAP

CLAP

CLAP

CLAP

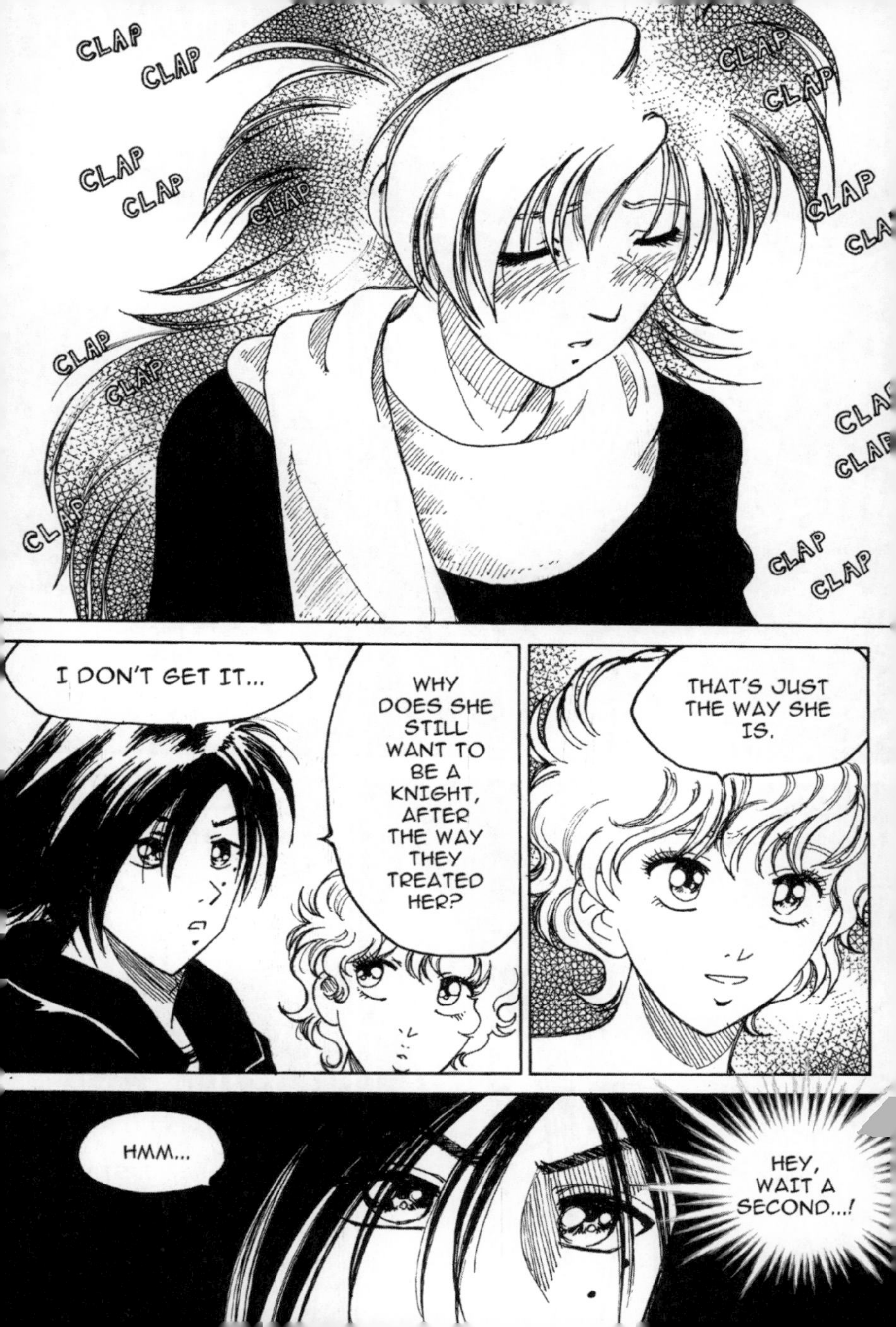
CLAP
CLAP
CLAP
CLAP
CLAP
CLAP
CLAP
CLAP
CLAP
CLAP
CLAP
CLAP
CLAP
CLAP
I DON'T GET IT...
WHY DOES SHE STILL WANT TO BE A KNIGHT, AFTER THE WAY THEY TREATED HER?
THAT'S JUST THE WAY SHE IS.
HMM...
HEY, WAIT A SECOND...!

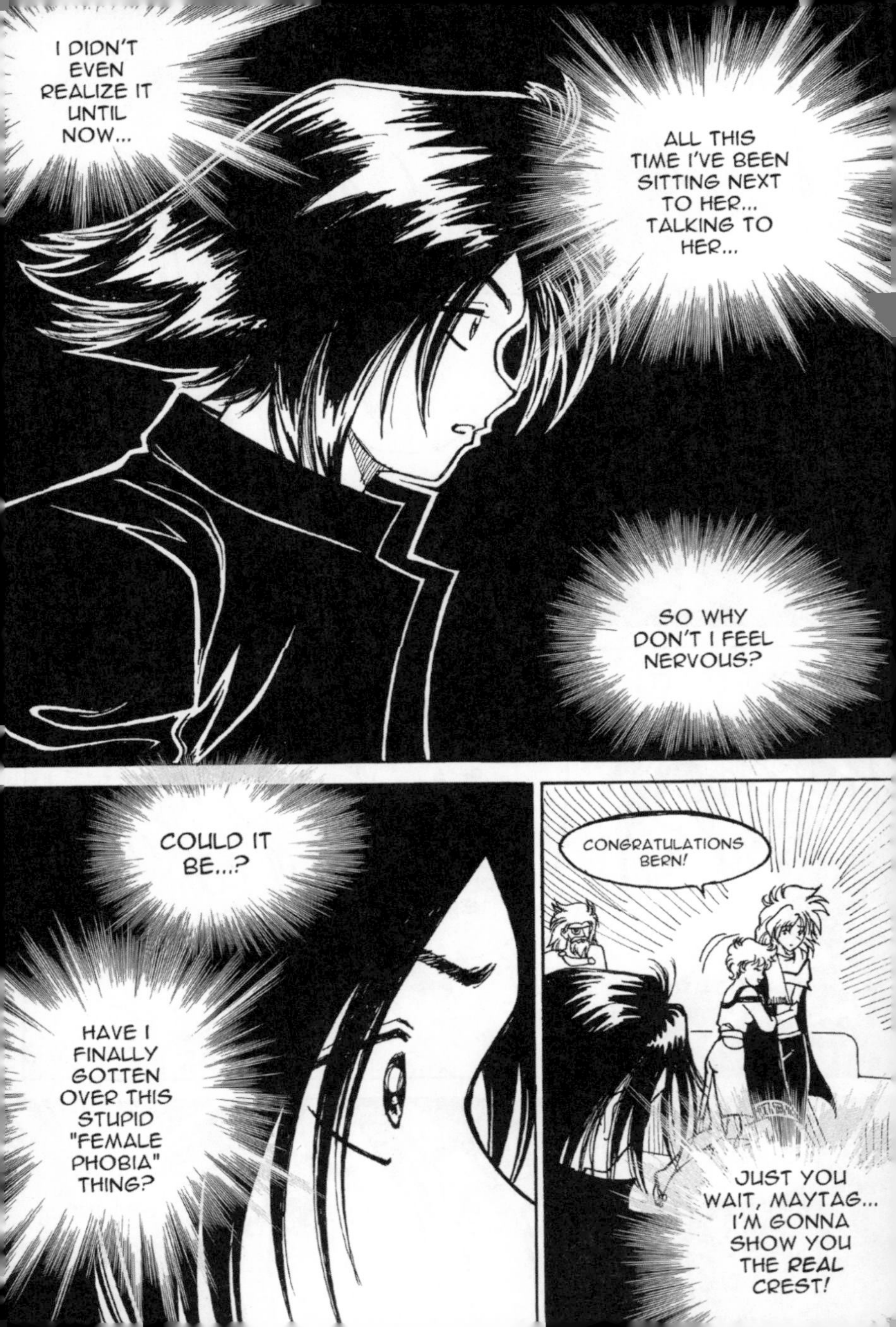

I DIDN'T EVEN REALIZE IT UNTIL NOW...
ALL THIS TIME I'VE BEEN SITTING NEXT TO HER... TALKING TO HER...
SO WHY DON'T I FEEL NERVOUS?
COULD IT BE...?
HAVE I FINALLY GOTTEN OVER THIS STUPID "FEMALE PHOBIA" THING?
CONGRATULATIONS BERN!
JUST YOU WAIT, MAYTAG... I'M GONNA SHOW YOU THE REAL CREST!

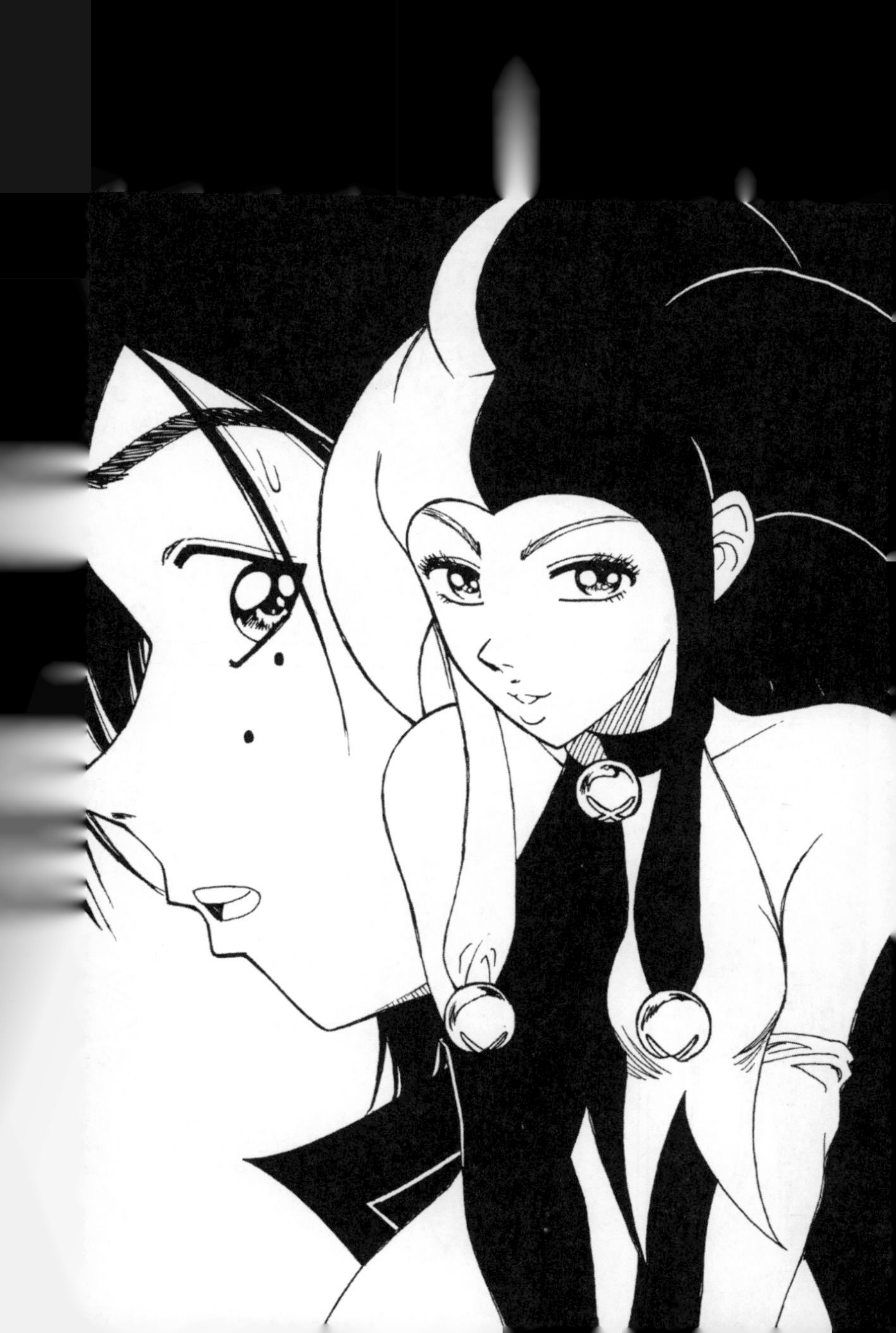

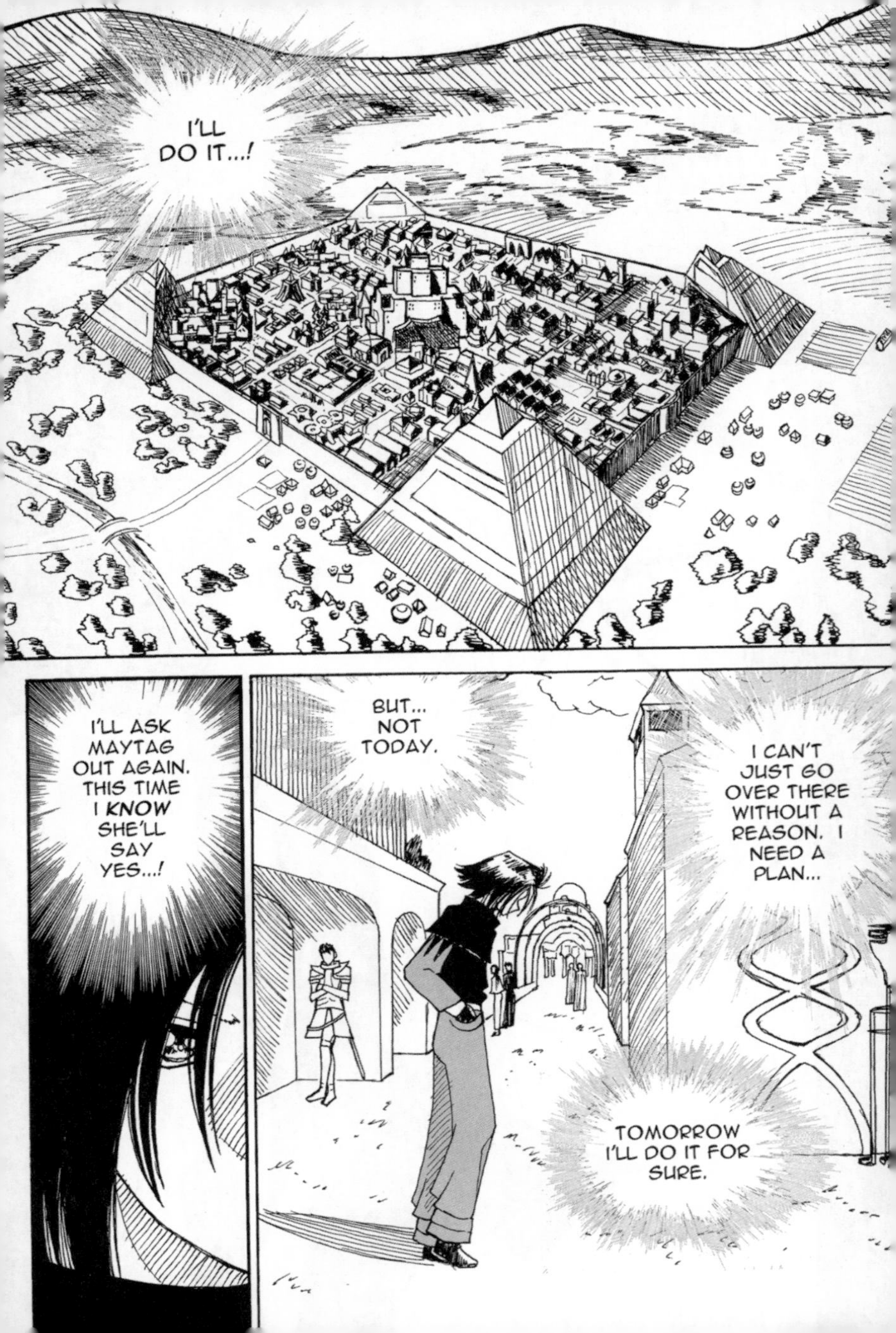
I'LL DO IT...!
I'LL ASK MAYTAG OUT AGAIN. THIS TIME I **KNOW** SHE'LL SAY YES...!
BUT... NOT TODAY.
I CAN'T JUST GO OVER THERE WITHOUT A REASON. I NEED A PLAN...
TOMORROW I'LL DO IT FOR SURE.

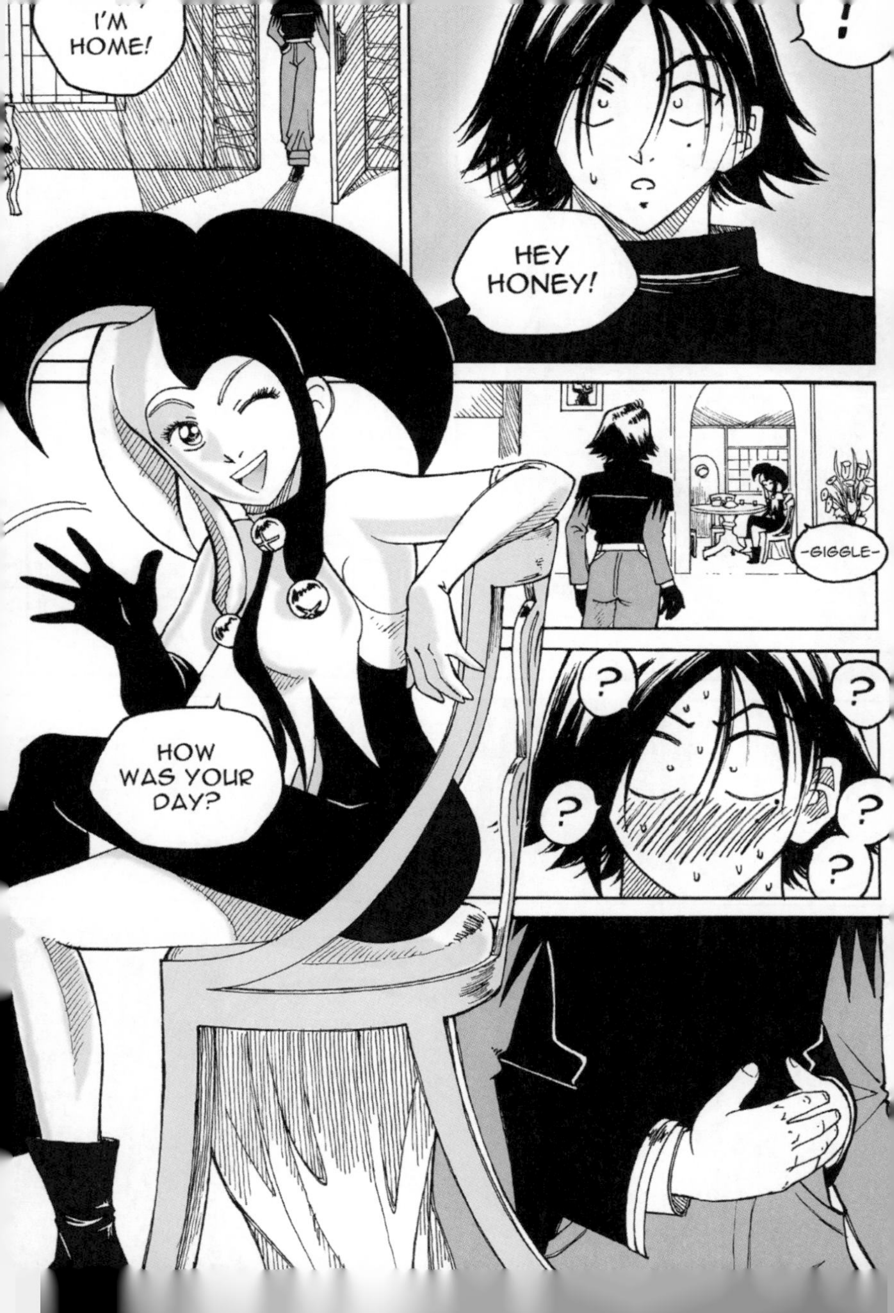
I'M HOME!
!
HEY HONEY!
HOW WAS YOUR DAY?
-GIGGLE-
?
?
?
?
?
?

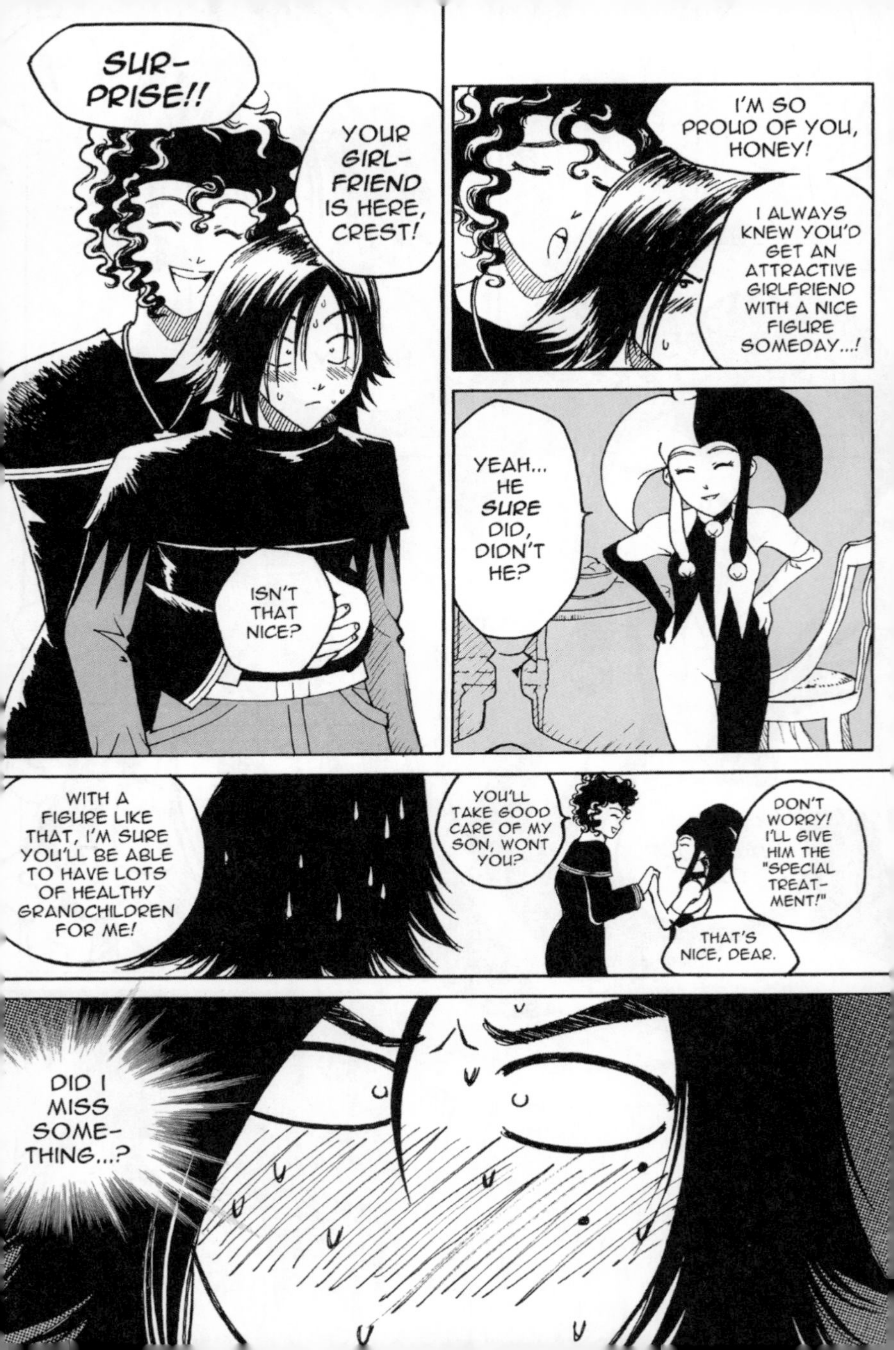
SUR-PRISE!!
YOUR GIRL-FRIEND IS HERE, CREST!
ISN'T THAT NICE?
I'M SO PROUD OF YOU, HONEY!
I ALWAYS KNEW YOU'D GET AN ATTRACTIVE GIRLFRIEND WITH A NICE FIGURE SOMEDAY...!
YEAH... HE SURE DID, DIDN'T HE?
WITH A FIGURE LIKE THAT, I'M SURE YOU'LL BE ABLE TO HAVE LOTS OF HEALTHY GRANDCHILDREN FOR ME!
YOU'LL TAKE GOOD CARE OF MY SON, WONT YOU?
DON'T WORRY! I'LL GIVE HIM THE "SPECIAL TREAT-MENT!"
THAT'S NICE, DEAR.
DID I MISS SOME-THING...?

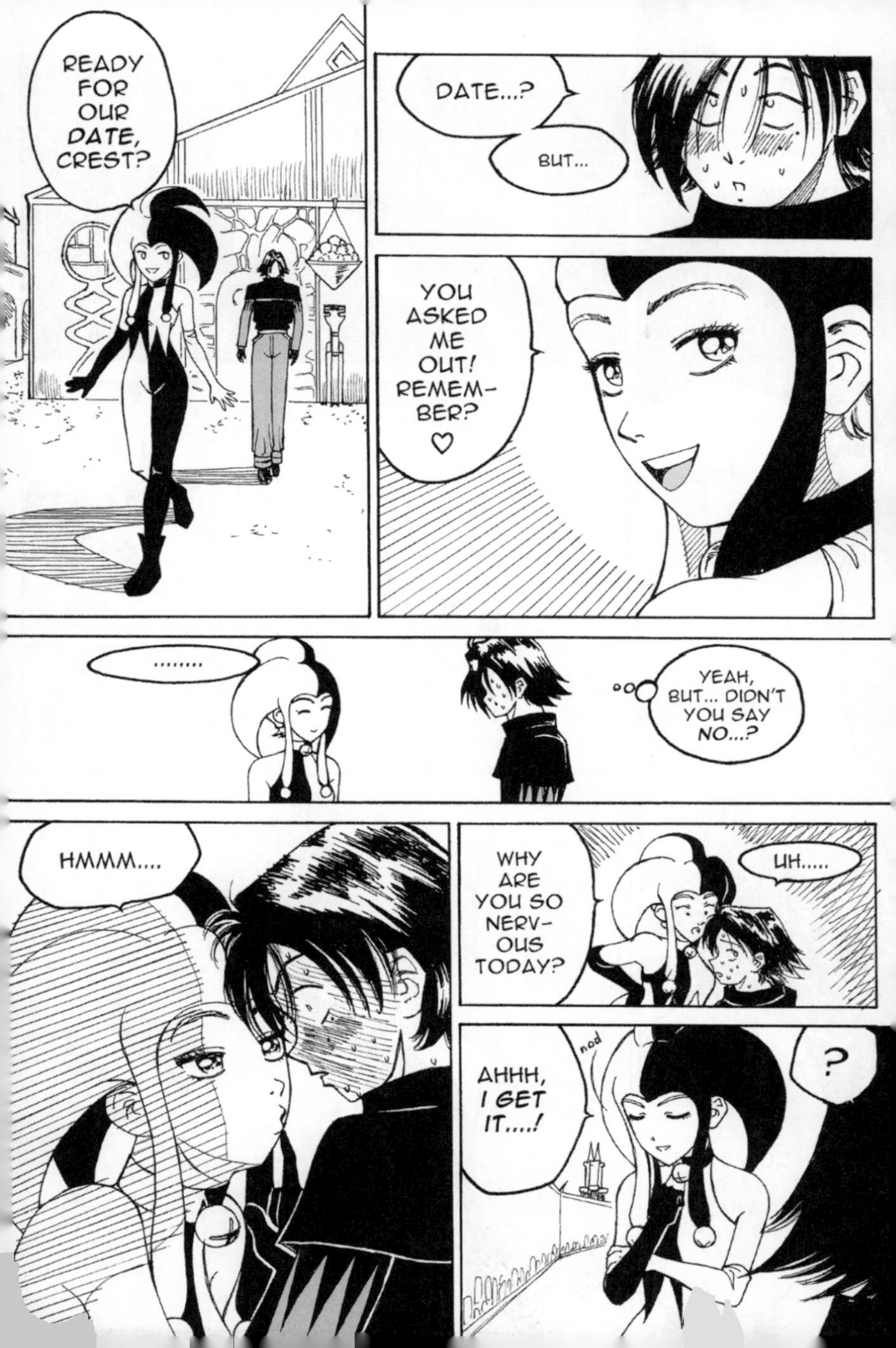
READY FOR OUR DATE, CREST?
DATE...?
BUT...
YOU ASKED ME OUT! REMEMBER? ♡
....
YEAH, BUT... DIDN'T YOU SAY NO...?
HMMM....
WHY ARE YOU SO NERVOUS TODAY?
UH.....
nod
AHHH, I GET IT....!
?

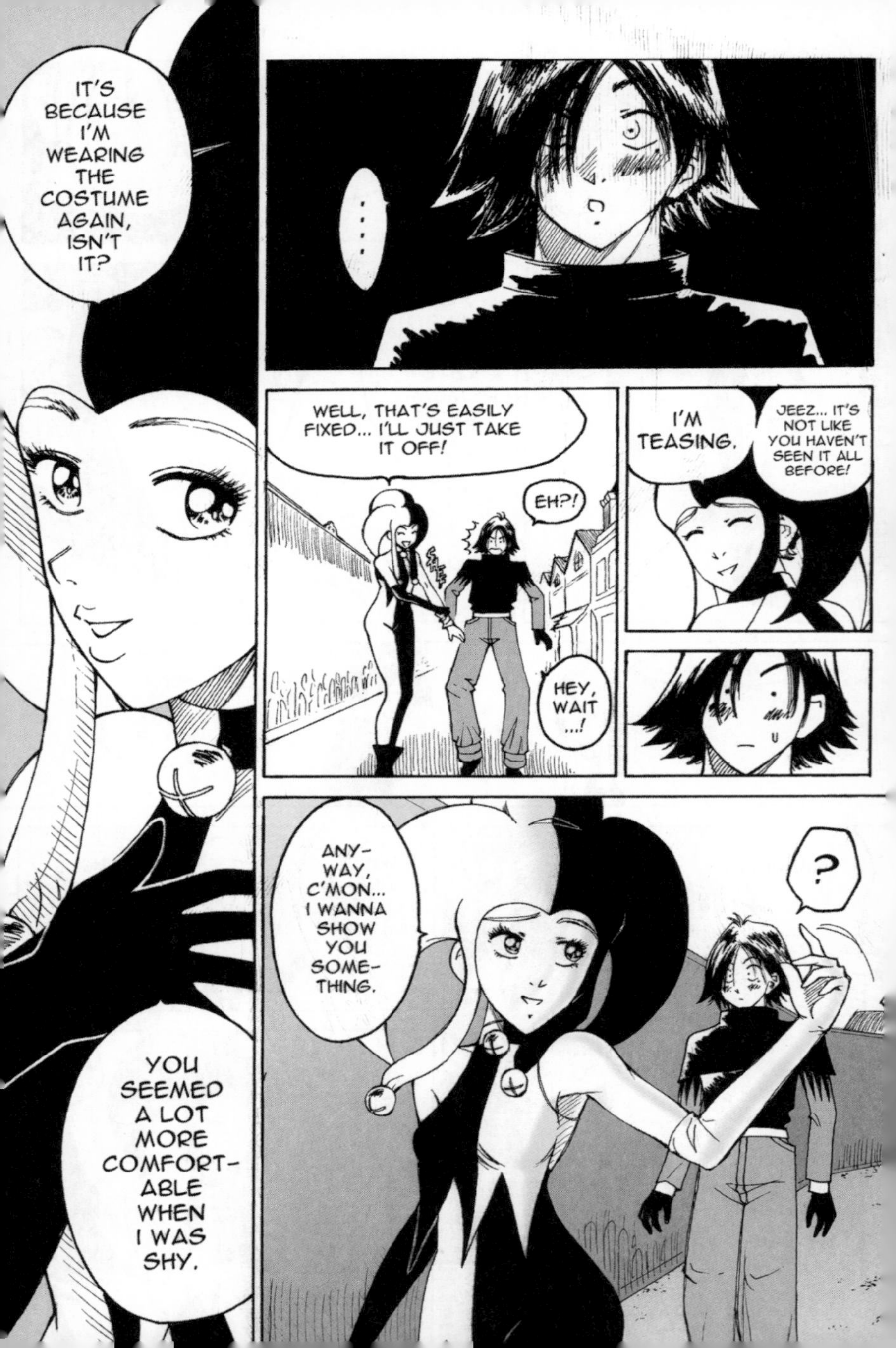
IT'S BECAUSE I'M WEARING THE COSTUME AGAIN, ISN'T IT?
YOU SEEMED A LOT MORE COMFORT-ABLE WHEN I WAS SHY.
.....
WELL, THAT'S EASILY FIXED... I'LL JUST TAKE IT OFF!
EH?!
HEY, WAIT ...!
JEEZ... IT'S NOT LIKE YOU HAVEN'T SEEN IT ALL BEFORE!
I'M TEASING.
ANY-WAY, C'MON... I WANNA SHOW YOU SOME-THING.
?

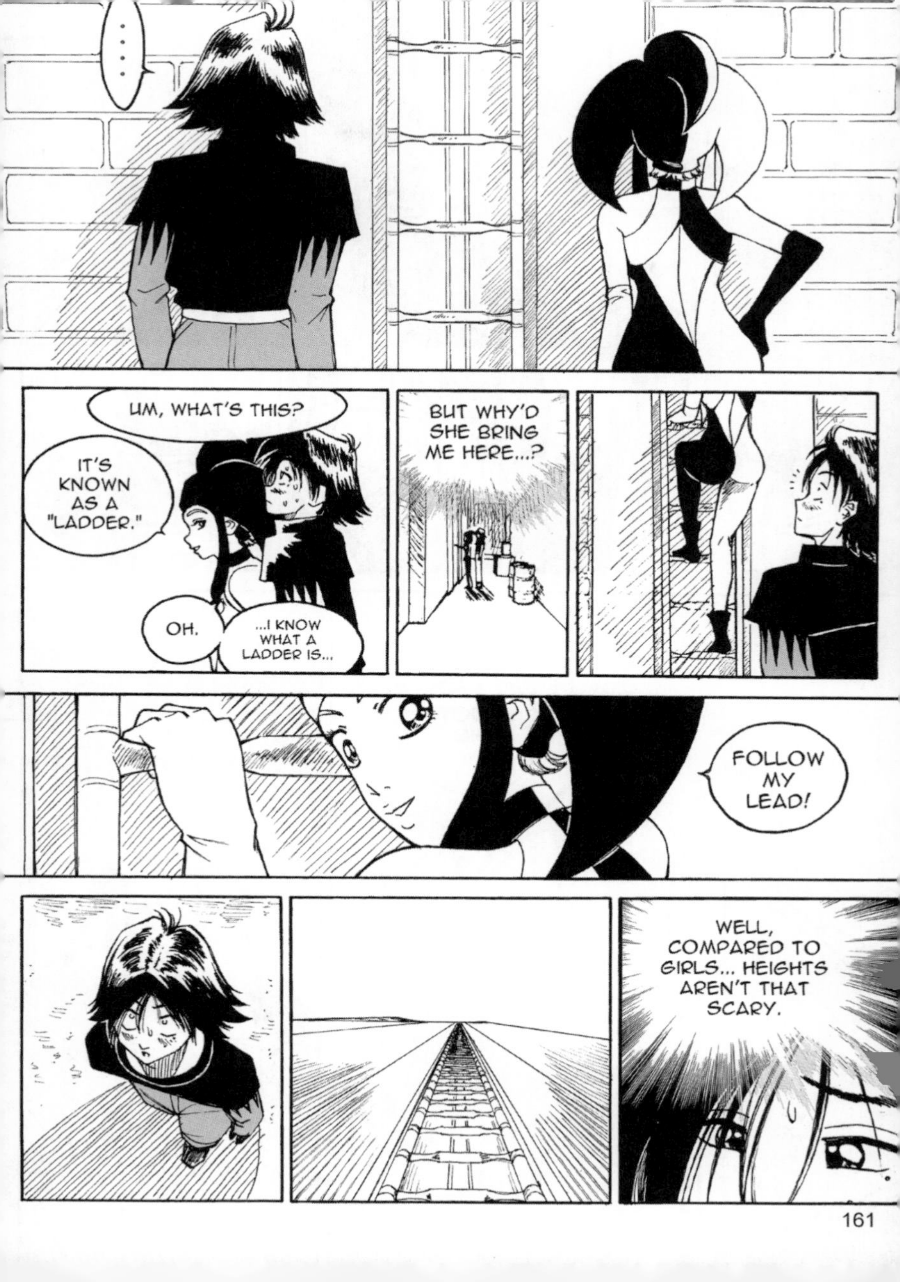
....
UM, WHAT'S THIS?
IT'S KNOWN AS A "LADDER."
OH.
...I KNOW WHAT A LADDER IS...
BUT WHY'D SHE BRING ME HERE...?
FOLLOW MY LEAD!
WELL, COMPARED TO GIRLS... HEIGHTS AREN'T THAT SCARY.

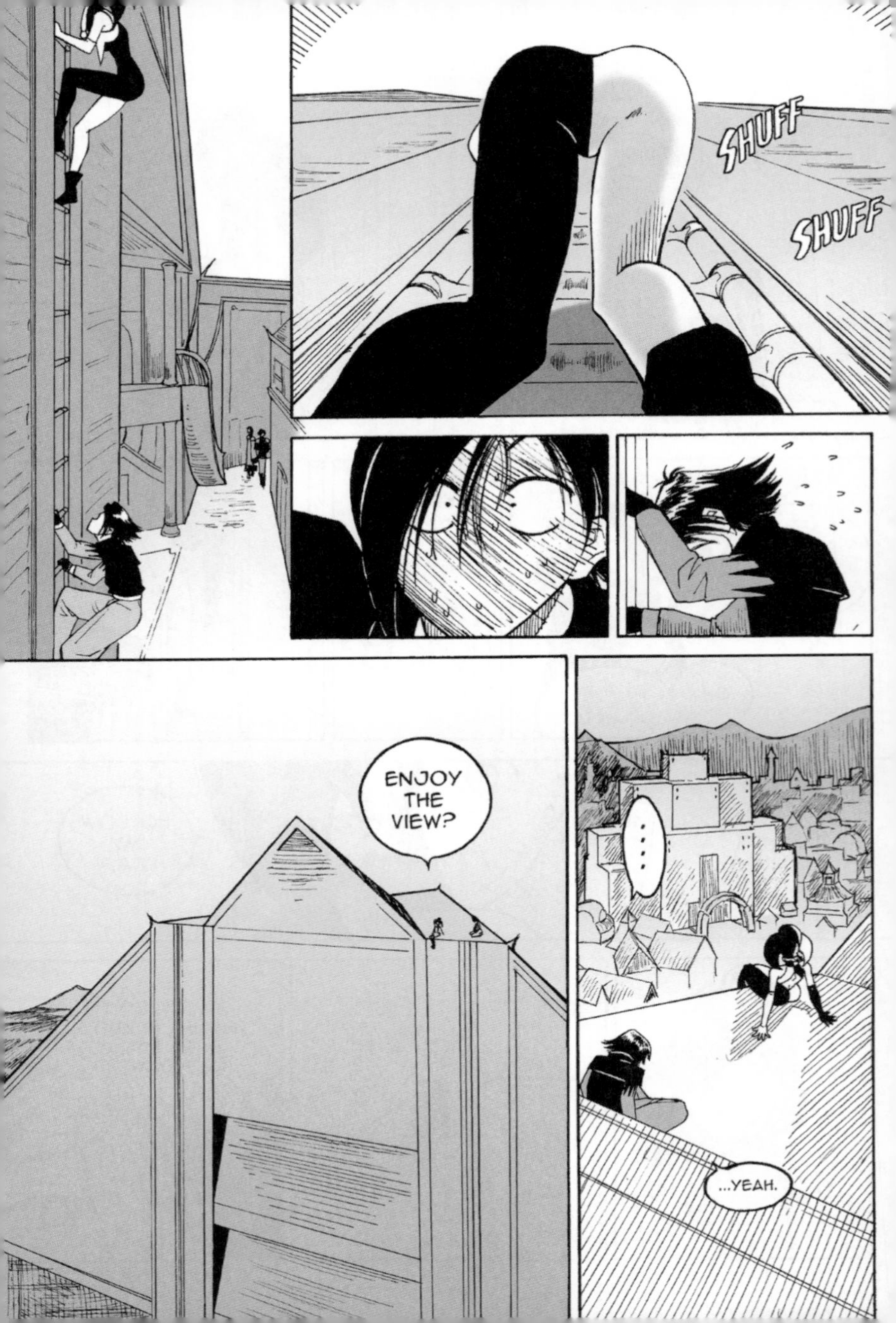
SHUFF
SHUFF
ENJOY THE VIEW?
....
...YEAH.

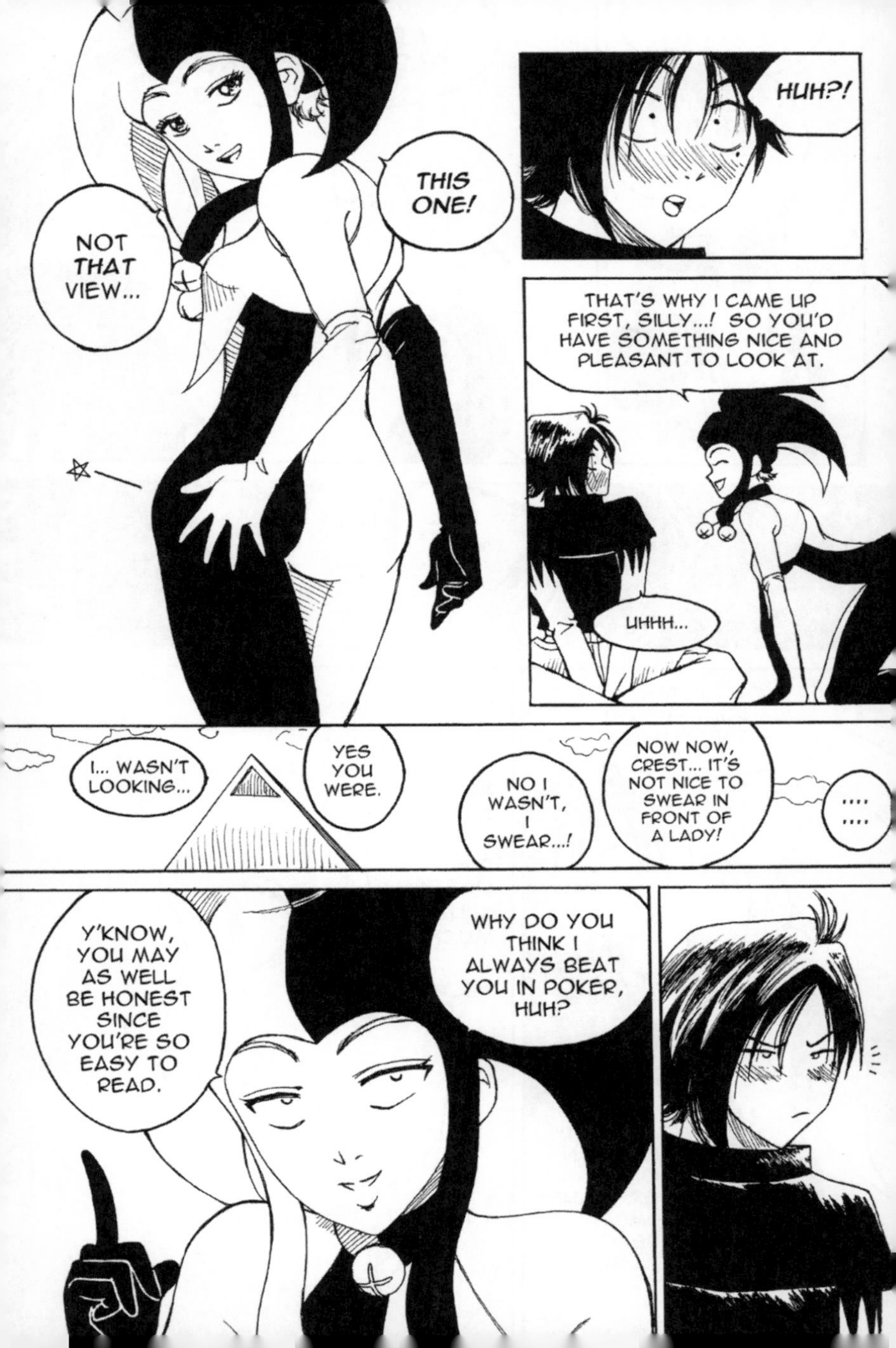

NOT THAT VIEW...
THIS ONE!
HUH?!
THAT'S WHY I CAME UP FIRST, SILLY...! SO YOU'D HAVE SOMETHING NICE AND PLEASANT TO LOOK AT.
UHHH...
I... WASN'T LOOKING...
YES YOU WERE.
NO I WASN'T, I SWEAR...!
NOW NOW, CREST... IT'S NOT NICE TO SWEAR IN FRONT OF A LADY!
....
....
Y'KNOW, YOU MAY AS WELL BE HONEST SINCE YOU'RE SO EASY TO READ.
WHY DO YOU THINK I ALWAYS BEAT YOU IN POKER, HUH?

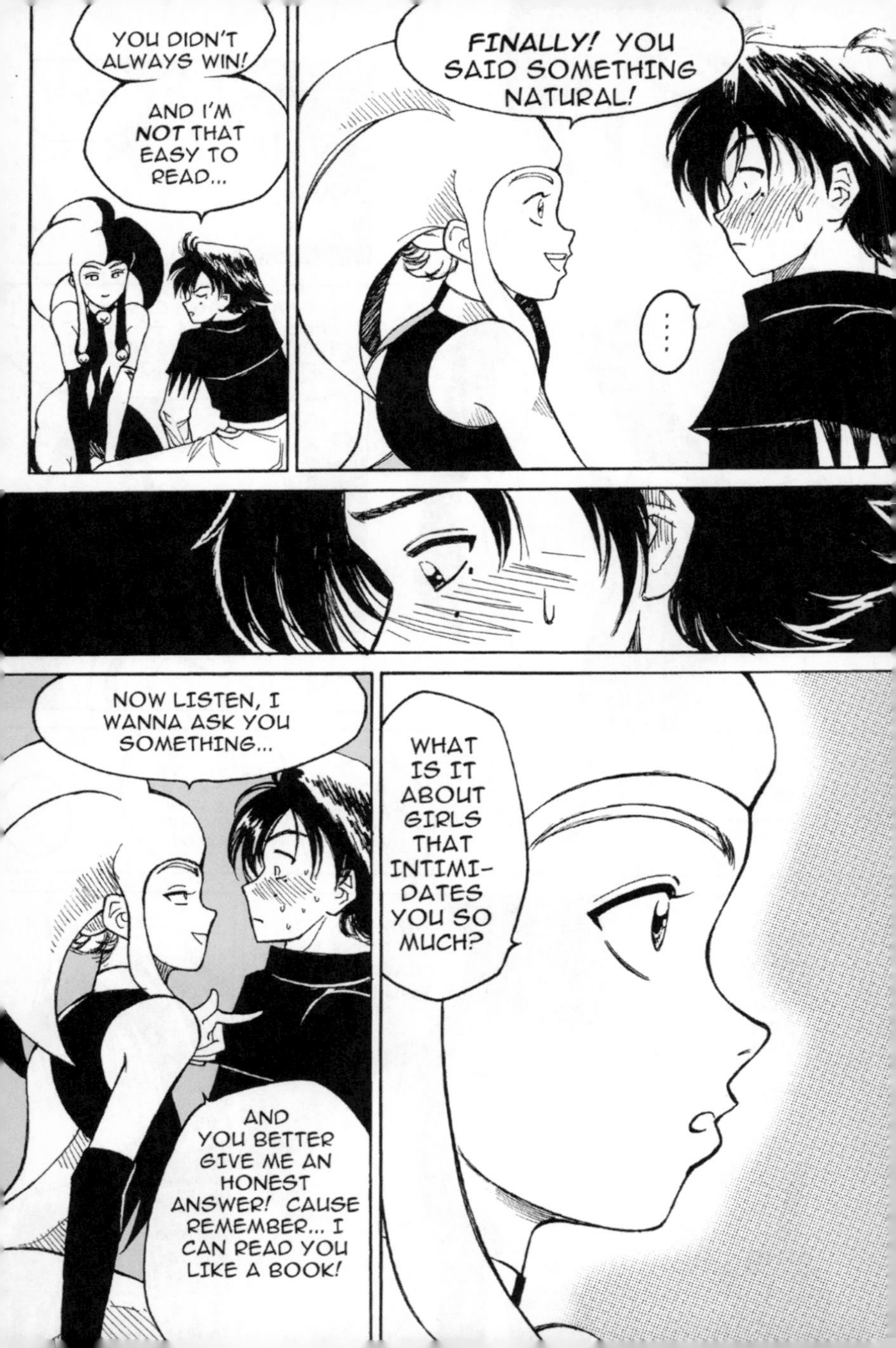
YOU DIDN'T ALWAYS WIN!
AND I'M **NOT** THAT EASY TO READ...
FINALLY! YOU SAID SOMETHING NATURAL!
....
NOW LISTEN, I WANNA ASK YOU SOMETHING...
AND YOU BETTER GIVE ME AN HONEST ANSWER! CAUSE REMEMBER... I CAN READ YOU LIKE A BOOK!
WHAT IS IT ABOUT GIRLS THAT INTIMI-DATES YOU SO MUCH?

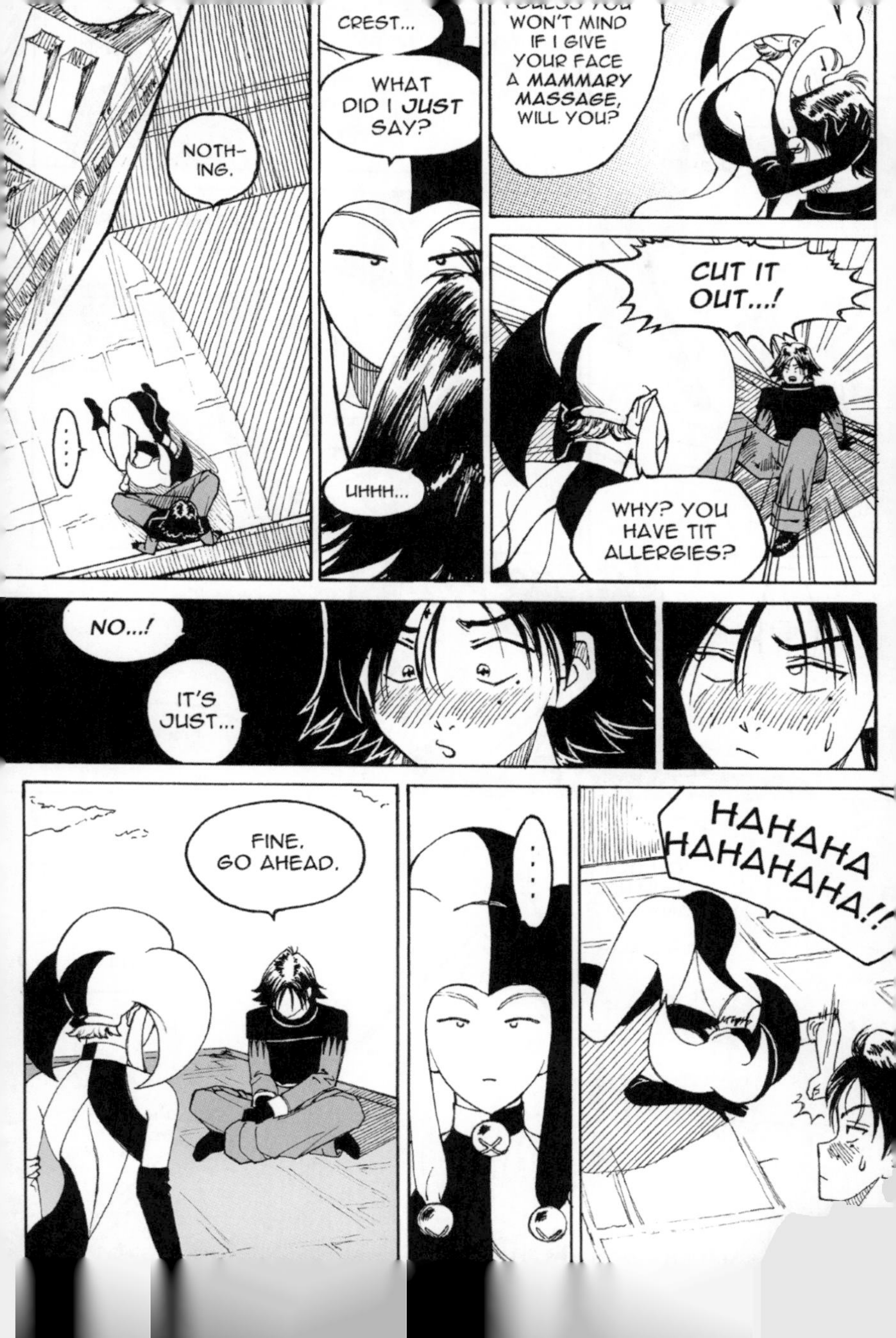
NOTH-ING.
....
CREST...
WHAT DID I JUST SAY?
UHHH...
WON'T MIND IF I GIVE YOUR FACE A MAMMARY MASSAGE, WILL YOU?
CUT IT OUT...!
WHY? YOU HAVE TIT ALLERGIES?
NO...!
IT'S JUST...
FINE. GO AHEAD.
....
HAHAHA HAHAHAHA!!

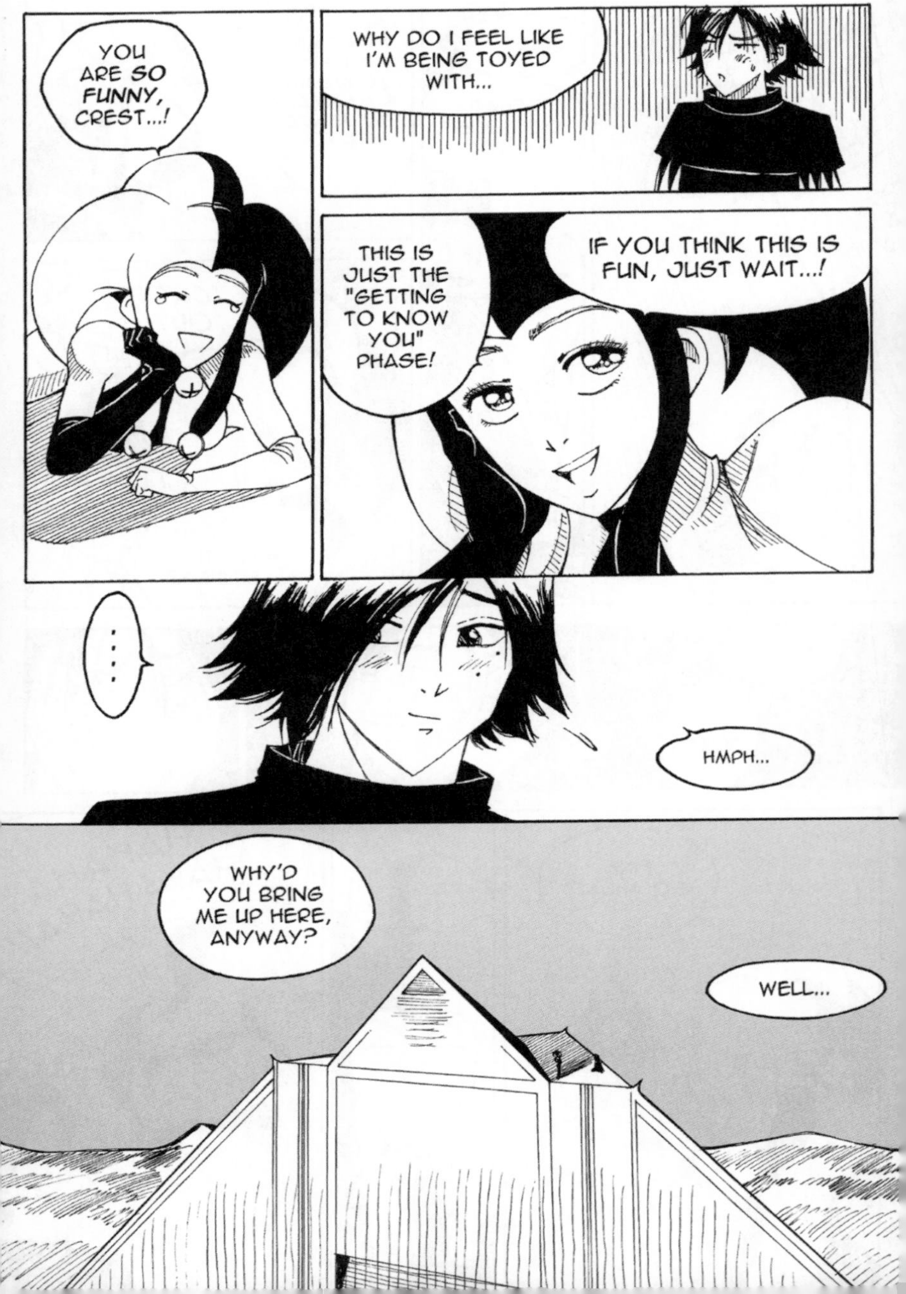
YOU ARE SO FUNNY, CREST...!
WHY DO I FEEL LIKE I'M BEING TOYED WITH...
IF YOU THINK THIS IS FUN, JUST WAIT...!
THIS IS JUST THE "GETTING TO KNOW YOU" PHASE!
....
HMPH...
WHY'D YOU BRING ME UP HERE, ANYWAY?
WELL...

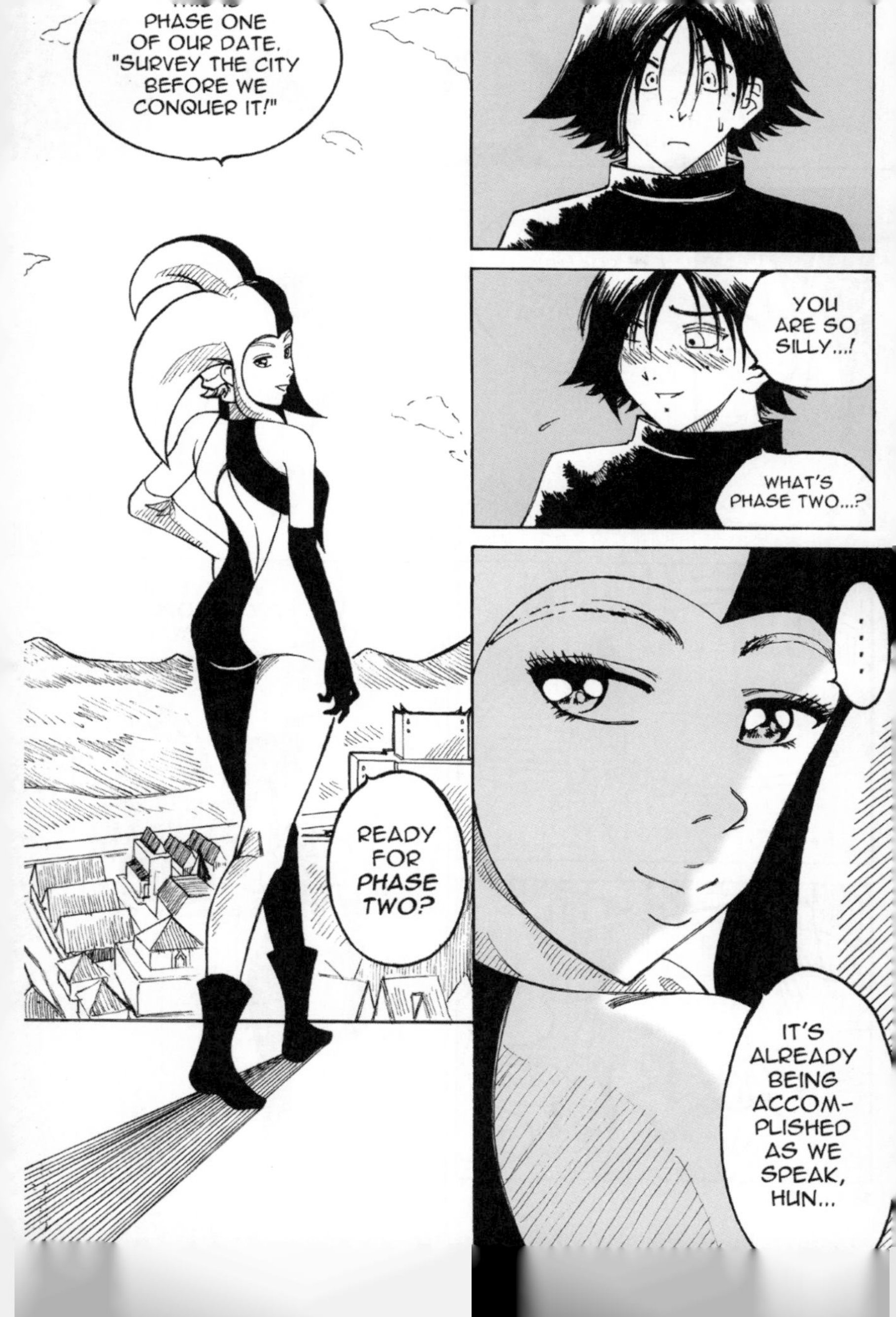
PHASE ONE OF OUR DATE. "SURVEY THE CITY BEFORE WE CONQUER IT!"
YOU ARE SO SILLY...!
READY FOR PHASE TWO?
WHAT'S PHASE TWO...?
....
IT'S ALREADY BEING ACCOM-PLISHED AS WE SPEAK, HUN...

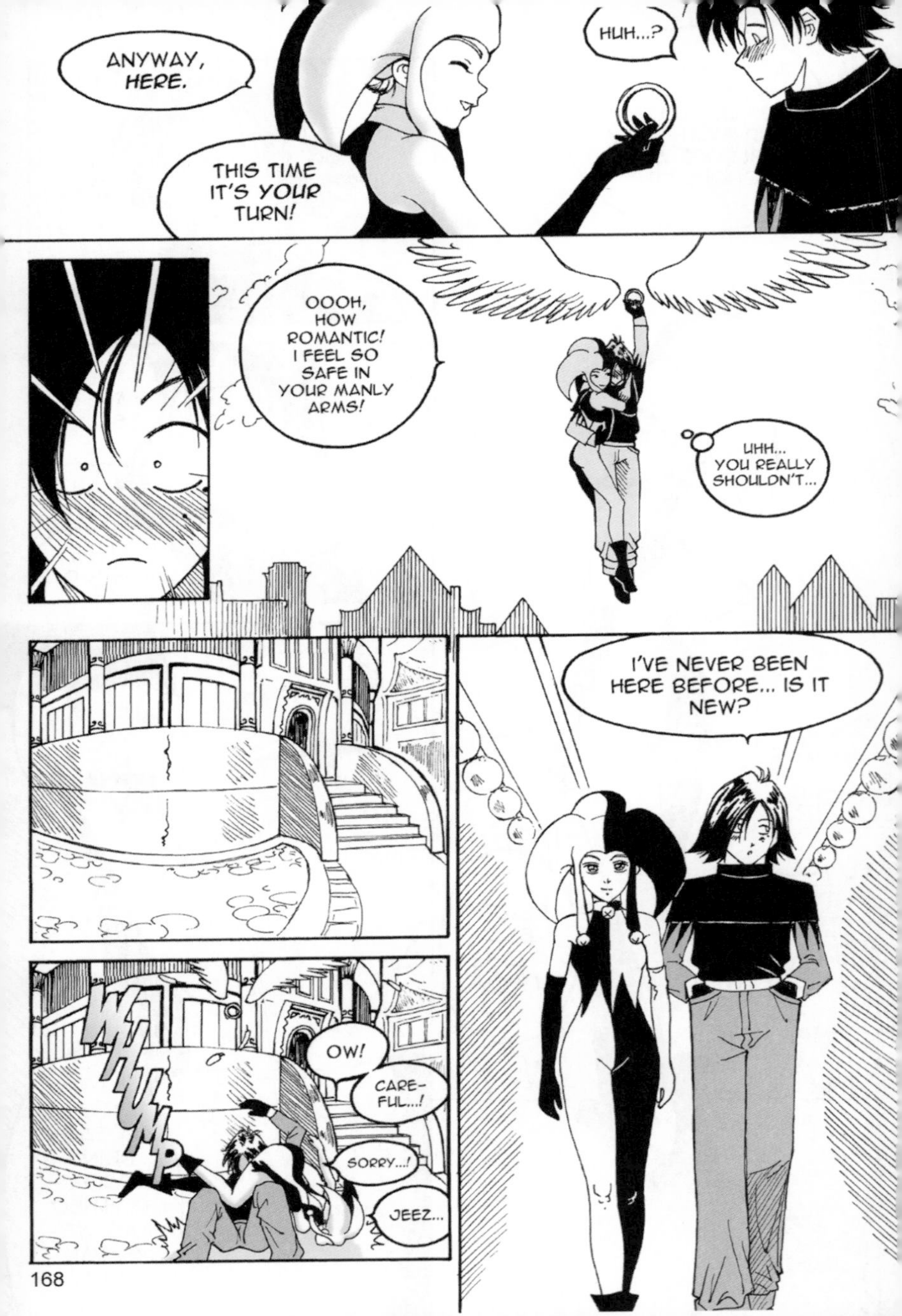
ANYWAY, HERE.
HUH...?
THIS TIME IT'S YOUR TURN!
OOOH, HOW ROMANTIC! I FEEL SO SAFE IN YOUR MANLY ARMS!
UHH... YOU REALLY SHOULDN'T...
WHUMP
OW!
CARE-FUL...!
SORRY...!
JEEZ...
I'VE NEVER BEEN HERE BEFORE... IS IT NEW?

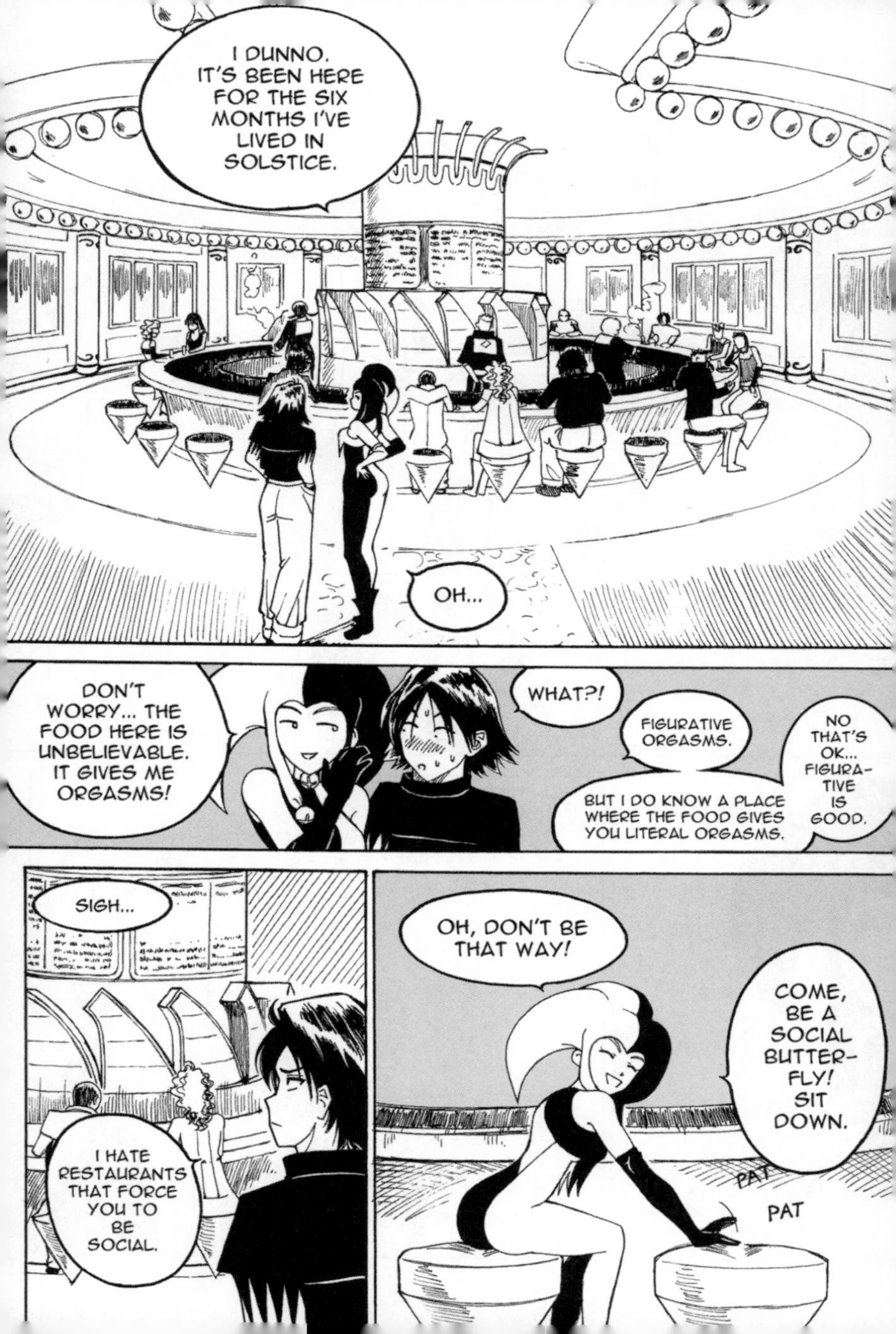
I DUNNO. IT'S BEEN HERE FOR THE SIX MONTHS I'VE LIVED IN SOLSTICE.
OH...
DON'T WORRY... THE FOOD HERE IS UNBELIEVABLE. IT GIVES ME ORGASMS!
WHAT?!
FIGURATIVE ORGASMS.
BUT I DO KNOW A PLACE WHERE THE FOOD GIVES YOU LITERAL ORGASMS.
NO THAT'S OK... FIGURA-TIVE IS GOOD.
SIGH...
I HATE RESTAURANTS THAT FORCE YOU TO BE SOCIAL.
OH, DON'T BE THAT WAY!
COME, BE A SOCIAL BUTTER-FLY! SIT DOWN.
PAT
PAT

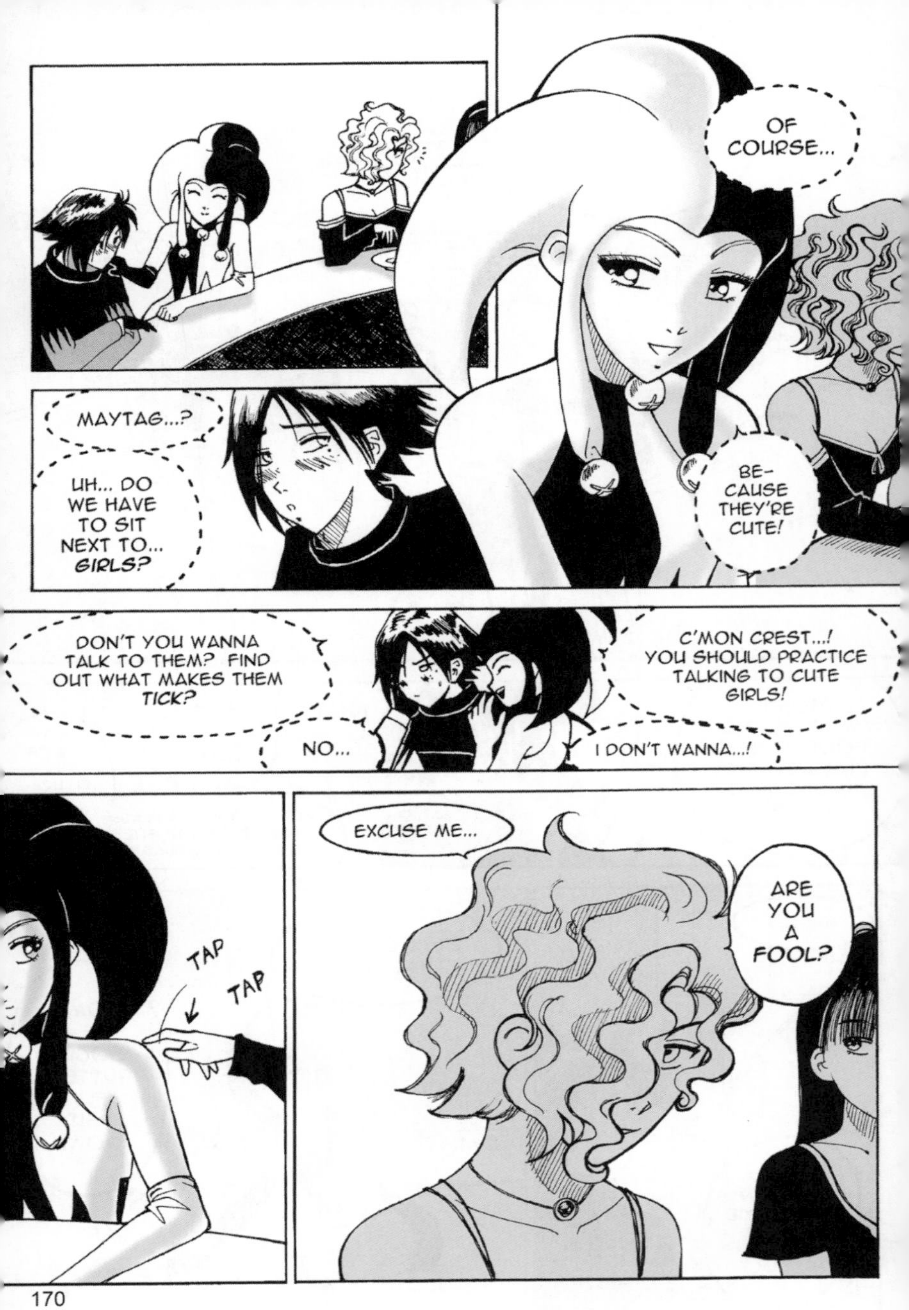

OF COURSE...
MAYTAG...?
UH... DO WE HAVE TO SIT NEXT TO... GIRLS?
BE-CAUSE THEY'RE CUTE!
DON'T YOU WANNA TALK TO THEM? FIND OUT WHAT MAKES THEM TICK?
NO...
C'MON CREST...! YOU SHOULD PRACTICE TALKING TO CUTE GIRLS!
I DON'T WANNA...!
TAP
TAP
EXCUSE ME...
ARE YOU A FOOL?

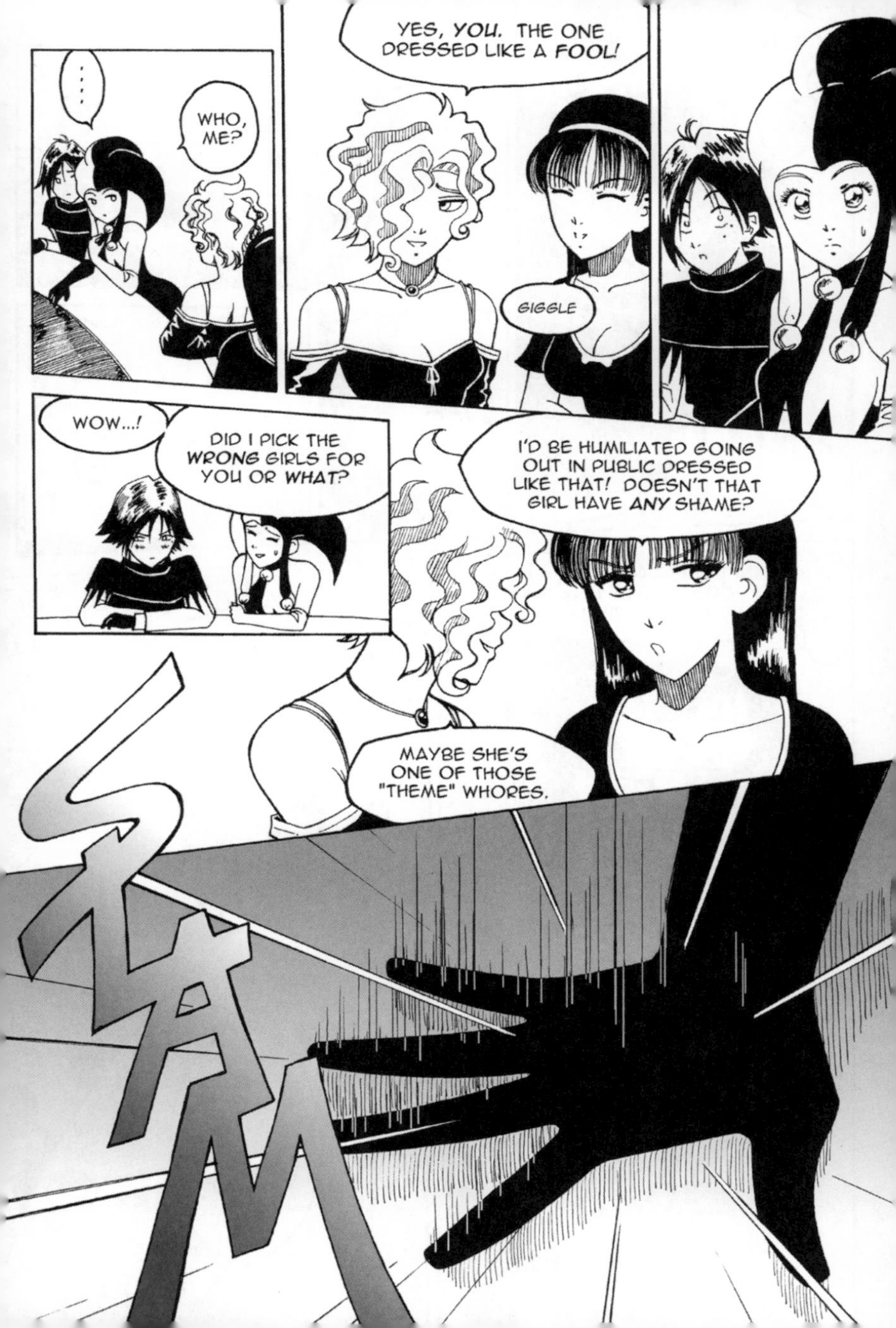
. . . .
WHO, ME?
YES, YOU. THE ONE DRESSED LIKE A FOOL!
GIGGLE
WOW...!
DID I PICK THE WRONG GIRLS FOR YOU OR WHAT?
I'D BE HUMILIATED GOING OUT IN PUBLIC DRESSED LIKE THAT! DOESN'T THAT GIRL HAVE ANY SHAME?
MAYBE SHE'S ONE OF THOSE "THEME" WHORES.
SLAM

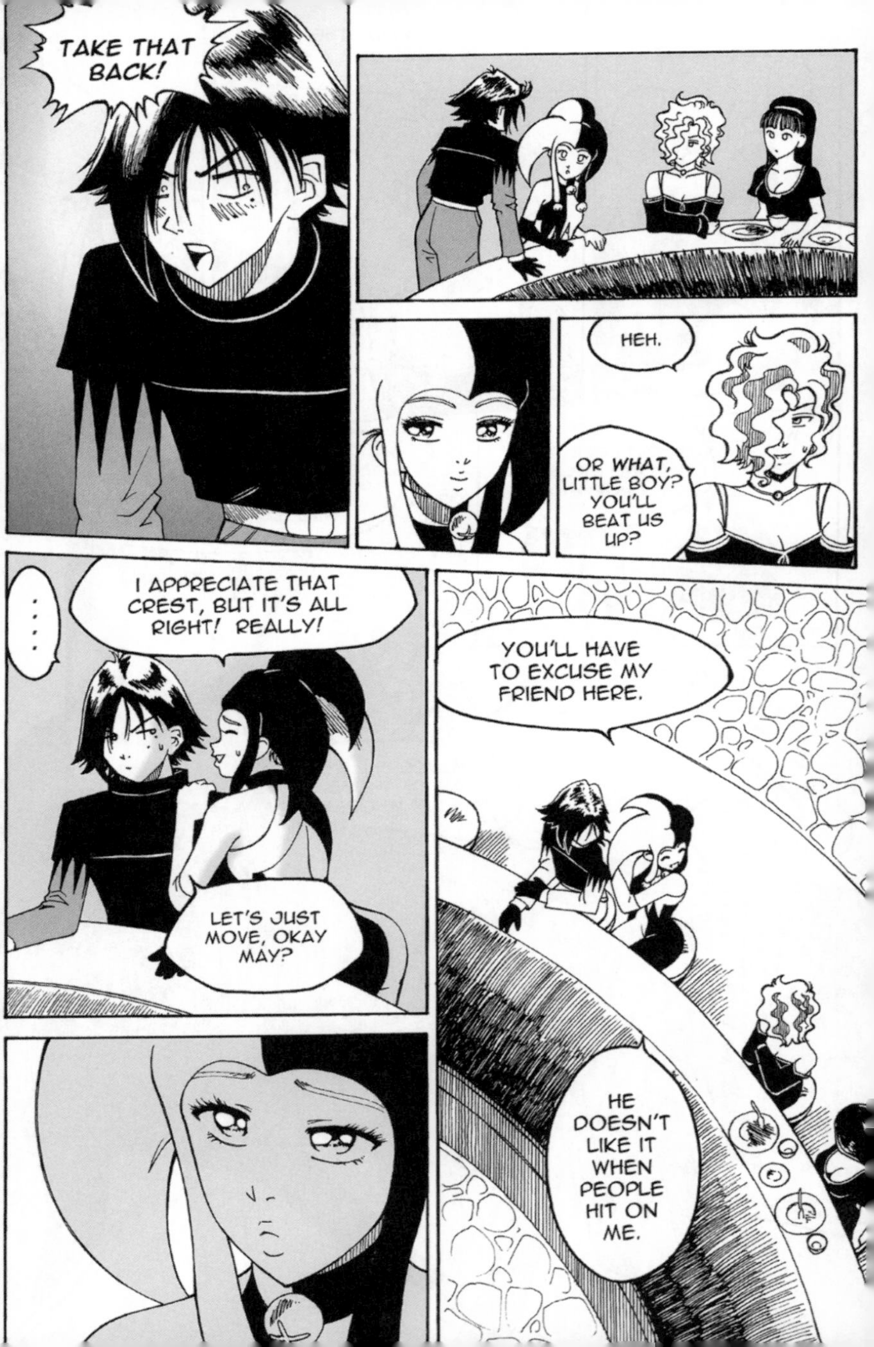
TAKE THAT BACK!
HEH.
OR WHAT, LITTLE BOY? YOU'LL BEAT US UP?
I APPRECIATE THAT CREST, BUT IT'S ALL RIGHT! REALLY!
. . . . .
LET'S JUST MOVE, OKAY MAY?
YOU'LL HAVE TO EXCUSE MY FRIEND HERE.
HE DOESN'T LIKE IT WHEN PEOPLE HIT ON ME.

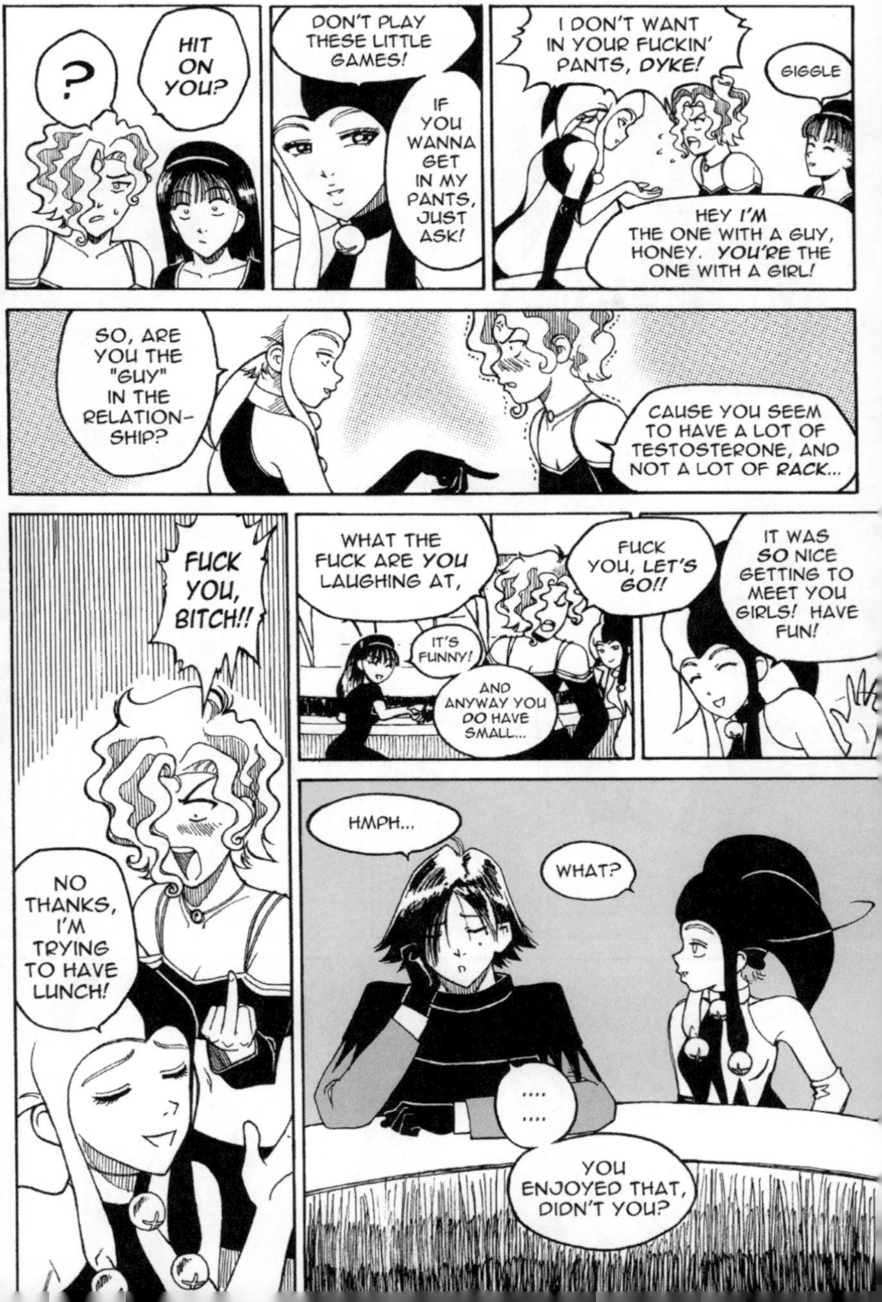
?
HIT ON YOU?
DON'T PLAY THESE LITTLE GAMES!
IF YOU WANNA GET IN MY PANTS, JUST ASK!
I DON'T WANT IN YOUR FUCKIN' PANTS, DYKE!
GIGGLE
HEY I'M THE ONE WITH A GUY, HONEY. YOU'RE THE ONE WITH A GIRL!
SO, ARE YOU THE "GUY" IN THE RELATION-SHIP?
CAUSE YOU SEEM TO HAVE A LOT OF TESTOSTERONE, AND NOT A LOT OF RACK...
FUCK YOU, BITCH!!
NO THANKS, I'M TRYING TO HAVE LUNCH!
WHAT THE FUCK ARE YOU LAUGHING AT,
FUCK YOU, LET'S GO!!
IT'S FUNNY!
AND ANYWAY YOU DO HAVE SMALL...
IT WAS SO NICE GETTING TO MEET YOU GIRLS! HAVE FUN!
HMPH...
WHAT?
....
....
YOU ENJOYED THAT, DIDN'T YOU?

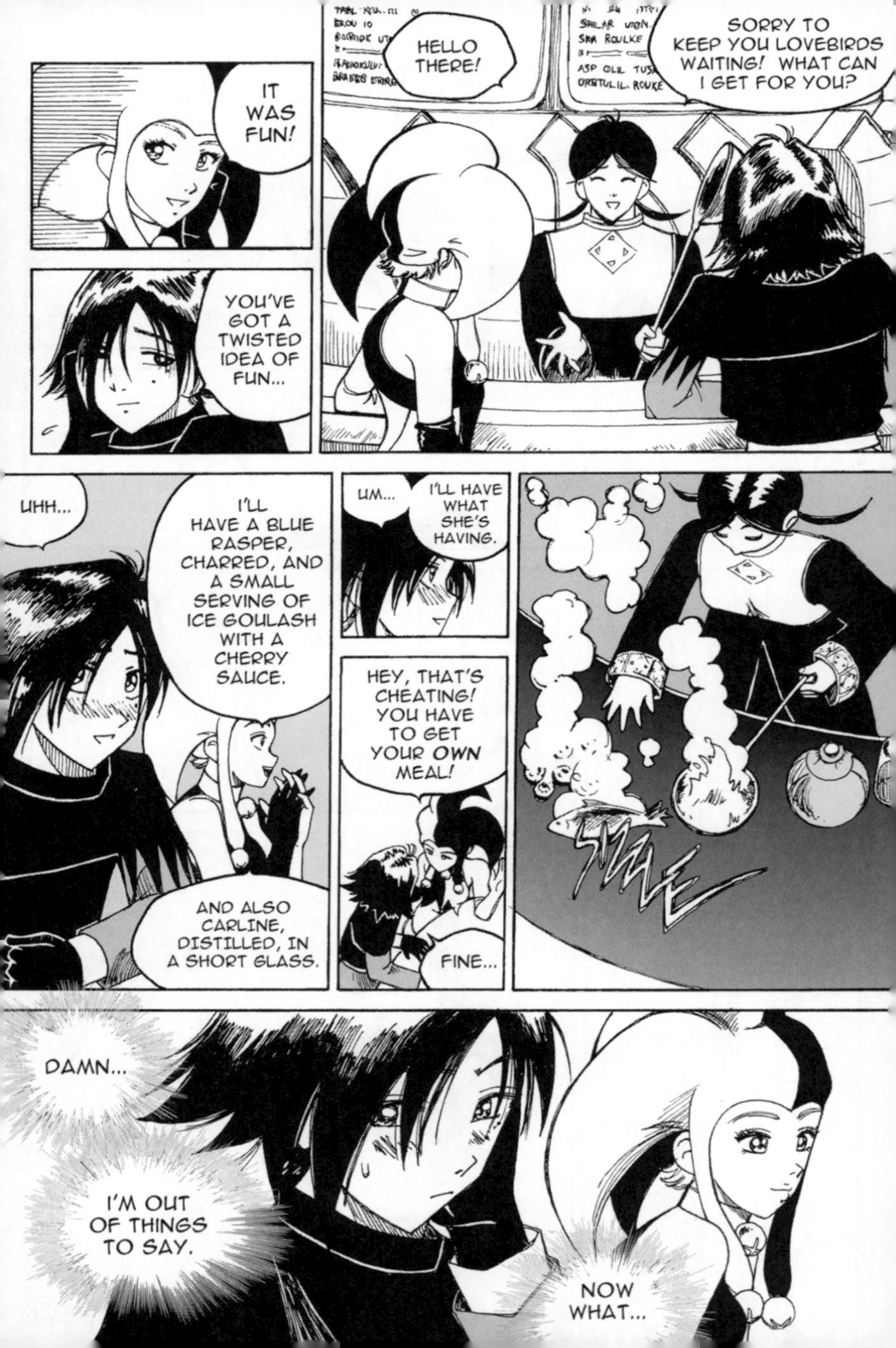
IT WAS FUN!
YOU'VE GOT A TWISTED IDEA OF FUN...
HELLO THERE!
SORRY TO KEEP YOU LOVEBIRDS WAITING! WHAT CAN I GET FOR YOU?
UHH...
I'LL HAVE A BLUE RASPER, CHARRED, AND A SMALL SERVING OF ICE GOULASH WITH A CHERRY SAUCE.
AND ALSO CARLINE, DISTILLED, IN A SHORT GLASS.
UM...
I'LL HAVE WHAT SHE'S HAVING.
HEY, THAT'S CHEATING! YOU HAVE TO GET YOUR OWN MEAL!
FINE...
DAMN...
I'M OUT OF THINGS TO SAY.
NOW WHAT...

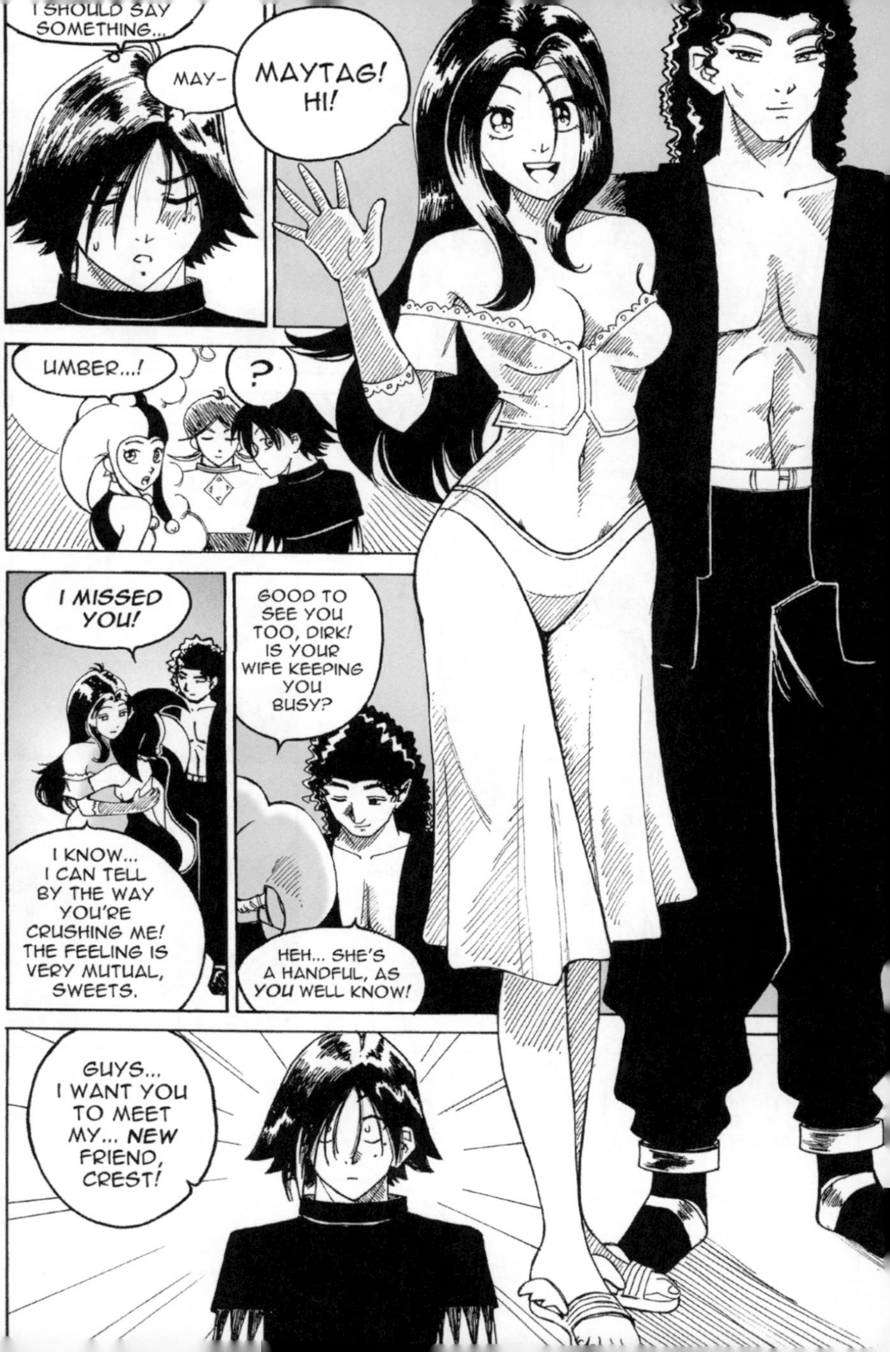
I SHOULD SAY SOMETHING...
MAY-
MAYTAG! HI!
UMBER...!
?
I MISSED YOU!
GOOD TO SEE YOU TOO, DIRK! IS YOUR WIFE KEEPING YOU BUSY?
I KNOW... I CAN TELL BY THE WAY YOU'RE CRUSHING ME! THE FEELING IS VERY MUTUAL, SWEETS.
HEH... SHE'S A HANDFUL, AS YOU WELL KNOW!
GUYS... I WANT YOU TO MEET MY... NEW FRIEND, CREST!

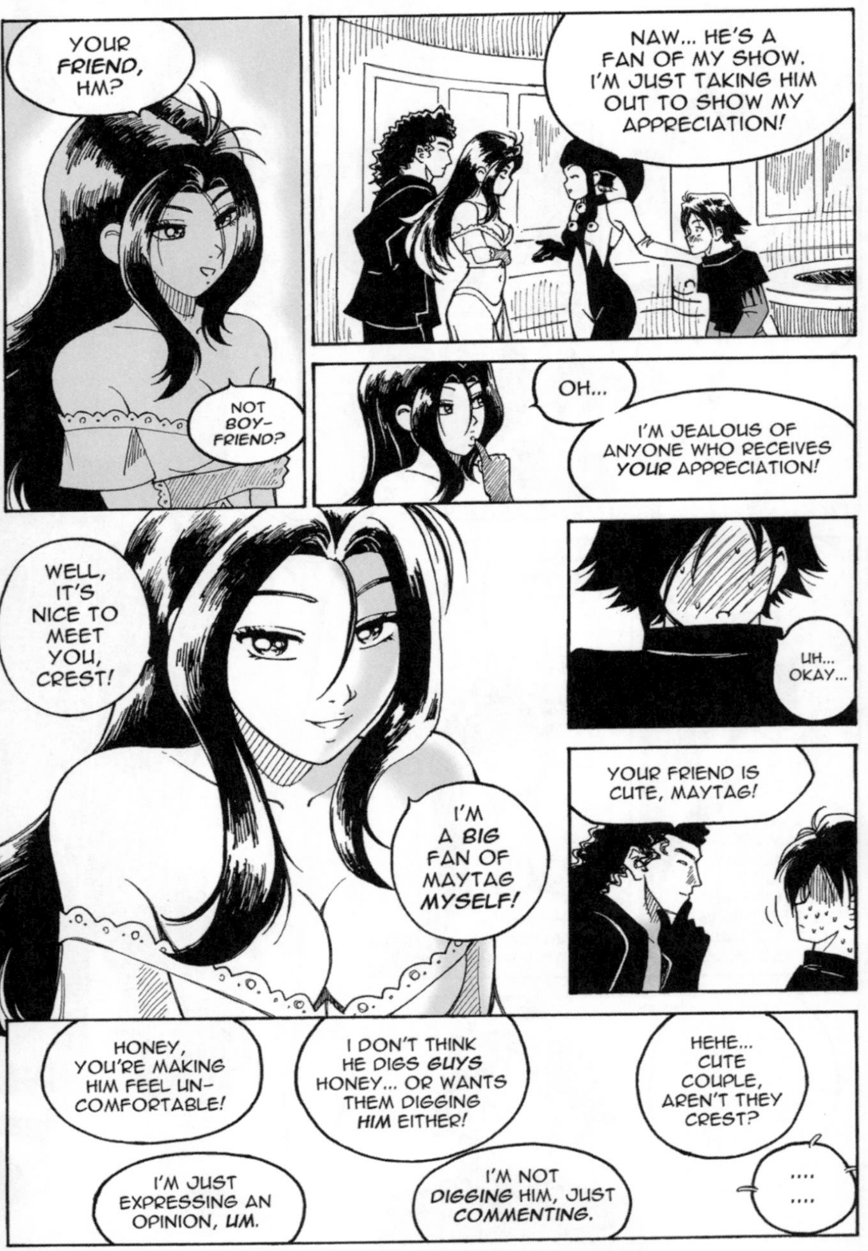
YOUR FRIEND, HM?
NOT BOY-FRIEND?
NAW... HE'S A FAN OF MY SHOW. I'M JUST TAKING HIM OUT TO SHOW MY APPRECIATION!
OH...
I'M JEALOUS OF ANYONE WHO RECEIVES YOUR APPRECIATION!
WELL, IT'S NICE TO MEET YOU, CREST!
I'M A BIG FAN OF MAYTAG MYSELF!
UH... OKAY...
YOUR FRIEND IS CUTE, MAYTAG!
HONEY, YOU'RE MAKING HIM FEEL UN-COMFORTABLE!
I'M JUST EXPRESSING AN OPINION, UM.
I DON'T THINK HE DIGS GUYS HONEY... OR WANTS THEM DIGGING HIM EITHER!
I'M NOT DIGGING HIM, JUST COMMENTING.
HEHE... CUTE COUPLE, AREN'T THEY CREST?
....
....

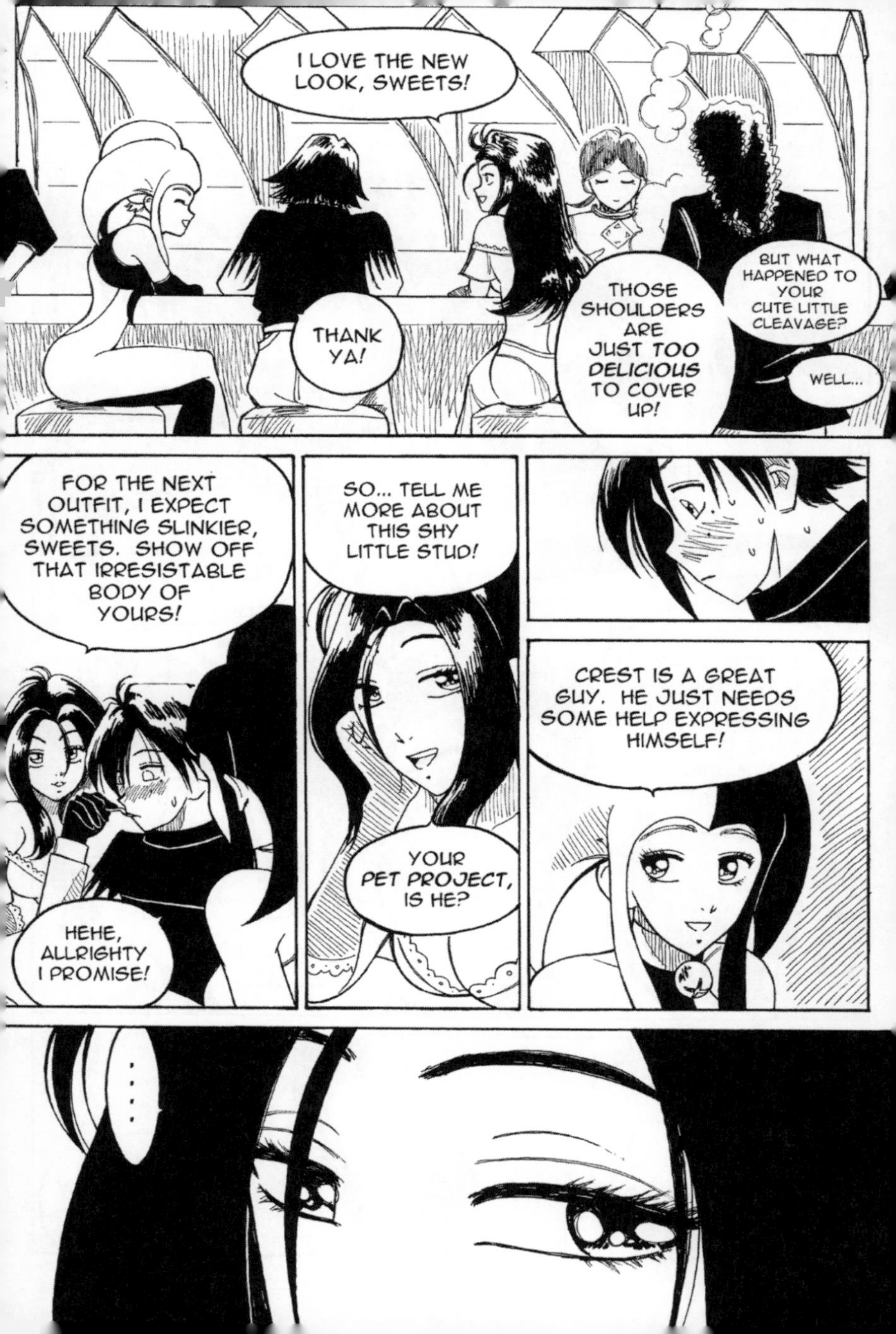
I LOVE THE NEW LOOK, SWEETS!
THANK YA!
THOSE SHOULDERS ARE JUST TOO DELICIOUS TO COVER UP!
BUT WHAT HAPPENED TO YOUR CUTE LITTLE CLEAVAGE?
WELL...
FOR THE NEXT OUTFIT, I EXPECT SOMETHING SLINKIER, SWEETS. SHOW OFF THAT IRRESISTABLE BODY OF YOURS!
HEHE, ALLRIGHTY I PROMISE!
SO... TELL ME MORE ABOUT THIS SHY LITTLE STUD!
YOUR PET PROJECT, IS HE?
CREST IS A GREAT GUY. HE JUST NEEDS SOME HELP EXPRESSING HIMSELF!
....

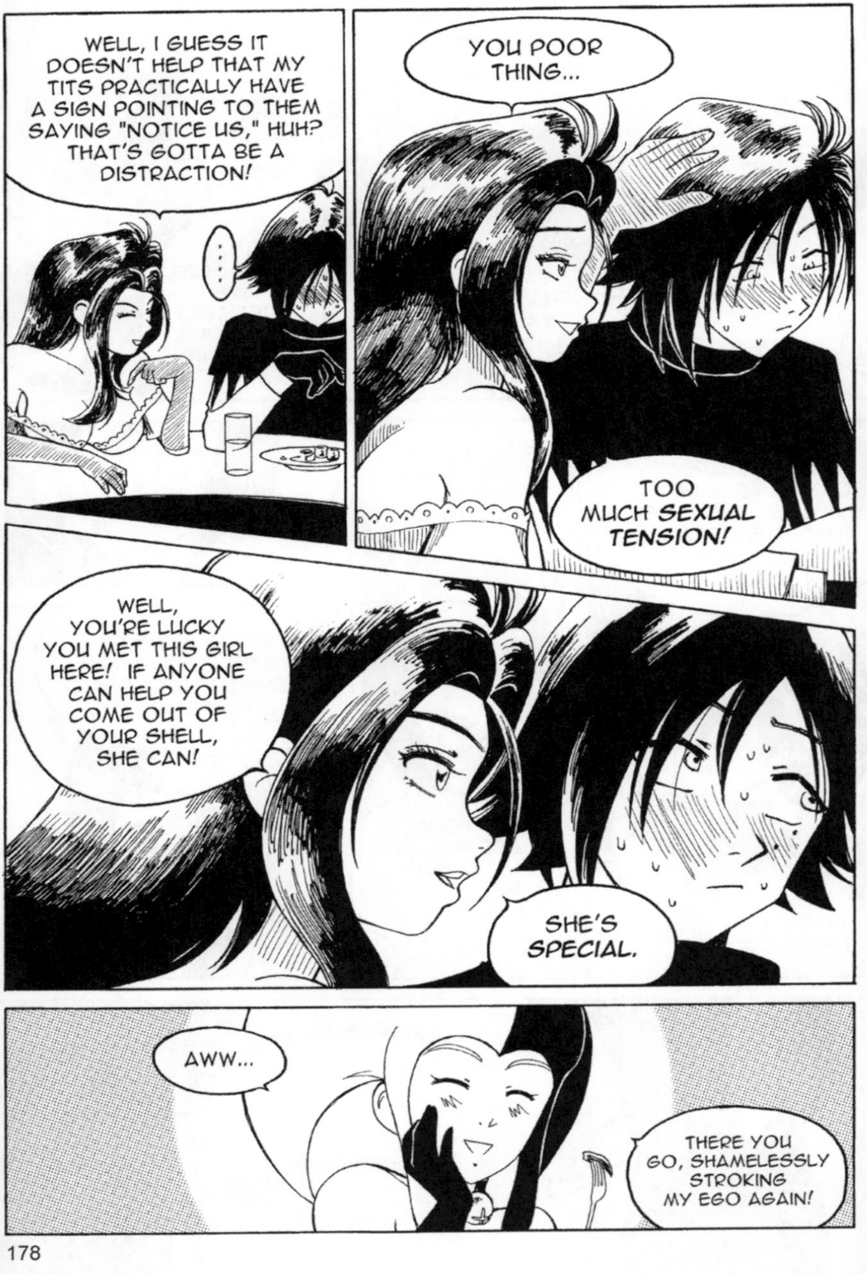
WELL, I GUESS IT DOESN'T HELP THAT MY TITS PRACTICALLY HAVE A SIGN POINTING TO THEM SAYING "NOTICE US," HUH? THAT'S GOTTA BE A DISTRACTION!
....
YOU POOR THING...
TOO MUCH **SEXUAL TENSION!**
WELL, YOU'RE LUCKY YOU MET THIS GIRL HERE! IF ANYONE CAN HELP YOU COME OUT OF YOUR SHELL, SHE CAN!
SHE'S SPECIAL.
AWW...
THERE YOU GO, SHAMELESSLY STROKING MY EGO AGAIN!

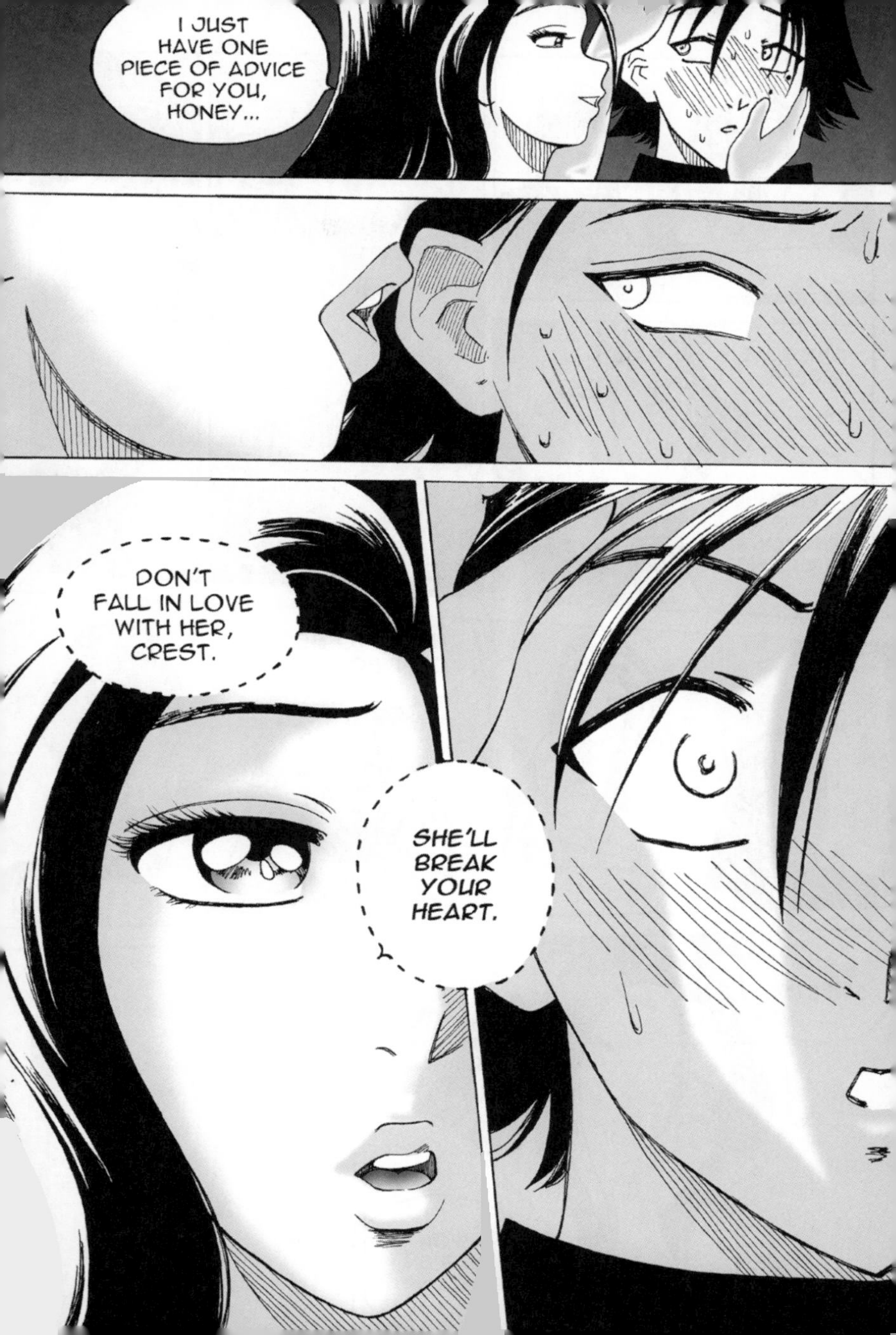
I JUST HAVE ONE PIECE OF ADVICE FOR YOU, HONEY...
DON'T FALL IN LOVE WITH HER, CREST.
SHE'LL BREAK YOUR HEART.

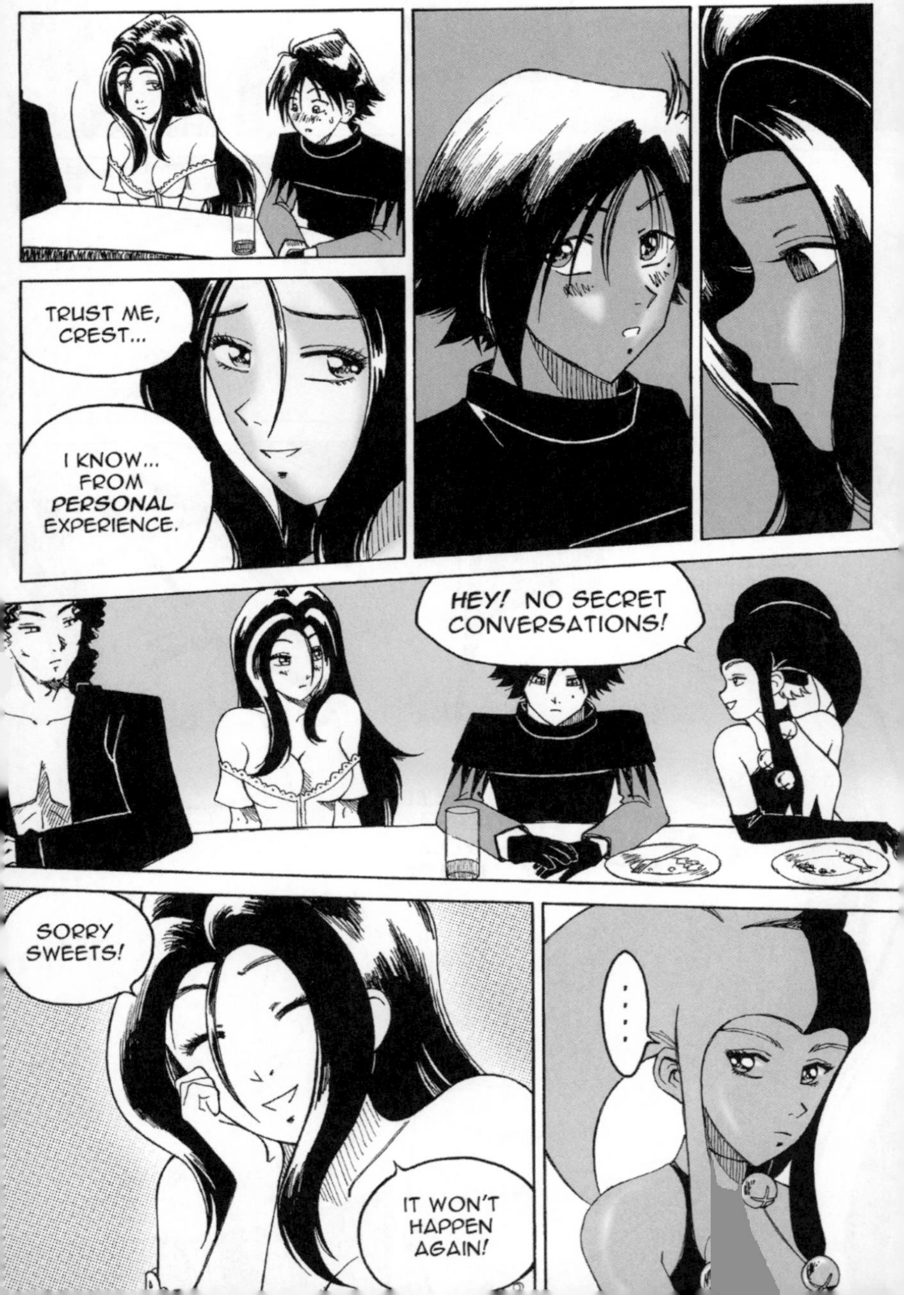
TRUST ME, CREST...
I KNOW... FROM PERSONAL EXPERIENCE.
HEY! NO SECRET CONVERSATIONS!
SORRY SWEETS!
IT WON'T HAPPEN AGAIN!
...

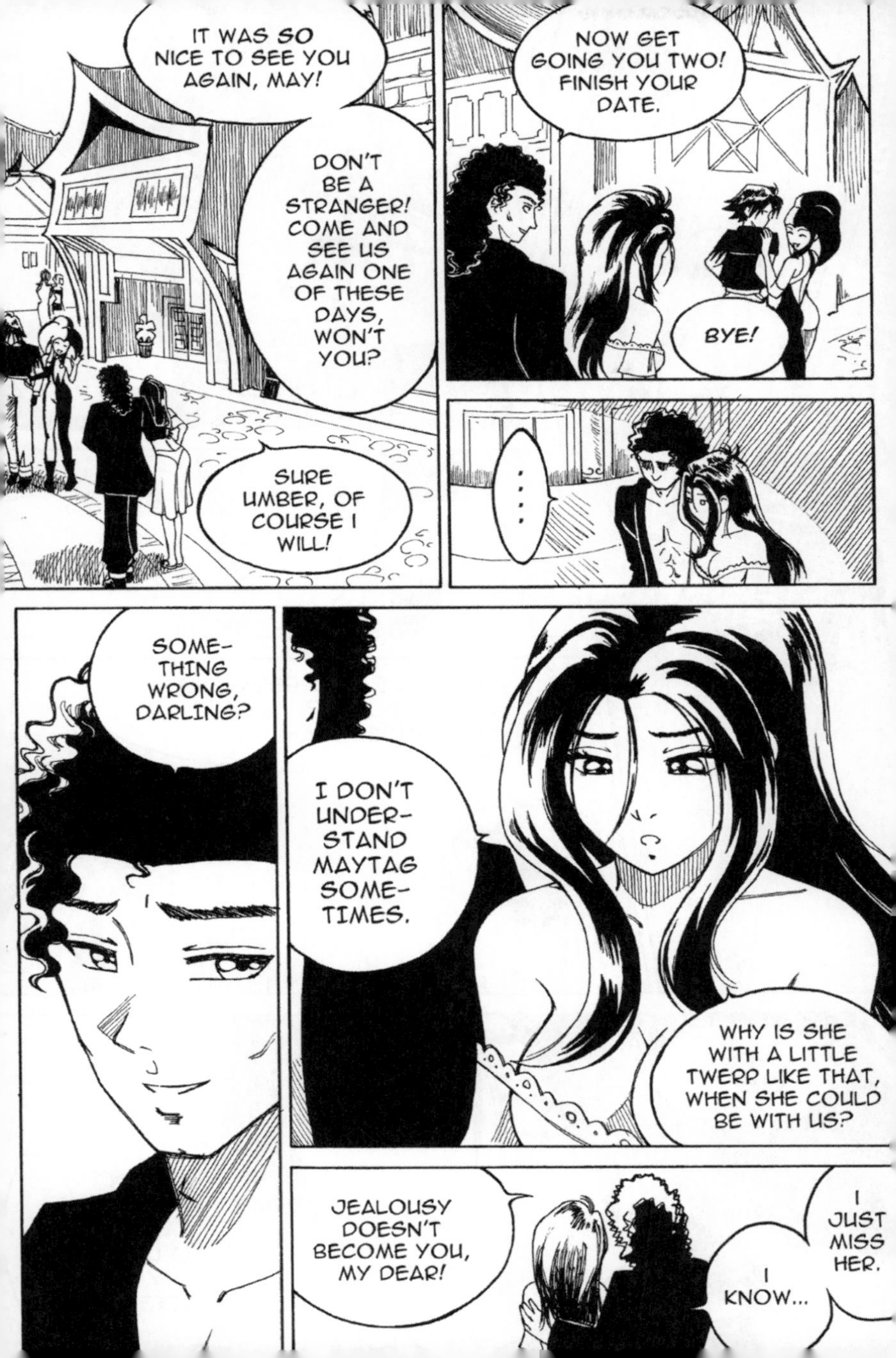

IT WAS SO NICE TO SEE YOU AGAIN, MAY!
DON'T BE A STRANGER! COME AND SEE US AGAIN ONE OF THESE DAYS, WON'T YOU?
SURE UMBER, OF COURSE I WILL!
NOW GET GOING YOU TWO! FINISH YOUR DATE.
BYE!
....
SOME-THING WRONG, DARLING?
I DON'T UNDER-STAND MAYTAG SOME-TIMES.
WHY IS SHE WITH A LITTLE TWERP LIKE THAT, WHEN SHE COULD BE WITH US?
JEALOUSY DOESN'T BECOME YOU, MY DEAR!
I KNOW...
I JUST MISS HER.

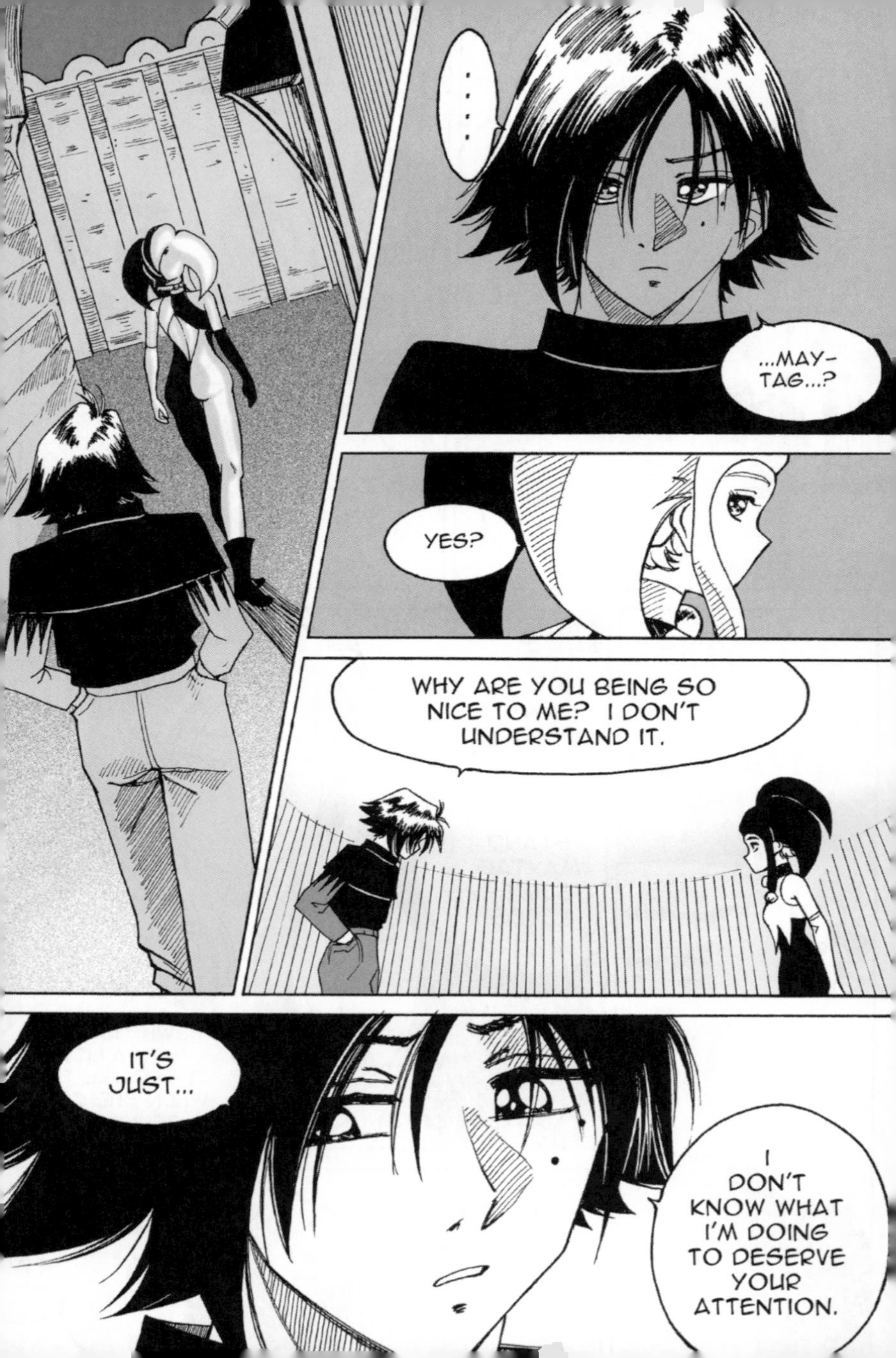
. . . .
...MAY-TAG...?
YES?
WHY ARE YOU BEING SO NICE TO ME? I DON'T UNDERSTAND IT.
IT'S JUST...
I DON'T KNOW WHAT I'M DOING TO DESERVE YOUR ATTENTION.

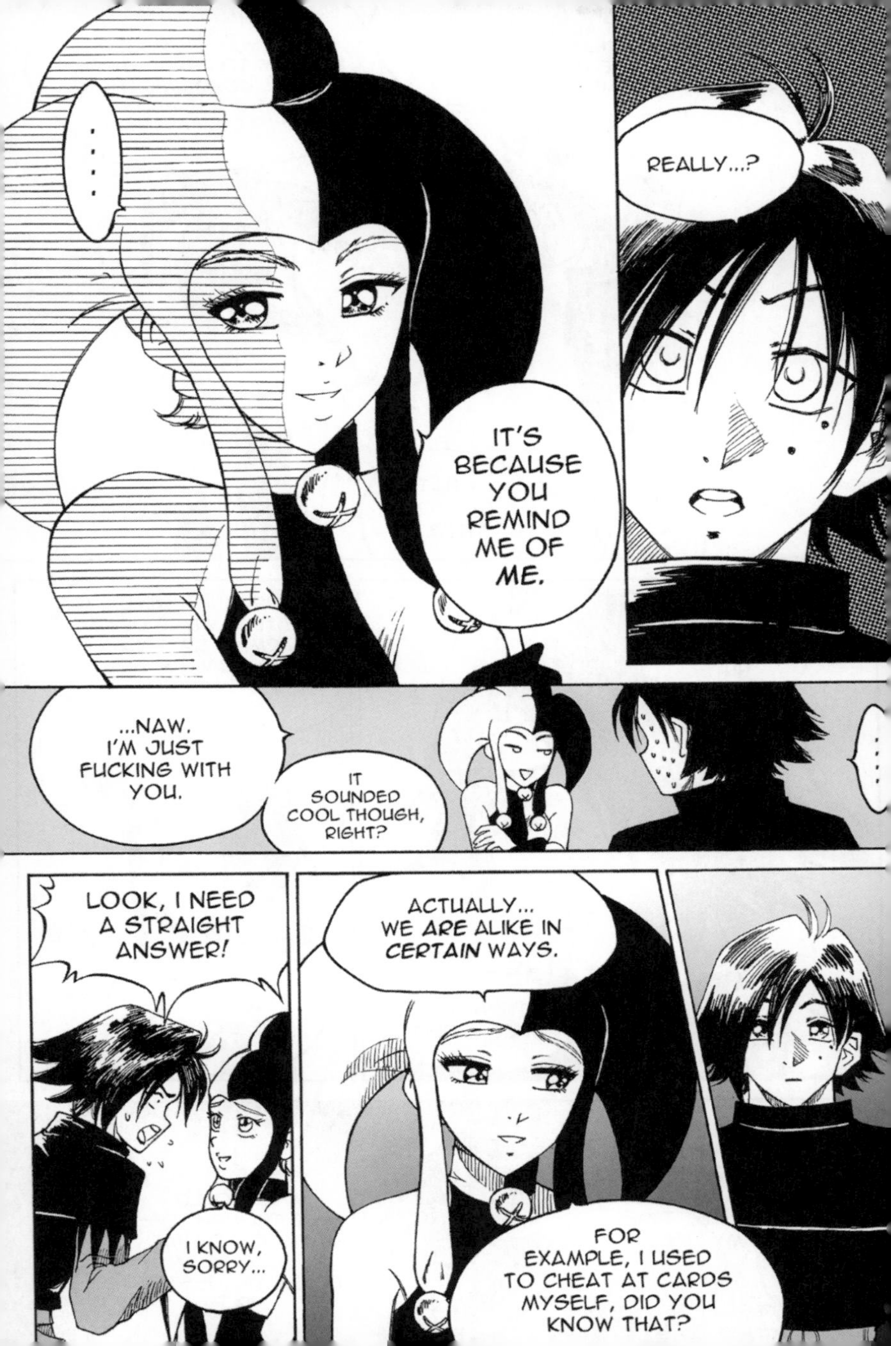
....
REALLY...?
IT'S BECAUSE YOU REMIND ME OF ME.
...NAW. I'M JUST FUCKING WITH YOU.
IT SOUNDED COOL THOUGH, RIGHT?
...
LOOK, I NEED A STRAIGHT ANSWER!
I KNOW, SORRY...
ACTUALLY... WE ARE ALIKE IN CERTAIN WAYS.
FOR EXAMPLE, I USED TO CHEAT AT CARDS MYSELF, DID YOU KNOW THAT?

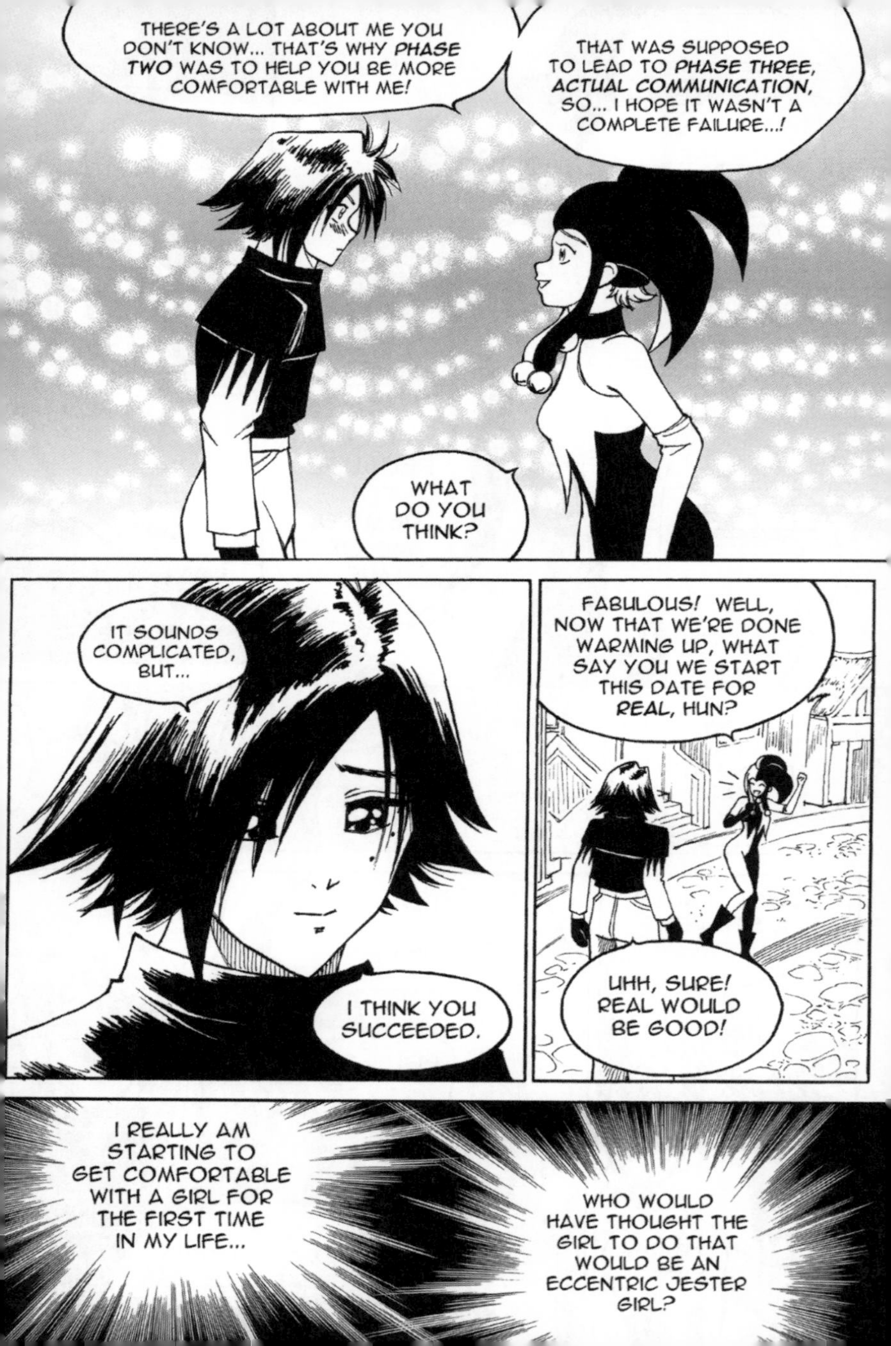
THERE'S A LOT ABOUT ME YOU DON'T KNOW... THAT'S WHY *PHASE TWO* WAS TO HELP YOU BE MORE COMFORTABLE WITH ME!
THAT WAS SUPPOSED TO LEAD TO *PHASE THREE, ACTUAL COMMUNICATION,* SO... I HOPE IT WASN'T A COMPLETE FAILURE...!
WHAT DO YOU THINK?
IT SOUNDS COMPLICATED, BUT...
I THINK YOU SUCCEEDED.
FABULOUS! WELL, NOW THAT WE'RE DONE WARMING UP, WHAT SAY YOU WE START THIS DATE FOR *REAL*, HUN?
UHH, SURE! REAL WOULD BE GOOD!
I REALLY AM STARTING TO GET COMFORTABLE WITH A GIRL FOR THE FIRST TIME IN MY LIFE...
WHO WOULD HAVE THOUGHT THE GIRL TO DO THAT WOULD BE AN ECCENTRIC JESTER GIRL?

NEXT:

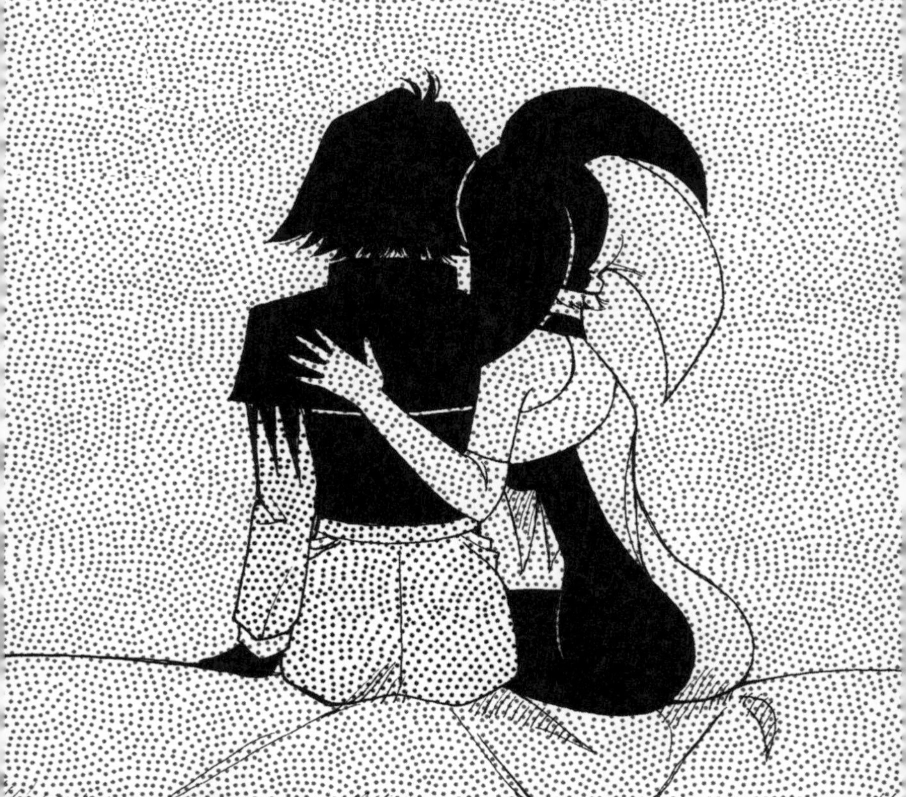

In Volume 2:

As Crest's date with Maytag continues, things start to heat up and get more personal. Finding himself in a hotel room with her turns out to be the easy part, it's what she tells him that really stirs up trouble... she has a boyfriend! How will Crest react, and what does Bernadette have to do with all this?

Coming in 2007!

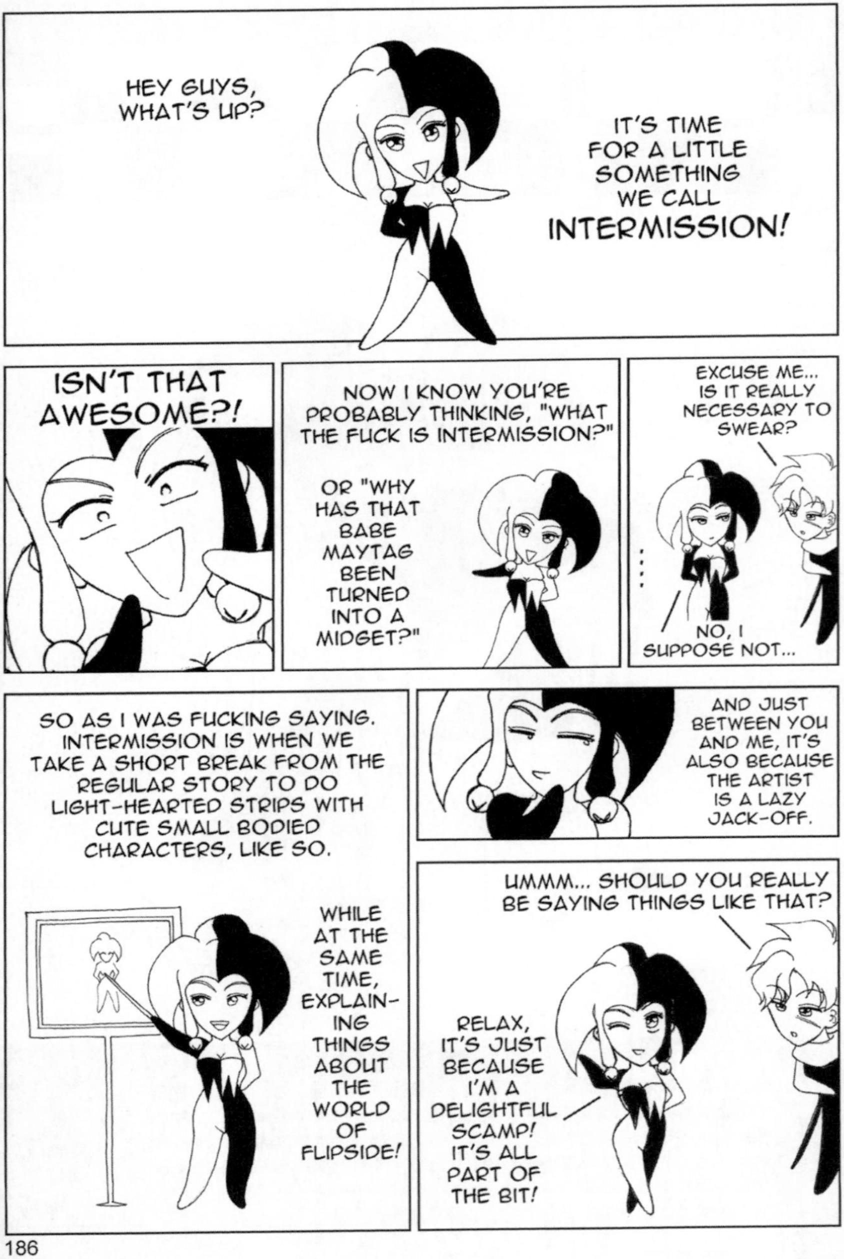

HEY GUYS, WHAT'S UP?
IT'S TIME FOR A LITTLE SOMETHING WE CALL INTERMISSION!
ISN'T THAT AWESOME?!
NOW I KNOW YOU'RE PROBABLY THINKING, "WHAT THE FUCK IS INTERMISSION?"
OR "WHY HAS THAT BABE MAYTAG BEEN TURNED INTO A MIDGET?"
EXCUSE ME... IS IT REALLY NECESSARY TO SWEAR?
....
NO, I SUPPOSE NOT...
SO AS I WAS FUCKING SAYING. INTERMISSION IS WHEN WE TAKE A SHORT BREAK FROM THE REGULAR STORY TO DO LIGHT-HEARTED STRIPS WITH CUTE SMALL BODIED CHARACTERS, LIKE SO.
WHILE AT THE SAME TIME, EXPLAIN-ING THINGS ABOUT THE WORLD OF FLIPSIDE!
AND JUST BETWEEN YOU AND ME, IT'S ALSO BECAUSE THE ARTIST IS A LAZY JACK-OFF.
UMMM... SHOULD YOU REALLY BE SAYING THINGS LIKE THAT?
RELAX, IT'S JUST BECAUSE I'M A DELIGHTFUL SCAMP! IT'S ALL PART OF THE BIT!

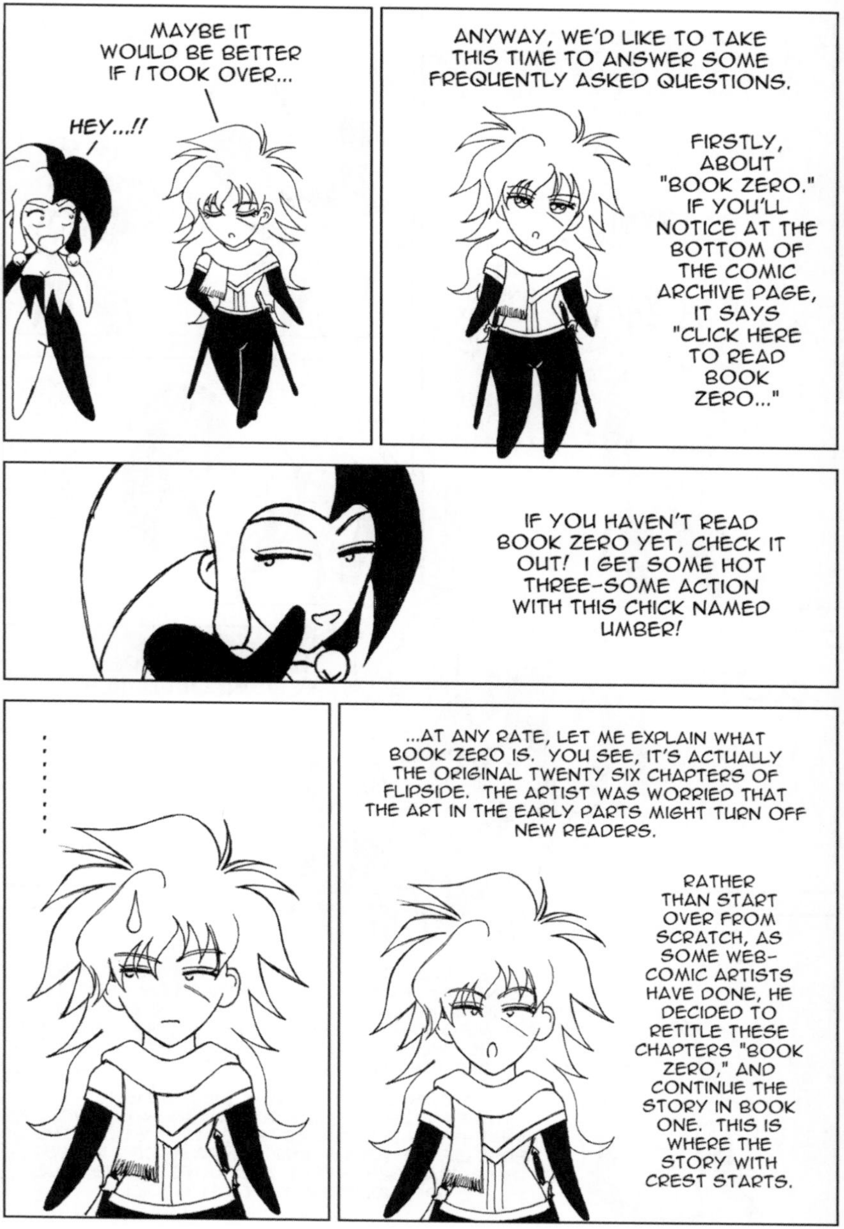

MAYBE IT WOULD BE BETTER IF I TOOK OVER...
HEY...!!
ANYWAY, WE'D LIKE TO TAKE THIS TIME TO ANSWER SOME FREQUENTLY ASKED QUESTIONS.
FIRSTLY, ABOUT "BOOK ZERO." IF YOU'LL NOTICE AT THE BOTTOM OF THE COMIC ARCHIVE PAGE, IT SAYS "CLICK HERE TO READ BOOK ZERO..."
IF YOU HAVEN'T READ BOOK ZERO YET, CHECK IT OUT! I GET SOME HOT THREE-SOME ACTION WITH THIS CHICK NAMED UMBER!
......
...AT ANY RATE, LET ME EXPLAIN WHAT BOOK ZERO IS. YOU SEE, IT'S ACTUALLY THE ORIGINAL TWENTY SIX CHAPTERS OF FLIPSIDE. THE ARTIST WAS WORRIED THAT THE ART IN THE EARLY PARTS MIGHT TURN OFF NEW READERS.
RATHER THAN START OVER FROM SCRATCH, AS SOME WEB-COMIC ARTISTS HAVE DONE, HE DECIDED TO RETITLE THESE CHAPTERS "BOOK ZERO," AND CONTINUE THE STORY IN BOOK ONE. THIS IS WHERE THE STORY WITH CREST STARTS.

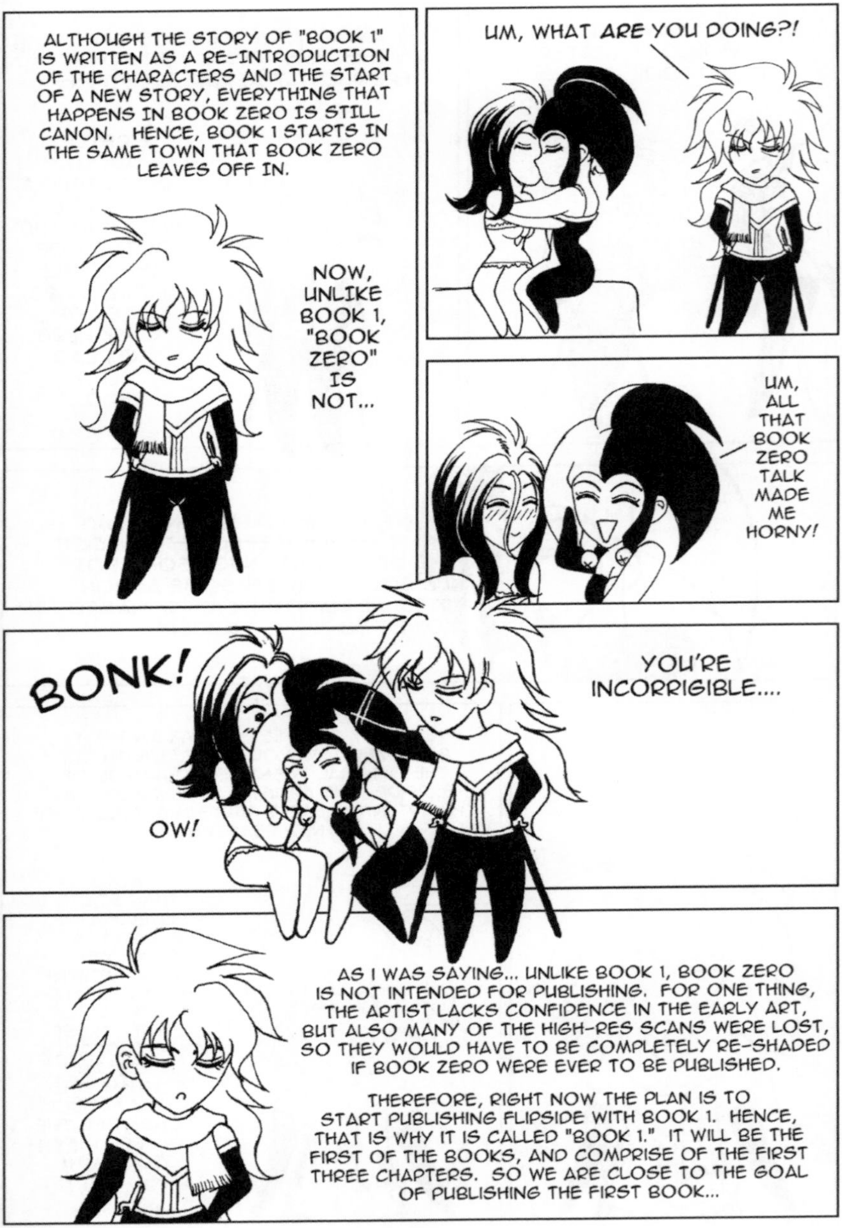
ALTHOUGH THE STORY OF "BOOK 1" IS WRITTEN AS A RE-INTRODUCTION OF THE CHARACTERS AND THE START OF A NEW STORY, EVERYTHING THAT HAPPENS IN BOOK ZERO IS STILL CANON. HENCE, BOOK 1 STARTS IN THE SAME TOWN THAT BOOK ZERO LEAVES OFF IN.
NOW, UNLIKE BOOK 1, "BOOK ZERO" IS NOT...
UM, WHAT ARE YOU DOING?!
UM, ALL THAT BOOK ZERO TALK MADE ME HORNY!
BONK!
YOU'RE INCORRIGIBLE....
OW!
AS I WAS SAYING... UNLIKE BOOK 1, BOOK ZERO IS NOT INTENDED FOR PUBLISHING. FOR ONE THING, THE ARTIST LACKS CONFIDENCE IN THE EARLY ART, BUT ALSO MANY OF THE HIGH-RES SCANS WERE LOST, SO THEY WOULD HAVE TO BE COMPLETELY RE-SHADED IF BOOK ZERO WERE EVER TO BE PUBLISHED.
THEREFORE, RIGHT NOW THE PLAN IS TO START PUBLISHING FLIPSIDE WITH BOOK 1. HENCE, THAT IS WHY IT IS CALLED "BOOK 1." IT WILL BE THE FIRST OF THE BOOKS, AND COMPRISE OF THE FIRST THREE CHAPTERS. SO WE ARE CLOSE TO THE GOAL OF PUBLISHING THE FIRST BOOK...

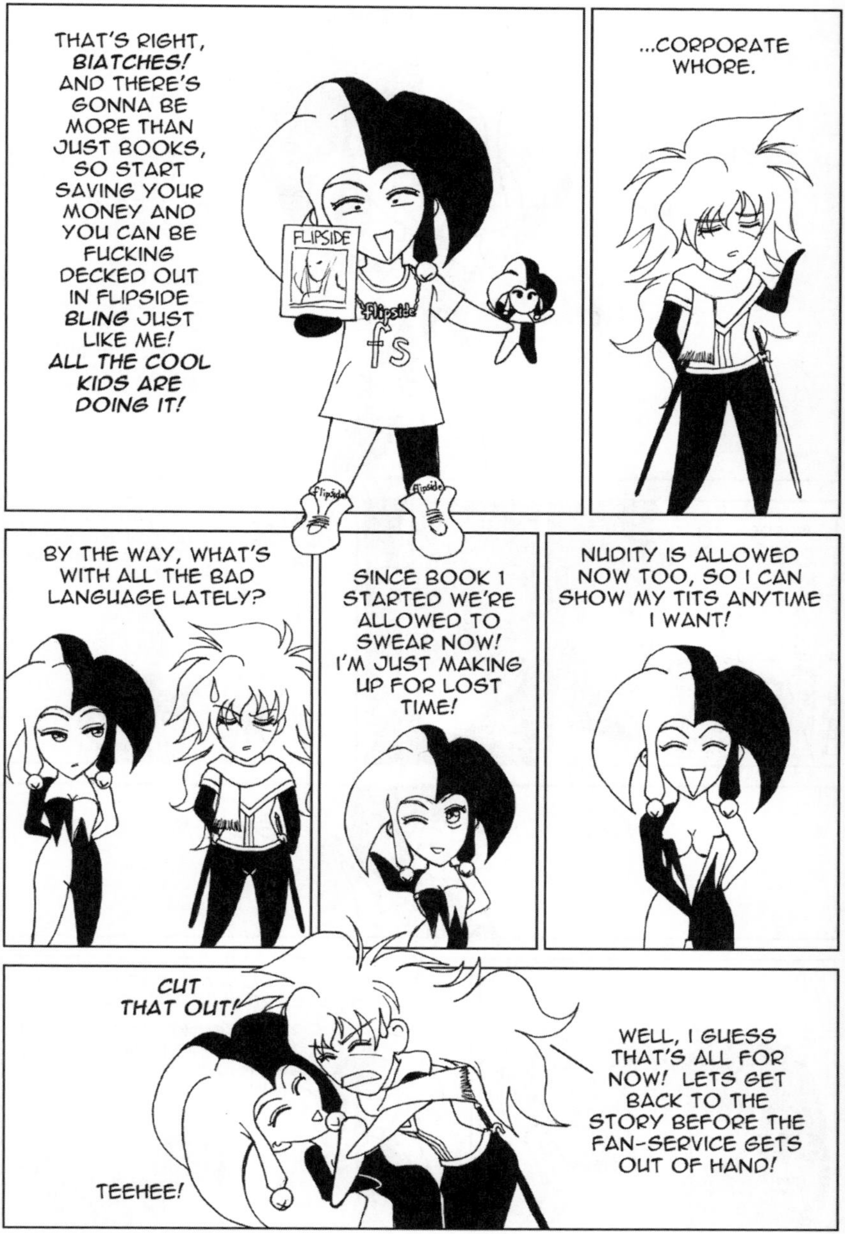
THAT'S RIGHT, BIATCHES! AND THERE'S GONNA BE MORE THAN JUST BOOKS, SO START SAVING YOUR MONEY AND YOU CAN BE FUCKING DECKED OUT IN FLIPSIDE BLING JUST LIKE ME! ALL THE COOL KIDS ARE DOING IT!
FLIPSIDE
flipside
fs
flipside
flipside
...CORPORATE WHORE.
BY THE WAY, WHAT'S WITH ALL THE BAD LANGUAGE LATELY?
SINCE BOOK 1 STARTED WE'RE ALLOWED TO SWEAR NOW! I'M JUST MAKING UP FOR LOST TIME!
NUDITY IS ALLOWED NOW TOO, SO I CAN SHOW MY TITS ANYTIME I WANT!
CUT THAT OUT!
TEEHEE!
WELL, I GUESS THAT'S ALL FOR NOW! LETS GET BACK TO THE STORY BEFORE THE FAN-SERVICE GETS OUT OF HAND!

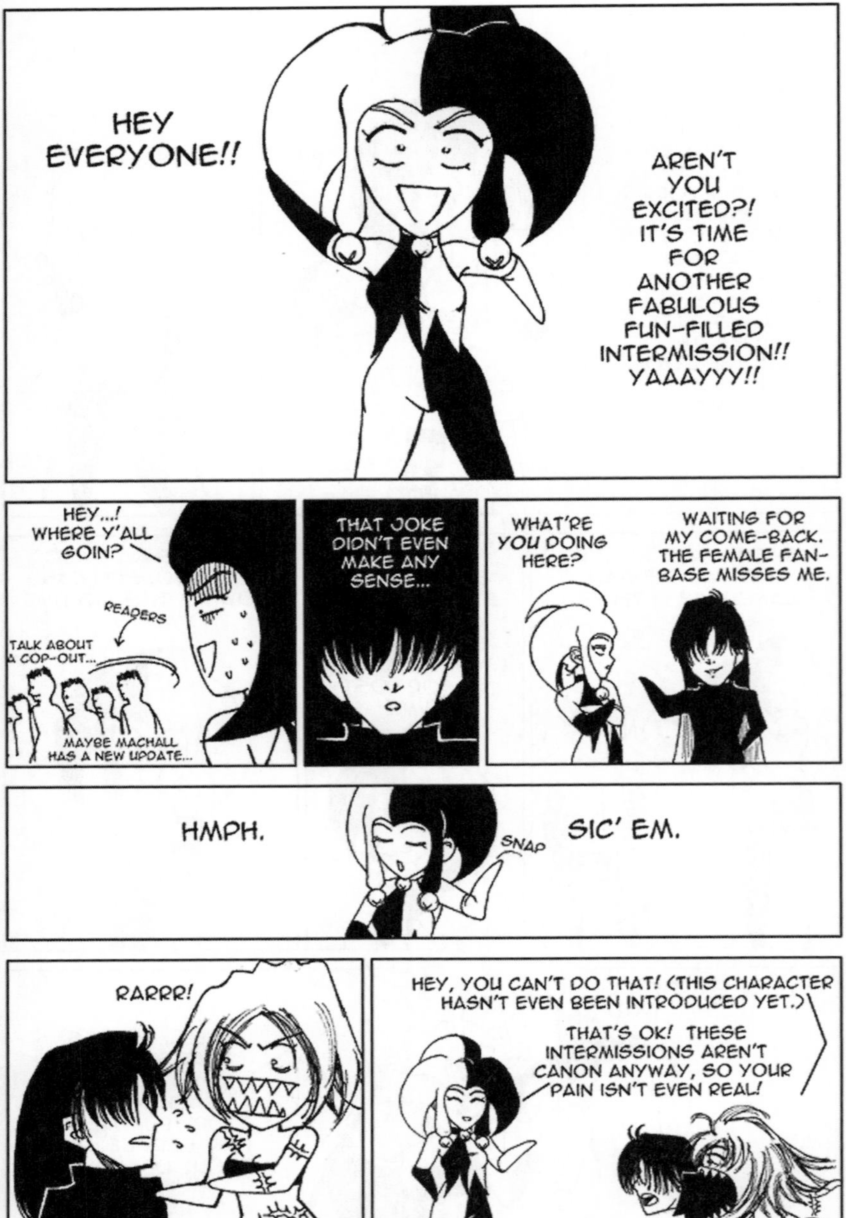
HEY EVERYONE!!
AREN'T YOU EXCITED?! IT'S TIME FOR ANOTHER FABULOUS FUN-FILLED INTERMISSION!! YAAAYYY!!
HEY...! WHERE Y'ALL GOIN?
READERS
TALK ABOUT A COP-OUT...
MAYBE MACHALL HAS A NEW UPDATE...
THAT JOKE DIDN'T EVEN MAKE ANY SENSE...
WHAT'RE YOU DOING HERE?
WAITING FOR MY COME-BACK. THE FEMALE FAN-BASE MISSES ME.
HMPH.
SNAP
SIC' EM.
RARRR!
HEY, YOU CAN'T DO THAT! (THIS CHARACTER HASN'T EVEN BEEN INTRODUCED YET.)
THAT'S OK! THESE INTERMISSIONS AREN'T CANON ANYWAY, SO YOUR PAIN ISN'T EVEN REAL!

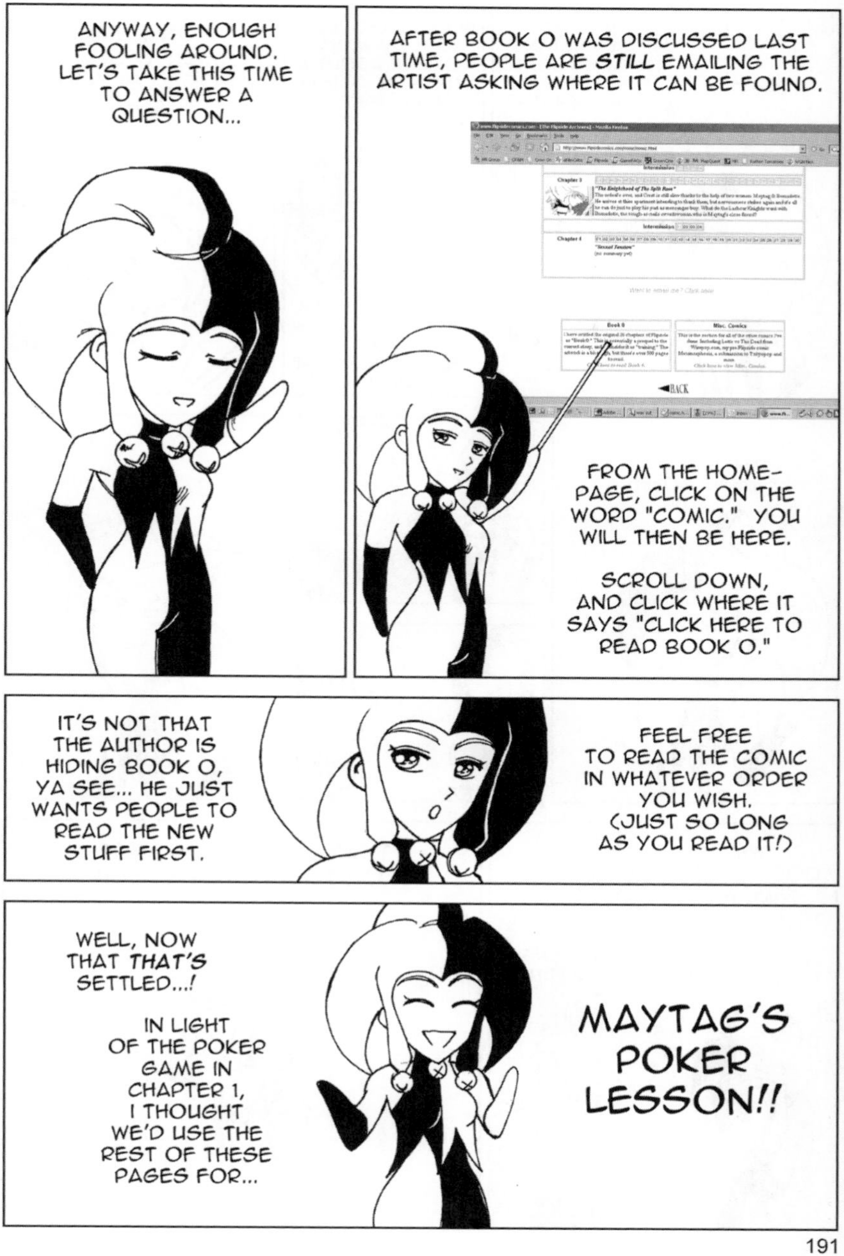
ANYWAY, ENOUGH FOOLING AROUND. LET'S TAKE THIS TIME TO ANSWER A QUESTION...
AFTER BOOK 0 WAS DISCUSSED LAST TIME, PEOPLE ARE *STILL* EMAILING THE ARTIST ASKING WHERE IT CAN BE FOUND.
FROM THE HOME-PAGE, CLICK ON THE WORD "COMIC." YOU WILL THEN BE HERE.
SCROLL DOWN, AND CLICK WHERE IT SAYS "CLICK HERE TO READ BOOK 0."
IT'S NOT THAT THE AUTHOR IS HIDING BOOK 0, YA SEE... HE JUST WANTS PEOPLE TO READ THE NEW STUFF FIRST.
FEEL FREE TO READ THE COMIC IN WHATEVER ORDER YOU WISH. (JUST SO LONG AS YOU READ IT!)
WELL, NOW THAT *THAT'S* SETTLED...!
IN LIGHT OF THE POKER GAME IN CHAPTER 1, I THOUGHT WE'D USE THE REST OF THESE PAGES FOR...
MAYTAG'S POKER LESSON!!

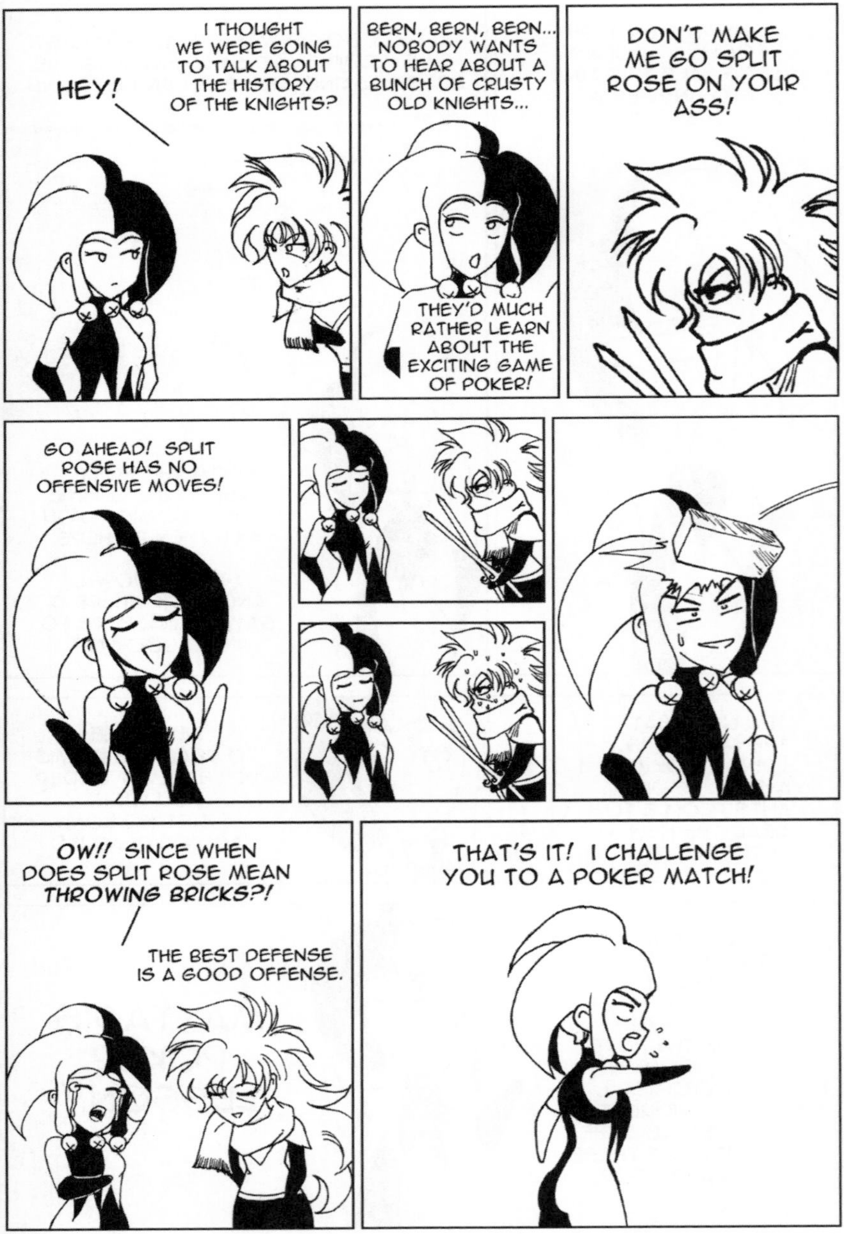
HEY!
I THOUGHT WE WERE GOING TO TALK ABOUT THE HISTORY OF THE KNIGHTS?
BERN, BERN, BERN... NOBODY WANTS TO HEAR ABOUT A BUNCH OF CRUSTY OLD KNIGHTS...
THEY'D MUCH RATHER LEARN ABOUT THE EXCITING GAME OF POKER!
DON'T MAKE ME GO SPLIT ROSE ON YOUR ASS!
GO AHEAD! SPLIT ROSE HAS NO OFFENSIVE MOVES!
OW!! SINCE WHEN DOES SPLIT ROSE MEAN THROWING BRICKS?!
THE BEST DEFENSE IS A GOOD OFFENSE.
THAT'S IT! I CHALLENGE YOU TO A POKER MATCH!

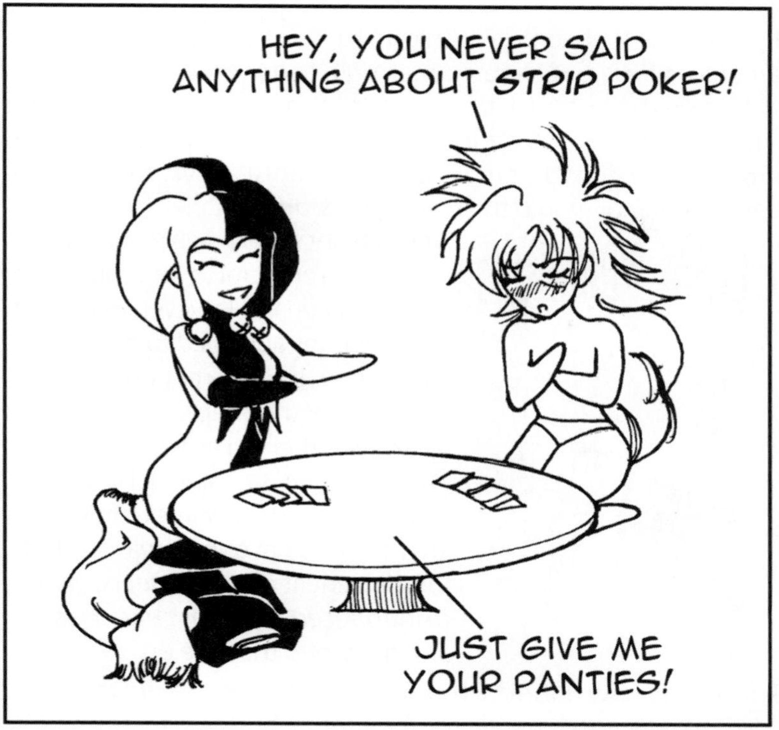
HEY, YOU NEVER SAID ANYTHING ABOUT STRIP POKER!
JUST GIVE ME YOUR PANTIES!

THE INTERMISSIONS ARE SHORT LITTLE INTERLUDES WHICH BREAK UP THE MAIN STORY TO PROVIDE A QUICK BREAK AND COMIC RELIEF.

SOMETIMES I USE THEM TO GIVE PEOPLE INFORMATION ABOUT THE WORLD OF FLIPSIDE, OR ABOUT THE WEBSITE IN GENERAL... MOST OF THE TIME I JUST USE THEM FOR SILLY JOKES LIKE THE ONE ABOVE.

SINCE THE COMIC GETS FAIRLY SERIOUS AT POINTS, I THINK IT'S GOOD TO HAVE A LITTLE WACKY HUMOR ONCE IN AWHILE TO LIGHTEN THE MOOD AND KEEP THE AUDIENCE ENTERTAINED.

The History of Flipside

I started the webcomic Flipside in 1999. It started out as an amateur effort, but I figured making a comic and putting it online would be the best way to get feedback and improve my art skills. After doing over 500 pages, I had improved quite a bit, and now I had the concern that most webcomic artists have: that the earlier material would turn off new readers.

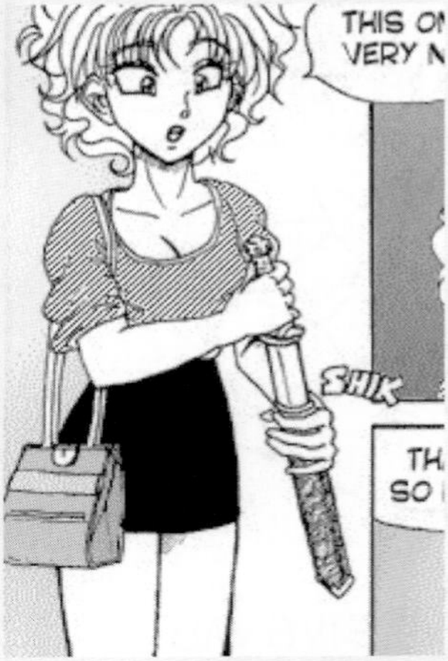
SHIK

At this point, many webcomic artists start over from scratch, or redraw their earliest material. However, neither of these options appealed to me, so I came up with a different one. I retitled all of the chapters I did as Book 0, and put them in a separate section. I started a new storyline, taking place with the same characters 6 months after the original one. It was written for the benefit of new readers, as it re-introduced the main characters and the world they live in.

This way, I felt that new readers would have an entrance point into the story with the benefit of better art. This new material was called Book 1, and is the material you now possess in this book. (As of now, 2006, I am currently working on Book 2 which can be read at www.flipsidecomics.com).

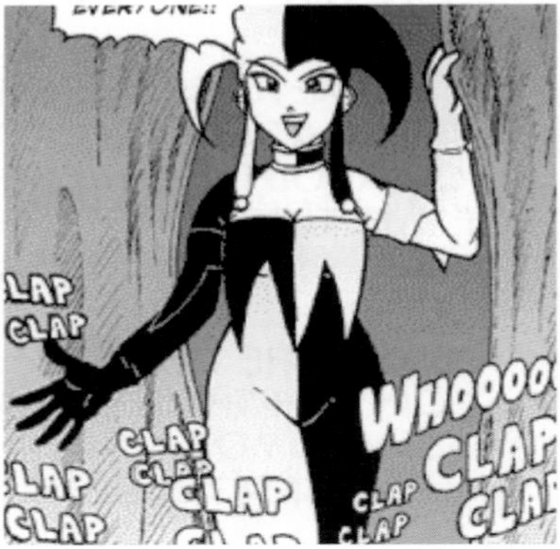
CLAP
CLAP
CLAP
CLAP

If you've never been to the website, or just haven't gotten around to reading Book 0, here is a short summary of what took place. I still consider this book practice, and it is not necessary to read it to understand the current storyline, but it will give certain insights into the happenings of this book.

Summary of Book 0

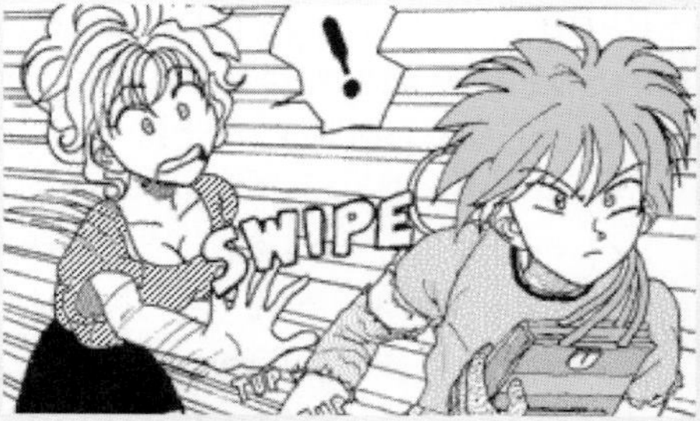
!
SWIPE

Originally, I started Flipside with the intention of doing sort of a farcical, Slayers-like fantasy comedy. This is reflected in the first few chapters of Book 0. We are introduced to Maytag without her costume, wandering the streets of a town called Vestige (located a little south of book 1's starting town, Solstice). Her purse is snatched by a thief, but a wandering mercenary gets it back for her. He asks her out on a date, but is surprised later on when the costumed Maytag shows up and wackiness ensues.

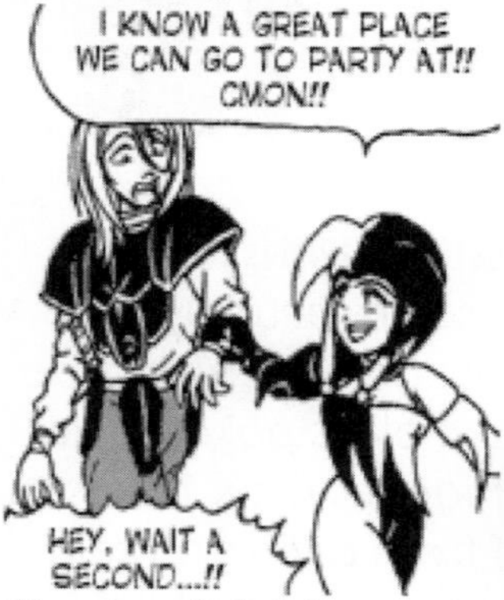
I KNOW A GREAT PLACE WE CAN GO TO PARTY AT!! CMON!!
HEY, WAIT A SECOND...!!

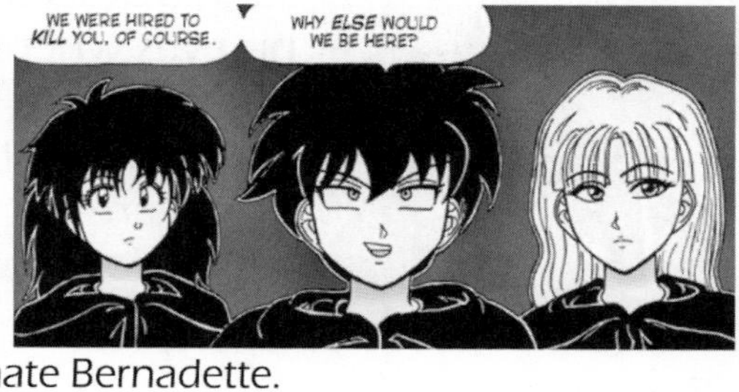
WE WERE HIRED TO KILL YOU, OF COURSE.
WHY ELSE WOULD WE BE HERE?

Chapters 3 & 4 focus on a group of assassins, The Black Poison Angels, and their attempt to assinate Bernadette.

In chapter 5, it is revealed that they were hired by a man named Seraph, to test Bernadette's skills. He then hires Bernadette to be his bodyguard. We are introduced to his assistant, Lucient, as well as two of his pupils, Regina & Moss.

From there, the rest of the storyline slowly uncovers the real reason why Seraph needs a bodyguard. It turns out that his estranged wife wants to kill him, and has sent an assassin called the Man-Eater after him. Any man who looks at this woman is paralyzed, which explains why Seraph wanted a skilled female bodyguard.

There are hints and allusions hidden in Book 0 as to what the future storyline will be. I hope that you'll check it out!

Secrets

Page 7: (Maytag's job) Since arriving in Solstice, Maytag was able to get a job quickly because of Umber's recommendation. Maytag's shows generally last an hour, and she works typically 3 days a week. One act consists of jokes, funny observations, dancing and juggling. She makes 11 gold per show, plus tips, which is a pretty decent wage. However, Maytag makes most of her money from playing poker.

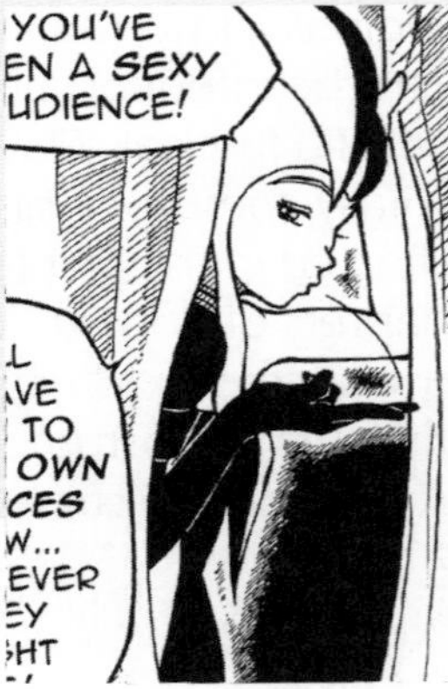
YOU'VE
EN A SEXY
UDIENCE!

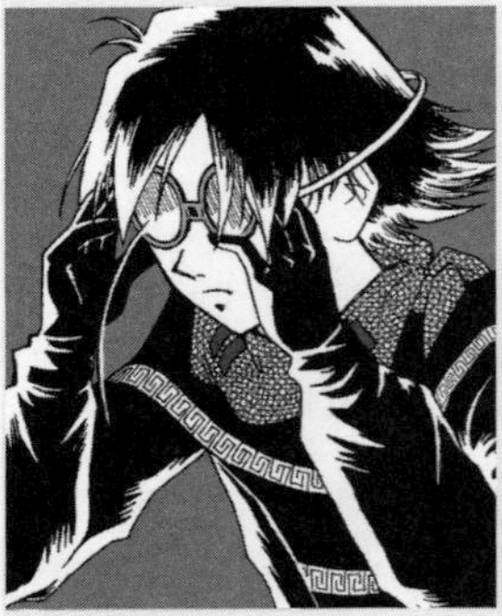

Page 15: (Crest's Glasses + Bandanna) These are actually sunglasses. Crest uses them to hide his eyes when he plays poker. The bandana is to hide his face. This is to protect himself from giving off tells, which are unconscious facial expressions that may give away a player's hand.

Page 19: (Crest's Home) Crest's home is paid for by the knights. They have been supporting him and his mother, Sierra, ever since her husband was killed and she became blind.

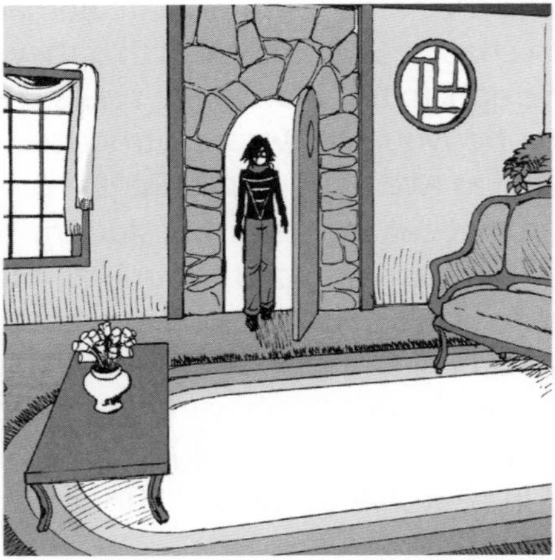

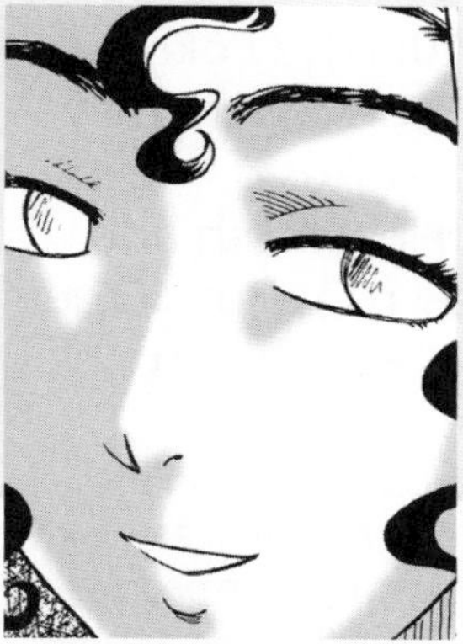

Page 23: (Sierra's Blindness) Sierra (Crest's mother) lost her sight in an accident when Crest was 4 years old. She was at a "sorcery demonstration" (where a variety of magical products are shown off.) One of these products happened to be defective and an explosion damaged the eyesight of several bystanders, one of which was Crest's mother. Since the knights frown on Sierra having anything to do with sorcery, she and Crest often just say that she has a "disease."

Page 24: (Crest the Fan) Notice the poster of Maytag on Crest's wall.

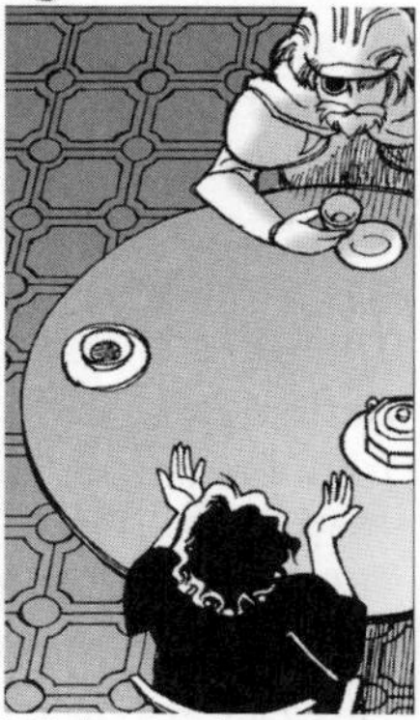

Page 26: (Crest the Thief) For a while, Crest was in a juvenile gang. He was involved with pickpocketing, shoplifting, and generally hanging out in the not so nice areas of town. This happened after the fallout between him and Orransong.

Page 34: (Adaperio & Septem) Latin words meaning open and seven, respectively. Magical elevators are not uncommon in taller buildings in the world of Flipside.

Page 38: (Accipio) Latin word meaning "accept." This device they are using is a sorcery detector. When Dice says "just the ordinary enchantments," she is talking about things like enchantments on

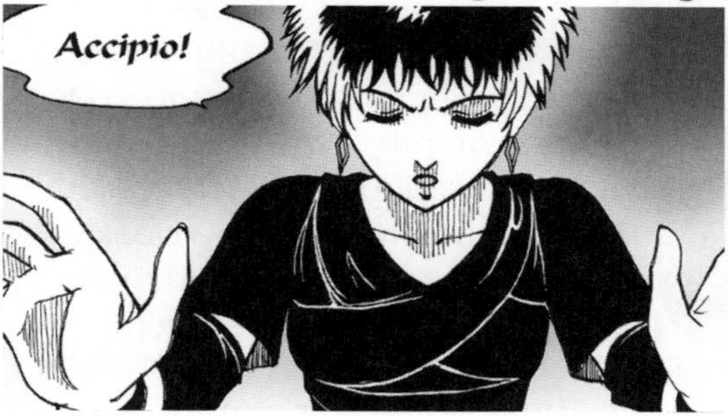
Accipio!

the clothes to keep them from getting dirty, bath enchantments to keep people clean, and so on. This is to prevent people from cheating magically.

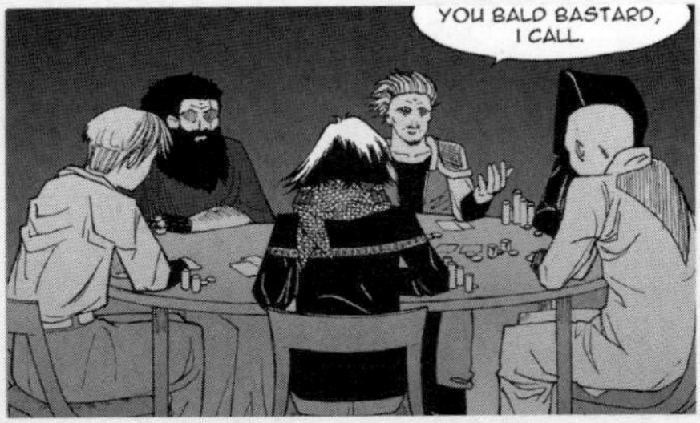
YOU BALD BASTARD,
I CALL.

Page 40: (The Poker Game) This is generally highest stakes game in town. Hellmouth and Brunson run a lot of the criminal activities in Solstice.

Page 44: (Poker) Crest is playing No Limit Texas Hold-em...but in the Flipside world, obviously there is no Texas so we just refer to it as Hold-em. Here is the strategy of this hand from Maytag's perspective: normally you should raise with two queens before the flop, but Maytag simply calls because she reads Crest for two high cards, and wants to get more action. On the flop, Crest has a pair of kings, but Maytag has flopped three Queens. She decides to slowplay the hand and merely calls, in order to get more money from Crest. When the turn comes an ace, she gets a sense that Crest has improved his hand. (Note that Crest gives this away by saying "I guess I'll bet again." This is a tell.) Therefore she check-raises, knowing that Crest will probably not check behind her. This allows her to extract the maximum amount of money from Crest

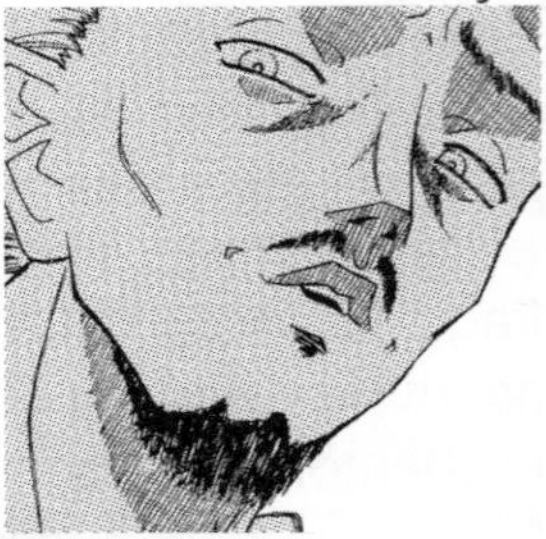

Page 48: (Hellmouth and Brunson) "Hellmouth" is a tribute to Phil "The Brat" Hellmuth, who is known for his trash-talking at the table as much as he is for his 9 World Series Bracelets. "Brunson" is named after Doyle "Texas Dolly" Brunson, a legend of poker.

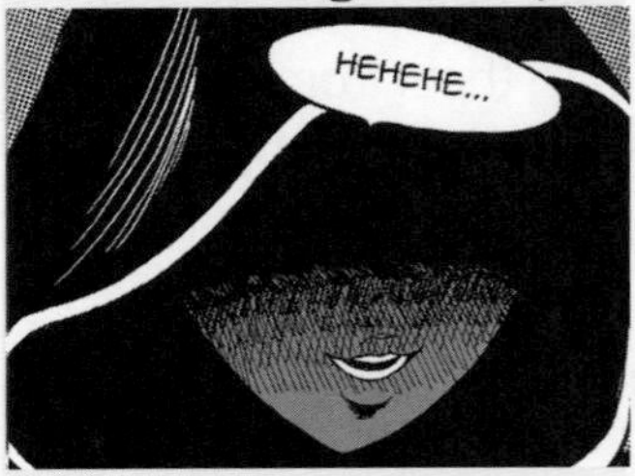
HEHEHE...

Page 55: (Maytag) Maytag has been playing poker with Hellmouth's gang for three months. She was able to join them by creating a character called "The Whisperer," a guy in a cloak who only speaks in whispers. When this character first approaches them, Maytag has one of her guy friends underneath the cloak, so that they are lead to believe The Whisperer is a man.

Angel Breath!

Page 65: (Magic Items) It should be noted that Maytag is not a sorcerer... the items she is using have a codeword that will activate it, which can be used by anyone.

Page 73: (Dice) Dice is a level 2 sorceress. She is older than she looks at 27. She also happens to be Hellmouth's girlfriend, although they don't have a very healthy relationship.

Page 166: (Girlfriend) Maytag never actually told her she was his girlfriend, Crest's mom just jumps to this conclusion.

Page 177: (Magic Grill) The chairs in this restaurant are enchanted to stay upright on their own. The cooks also happen to be sorcerers, they heat up only certain portions of the grill they wish to use.

AG!

SHE'S FUL AS L KNOW!

Page 183: (Umber & Dirk) These two characters first appeared in Book 0. Maytag had a one night stand with both of them. (Dirk used to have a mustache.)

Page 187: (Heartbreaker) Umber dances under the name "Heartbreaker."

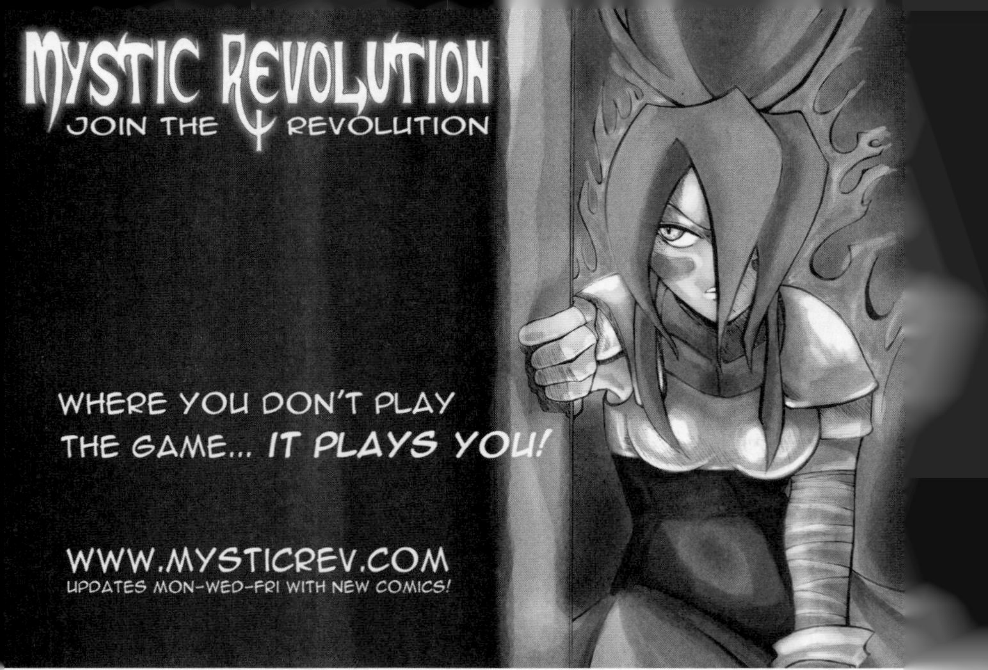
MYSTIC REVOLUTION
JOIN THE REVOLUTION
WHERE YOU DON'T PLAY THE GAME... IT PLAYS YOU!
WWW.MYSTICREV.COM
UPDATES MON-WED-FRI WITH NEW COMICS!

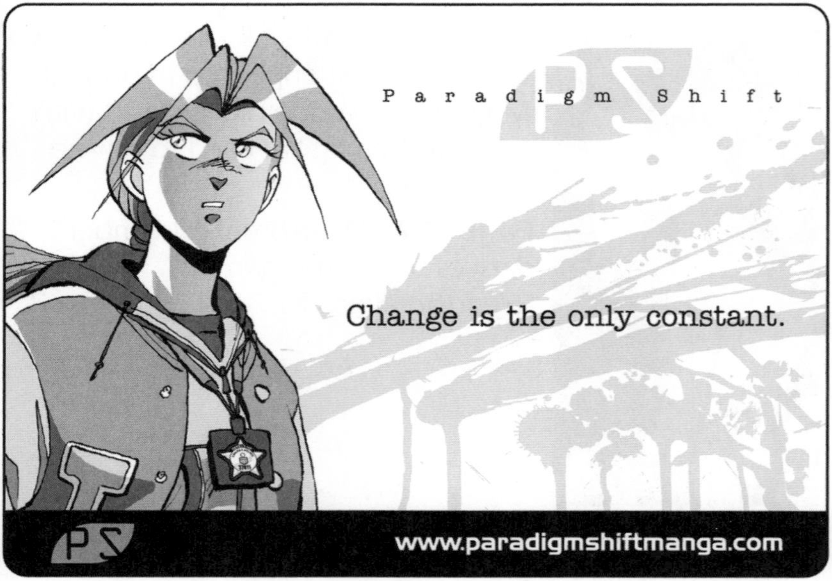
Paradigm Shift
Change is the only constant.
www.paradigmshiftmanga.com